Living and Working in

Italy

A Survival Handbook

edited by
Graeme Chesters

SURVIVAL BOOKS • LONDON • ENGLAND

First published 2001
2nd Edition 2003

Survival Books Limited, 1st Floor,
60 St James's Street, London SW1A 1ZN, United Kingdom
☎ +44 (0)20-7493 4244, ▤ +44 (0)20-7491 0605
✉ info@survivalbooks.net
💻 www.survivalbooks.net
To order books, please refer to page 472.

British Library Cataloguing in Publication Data.
A CIP record for this book is available
from the British Library.
ISBN 1 901130 67 3

Printed and bound in Finland by WS Bookwell Ltd

ACKNOWLEDGEMENTS

My sincere thanks to all those who contributed to the successful publication of the second edition of this book, in particular Heather Matuozzo (research), Louise Chesters (word processing), and Joe and Kerry Laredo (revising, proof-reading and desktop publishing). Also a special mention to the many people who assisted with the first edition – written by Nick Daws – including Joanna Styles, Mary Jane Cryan, Laura Jane Pancani, Fulvio Ferri, Patricia Aptowitz, Val Fox, Tracey Gambarotta, Paulo Puppo, Heather Matuozzo, Alan and Fiona Tankard, Nicola Meecham, Karbalaei Hassan Ali (Farrokh) and Börje Kyrklund. I also wish to acknowledge the assistance provided by Geoffrey Watson (British Embassy in Rome, press department), John Murphy (*The Informer*) and Susan Jarman (*The Grapevine*). Finally a special thank you to Jim Watson for the superb cover, illustrations, cartoons and maps.

OTHER TITLES BY SURVIVAL BOOKS

Living and Working Series

Abroad; America; Australia; Britain; Canada; France; Germany; the Gulf States & Saudi Arabia; Holland, Belgium & Luxembourg; Ireland; London; New Zealand; Spain; Switzerland

Buying a Home Series

Abroad; Britain; Florida; France; Greece & Cyprus; Ireland; Italy; Portugal; Spain

Other Titles

The Alien's Guide to Britain; The Alien's Guide to France; The Best Places to Live in France; The Best Places to Live in Spain; How to Avoid Holiday & Travel Disasters; Retiring Abroad; Rioja and its Wines; The Wines of Spain

Order forms are on page 472.

WHAT READERS & REVIEWERS

When you buy a model plane for your child, a video recorder, or some new computer gizmo, you get with it a leaflet or booklet pleading 'Read Me First', or bearing large friendly letters or bold type saying 'IMPORTANT – follow the instructions carefully'. This book should be similarly supplied to all those entering France with anything more durable than a 5-day return ticket. It is worth reading even if you are just visiting briefly, or if you have lived here for years and feel totally knowledgeable and secure. But if you need to find out how France works then it is indispensable. Native French people probably have a less thorough understanding of how their country functions. – Where it is most essential, the book is most up to the minute.

LIVING FRANCE

Rarely has a 'survival guide' contained such useful advice. This book dispels doubts for first-time travellers, yet is also useful for seasoned globetrotters – In a word, if you're planning to move to the USA or go there for a long-term stay, then buy this book both for general reading and as a ready-reference.

AMERICAN CITIZENS ABROAD

It is everything you always wanted to ask but didn't for fear of the contemptuous put down – The best English-language guide – Its pages are stuffed with practical information on everyday subjects and are designed to complement the traditional guidebook.

SWISS NEWS

A complete revelation to me – I found it both enlightening and interesting, not to mention amusing.

CAROLE CLARK

Let's say it at once. David Hampshire's *Living and Working in France* is the best handbook ever produced for visitors and foreign residents in this country; indeed, my discussion with locals showed that it has much to teach even those born and bred in l'Hexagone. – It is Hampshire's meticulous detail which lifts his work way beyond the range of other books with similar titles. Often you think of a supplementary question and search for the answer in vain. With Hampshire this is rarely the case. – He writes with great clarity (and gives French equivalents of all key terms), a touch of humour and a ready eye for the odd (and often illuminating) fact. – This book is absolutely indispensable.

THE RIVIERA REPORTER

A mine of information – I may have avoided some embarrassments and frights if I had read it prior to my first Swiss encounters – Deserves an honoured place on any newcomer's bookshelf.

ENGLISH TEACHERS ASSOCIATION, SWITZERLAND

HAVE SAID ABOUT SURVIVAL BOOKS

What a great work, wealth of useful information, well-balanced wording and accuracy in details. My compliments!

THOMAS MÜLLER

This handbook has all the practical information one needs to set up home in the UK – The sheer volume of information is almost daunting – Highly recommended for anyone moving to the UK.

AMERICAN CITIZENS ABROAD

A very good book which has answered so many questions and even some I hadn't thought of – I would certainly recommend it.

BRIAN FAIRMAN

We would like to congratulate you on this work: it is really super! We hand it out to our expatriates and they read it with great interest and pleasure.

ICI (SWITZERLAND) AG

Covers just about all the things you want to know on the subject – In answer to the desert island question about the one how-to book on France, this book would be it – Almost 500 pages of solid accurate reading – This book is about enjoyment as much as survival.

THE RECORDER

It's so funny – I love it and definitely need a copy of my own – Thanks very much for having written such a humorous and helpful book.

HEIDI GUILIANI

A must for all foreigners coming to Switzerland.

ANTOINETTE O'DONOGHUE

A comprehensive guide to all things French, written in a highly readable and amusing style, for anyone planning to live, work or retire in France.

THE TIMES

A concise, thorough account of the DOs and DON'Ts for a foreigner in Switzerland – Crammed with useful information and lightened with humorous quips which make the facts more readable.

AMERICAN CITIZENS ABROAD

Covers every conceivable question that may be asked concerning everyday life – I know of no other book that could take the place of this one.

FRANCE IN PRINT

Hats off to *Living and Working in Switzerland*!

RONNIE ALMEIDA

CONTENTS

12. HEALTH   251

13. INSURANCE   271

IMPORTANT NOTE

Italy is a diverse country with many faces, a variety of ethnic groups, languages, religions and customs, and continuously changing rules, regulations (particularly regarding business, social security and taxes), interest rates and prices. Note that a change of government in Italy, which happens frequently, can have far-reaching effects on many important aspects of life. **I cannot recommend too strongly that you check with an official and reliable source (not always the same) before making any major decisions or taking an irreversible course of action. However, don't believe everything you're told or read – even, dare I say it, herein!**

Useful addresses and references to other sources of information have been included in all chapters and in **Appendices A to C** to help you obtain further information and verify details with official sources. Important points have been emphasised, in **bold** print, some of which it would be expensive, or even dangerous, to disregard. **Ignore them at your peril or cost!** Unless specifically stated, the reference to any company, organisation or product in this book doesn't constitute an endorsement or recommendation.

EDITOR'S NOTES

- Frequent references are made in this book to the European Union (EU), which comprised (in summer 2003) Austria, Belgium, Denmark, Finland, France, Germany, Greece, Ireland, Italy, Luxembourg, the Netherlands, Portugal, Spain, Sweden and the United Kingdom, and the European Economic Area (EEA), which includes the EU countries plus Iceland, Liechtenstein and Norway.

- Names of major Italian cities are written in English (the Italian names are given here in brackets), e.g. Florence (*Firenze*), Milan (*Milano*), Naples (*Napoli*), Padua (*Padova*), Rome (*Roma*), Turin (*Torino*) and Venice (*Venezia*).

- Times are shown using am for before noon and pm for after noon (see also **Time Difference** on page 427).

- Prices should be taken as guides only, although they were mostly correct at the time of publication. Unless otherwise stated, all prices quoted usually include value added tax (*imposta sul valore aggiunto/IVA*) at 4, 10 or 20 per cent (see page 307).

- His/he/him also means her/she/her (please forgive me ladies). This is done to make life easier for both the reader and (in particular) the author, **and isn't intended to be sexist.**

- The Italian translation of many key words and phrases is shown in brackets in italics.

- All spelling is (or should be) British and not American English.

- Warnings and important points are shown in **bold** type.

- The following symbols are used in this book: ☎ (telephone), 🖷 (fax), 🖳 (Internet) and ✉ (e-mail).

- Lists of **Useful Addresses**, **Further Reading** and **Useful Websites** are contained in **Appendices A**, **B** and **C** respectively.

- For those unfamiliar with the metric system of weights and measures, imperial conversion tables are included in **Appendix D**.

- A map of Italy showing the regions is included in **Appendix E**.

INTRODUCTION

Whether you're already living or working in Italy or just thinking about it, this is **THE BOOK** for you. Forget about all those glossy guide books, excellent though they are for tourists; this amazing book was written particularly with you in mind and is worth its weight in *parmigiano*. *Living and Working in Italy* is designed to meet the needs of anyone wishing to know the essentials of Italian life, including immigrants, temporary workers, businessmen, students, retirees, long-stay tourists, holiday homeowners and even extra-terrestrials. However long your intended stay in Italy, you will find the information contained in this book invaluable.

General information isn't difficult to find in Italy (provided you speak Italian) and a multitude of books is published on every conceivable subject. However, reliable and up-to-date information in English specifically intended for foreigners living and working in Italy isn't so easy to find, least of all in one volume. Our aim in publishing this book was to help fill this void and provide the comprehensive **practical** information necessary for a relatively trouble-free life.

You may have visited Italy as a tourist, but living and working there is a different matter altogether. Adjusting to a different environment and culture and making a home in any foreign country can be a traumatic and stressful experience, and Italy is no exception. You need to adapt to new customs and traditions and discover the Italian way of doing things, e.g. finding a home, paying bills and obtaining insurance. For most foreigners in Italy, overcoming the everyday obstacles of life has previously been a matter of luck. **But no more!** With a copy of *Living and Working in Italy* to hand you'll have a wealth of information at your fingertips – information derived from a variety of sources, both official and unofficial, not least the hard won personal experiences of the author and editor, their family, friends, colleagues and acquaintances.

Living and Working in Italy is a comprehensive handbook on a wide range of everyday subjects and represents the most up-to-date source of general information available to foreigners in Italy. It isn't, however, simply a monologue of dry facts and figures, but a practical and entertaining look at life in Italy.

Adapting to life in a new country is a continuous process and, although this book will help reduce your beginner's phase and minimise the frustrations, it doesn't contain all the answers. (Most of us don't even know the right questions to ask!) What it **will** do, however, is help you to make informed decisions and calculated judgements, instead of uneducated guesses and costly mistakes. **Most important, it will help save you time, trouble and money, and repay your investment many times over.**

Although you may find some of the information in this book a bit daunting, don't be discouraged. Most problems occur only once and fade into insignificance after a short time (as you face the next half a dozen!). The majority of foreigners in Italy would agree that, all things considered, they love living there.

A period spent in Italy is a wonderful way to enrich your life, broaden your horizons and hopefully please your bank manager. I trust that this book will help you to avoid the pitfalls of life in Italy and smooth your way to a happy and rewarding future in your new home.

Buona fortuna!

1.

FINDING A JOB

Finding a job in Italy isn't always as difficult as the unemployment figures may suggest, particularly in Rome, Milan and other large cities, depending of course on your qualifications and Italian language ability. However, if you don't qualify to live and work in Italy by birthright or as a national of a European Union (EU) country, obtaining a work permit (*permesso di soggiorno per motive di lavoro* – see page 80) may be more difficult than finding a job. Americans and other nationalities without the automatic right to work in Italy must have their employment approved by the Italian Ministry of Labour and they would need an employment visa before arriving in Italy. High unemployment in Italy has made hiring non-EU workers a sensitive and emotive issue in some regions. The 1998 Immigration Law introduced a quota system that restricts the number of freelance people of any nationality and category allowed into the country each year (see **Employees** on page 45). However, despite the difficulties, foreigners are found in large numbers in almost every walk of life, particularly in the major cities.

Although Italy isn't a country that's usually associated with immigration, it has a long tradition of welcoming immigrants, particularly political refugees. In 1972, for the first time, it registered more people entering the country than leaving, although many of these were Italians returning home from northern Europe and the USA. However, Italy has received an increasing numbers of migrants from Asia, Africa, and Latin America in the last few decades and by 1989 the foreign population numbered 1.1 million, most from outside the EU. The majority of foreigners settle in the centre or the north, in the major urban conurbations of Milan, Rome, Turin and Genoa, although Florence and Palermo are also popular, particularly among African immigrants. In recent years, Italy's rapid economic growth has attracted further immigrants to the country, mainly from North and sub-Saharan Africa, but also from the Philippines, China, South America and most recently from Poland, Romania, Albania and the former Yugoslavia after the collapse of communist regimes in eastern Europe. In the last census (in 2000), there were 1,520,000 registered immigrants, and it's estimated that there are another 1 million living there illegally (*clandestini*), which has led to tougher immigration rules and a more forceful programme of expulsion.

EMPLOYMENT PROSPECTS

Being attracted to Italy by its weather, cuisine, wine and lifestyle is laudable, but doesn't rate highly as an employment qualification. You should have a positive reason for living and working in Italy; simply being fed up with your boss or the weather isn't the best motive (although thoroughly understandable). It's extremely difficult to find work in rural areas and isn't easy in cities (even Rome or Milan), especially if your Italian isn't fluent. You shouldn't plan on obtaining employment in Italy unless you have a firm job offer or special qualifications or experience for which there's a strong demand. If you want a good job, you must usually be well qualified and speak fluent Italian. If you plan to arrive in Italy without a job, it's wise to have a plan for finding employment on arrival and to try to make some contacts before you arrive.

There's a huge difference between northern and southern Italy in terms of wealth and job opportunities. The *Mezzogiorno* (the name given to the southern area of the country comprising the regions of Abruzzo, Molise, Campania, Calabria and Basilicata, and the islands of Sicily and Sardinia), which constitutes some 40 per cent of Italy's total land area and 35 per cent of its population, creates only around 25 per cent of the country's Gross Domestic Product (GDP). Unemployment in the south is around three times the northern rate and wages are some 40 per cent below the national average.

Many people turn to self-employment or starting a business to make a living, although this path is strewn with pitfalls for the newcomer. **Most foreigners don't do sufficient homework before moving to Italy.** While hoping for the best, you should plan for the worst case scenario and have a contingency plan and sufficient funds to last until you're established (this also applies to prospective employees). If you're planning to start a business in Italy, you must also do battle with the notoriously obstructive Italian bureaucracy (*buona fortuna!*).

Unemployment

Italy has a relatively high unemployment rate, which was officially running at around 8.9 per cent (in the north around 5 per cent, in central Italy 6 per cent and in the south 21 per cent) of the workforce in October 2002. As already indicated, unemployment varies according to the region and in the impoverished south it's as high as 50 per cent in some areas, where the youth has traditionally migrated to the north or abroad in search of work. Unemployment is a disaster for Italy's youth; some 30 per cent of young people in the under 25-age group are unemployed, many of whom have little prospect of finding a job. It's difficult for young Italians to get a foothold on the employment ladder due to lack of experience and many young people, even university graduates, attend vocational high schools or special programmes to gain work experience.

Although unemployment has hit manufacturing industries the hardest, no sector has survived unscathed, including the flourishing service industries. Some of the hardest-hit industries have been construction, electronics, communications, the media and banking, all traditionally strong sectors. Many companies have periodic bans on recruitment and expect many employees to accept short-term contracts, rather than life-long security (Italian job security had traditionally been among the best in Europe). Over a quarter of Italy's working population have short-term contracts.

Unemployment benefits are virtually non-existent in Italy and less than 25 per cent of the country's unemployed are eligible for any form of unemployment compensation, and families have traditionally been expected to support their unemployed members. There's no national scheme or assistance for the long-term unemployed in Italy, although there's a limited degree of support for low-income families in the south.

Economy

Italy has Europe's fourth-largest economy (after the UK, Germany, and France), but is around 12th out of the 15 EU countries in terms of gross domestic product (GDP) per head. The country had an estimated per capita GDP in 2002 of US$24,700, compared with US$29,360 in the UK, US$29,210 in Germany, US$27,890 in France and US$37,600 in the US (figures from the Economist Intelligence Unit). However, Italy has huge extremes of wealth and poverty, and there's a vast difference in incomes between the rich northern region and the poor southern *Mezzogiorno* – an imbalance that vast injections of central government and EU cash have done little to alleviate. Not surprisingly, given Italy's woeful fiscal mismanagement, the rules to allow Italy entry to the euro were fudged (Italy had a public debt well above the level specified in the Maastricht Treaty) and it's one of the weakest links in the euro group of 12 countries. However, it's hoped that the discipline imposed by the euro (and the possibility of Italy being thrown out if it doesn't stick to the rules) will knock the Italian financial system into shape. Italy was badly hit by the recession in the early 1990s and, although the economy has recovered, unemployment remains relatively high, the cost of living has increased in recent years and per capita personal debt has risen considerably.

The percentage of the working population engaged in agriculture is around 7 per cent, compared to some 33 per cent in industry and around 60 per cent in the service sector. The fast-growing service industry is the most important and includes tourism, the hotel industry, restaurants, transport and communications, domestic workers, financial services, and public administration. Factors that have contributed to the growth of the service sector in recent years include the rise in the standard of living in Italy (and Europe in general), leading to an increase in mobility, financial transactions, business, demand for leisure activities and tourism.

Industrial production in Italy is typified by the many small and medium-sized companies engaged in sectors such as the clothing, mechanical engineering and textile industries. However, there are also many large multi-national companies, a number of which are still family-dominated, such as Benetton, Fiat and Pirelli. Italy is also at the forefront of many hi-tech industries such as aviation, computing, electronics and telecommunications. Olivetti is one of the world's leading suppliers of computers and software products. Other prominent Italian industries include ceramics, glass, furniture, household goods and leather articles, which are world renowned for their design and quality. The country's most significant industries are based in the northern cities of Milan, Turin and the Veneto Region. For the last 50 years there's been a concerted effort to redress the long-standing economic imbalance between the north and the south of the country, although it has had little impact.

Industrial Relations: There has been a reduction in strikes (*scioperi*) in recent years, with the power of the trade unions lessening, although Italy still has the worst industrial relations in the European Union. At one time, strikes were so frequent (a day's holiday is jokingly referred to as *è giorno di sciopero*) that a space was reserved in newspapers for announcements about public services that wouldn't be operating (nowadays you can obtain the latest information via the TV televideo service). The majority of strikes are in the public sector and the transportation industries.

Italy & The European Union

Italy was one of the six founder members of the European Union (EU) in 1957 along with Belgium, France, Germany, Luxembourg and the Netherlands, and the original Common Market agreement was signed in Italy and dubbed the 'Treaty of Rome'. Since then Austria, Denmark, Finland, Greece, Ireland, Portugal, Spain, Sweden and the United Kingdom have increased the number of members to 15. The EU countries plus Iceland, Liechtenstein and Norway also make up the European Economic Area (EEA). Nationals of EU (and EEA) countries have the right to work in Italy or any other member state without a work permit, provided they have a valid passport or national identity card and comply with the member state's laws and regulations on employment. EU nationals are entitled to the same treatment as Italian citizens in matters of pay, working conditions, access to housing, vocational training, social security and trade union rights, and their families and immediate dependants are entitled to join them and enjoy the same rights. The Single European Act, which came into effect on 1st January 1993, created a single market with a more favourable environment for stimulating enterprise, competition and trade, and made it easier for EU nationals to work in other EU countries.

There are still barriers to full freedom of movement and the right to work within the EU, for example some jobs in member states require applicants to have specific skills or vocational qualifications, and qualifications obtained in some member states aren't recognised in others. However, in most trades and professions, member states are required to recognise qualifications and experience obtained elsewhere in the EU (see **Qualifications** below). There are restrictions on employment in the civil service, when the right to work may be limited in individual cases on the grounds of public policy, security or public health.

QUALIFICATIONS

The most important qualification for working in Italy is the ability to speak Italian (see **Language** on page 49 and **Language Schools** on page 191). Once you've overcome this hurdle you should establish whether your trade or professional qualifications and experience are recognised in Italy. If you aren't experienced, Italian employers expect studies to be in a relevant subject and to have included work experience. Professional or trade qualifications are necessary to work in most fields in Italy and qualifications are also often needed to be self-employed or start a business. It isn't just a matter of hanging up a sign and waiting for the stampede of customers to your door. Many foreign artisans and traders are required to undergo a 'business' course before they can start work in Italy (see **Self-Employment** on page 41).

Under EU regulations, when a qualified professional from another European member state wishes to pursue his career in Italy or another member state, all qualifications and professional experience are to be taken into consideration. If the diplomas held are equivalent to those required under national legislation for working in a specified field, then a qualified professional is authorised to set up a practice. Italy defines the rules and regulations to be followed when setting up a practice and rights concerning trade unions, working conditions and employee contracts are the same as for Italian nationals. You must apply to the professional body for your profession for permission to set up a practice and to have your qualifications recognised.

Theoretically, qualifications recognised by professional and trade bodies in one EU country should be recognised in Italy. However, recognition varies from country to country and in some cases foreign qualifications aren't recognised by Italian employers or professional and trade associations. All academic qualifications should also be recognised, although they may be given less prominence than equivalent Italian qualifications, depending on the country and the educational establishment. A ruling by the European Court in 1992 declared that where EU examinations are of a similar standard with just certain areas of difference, then individuals should be required to take exams only in those particular areas. In some trades and professions, you must prove that you've been practising as a self-employed person for a certain period of time, generally five or six years.

In order to set up and operate a professional practice, you must produce (in Italian) a certificate of equivalence (*certificato di equipollenza*) document from the ministry concerned, stating that your qualifications are equivalent to Italian qualifications. You must provide evidence that you satisfy the requirements regarding character and repute, and have not been declared bankrupt. You need a residence permit (*certificato di residenza* – see page 86), an identity document and proof of citizenship, and are informed within 30 days if further documents or evidence are required. **In certain cases, you may be required to take an aptitude test or in exceptional cases undergo a period of training for up to three years.** The recognition of your qualifications entitles you to register in the professional rolls and to practise your profession according to the requirements of the Italian state. If, however, your profession isn't regulated in Italy, you don't need to apply for recognition of your qualifications and can begin practising under the same conditions as Italian nationals.

Italy (and other EU states) may reserve certain posts for their nationals if the jobs involve the exercise of powers conferred by public law and the safeguarding of the general interests of the state or local authorities, for example, the diplomatic service, police, judiciary and the armed forces. However, most public sector jobs in the areas of health, education, the provision of commercial services and research for civil purposes are open to all EU nationals and aren't subject to any restrictions on the grounds of nationality. Access to public sector jobs varies from one country to another and you should contact the Italian authorities for information regarding specific jobs.

All EU member states publish occupation information sheets containing a common job description with a table of qualifications. These cover a large number of trades and are intended to help someone with the relevant qualifications look for a job in another EU country. You can obtain a direct comparison between any EU qualification and those recognised in Italy from the Italian branch of the National Academic Recognition Information Centre (NARIC). For information about equivalent academic and professional qualifications in Italy contact CIMEA, Fondazione Rui, Viale Ventuno Aprile, 36, 00162 Rome (☎ 06-8632 1281) or the Presidenza Consiglio Ministri, Ministerio Coordinamento Politiche Communitarie, Via Giardino Theodoli, 66, 00186 Rome (☎ 06-6779 5322).

In Britain, information about academic qualifications can be obtained from NARIC, ECCTIS, Oriel House, Oriel Road, Cheltenham, Glos. GL50 1XP (☎ 01242-260010, 🖳 www.naric.org.uk) and information about the recognition of professional qualifications from the Department of Trade and Industry, DTI Enquiry Unit, 1 Victoria Street, London SW1H 0ET (☎ 020-7215 5000, 🖳 www. dti.gov.uk). You can also check whether trades and professions are officially recognised on the European Union website (🖳 http://citizens.eu.int).

EMPLOYMENT SERVICES

Job seekers in Italy should register at the nearest employment office (*ufficio di collocamento*) of the government employment service (Sezione Circoscrizionate per l'Impiego). You can register without being a resident (and should be given the same help as Italian nationals and residents), but require a permit to stay (see page 79) and a workers' registration card (*libretto di lavoro*). Employment offices provide information about registration, unemployment cards, agricultural jobs, residency, apprenticeships, public bodies, and benefit applications and payments. They organise seminars about job hunting and have trained counsellors to help you find an appropriate job. Some centres have Internet access.

Regional employment agencies are operated by the Ministry of Labour and Social Welfare (Ministero del Lavoro e della Previdenza Sociale) and there are also local employment centres (*centri di iniziativa locale per l'occupazione/CILO*) in cities and large towns, which provide help and advice about work-related problems and self-employment. There are also information centres for the unemployed (*centro infomazione disoccupati*) in major cities run by the larger trade unions. Here you can obtain information about job vacancies, finding work and employment regulations; some offices also offer advice on job interviews, writing application letters, setting up a business, self-employment, income tax and social security.

Young people can obtain information about jobs and training at local information centres (*informagiovani*), found in most towns and cities. These centres have situations vacant boards for temporary (*lavoro interinale*) and part-time (*lavoro a tempo parziale* or *lavoro part-time*) jobs such as baby-sitting, teaching children, gardening and domestic work. They maintain job listings (you can also place a 'work wanted' ad.) and distribute leaflets, flyers and booklets about finding work in Italy. They provide help and advice on finding temporary work, information about courses and training, evening classes, scholarships, enrolment at university, cultural events and hobbies. You can lodge your curriculum vitae (CV) on their website (🖳 www.informagiovani.it), check job offers, contact agencies offering part-time work and apply directly to companies offering employment. There's also a section listing employment laws, working conditions and employment contracts.

There's also a European Employment Service (EURES) network, members of which include all EU countries plus Norway and Iceland. Member states exchange information regularly on job vacancies, and local EURES offices have access to information on how to apply for a job and living and working conditions in each country. The international department of your home country's employment service can put you in touch with a 'Euroadviser' who can provide advice on finding work in Italy. Euroadvisers have permanent links with EURES services in other member states and also have permanent access to two databases. One database contains details of job offers in all member states and the other provides information on living and working conditions, and a profile of the trends for regional labour markets.

Euroadvisers can also arrange to have your personal details forwarded to the Italian Job Centre (Sezione Circoscrizionale per l'Impiego Collocamento in Agricola/SCICA) in Italy. However, given the high level of unemployment in Italy, this is rarely the fastest or the most efficient method for finding a job there, particularly from abroad. As would be expected, national employment services give priority to their own nationals and jobs aren't generally referred to EURES or other national agencies until after prospective local candidates have been considered. The Citizens First website (🖳 http://citizens.eu.int) contains information about EURES and EURES-related agencies in many European countries and you can also consult 🖳 http://europa.eu.int/eures/index.jsp.

For further information contact the Ministero del Lavoro e della Previdenza Sociale, Via Flavia, 6, 00187 Rome (☎ 06-4788 7174, 🖳 www.minlavoro.it).

PRIVATE RECRUITMENT AGENCIES

There are two main kinds of recruitment agency in Italy, temporary agencies (*lavori ad interim*) and executive search companies (*ricerca personale*).

Temporary Agencies

Unlike many other European countries, Italy officially prohibited temporary employees until January 1998, when a new law came into effect. Under the new law, an agency can only place workers with an employer to satisfy a temporary demand and agencies must have fulfilled certain criteria and received authorisation. A temporary contract (*contratto per prestazioni di lavoro temporaneo*) is a fixed-term contract or an open-ended contract, where an agency must pay compensation to a worker for the periods when he isn't working. The agency must pay workers' social security contributions and work accident insurance. Temporary workers have pro rata rights to annual and public holidays, a 13th month's salary and any other payments which other workers employed by the same company are entitled to.

To sign up with an agency you need a permit to stay, a fiscal code (*codice fiscale*) and your work record book (*libretto di lavoro*). You're required to complete a form in Italian and must supply a CV (in Italian) and a passport-size photograph. You will be interviewed by the agency and probably again by a prospective employer. Temporary work is most common in the secretarial, computer and industrial fields, and work in other sectors is limited, although it may still be worth enquiring and registering with agencies. Always ensure that you know exactly how much, when and how you will be paid. Because of the long annual holidays in Italy and generous maternity leave, companies often require temporary staff, and a temporary job can frequently be used as a stepping stone to a permanent position (companies often hire temporary workers for a 'trial' period before offering them a full-time contract).

Temporary agencies with offices in most Italian cities include Adecco (🖥 www.adecco.it), ALI (🖥 www.alispa.it), Eurointerim (🖥 www.euro interim.it), Kelly (🖥 www.kellyservices.it), Manpower (🖥 www.manpower.it), Sinterim (🖥 www.sinterim.it) and Vedior (🖥 www.vedior.it). You can also find local agencies in the yellow pages under *Lavoro Interinale e Temporaneo*.

Executives

Executive recruitment and search companies are common in the major cities and are mainly used by large Italian companies to recruit staff, particularly executives, managers and professionals. Agents place advertisements in daily and weekly newspapers and trade magazines, but don't usually mention the client's name, not least to prevent applicants from approaching a company directly, thus depriving the agency of its fat fee. Recruitment agencies were hard hit by the recession in the 1990s, particularly those dealing with executives and senior managers, and many Italian companies now do their own recruiting or promote in-house. Unless you're a particularly outstanding candidate with half a dozen degrees, are multi-lingual and have valuable experience, sending an unsolicited CV to an agent is usually a waste of time. There are also recruitment agencies in many countries that specialise in recruiting executives, managers and professionals for employers in Italy.

Internet

The rapid development of the Internet has led to a huge increase in the number of online recruitment agencies and job search sites. Some sites charge a subscription fee to access their vacancy listings, but many allow job seekers to review and respond to listings free of charge. It's also possible to submit your CV online (usually free), but it's wise to consider the security implications of this move. By giving your home address or phone number, you could lay yourself open to nuisance phone calls or even worse. A number of websites that list vacancies in Italy are listed below:

- www.alispa.it
- www.bancalavoro.com
- www.executivenetwork.it
- www.fionline.it
- www.informagiovani.it
- www.job-net.it
- www.jobline.it
- www.jobs.it
- www.monster.it
- www.obiettivolavoro.it
- www.quilavoro.com

It's worth noting that you may not find any information in English on Italian websites (those which end .it). However, if your Italian skills are poor, you can obtain a rough translation using the (free) Babel Fish translator provided by the search engine company Alta Vista. Enter http://babelfish.altavista.com in your browser, then enter the address of the website that you wish to visit in the Babel Fish dialogue box that appears. You will be presented with an instant translation of the web page in question into the language selected.

SEASONAL JOBS

Seasonal jobs (*lavoro stagionale*) are available throughout the year in Italy, the vast majority in the tourist industry. Many jobs last for the duration of the summer or winter tourist seasons, May to September and December to April respectively, although some are simply casual or temporary jobs for a number of weeks. Italian fluency is required for all but the most menial and worst paid jobs, and is equally or more important than experience and qualifications (although fluency in Italian alone won't guarantee you a well paid job). Seasonal jobs include most trades in hotels and restaurants, couriers and travel company representatives, a variety of jobs in ski resorts, sports instructors, jobs in bars and clubs, fruit and grape picking, and various jobs in the construction industry.

If you aren't an EU national, it's essential to check whether you're eligible to work in Italy before making plans and you may also be required to obtain a visa (see page 76). Check with an Italian embassy or consulate in your home country well in advance of your visit. Foreign students in Italy can obtain a temporary work permit (*autorizzazione di lavoro provvisoria*) for part-time work during the summer holiday period and school terms (see page 80). The main seasonal jobs available in Italy are mentioned below.

Holiday Company Representatives

The duties of holiday representatives include ferrying tourist groups back and forth from airports, organising excursions and social events, arranging ski passes and equipment rental, and generally playing the role of Jack of all trades. A job as a representative is tough and demanding, and requires resilience and resourcefulness to deal with the chaos associated with the package holiday business. The necessary requirements include the ability to answer many questions simultaneously (often in different languages), to remain calm and charming under extreme pressure, and above all, to maintain a keen sense of humour. Lost passengers, tickets, passports and tempers are everyday occurrences. It's an excellent training ground for managerial and leadership skills, pays well and often offers opportunities to supplement your earnings with tips.

Representatives are required by many local and foreign tour companies in both winter and summer resorts. Competition for jobs is fierce and local language ability is usually required, even for employment with British tour operators. Most companies have age requirements, the minimum usually being 21, although many companies prefer employees to be a few years older.

The majority of representative jobs in Italy are available during the winter ski season with British ski-tour companies and school ski-party organisers. A useful source of information is ski magazines, which contain regular listings of tour companies showing who goes to which resorts. It's wise to find out the kind of clients you're likely to be dealing with, particularly if you're allergic to children or yuppies (young urban professionals, similar to children but more immature). In order to survive a winter in a ski resort, it helps to be a keen skier or a dedicated learner, otherwise you risk being bored to death by ski bums.

Some companies operate both summer and winter hotels and camps throughout Italy. Employees are required to speak good Italian. Representatives are also required for summer camps, which are organised for both adults and children. Among the main employers are Alpitour Italia, Viale Maino, 42, 20129 Milan (🖳 www.alpitour.it), Club Med. (🖳 www.clubmedjobs.com), Francorosso International (🖳 www.francorosso.it) and Valtur (🖳 www.valtur.it).

Hotels & Catering

Hotels and restaurants are the largest employers of seasonal workers, from hotel managers to kitchen hands, with jobs which are available all year round. Experience, qualifications and fluent Italian are required for all the best and highest paid positions, although a variety of jobs are available for the untrained and inexperienced. **If accommodation with cooking facilities or full board isn't provided with a job, it can be expensive and difficult to find.** Ensure that your salary is sufficient to pay for accommodation, food and other living expenses, and to hopefully save some money. The best way to find work is to contact hotel chains directly (see **Hotels** on page 329), preferably at least six months before you wish to start work.

Grape & Fruit Picking

To find a fruit or vegetable picking job, visit the local information centre, which will provide you with a list of farms in the area taking on temporary workers for the harvest season. Local employment offices (*uffici di collocamento*) and agricultural co-operatives (Sezione Circoscrizionale per l'Impiego Collocamento in Agricola/SCICA) may also be helpful, although it's generally best to contact farms directly. You may not be provided with accommodation and students normally camp while working. Pay is usually on a piece work (*lavoro a cottimo*) basis, where the more you pick, the more you earn.

One of the most popular summer jobs in Italy is grape picking. Goodness knows why, because it's boring, badly paid and involves hard physical work, although a surprising number of young people find it appealing. Occupational hazards include mosquito and other insect bites, cuts from secateurs, rashes on your arms and legs from chemical sprays, and incessant back pain from bending all day long. Accommodation and cooking facilities can be extremely primitive, and the cost of food and accommodation is usually deducted from your pay. The main grape-picking areas are Emilia Romagna, Lazio, Marche, Piedmont, Puglia, Trentino, Tuscany and Veneto, where the harvest (*vendemmia*) is in September or October. The seasons and regions for some other crops are shown below:

- Apples and pears – Emilia Romagna, Trentino and Veneto from August to October;
- Cherries, peaches, plums and strawberries: Emilia Romagna and Piedmont from May to August;
- Flowers – Liguria and Tuscany year round;
- Olives – southern Italy, Marche, Sardinia, Sicily, Tuscany, Umbria, Veneto from November to January;
- Tobacco – Campania, Puglia and Umbria from November to December;
- Vegetables – Emilia Romagna and Veneto from spring to late autumn.

Ski Resorts

A seasonal job in an Italian ski resort can be a lot of fun and very satisfying. You will get fit, improve your Italian, make some friends, and may even save some money. **Although a winter job may be a working holiday to you (with lots of skiing and little work), to your employer it means exactly the opposite!** Ski resorts require an army of temporary workers to cater for the annual invasion of winter sports enthusiasts. As well as the jobs in the hotel and catering trades already mentioned above, a variety of other jobs are available, including resort representatives, chalet girls, ski technicians, ski instructors and guides. As a general rule, the better paid the job, the longer the working hours and the less time there is for skiing. Employment in a winter resort usually entitles employees to a discounted ski-pass.

An invaluable book for anyone looking for a job in a ski resort is *Working in Ski Resorts – Europe*, by Victoria Pybus & Charles James (Vacation Work).

Sports Instructors

Sports instructors are required for a variety of sports, including badminton, canoeing, diving, golf, gymnastics, hang-gliding, horse riding, mountaineering, parachuting, rock-climbing, sailing, squash, sub-aquatic sports, swimming, tennis and windsurfing. Whatever the sport, it's probably played and taught somewhere in Italy. Most jobs for are available in the summer months. If you're a qualified winter sports instructor, you should contact Italian ski resorts. Ski instructors and guides should also contact tour operators, large luxury hotels, and ski rental and service shops.

You should start applying for work from May onwards. Interviews usually take place from early September through to early November and successful candidates are on the job by mid-December. If you miss the May deadline, you should still apply, because many applicants who have been offered jobs drop out at the last minute.

Books

There are many books for those seeking holiday jobs (see also page 28), including *Summer Jobs Abroad* by David Woodworth and *Work Your Way Around the World* by Susan Griffith (both published by Vacation Work). *A Year Off, A Year On* is published by CRAC Learning Materials, Hobson Publishing plc, Bateman Street, Cambridge CB2 1LZ, UK (🖥 www.hobsons.com).

If you're a sports or ski instructor, tour guide, holiday representative or are involved in any job that gives you responsibility for groups of people or children, you should be extremely wary of accepting an illegal job without a contract, as you won't be insured for injuries to yourself, the public or accidents while travelling. Bear in mind that seasonal workers have few rights and little legal job protection in Italy, and can generally be fired without compensation at any time.

See also **Recruitment Agencies** on page 26 and **Temporary, Casual & Part-Time Work** below.

TEMPORARY, CASUAL & PART-TIME WORK

Temporary (*lavoro temporaneo*) and casual work (*lavoro occasionale*) is usually for a limited or fixed period, ranging from a few hours to a few months, or work may be intermittent. Part-time work (*lavoro a tempo parziale* or *lavoro part-time*), however, may be a temporary or permanent job but with reduced working hours, e.g. up to 20 hours per week. Casual workers are often employed on a daily, first-come, first-served basis. Anyone looking for casual unskilled work in Italy must usually compete with Albanians, North Africans and other unemployed foreigners, who are usually prepared to work for less money than anyone else, although nobody should be paid less than the minimum wage (see page 40) for a particular job, which should be aligned with that of permanent employees. Many employers illegally pay temporary staff in cash without making deductions for social security (see **Illegal Working** on page 48). Temporary and casual work usually includes the following:

- Office and secretarial work, which is well paid if you're qualified and the easiest work to find in cities and large towns.

- Work in the building trade, which can be found by applying at building sites and through industrial recruitment agencies (such as Manpower).

- Jobs in shops and stores, which are often available over Christmas and during sales periods.

- Gardening jobs in private gardens (possibly working for a landscape gardener), public parks and garden centres, particularly in spring and summer.

- Peddling ice cream, cold drinks and fast food in summer, e.g. on beaches.

- Working as a deck-hand on a yacht operating from one of Italy's fashionable coastal resorts.

- A wide variety of jobs can be found on board ships. Most cruise and some ferry companies are happy to take on foreign staff, although you stand a better chance if you can speak another European language fluently.

- Writers and translators can find work with Italian businesses wishing to do business with the English-speaking world.

- Market research, which entails asking people personal questions, either in the street or door to door.

- Modelling at art colleges; both sexes are usually required and not just the body beautiful.

- Work as a security guard (long hours for low pay).

- Nursing and auxiliary nursing in hospitals, clinics and nursing homes.

- Newspaper, magazine and leaflet distribution.

- Courier work (own transport required – motorcycle, car or van).
- Driving jobs, including coach and truck drivers, and ferrying cars for manufacturers and car hire companies.
- Miscellaneous jobs such as office cleaners, baby-sitters and labourers, are available from a number of agencies specialising in temporary work.

Temporary jobs are advertised in employment offices, on notice boards in expatriate clubs, churches and organisations, and in expatriate newsletters and newspapers. See also **Private Recruitment Agencies** on page 26 and **Seasonal Jobs** on page 28.

ENGLISH TEACHERS & TRANSLATORS

There's a high demand for English teachers, translators and interpreters in the major cities in Italy, particularly in Rome and the north of the country. There's a high turnover of teachers in language schools and a constant demand for translators (and sometimes writers) from Italian companies.

Language Schools

There are literally hundreds of English-language schools (*scuole di lingua*) in Italy, many of which expect teachers to have a TEFL (Teacher of English as a Foreign Language) certificate or its equivalent, although this isn't always the case. Some schools employ anyone whose mother tongue is English provided they've had experience in teaching, while others have their own teaching methods and prefer to train teachers to their own standards. Many of the best schools are members of the Italian Association of English Language Schools (Associazione Italiana Scuole di Lingua Inglese/AISLI), a list of which is available from the Cambridge Centre of English, Via Campanella, 16, 41100 Modena (☎ 059-241 004). Language schools generally pay less than you can earn giving private lessons, but they provide a contract and pay your taxes and social security. However, you may be able to obtain only a short-term contract or freelance work. You're usually paid by the hour and therefore should ensure that you have a guaranteed number of hours per week. Schools are listed under *Scuole di Lingua* in the yellow pages.

Private Lessons

Italians tend to favour learning lots of grammar and you also find that students know a lot about English literature, but cannot speak a word of it correctly! If you aren't up-to-date with grammar and you want to teach privately, you should stick to teaching conversation or children. Work is generally easy to find, particularly in university cities and towns, as students must usually study English as part of their course work. Many foreigners teach English privately and are paid cash-in-hand by students, much of which is never declared. Most people find that when they have a few students they spread the word and before you know it you have as much work as you can handle. You could also try placing an advertisement in local newspapers and magazines offering private English lessons, although replies may be received from Italian men who think that 'English lessons' implies something other than language lessons! The going rate for private lessons varies, but averages around €30 per hour (it's usually higher in major cities than small towns).

Translators & Interpreters

These are other occupations that tend to come under the heading of English teaching, with many expatriates moving between the three professions quite easily. Professional translators and interpreters are in huge demand and are usually employed by agencies. For anyone speaking fluent Italian and wanting to work in Italy, it would be worthwhile training as a professional translator or interpreter. Professional translators are paid by the page (or line) and the average rate is €15 per page, although this varies according to the kind of translation. Rates are higher in Rome and the northern cities than in the south. Translating is a long and tiresome business, you must usually work to stringent deadlines, the subject matter can be highly technical (requiring special vocabulary) and translations must be precise. If you don't translate medical notes, legal papers or business documents accurately, any mistakes could have serious consequences! Interpreters are employed mainly for exhibitions, congresses and seminars. You may be paid a flat rate for the day, e.g. between €35 and €55, or by the hour, e.g. €8.

University Teaching

English is taught in most universities in Italy and positions for assistants (*lettori*) in the English-language departments of Italian Universities are open to foreigners with university degrees. Applications should be made directly to the Rector of the University, followed by the name of the town or city, e.g. '*Al Magnifico Rettore, Università di . .*'. The same procedure should be followed for the University Institute of Modern Languages at Feltre and Milano, and also for the Università Cattolica del Sacro Cuore di Milano and the Istituto Universitario Orientale di Napoli.

Further Information

An excellent source of information is *Teaching English in Italy* by Martin Penner. For a more general overview you could try *Teaching English Abroad* by Susan

Griffith (Vacation Work) or *Teaching English as a Foreign Language and Teaching Abroad* published by AGCAS, Direct Prospects, CSU, Prospects House, Booth Street East, Manchester M13 9EP, UK (💻 www.prospects.ac.uk). Another useful resource for English teachers is the monthly *El Gazette*, PO Box 464, Berkhamsted, Hertfordshire HP4 2UR, UK (☎ 01442-879 097, 💻 www.elga zette.com). Finally, make use of the British Council (💻 www.britishcouncil.org), which recruits English language teachers and supervisory staff for placements in its language centres. It's necessary to have an RSA diploma or PGCE in TEFL and two years experience for most positions. For managerial posts, postgraduate qualifications and a minimum of five years experience are required. For information contact The British Council, Teacher Recruitment Unit, ELT Group, 10 Spring Gardens, London SW1A 2BN, UK (☎ 020-7389 4167).

VOLUNTARY WORK

Voluntary work (as described here) is primarily to enable students and young people to visit Italy for a few weeks or months, and learn about the country and its people at first hand. The minimum age limit for volunteers is 16 to 18 and they must usually be under 30, although some organisations have no upper age limit. No special qualifications are required and the minimum length of service is usually a few weeks. Handicapped volunteers are welcomed by many organisations. **Voluntary work (*lavori socialmente utili*) is unpaid and you must usually pay a registration fee that includes liability and health insurance, and your travel costs both to and from Italy and to the workcamp.** Although meals and accommodation are normally provided, you may be expected to contribute towards the cost of board and lodging. The usual visa regulations apply to voluntary workers and you're informed when applying whether you need one. A work permit isn't necessary.

There are over 35,000 volunteer associations, co-operatives and foundations in Italy, including some 75 workcamps organised by Volunteers for Peace. Much voluntary work in Italy takes place in international workcamps, which provide the opportunity for young people to live and work together on a range of projects, including agriculture, archaeology, building, conservation, environmental, gardening, handicrafts, restoration of buildings and monuments, social welfare and community projects. Camps are usually run for two to four weeks between April and October, although some operate all year round (you must usually apply before March to find a position the same year). Work is unskilled or semi-skilled and is for around five to eight hours per day, five or six days per week. The work is usually quite physically demanding and accommodation, shared with your fellow 'slaves', is fairly basic. Most workcamps consist of volunteers from several countries and English may be the common language.

Many organisations, both Italian and international, host volunteer programmes for students and young people, some of which are listed below:

- The Belgian-based Association of Voluntary Service Organisations maintains a directory of volunteer opportunities throughout the world, and the group Action Without Borders has a directory website (⌨ www.idealist.org);

- Earthwatch Europe, 267 Banbury Road, Oxford OX2 7HT, UK (☎ 01865-318 838, ⌨ www.earthwatch.org);

- Italian Foundation of Volunteering (Fondazione Italiana per il Volontariato), Via Nazionale, 39, 00184 Rome (☎ 06-4748 1230, ⌨ www.fivol.it);

- Mani Tese, Piazza Gambara, 7/9, 20146 Milan (☎ 02-4075 165, ⌨ www.manitese.it);

- National Coordination of Welcoming Communities (CNCA), Via G Baglivi, 8, 00161 Rome, (☎ 06-4423 0395, ⌨ www.cnca.it);

- National Public Assistance Association (ANPAS), Via Baracca, 209, 50127 Florence (☎ 055-374 887, ⌨ www.anpas.org);

- Servizio Civile Internazionale, Via G Cardano, 135, 00146 Rome (☎ 06-5580 644, ⌨ www.sci-italia.it).

Useful websites for prospective volunteers include ⌨ www.citinv.it, ⌨ www.greenpeace.org, ⌨ www.quinonprofit.it and ⌨ www.assofa.org.

In addition to workcamps, there are a variety of unpaid voluntary jobs in Italy, particularly in Rome and other major cities. Voluntary work is an excellent way to improve your Italian and gain valuable work experience, and may even be an entry to a permanent salaried job. Whatever your motive, whether it's a desire to make new friends, boredom, or a stepping stone to a new career, voluntary work is highly rewarding. Whenever you find yourself wondering what to do, contact your local expatriate organisations – they will put those idle hands to work!

JOB HUNTING

When looking for a job in Italy, it's best not to put all your eggs in one basket – the more jobs you apply for, the better your chances are of finding one. Contact as many prospective employers as possible, either by writing, telephoning or calling on them in person. Whatever job you're looking for, it's important to market yourself correctly and appropriately, which depends on the kind of job or position you're seeking. For example, the recruitment of executives and senior managers is handled almost exclusively by executive search companies which advertise in the Italian 'national' press and trade magazines. At the other end of the scale, manual jobs requiring no previous experience may be advertised at local employment offices (*uffici di collocamento*), in local newspapers and on notice boards, and the first suitable applicant may be offered the job on the spot. Job hunting includes the following resources:

Newspapers

Most national, regional and local newspapers (see page 392) contain a situations vacant or jobs section (*Offerte di Lavoro* or *Offerte di Collaborazione*) on certain days of the week. The Milan daily newspaper, *Corriere della Sera*, publishes a *Corriere Lavoro* (💻 www.corriere.it/corrierelavoro) job supplement on Fridays and the financial newspaper, *Il Sole 24 Ore*, publishes *Cerco Lavoro – Giovani* for college graduates on Mondays and also publishes a *Lavoro & Carriere* supplement. There are also specialised local and national newspapers for job seekers such as *Il Posto* (the job) and *Il Concorso* (which lists civil service and local government jobs) in Naples, *Trova Lavoro* and *Bollettino Del Lavoro* (💻 www.bollettinodellavoro.it), a monthly publication available at employment offices and libraries. Jobs are also advertised in industry and trade newspapers and magazines. Ask the locals which publications and days are best for job ads. in your area.

Most major newspapers and magazines have websites where you can usually access their 'situations vacant' sections free of charge and local and national newspapers are available in libraries, bars and cafés in Italy, so you don't always need to buy them. Italian newspapers are also available abroad from international news agencies, trade and commercial centres, expatriate organisations and social clubs (although they don't always contain the 'appointments' or 'situations vacant' sections).

Most professions and trade associations publish journals containing job offers (see *Benn's Media Directory Europe*) and jobs are also advertised in various English-language publications, including the *International Herald Tribune, Wall Street Journal Europe, Wanted in Rome* and other local publications (see **Appendix A**). You can also place an advertisement in the 'situations wanted' section of a local newspaper in Italy in an area where you would like to work. If you're a member of a recognised profession or trade, you could place an advertisement in a newspaper or magazine dedicated to your profession or industry. It's best to place an advert in the middle of the week and avoid the summer and other holiday periods.

Employment Offices

Visit local employment offices (*uffici di collocamento*) and other offices in Italy (see page 25). Jobs on offer are mainly non-professional skilled, semi-skilled and unskilled jobs, particularly in industry, retailing and catering.

Information Centres And Libraries

Local information centres (*informagiovani*) are useful for information about jobs, job hunting, education and training, for more details visit their website (💻 www.informagiovani.it). Main libraries also provide a range of resources for job seekers, although they don't specifically provide advice and assistance for the unemployed, as in some other countries.

Recruitment Agencies

Apply to international recruitment agencies acting for Italian companies and foreign companies in Italy. These companies chiefly help to recruit executives and key personnel, and many have offices world-wide, including in many Italian cities (see page 26). **Some Italian agencies may find positions only for Italian and EU nationals or foreigners with a residence permit.**

Chambers Of Commerce

Foreign chambers of commerce (camera di commercio) in Italy maintain lists of their member companies doing business (or with subsidiaries) in Italy. British nationals can join the British chamber of commerce in Italy, Via Dante, 12, 20121 Milan (☎ 02-877 798 or 8056 094, 💻 www.britchamitaly.com) for between €140 and €1,200, for a range of different memberships and benefits. Italian chambers of commerce abroad are also a useful source of information, as are Euro Info Centres (EIC) found in the major cities of EU countries. Infoimprese (💻 www. infoimprese.it) is a useful website of Italian chambers of commerce with information on companies.

Internet

The Internet provides access to hundreds of sites for job-seekers, including corporate websites, recruitment companies (see page 26) and newspaper job advertisements (you can use a search engine to find them).

Unsolicited Applications To Companies

Apply to American, British and other multi-national companies with offices or subsidiaries in Italy, and make written applications direct to Italian companies. Italian companies are listed by products, services and province in *Kompass Italy* and directories, available at libraries in Italy, and main libraries and Italian chambers of commerce abroad. Making unsolicited job applications is naturally a hit and miss affair. It can, however, be more successful than responding to advertisements, as you aren't usually competing with other applicants. Some companies recruit a large percentage of employees through unsolicited applications. When applying for jobs, address your letter to the personnel director (*capo del personale*) and include your CV (in Italian), and copies of references and qualifications. If possible, offer to attend an interview and tell them when you're available. Letters should be tailored to individual companies and professionally translated if your Italian isn't perfect. **Some Italian**

companies require hand-written letters from job applicants and may submit them to graphologists. When writing from abroad, enclosing an international reply coupon may help to elicit a response.

Networking

Networking basically involves getting together with like-minded people to discuss business. It's particularly useful in Italy, where people use personal contacts for everything from looking for jobs to finding accommodation. In fact, a personal recommendation (*raccomandati*) is often the best way to find employment in Italy, where nepotism and favouritism are rife. When looking for a job in Italy, it isn't necessarily **what** you know but **who** you know. It's difficult for most foreigners to make contacts among Italians and therefore many turn to the expatriate community, particularly in Rome and Milan. If you're already in Italy, you can contact or join local expatriate social clubs, churches, societies and professional organisations (see also **Appendix A**). Finally, don't forget to ask your friends and acquaintances working in Italy if they know of an employer seeking someone with your experience and qualifications.

Personal Applications

Your best chance of obtaining certain jobs in Italy is to apply in person, when success is often simply a matter of being in the right place at the right time. Many companies don't advertise at all, but rely on attracting workers by word of mouth and by their own vacancy boards. Shops and supermarkets often put vacancy notices in their windows or have notice boards where employers can advertise jobs, although these are generally for temporary or part-time help only.

It's recommended to leave your name and address with a prospective employer and, if possible, a telephone number where you can be contacted, particularly when a job may become vacant at a moment's notice. Advertise the fact that you're looking for a job, not only with friends, relatives and acquaintances, but with anyone you come into contact with who may be able to help. You can give lady luck a helping hand with your persistence and enterprise by:

- cold calling on prospective employers;
- checking 'wanted' boards;
- looking in local newspapers;
- checking notice and bulletin boards in large companies, shopping centres, embassies, clubs, sports centres and news agencies;
- asking other foreign workers.

When leaving a job in Italy, it's wise to ask for a written reference (which isn't usually provided automatically), particularly if you plan to look for further work in Italy or you think your work experience will help you find work in another country.

SALARIES

It isn't usually difficult to determine the salary you should command in Italy, where salaries in most industries are decided by collective bargaining between employers and unions. Agreements specify minimum wage (see page 40) levels for each position within main employment categories in a particular industry or company. This means that wage levels are effectively fixed, although it also ensures that they keep pace with inflation. When there's a collective agreement, employers must offer at least the minimum wage agreed, although these are exceeded by most major companies. However, salaries vary considerably for the same job in different regions of Italy. Those working in Milan and other northern cities are generally the highest paid, primarily due to the high cost of living, particularly accommodation. Women are generally paid less than men, even when they're doing the same job.

Most employees in Italy receive an extra month's salary at Christmas, known as the 13th month's salary (*tredicesima mesilità*) or a Christmas bonus (*gratifica natalizia*), and many employees also receive a 14th month's salary (*quattordicesima mesilità*) prior to the summer holiday period. Some employees, such as those in the banking and petroleum industries, even receive 15th and 16th months' salary!

If you're able to negotiate your own salary you should ensure that you receive the salary and benefits commensurate with your qualifications and experience (or as much as you can get!). If you have friends or acquaintances working in Italy or who have worked there, ask them what an average or good salary is for your particular trade or profession. When comparing salaries you must take into account compulsory deductions such as tax and social security, and also compare the cost of living (see page 321). Italian salaries for executives and managers compare favourably with other western countries and are among the highest in Europe, although wages are below average for many other workers. In recent years, university graduates and school-leavers have had to accept almost any wage in order to get a foot on the career ladder.

Salaries are generally similar to those in Britain, but lower than those in the USA. In the managerial category, staff may receive from €2,900 per month, office staff receive from around €1,300 per month, while manual workers receive from €1,100 and agricultural workers around €1,600. A foreign executive may find that his salary is much higher in Italy. Italian executive salaries were lower than the international average in the 1970s and 1980s, but have since caught up and even surpassed some of their competitors. Executive salaries rose much faster than the rate of inflation over the last few decades and are augmented by lucrative bonuses and profit-sharing schemes.

For many employees, particularly executives and senior managers, their remuneration is much more than what they receive in their monthly pay packets. Many companies offer a range of benefits for executives and managers that may include a company car (although rare in Italy), private health insurance and health screening, expenses-paid holidays, private school fees, inexpensive or interest-free home and other loans, rent-free accommodation, free or subsidised public transport tickets, free or subsidised company restaurant, sports or country club membership, non-contributory company pension, stock options, bonuses and profit-sharing schemes, tickets for sports events and shows, and 'business' conferences in exotic places (see also **Executive Positions** on page 70).

SELF-EMPLOYMENT

If you're an EU national or a permanent resident with a *certificato di residenza,* you can work as self-employed (*lavoro autonomo* or *lavora in proprio*), freelance (*lavoro indipendente* or *libero professionista*) or as a sole trader (*commerciante in proprio, imprenditore* or *ditta individuale*) in Italy. If you wish to work as self-employed in a profession or start a freelance business in Italy, you must meet certain legal requirements and register with the appropriate organisations. For example, you must be included on the Register of Enterprises (Registro delle Imprese) maintained by the local chamber of commerce (Camera di Commercio) and obtain a certificate of registration (*certificato di iscrizione*). **A permit to stay (see page 79) doesn't automatically allow you to work as self-employed and it needs to be changed to a** *permesso di soggiorno per lavoro autonomo/indipendente* (how easy this will be depends on your nationality and status). Before starting work you must also register with the local tax office (*intendenza di finanza*) and be registered for VAT (*imposta sul valore aggiunto/IVA* – see page 307).

Under Italian law, a self-employed person must have an official status and it's illegal to simply hang up a sign and start business. Members of some professions and trades must have certain qualifications and certificates recognised in Italy. You should **never** be tempted to start work before you're registered, for which there are stiff penalties, which may include a large fine, confiscation of machinery or tools, deportation and even a ban from entering Italy for a number of years.

If you're self-employed and operate as a sole trader, you must register with the local tax office and are taxed in the same way as any other individual. **Note, however, that the liabilities of a sole trader aren't deemed to be separate from his personal debts and should you become insolvent you would be declared bankrupt.** Therefore you may find it advantageous to operate as a limited company (see page 45), for example a *società a responsabilità limitata* (*Srl*) or *società per azioni* (*SpA*). Always obtain professional advice before deciding whether to operate as a sole trader or form a company, as it has far-reaching social security, tax and other consequences.

Self-employed people may wish to join the Unione di Commercio, which provides a range of information and assistance for the self-employed and those running their own businesses, including supplementary health insurance, help in dealing with Italian bureaucracy, taxation and social security.

STARTING A BUSINESS

The bureaucracy associated with starting a business (*azienda*) in Italy is horrendous and rates among the most pernicious in the world. Italy is an almost impenetrable red tape jungle and Italian civil servants (*impiegati*) can be inordinately obstructive, endlessly recycling bits of paper to create 'employment' for themselves. For foreigners, Italy is a bureaucratic nightmare, particularly if you don't speak Italian, and you will be inundated with official documents and must be able to understand them. It's only when you come up against the full force of Italian bureaucracy that you understand what it **really** means to be a foreigner! You should expect to spend most of your time battling with civil servants when establishing a new business. However, despite the red tape, Italy is traditionally a land of small companies (there are over three million employing less than 50 people) and individual traders, where the culture and economic philosophy actually encourages and even nurtures the creation of small businesses.

Professional Assistance

Due to the difficulties in complying with (or understanding) Italian laws and bureaucracy, there are agencies (colloquially called *galoppini*) that specialise in obtaining documents and making applications for individuals and businesses, listed in the yellow pages under *Certificati, Agenzie*. They act as a buffer between you and officialdom, and register your business with the tax registrar's office (*ufficio registro*), registrar of enterprises (*registro delle imprese*), the registrar of companies at the local chamber of commerce (*ufficio delle ditte*), local tax office (*intendenza di finanza*) and obtain a value added tax (*imposta sul valore aggiunto/IVA*) number from your local vat office (*ufficio IVA*). A notary (*notiao*) can also do this, but is much more expensive. If you're a professional, you may need to take a routine examination before you can be included on the professional register (*albo professionale*) with the chamber of commerce. There are also business consultants and relocation agencies in many areas that provide invaluable local assistance. International accountants such as PricewaterhouseCoopers and Ernst & Young have offices throughout Italy, and are an invaluable source of information (in English) on subjects such as forming a company, company law, taxation and social security. Many countries maintain chambers of commerce in Italy, which are also a good source of information and assistance.

Italian Trade Organisations

There are a number of Italian trade organisations, including the Istituto Nazionale per il Commercio Estero (ICE), Via Lizst, 21, 00144, Rome (☎ 06-59921, 🖥 www. ice.it), which is a public organisation (with over 30 offices in Italy and some 80 abroad) that promotes Italian trade throughout the world. Confcommercio, Confederazione Generale Italiana del Turismo dei Servizi e delle PMI, Piazza G G Belli 2, 00153 Rome (☎ 06-58661, 🖥 www.confcommercio.it) is another trade organisation specialising in certain industries, such as construction, computers (hardware and software), cosmetics, fashion, retailing, and import and export, which organises trade fairs and other promotional activities, and provides free financial and legal advice to its members.

Legal Advice

Before undertaking any business transactions in Italy, it's important to obtain legal advice to ensure that you're operating within the law. There are severe penalties for anyone who ignores the regulations and legal requirements. It's also important to obtain legal advice before establishing a limited company. Businesses must also register for value added tax. Non-EU nationals require a special licence to start a business in Italy and no commitments should be made until permission has been granted. Among the best sources of help and information are local chambers of commerce and town halls (*municipio*).

Experience

Generally speaking you shouldn't consider running a business in Italy in a field in which you don't have previous experience (excluding 'businesses' such as bed and breakfast, where experience isn't really necessary). It's often wise to work for someone else in the same line of business in order to gain experience, rather than jump in at the deep end. Always thoroughly investigate an existing or proposed business before investing any money. **As any expert will tell you, Italy isn't a country for amateur entrepreneurs, particularly amateurs who don't speak fluent Italian!** Many small businesses in Italy exist on a shoe-string and certainly aren't what would be considered thriving enterprises. As in many countries, most people are self-employed for the lifestyle and freedom it affords (no clocks or bosses!), rather than the financial rewards. It's important to keep your plans small and manageable, and stay well within your budget, rather than undertaking some grandiose scheme.

Avoiding The Crooks

In addition to problems with the Italian authorities, you may also come into contact with assorted crooks and swindlers who will try to relieve you of your money. You should have a healthy suspicion regarding the motives of anyone you do business with in Italy, particularly your fellow countrymen. It's also generally best to avoid partnerships, as they rarely work and can be a disaster. In general, you should trust nobody and shouldn't sign anything or pay any money before having a contract checked by a lawyer. It's a sad fact of life that foreigners who prey on their fellow countrymen are commonplace in Italy. In most cases you're better off dealing with a long-established Italian company with roots in the local community (and therefore a good reputation to protect), rather than your compatriots. **If things go wrong, you may be unprotected by Italian law**, the wheels of which grind extremely slowly – when they haven't fallen off completely!

Buying An Existing Business

It's much easier to buy an existing business in Italy than to start a new one and it's also less of a risk. The paperwork for taking over an existing business is also simpler, although still complex. Buying a business that's a going concern is difficult as Italians aren't in a habit of buying and selling businesses, which are usually passed down from generation to generation. If you plan to buy a business, obtain an independent valuation (or two) and employ an accountant (*commercialista*) to audit the books. **Never sign anything that you don't understand 110 per cent, and even if you think you understand it, you should still obtain unbiased professional advice, e.g. from local experts such as banks and accountants, before buying a business.** In fact, it's best not to start a business until you have the infrastructure established, including an accountant, lawyer and banking facilities. There are various ways to set up a small business and it's essential to obtain professional advice regarding the best method of establishing and registering a business in Italy, which can dramatically affect your tax position. It's also important to employ an accountant to do your books.

Starting A New Business

Most people are far too optimistic about the prospects for a new business in Italy and overestimate income levels (it often takes years to make a profit). Be realistic or even pessimistic when estimating your income and overestimate the costs and underestimate the revenue (then reduce it by 50 per cent!). While hoping for the best, you should plan for the worst and have sufficient funds to last until you're established (under-funding is the major cause of business failures). New projects are rarely, if ever, completed within budget and you need to ensure that you have sufficient working capital and can survive until a business takes off. Italian banks are extremely wary of lending to new businesses, particularly businesses run by foreigners, and it's almost impossible for foreigners to obtain finance in Italy. If you wish to borrow money to buy property or for a business venture in Italy, you should carefully consider where and in what currency to raise the finance.

Location

Choosing the location for a business is even more important than the location for a home. Depending on the type of business, you may need access to motorways (*autostrade*) and rail links, or to be located in a popular tourist area or near local attractions. Local plans regarding communications, industry and major building developments, e.g. housing complexes and new shopping centres, may also be important. Plans regarding new motorways and rail links are normally available from local town halls.

Employees

Hiring employees shouldn't be undertaken lightly in Italy and must be taken into account before starting a business. You must enter into a contract under Italian labour law and employees enjoy extensive rights. If you buy an existing business, you may be required to take on existing (possibly inefficient) staff who cannot be dismissed, or be faced with paying high redundancy compensation. It's **very** expensive to hire employees, because, in addition to salaries, you must pay an additional amount of around 50 per cent in social security contributions, 13 and possibly 14 months' salary, five or six weeks paid annual holiday, plus pay for public holidays, sickness, maternity, etc.

Type Of Business

The most common businesses operated by foreigners in Italy include holiday accommodation, caravan and camping sites, building and allied trades (particularly restoring old houses in Tuscany and Umbria), farming, catering, hotels, shops, franchises, estate agencies, translation and interpreting bureaux, language and foreign schools, landscape gardening, and holiday and sports centres. The majority of businesses established by foreigners are linked to the leisure and catering industries, followed by property investment and development. Many professionals such as doctors and dentists have also set up practices in Italy to serve the expatriate community. There are also opportunities in import and export, e.g. importing foreign foods (e.g. health foods) for the Italian and expatriate market, and exporting Italian goods such as handicrafts and fashion. You can also find niche markets in providing services for expatriates and Italians that are unavailable in Italy.

Companies

Companies cannot be purchased 'off the shelf' in Italy and it usually takes a number of months to establish one. Incorporating a company in Italy takes longer and is more expensive and more complicated than in many other European countries. There are many different kinds of 'limited companies' or business entities in Italy and choosing the right one is important. The most common kinds of companies in Italy are a *società a responsibilità limitata* (*Srl*) and a *società per azioni* (*SpA*), with a minimum share capitalisation of €10,000 and €100,000 respectively. **Always obtain professional legal advice regarding the advantages and disadvantages of different limited companies.**

Grants & Incentives

Many different grants and incentives are available for new businesses in Italy, particularly in rural areas and the south of the country (the *Mezzogiorno*). Grants include EU subsidies, central government grants, regional development grants, redeployment grants, and grants from provincial authorities and local communities. Grants may include assistance to buy buildings and equipment (or the provision of low-cost business premises), research and technological assistance, subsidies for job creation, low-interest loans and tax incentives (ten years for new companies established in the *Mezzogiorno*). Contact Italian chambers of commerce and embassies for information (see **Appendix A**). Information about chambers of commerce in Italy and a list of offices is provided on the Internet (🖳 www.camcom.it).

Whatever people may tell you, working for yourself isn't easy and requires a lot of hard work (self-employed people generally work much longer hours than employees), a sizeable investment and sufficient operating funds (most new businesses fail due to a lack of capital), good organisation (e.g. bookkeeping and planning), excellent customer relations, and a measure of luck – although generally the harder you work, the more 'luck' you have. Don't be seduced by the apparent laid-back way of life in Italy – if you want to be a success in business you cannot play at it. Bear in mind that some two-thirds of all new businesses fail within three to five years and that the self-employed enjoy far fewer social security benefits than employees.

AU PAIRS

Single males and females aged between 18 and 30 are eligible for a position as an au pair (*alla pari*) for up to 12 months. The au pair system provides an excellent opportunity to travel, improve your Italian, and generally broaden your education by living and working in Italy. The main aim of the au pair system is to give young people the opportunity to learn a foreign language in a typical family environment. Au pairs are accepted from most countries. If you're an EU national you need only a valid passport and aren't required to arrange a position before arriving, although it's usually wise. Some agencies allow you to meet families in Italy before making a final decision, which is highly desirable as you can interrogate the family, inspect their home and your accommodation, and meet the children who will make your life heaven or hell! However, applicants from non-EU countries need a visa (see page 76), an agreement with a Italian family and a certificate of registration for Italian classes at a language school. These must be presented to your local Italian embassy or consulate with your passport when applying for a visa.

Au pairs are usually contracted to work for a minimum of six and a maximum of 12 months. Most families require an au pair for at least the whole school year, from September to June. The best time to look for an au pair position is therefore before the beginning of the school year in September. You should apply as early as possible and not later than one month prior to your preferred start date or at least two months if you need a visa.

Au pairs are usually placed in Italian-speaking families with children, although non-Italian-speaking families without children can also engage an au pair. An au pair's duties consist of light housework, including simple cooking for children, clothes washing (with a machine) and ironing, washing and drying dishes (if the family doesn't have a dishwasher), making beds, dusting; vacuum cleaning, and other light jobs around the home. To enjoy life as an au pair you should be used to helping around the house and like working with children. An au pair isn't a general servant or cook (although you may be treated as one) and you aren't expected to look after physically or mentally handicapped children. As an au pair, you receive all meals and accommodation, usually with a study area, in lieu of a salary.

Working hours are officially limited to 30 per week, five hours per day (morning or afternoon), six days per week, plus a maximum of three evenings' baby-sitting. You should be given time off to attend Italian classes and religious services. In some families, au pairs holiday with the family or are free to take Christmas or Easter holidays at home. Choose a wealthy family and you may be taken on exotic foreign holidays, although they may be less likely to treat you as a close family member. For your labours you're paid the princely sum of around €6 per hour. You're required to pay your own fare from your country to Italy (and back). Your family is also required to pay for health insurance under the national health service (SSN).

An au pair position can be arranged privately with a family or through an agency. There are au pair agencies in Italy and many other countries and positions can also be found via magazines (such as the British *The Lady* magazine) and newspapers, but you're usually better off going through an agency. The better agencies vet families, make periodic checks on your welfare, help you overcome problems (either personal or with your family), and may organise cultural activities (particularly in major cities). An agency will send you an application form (questionnaire) and usually ask you to provide character (moral) and child-care references, a medical certificate and school references. Au pairs must usually have had a high school education or the equivalent, have a good knowledge of Italian and must attend Italian-language classes (see page 191) organised for foreign students. Agency registration fees vary, although there are maximum fees in some countries, e.g. around £50 in Britain.

Your experience as an au pair will depend entirely on your relationship with your family. If you're fortunate enough to work for a warm and friendly host family, you will have a wonderful experience, lots of free time and possibly some memorable holidays. Many au pairs grow to love their children and families, and form lifelong friendships. On the other hand, abuses of the au pair system are common in all countries and you may be treated as a servant rather than a member of the family, and be expected to work long hours and spend most evenings baby-sitting. Many families engage an au pair simply because it costs far less than employing a nanny. If you have any complaints about your duties, you should refer them to the agency that found you your position (if applicable). **There are many families to choose from and you shouldn't feel that you need to remain with a family that treats you badly.** You're usually required to give notice if you wish to go home before the end of your agreement, although this won't apply if the family has broken the contract.

Prospective au pairs should contact a number of agencies and compare registration fees and pocket money, both of which may vary considerably (although the terms of employment should be the same). Pocket money is usually higher in major cities (e.g. Milan and Rome) than in the provinces. Many British agencies are listed in the *Au Pair and Nanny's Guide to Working Abroad* by Susan Griffith (Vacation Work). Note that it's possible for responsible Italian-speaking young women with or without experience or training to obtain employment as a nanny in Italy. Duties are basically the same as an au pair, although a position as a nanny is a proper job with full employee rights and a real salary!

Italian au pair agencies include Agencia Intermediate, Via Bramante, 13, 00153 Rome (☎ 06-5747 444), Euro Au Pair, Corso dei Tintori, 8, Tintari, 50122 Florence (☎ 055-242 181), Jolly Italian Au Pair Agency, Via Giovanni XX111, 20, 36050 Monteviale (VI) (🖳 www.goldnet.it/jolly) and Mix Culture, Via Nazionale, 24, 00184 Rome (☎ 06-4788 2289).

ILLEGAL WORKING

Illegal working (*lavaro in nero*) thrives in Italy particularly in the south of the country (the *Mezzogiorno*) and among sections of the expatriate community and immigrants. It has been conservatively estimated that the black economy (*economia sommersa/nera*) is equal to as much as 30 per cent of the country's GDP – it's estimated that 30 per cent of all incomes are hidden from the taxman and up to 50 per cent in the south of the country! An employer may even ask you whether you want to be paid officially, with tax and social security deducted (*in regola*) or unofficially, e.g. cash in hand! It's most common in industries that employ itinerant workers such as the catering (bars and restaurants), construction, farming, tourism and textile industries, and in jobs such as domestic work and language teaching. Another aspect of illegal working is avoiding the payment of value added tax (*IVA*).

In many areas officials turn a blind eye, as the black economy keeps many small businesses alive and the unemployed in 'pocket money'. The government doesn't pay unemployment benefits to the long-term unemployed and any other benefits paid are usually too low to live on. Moonlighting by employees with second or third jobs is also widespread, particularly among those employed in the public sector, who are generally low paid. However, unscrupulous employers also use illegal labour in order to pay low wages (below the minimum wage) for long hours and poor working conditions.

It's strictly illegal for non-EU nationals to work in Italy without a work permit. **If you use illegal labour or avoid paying VAT, you have no official redress if goods or services are substandard.** If you work illegally, you have no entitlement to social security benefits such as insurance against work injuries, public health care, unemployment pay and a state pension. A foreigner who works illegally in Italy is liable to a heavy fine and deportation, while businesses can be fined, closed down and the owners imprisoned.

LANGUAGE

Although English is the *lingua franca* of international commerce and may help you secure a job in Italy, the most important qualification for anyone seeking employment is the ability to speak fluent Italian. English is the second language of young Italians and the ability to speak English confers prestige in Italy. It's widely spoken in the major cities such as Florence, Milan, Rome and Venice, which attract millions of foreign visitors each year, although it's unlikely to be spoken in the far south of the country and in many rural areas. Although not as proud or arrogant as the French where their language is concerned (Italy adopts foreign words with abandon), most Italians expect anyone living or working in Italy to speak it.

There are around 58 million Italian speakers in Italy plus 1.5 million in Croatia, France and Slovenia, some 500,000 in Switzerland, and large Italian immigrant groups in Argentina, Australia, Brazil and the USA. Dialects or foreign languages are used by some 60 per cent of Italians and spoken exclusively by around 15 per cent of the population. However, although many Italians converse in dialect at home, they tend to speak *italiano standard* when travelling outside their home region or speaking to foreigners. In reality, the universal language of Italy is sign language mainly using the hands (without which many Italians would be speechless), although the whole body is employed, including facial expressions. The first languages of some 2.5 million or 5 per cent of the population are languages such as French, German and Slovene. Italy is home to a number of linguistic minorities, some of which have been granted special privileges in autonomous or semi-autonomous regions, and their language given equal status with Italian. These include French (Valle d'Aosta), German (Alto Adige) and Slovene (Friuli-Venezia Giulia), which are all official languages taught in state schools in these regions.

Franco-provençal or Arpitano French dialects are spoken in Valle d'Aosta, and in certain Piedmont valleys and in the upper Val Argentina (IM), Provençal or Occitanian dialects are spoken. Most German-speaking minorities (some

300,000 speak the Bavarian-Austrian dialect) live in the Province of Bolzano, while Slovenes are generally restricted to the Val di Resia (UD), the upper Torre and Natisone valleys, Val Canale, the eastern part of Gorizia province and most of the province of Trieste (a total of around 50,000). Several groups speaking Serbo-Croat are found in Molise while Croatian, the smallest minority language spoken by some 2,000 people, has survived in Campobasso province in Molise.

Albanian-speaking colonies are concentrated mainly in Sicily and Calabria, but are also found in Molise, Abruzzo, Campania, Puglia and Basilicata, some of whom (descended from 15th century Albanian mercenaries) speak a dialect of Albanian known as Arbëresh.

There are Catalan-speaking groups in the town of Alghero in the north-west of Sardinia, dating from the island's capture by the crown of Aragon in 1354. Greek dialects are spoken in some parts of Calabria and Puglia. There are also gypsies who speak the *Sinti* dialect in the north and the *Rom* dialect in the centre and south of the country.

The main Italian dialects are *Sardo* (circa 1,350,000 speakers), *Friulano* (circa 700,000 speakers) and *Ladin* (circa 40,000 speakers). *Sardo*, spoken in Sardinia, is virtually another language entirely, similar to Catalan and dating back to Spanish rule. Variations in dialect can be particularly strong and include *Ligurian* (which employs a mixture of Italian, Catalan and French), *Neapolitan* and *Sicilian*.

Italian is one of the romance languages and is a beautiful tongue that's relatively easy to learn, particularly if you already know some French or Spanish (or Latin) – and have many hands. The Catholic Church still uses Latin as the official liturgical language and it's still taught in Italian schools from the 6th grade upwards (with the exception of technical establishments). Modern Italian is a descendant of 'vulgar' spoken Latin and was standardised in the late Middle Ages (14th century) by the literary triumvirate of Boccaccio, Dante and Petrarch, who wrote mainly in the Florentine dialect, which subsequently became the basis for today's standard Italian (*italiano standard*). This is the language taught in schools and used in the media, although it's often mixed with dialects. However, standard Italian has been in widespread use only since the unification of Italy in the 1860s and Italians were slow to adopt the language of the new nation-state, identifying much more strongly with their regional dialects.

If you don't already speak good Italian, don't expect to learn it quickly, even if you already have a basic knowledge and take intensive lessons. It's common for foreigners not to be fluent after a year or more of intensive lessons in Italy. If your expectations are unrealistic you will become frustrated, which can affect your confidence. It takes a long time to reach the level of fluency needed to be able to work in Italian and understand the various accents. If you don't speak Italian fluently, you should begin Italian lessons on arrival and consider taking a menial or even an unpaid voluntary job, as this is one of the quickest ways of improving your Italian.

If necessary you should have Italian lessons before arriving. A sound knowledge of Italian won't only help you find a job or perform your job better, but will make everyday life much simpler and more enjoyable. If you come to Italy without being able to speak Italian, you will be excluded from everyday life and will feel uncomfortable until you can understand what's going on around you. The most common reason for negative experiences among foreigners in Italy, both visitors and residents alike, is because they cannot or won't speak Italian. However terrible your Italian, your bad grammar, poor vocabulary and terrible accent will be much better appreciated than your fluent English. Italians will usually encourage you and greet your butchered attempts with appreciation and good humour. You **must** learn Italian if you wish to have Italian friends.

When doing business in Italy or writing letters to Italian businesses, communications should always be in Italian. Many Italians have a phobia about writing letters (most are unable to write grammatically correct Italian) and postpone replying to letters for as long as possible. However, if you write a letter to an Italian company applying for a job you should ensure that it's grammatically correct, even if it means employing a professional translator. When stating your Italian-language ability, it's important not to exaggerate, as it's easy to confirm the truth. If you state that your Italian is very good or fluent, you will almost certainly be interviewed in Italian (which is also possible even if you have only a little knowledge). Overstating your fluency is a waste of your and a prospective employer's time.

Those interested in the Italian language may like to check the Italian language website (🖥 www.italianlang.org) and http://italian.about.com. See also **Language** on page 49 and **Language Schools** on page 191.

2.

EMPLOYMENT CONDITIONS

Employment conditions (*condizioni di lavoro*) in Italy are generally good and employees are well protected by extensive social and labour laws (*statuto dei lavoratori*). In general, Italians enjoy among the best job security in the world; in Europe, only the Swiss have greater security. Italians also traditionally enjoy a wide range of benefits, which may include assistance towards housing, free transport, company canteens, children's nurseries and kindergartens, all of which are provided by many medium-size and large companies. Women are entitled to extensive maternity benefits, which are among the most generous in the world. Italian labour law is protective of an employee's welfare (particularly regarding dismissal) and tends to favour job security, although to a lesser extent than in the past. In recent years, the need for flexibility in the job market has become more widely accepted and temporary and part-time employment have become increasingly common.

Labour relations in various trades, industries and professions are governed by collective bargaining agreements (*contrattazione collettiva* or *contratto collettivo di lavoro*) negotiated between trade unions and employers' organisations. These cover around 75 per cent of the workforce and specify the rights and obligations of employers and employees in a particular industry or occupation. Collective bargaining agreements may be national (*contratto collettivo nazionale del lavoro/CCNL*), provincial or local in scope. Agreements are binding on all parties and establish the various categories of employee and the criteria and minimum limits for wages and benefits. Large enterprises usually have their own agreements or contracts (*accordi/contratti integrativi aziendali*), which operate within the framework of the collective agreements adopted at national level, but often improve upon the minimum requirements and take into account local circumstances.

If an employer doesn't abide by the laws or the regulations in a particular industry, employees can report him to unions or work syndicates. Where there's no union, a case is heard before an industrial tribunal (*tribunale del lavoro*) comprising employer and syndicate representatives (elected by the workforce).

Employment conditions are often dependent on the region where you work and the local economic conditions. In some regions – particularly the south of the country, where there's high unemployment – there's a tendency for employers to use the black market. Although legislation requires employees to be given a contract, this can often be difficult to obtain (see below).

EMPLOYMENT CONTRACT

Under Italian law every employee must have an employment contract (*contratto di lavoro*) for a job for which he expects to be paid. Although some employers are less than keen to provide one, you should insist on a written contract. You and your employer are obliged to follow the rules and regulations established under Italian law and to abide by the conditions laid down in your contract.

There are usually no hidden surprises or traps for the unwary in an Italian employment contract. Nevertheless, as with any contract, you should know exactly what it contains before signing it. If your Italian isn't fluent, you should try to obtain an English translation, as your language ability would need to be excellent to understand the legal jargon that goes into some contracts. Italian employers seldom provide foreigners with contracts in English, irrespective of the number of English-speaking foreigners employed. If you cannot obtain a written English translation of your contract, at least have it translated orally so that you don't receive any nasty surprises later – such as discovering you're required to give six months' notice.

There are two main kinds of contract: for employees (*dipendente*) and for apprentices (*contratto di appredistato/tirocinio* or *contratto di formazione*). Contracts may be for a fixed term (*contratto a termine* or *contratto a tempo determinato)* or permanent (*contratto a tempo indeterminato*), which is more common. A fixed-term contract lasts for a specified period and terminates automatically without requiring either party to give notice. A fixed-term contract may be renewed, but if it's renewed a second time it automatically becomes an unlimited duration contract and your job is then permanent. Contracts for a fixed term are possible only in certain cases provided for in collective agreements or by law, e.g. seasonal or unusual occupations or replacements for temporarily absent workers. Salaries are negotiated between employees and employers but may not be less than the minimum provided for in the relevant collective employment agreement.

Always obtain a written contract and ensure that it states the salary, holiday dates, pay details, sick pay entitlement and any bonuses. A contract should make reference to a national collective bargaining labour contract if appropriate. At the top of each contract there's a list of all the workers' union's agreement abbreviations, next to which is the word *stipula*, which means the date you were hired. *Decorrenza* means 'with effect from', under which will be the date you start work.

In most fields of employment in Italy, standard employment contracts are drafted by a professional body, based on collective labour contracts or legislation. These are usually applicable unless both employer and employee agree otherwise in writing. Your employment contract may contain your:

- job title;
- department name and manager;
- main duties;
- relationships with other departments;
- responsibility to the employer;
- place(s) of work;
- salary details, including extra month's salary and any agreed increases;
- the date employment starts;
- probationary and notice periods.

Apprenticeship contracts exist for young people between the ages of 16 and 24 and cover a training period during which employees have reduced benefits and lower pay. The duration of an apprenticeship cannot be less than 18 months or more than four years. Employers often take on staff using this contract to avoid paying taxes and certain benefits, which are paid by the state. When the contract expires, the employer must offer you a permanent contract if he wishes to retain your services.

'Work-training' contracts (*contratto di formazione e lavoro*) also exist and were introduced to facilitate the entrance of young workers into employment and only workers between 16 and 32 years of age are eligible. There are two kinds of work-training contract, neither of which is renewable: a one-year contract and a two-year contract leading to an intermediate or high professional level. One of the advantages of these contracts is reduced social security contributions, which vary according to the type of enterprise and region of the country, mainly favouring the depressed southern areas.

Other kinds of employment contract include those for positions such as seasonal work (*lavoro stagionale*) and temporary replacement (*lavoro interinale*) to cover maternity leave, illness, military service, etc., when it's necessary to hire temporary staff.

Employment contracts (particularly temporary contracts) are currently under review and you should check the latest legislation before signing a contract.

In addition to a contract, you should obtain a copy of your employer's general terms and conditions (*condizioni di impiego*), which govern such things as staff regulations and benefits and apply to all employees unless otherwise stated in individual contracts of employment. General conditions are usually referred to in employment contracts and employees usually receive a copy on starting a job (or in some cases beforehand).

SALARY & BENEFITS

Your salary (*stipendio* – the word *salario* means wage) is stated in your employment contact, and details of salary reviews, planned increases and cost of living rises may also be included. Salaries in job contracts are normally stated gross (*lordo*), i.e. before all deductions and withholdings for benefits, taxes and social security. Salaries are generally paid monthly, although they may be quoted in contracts on an hourly (*orario*), monthly (*mensile*) or annual (*annuale*) basis, depending on the type of job or position. If a bonus is paid, such as a 13th or 14th month's salary, it's stated in your employment contract. Points such as the payment of your salary into a bank or post office account and the date of salary payments are usually included in general terms and conditions. You receive a pay slip (*busta paga*) with your salary detailing your gross pay and deductions.

Salaries are fixed under collective agreements between unions and employers for each category of worker and may not be less than the minimum basic wage (*page base*) provided for in the relevant agreement. This basic wage may, however, be adjusted downwards for apprentices. Inexperienced employees may earn the minimum basic wage, although most employees are paid much more, particularly in the north of the country (wages are lower in the south, which has high unemployment). The basic salary may be supplemented by an 'above base payment' (*superminimo*), a seniority increase (*scatti di anzianità*), overtime (*straordinari*) and bonuses (*premi e gratificazioni*). Minimum wages are reviewed every few years and there's also a wage increase for inflation every two years. The government publishes a salary rate book (*tabella professionali*) for each category of employee, including operatives (*operai*), staff employees (*impiegati*) and managers (*dirigenti*), which have different pay scales.

13th Month's Salary & Bonuses

All employees in Italy are entitled to an additional month's remuneration – the so-called 13th month's salary (*tredicesima mesilità*) – usually paid in December before Christmas and referred to as a Christmas bonus (*gratifica natalizia*) when it applies to factory or manual workers. In addition, salaried employees in the commerce industry, managers, executives, and those who have worked for many years in the same company usually receive a 14th month's salary (*quattordicesima mesilità*) during the summer, usually in June. Some employees, such as those in the petroleum and banking industries, receive 15th and even 16th months' salary. In your first and last years of employment, your extra months' salary and other bonuses should be paid pro rata (calculated in twelfths or *dodicesimi*) if you don't work a full calendar year. Where applicable, extra months' salary are guaranteed bonuses and aren't pegged to the company's performance. Senior and middle managers often receive extra bonuses (*premi e gratificazioni*), perhaps linked to profits, equal to around 10 to 20 per cent of their annual salary.

Education & Training

Employee education (*educazione*) and training (*formazione*) isn't taken as seriously as in many other EU countries, and Italian employers aren't obliged to provide employee training programmes. Training may include seminars, conferences, special technical courses, language lessons or any other form of continuing education. If you need to learn or improve your Italian or another language in order to perform your job, the cost of language study is usually paid by your employer. Employers who are keen to attract the best employees, particularly those engaged in high-tech fields, usually allocate extra funds and provide excellent training schemes, although not all employees benefit equally from training, which is decided by the employer. It's in your interest to investigate courses of study, seminars and lectures that you feel will be of direct benefit to you and your employer. Most employers give reasonable consideration to a request to attend a course during working hours, provided you don't make it a full-time occupation.

RELOCATION & TRAVEL EXPENSES

Travel and relocation expenses (*spese per viaggio e trasferimento*) to Italy depend on your agreement with your employer and are usually included in your employment contract or conditions. If you're hired from outside Italy, your air ticket and other travel costs to Italy are usually booked and paid for by your employer or his local representative, although this doesn't usually apply to seasonal workers. In addition you can usually claim any incidental travel costs, e.g. the cost of transport to and from airports. If you travel by car to Italy, you can usually claim a mileage rate or the equivalent air fare.

An employer may pay a fixed relocation allowance based on your salary, position and size of family, or he may pay the total cost of removal; you may be required to sign a contract stipulating that if you leave the employer before a certain period (e.g. five years), you must repay a percentage of your removal costs. The allowance should be sufficient to move the contents of an average house (castles aren't usually catered for) and you must normally pay any excess costs yourself. If you don't want to bring your furniture to Italy or have only a few belongings to ship, it may be possible to purchase furniture locally up to the limit of your allowance. Check with your employer. When a company is liable for the total cost, they may ask you to obtain two or three removal estimates.

Generally, you're required to organise and pay for the removal in advance. Your employer usually reimburses the equivalent amount in local currency **after** you've paid the bill, although it may be possible to have him pay the bill directly or give you a cash advance. If you change jobs within Italy, your new employer may pay your relocation expenses when it's necessary for you to move house. Don't forget to ask, as they may not offer to pay (it may depend on how desperate they are to employ you).

WORKING HOURS

The standard working week is 40 hours. A couple of years ago, it was suggested that working hours (*orario di lavoro*) be reduced to 35 (in common with France), but the idea has been shelved. Under European Union law, you may not work more than eight hours per day or 48 hours per week. In general, Italians tend to work 40 hours per week divided into eight hours per day from Mondays to Fridays. The official working hours in most Italian companies are from 8.30am to 1pm and from 3 to 7pm, although some companies (including many foreign-owned businesses) work through (*orario continuato*) from 9am to 6pm with an hour for lunch. This is more common in the north of the country than in the south. Managers and executives generally work long hours, even allowing for their occasionally long lunch breaks. For example, in Milan executives often work from 8.30 or 9am until 7 or 8pm. Senior staff in the south generally work shorter hours than those in the north, particularly on hot summer days (when they sensibly go home early and jump in the swimming pool!).

Weekends are sacrosanct and almost nobody works on Saturdays and Sundays, except when necessary, e.g. shop staff. Employees cannot be obliged to work on Sundays unless collective agreements state otherwise. Official authorisation is usually required for employees to work on Sundays and time off in lieu must be granted during the normal working week.

There are usually no scheduled coffee or tea breaks in Italy, although drinks can usually be taken at an employee's workplace at any time. Many companies traditionally have a two-hour lunch break, particularly in the provinces, although this is no longer standard practice. Nevertheless, taking a long lunch break, perhaps for a game of tennis or a swim, isn't frowned upon, provided you put in the required hours and don't neglect your work.

It may come as a nasty surprise to some foreigners to discover that many Italian employers (including most large companies) require employees to clock in and out of work. If you're caught cheating the clock, you can be dismissed.

Flexi-Time

Many employers operate flexi-time working hours (*orario flessibile*), particularly in the north of the country and in the civil service. A flexi-time system usually requires all employees to be present between certain hours, known as the core or block time. For example, from 9 to 11.30am and from 1.30 to 4pm. Employees may make up their required working hours by starting earlier than the required core time, reducing their lunch break or working later. Most business premises are open from around 7am to 6pm and smaller companies may allow employees to work as late as they wish, provided they don't exceed the maximum permitted daily working hours (see above).

Overtime

Overtime (*lavoro straordinari*) earns you up to 130 per cent of your basic pay for daytime work and up to 150 per cent for work on public holidays or at night. Overtime must not exceed two hours per day, or 80 hours per quarter or 250 hours per year. Some companies have a limit of 200 overtime hours per year, and some unions don't permit overtime at all. Salaried employees, particularly executives and managers, aren't generally paid overtime, although this depends on their employment contracts.

HOLIDAYS & LEAVE

Annual Holidays

The amount of annual holiday (*ferie*) you're entitled to depends on your length of service, although employees in Italy are usually entitled to five or six weeks paid holiday per year, which must usually be taken during the year in which it's earned. Most people take a month in the summer (virtually the whole country closes down from 20th July to 20th August, except for the leisure industry) and two weeks around Christmas and the New Year. If your company closes in August, you **must** take holiday at that time. If you don't take all your holiday allowance, you may be paid in lieu, although some companies may insist that employees take all the holiday they've accrued.

Before starting a new job, you should check that any planned holidays will be honoured by a prospective employer. This is particularly important if they fall within your probationary period (see page 66), when holidays may not be permitted.

Public Holidays

Most collective agreements include the ten Italian national holidays (*feste nazionale*), which are as follows:

Date	Holiday
1st January	New Year's Day (*Capodanno* or *Primo dell'Anno*)
6th January	Epiphany (*La Befana* or *Epifania*)
March or April	Easter Monday (*Lunedì di Pasqua*)
25th April	Liberation Day (*Festa della Liberazione*)
1st May	Labour Day (*Primo Maggio* or *Festa del Lavoro*)
15th August	Feast of the Assumption (*Ferragosto*)
1st November	All Saints' Day (*Ognissanti* or *Tutti i Santi*)
8th December	Immaculate Conception (*Immacolata Concezione*)
25th December	Christmas Day (*Natale*)
26th December	Boxing Day (*Santo Stefano*)

Republic Day (*Festa della Repubblica*) and Armistice Day (*Caduti di Tutti le Guerre*), on the first Sundays in June and November respectively, aren't official national holidays but are widely allocated as paid holidays.

Employees generally also receive the local saint's day. The following are the saints' days in the major cities:

City	Date
Bologna	4th October (St. Petronio)
Florence	24th June (St. John)
Genoa	24th June (St. John)

Milan	7th December (St. Ambrose)
Naples	9th September (St. Gennaro)
Palermo	11th July (St. Rosalia)
Rome	29th June (St. Peter)
Turin	4th June (St. John)
Venice	25th April (St. Mark)

There are usually also a number of half-day holidays, which vary from region to region but may include Easter Friday, Christmas Eve, New Year's Eve and a spring festival in April.

When a holiday falls on a Saturday or Sunday, another day's holiday is usually granted in compensation. When a public holiday falls on a Tuesday or Thursday, the day before or the day after (i.e. Monday or Friday respectively) may also be declared a holiday depending on your employer – a practice known as making a bridge (*ponte*). If a holiday falls on a Wednesday, employees may take the two preceding or succeeding days off.

All public offices, banks, post offices, schools and most shops and businesses are closed on public holidays, when only essential work is carried out. Public transport remains in service, although schedules may be reduced.

Foreign embassies and consulates in Italy usually observe Italian public holidays **plus** their own country's national holidays.

Sick Leave

Employees in Italy don't receive a quota of sick days as in some countries (e.g. the US) and there's no limit on the amount of time you may take off work due to sickness or accidents. Sick leave for workers and staff employees in commerce and industry is paid by the employer and the National Institute for Social Security (INPS), to which contributions are automatically deducted from your salary (see **Sickness Benefit** on page 277). Some employers pay the full salary of sick employees for up to six months.

An application for sickness benefit must be made to an INPS office with a doctor's medical certificate (*certificato medico*) showing the diagnosis and how long you will be unable to work. Benefit is payable only after the certificate is received, so you should register immediately or get someone to do so on your behalf. If you're still unable to work after the date given on the original medical certificate, you must provide another certificate within two days.

Parental Leave

The maternity law and allowances were revised in 2000 and expectant mothers can now work until their eighth month of pregnancy (subject to medical approval) and are entitled to a total of five months' paid maternity leave (*congedo per maternità*), including at least one month before the birth. A new mother can take an additional six months' leave on 30 per cent of her salary (*congedo facoltativo*). If you choose not to extend their leave of absence and return to work three months after giving birth, you have the right to two hours' paid time off each day to nurse or feed your baby. A doctor may authorise additional time off, either before or after the birth, in which case a company must continue to pay the mother's salary.

Fathers normally receive a few days' compassionate leave when a child is born and can obtain a three-month leave of absence after a child is born if the mother is deceased or seriously ill. Maternity leave (for either parent) doesn't affect their state pension.

A woman cannot be dismissed from her job from the beginning of pregnancy (fixed at 300 days before the date when the baby is due) through to the baby's first birthday. If she is dismissed, she has the right to reinstatement (*il ripristino del rapporto di lavoro*), provided she presents the appropriate certificate of pregnancy or birth to her employer within 90 days of dismissal. A woman wishing to regain her job should take this step immediately, as she won't be paid for the interim period between dismissal and reinstatement. See also **Maternity Benefit** on page 277.

Compassionate & Special Leave

Most companies provide additional days off for certain occasions, e.g. moving house, your own or a family marriage, the birth of a child, the death of a family member or close relative and other compassionate reasons. Grounds for compassionate leave (*congedo per gravi motivi* or *congedo straordinario*) are usually defined in collective agreements, and the number of days' special leave granted varies with the reason. Employees who have worked for a company for a minimum number of years may be entitled to take a sabbatical of up to a year (usually without pay).

Notification Of Sickness Or Accident

You're usually required to notify your employer as soon as possible of sickness or an accident that prevents you from working, i.e. within a few hours of your normal starting time. Failure to do so may result in your not being paid for that day's absence. You're required to keep your boss or manager informed about your illness and when you expect to return to work.

For periods of more than a few days' sickness, you're usually required to provide your employer with a doctor's certificate (*certificato medico*); the period will be specified in your employment conditions. An employer cannot terminate an employee's contract during a period of sickness or when he's recovering from an accident.

INSURANCE

Social Security

All Italian and foreign employees of Italian companies and the self-employed must usually contribute to the Italian social security (*previdenza sociale*) system. Exceptions include some nationals of countries with a reciprocal social security agreement with Italy, which allows social security payments to be made abroad for a limited period. Social security includes sickness and maternity, accidents at work and occupational diseases, old-age, invalidity and survivor's pensions, unemployment benefits, and family allowances. It doesn't include the national heath service (Servizio Sanitario Nazionale/SSN), which is funded separately from general taxation. Contributions (*contributi*) are calculated as a percentage of your gross income and are deducted at source by your employer. Employees pay around 10 per cent of their gross earnings, while the employer pays around 35 per cent of an employee's salary, making a total of some 45 per cent. See **Social Security** on page 274 for details.

Health Insurance

Residents in Italy are eligible for health care under the Italian national heath service (Servizio Sanitario Nazionale/SSN) and many people have supplementary private health insurance. Many foreigners have an international private health insurance policy, which covers their families both in Italy and world-wide. Most companies provide private health insurance for employees transferred to Italy, and some employers, particularly foreign companies, provide free comprehensive private health insurance for executives, senior managers and their families. For further information see **National Health Service** on page 254 and **Health Insurance** on page 282.

Unemployment Insurance

Employees in Italy make obligatory contributions to the state unemployment fund in their monthly social security contributions. If you become unemployed, you're entitled to ordinary unemployment benefits (*indennità di disoccupazione*) if you've worked for at least a year and made contributions in the preceding two years. For details see **Unemployment Benefits** on page 278.

Accident Insurance

Accident insurance (*assicurazione contro gli infortuni*) is mandatory for all employees in Italy. It's paid for by employers and provided by the Instituto Nazionale per l'Assicurazione Contro gli Infortuni sul Lavaoro/INAIL. It covers accidents or illness at work and accidents that occur while travelling to and from work and on company business. Although the primary responsibility for safety rests with the employer, employees are required by law to ensure that they co-operate with their employers and that they don't endanger themselves or anyone else by their actions or negligence. There are usually specific regulations for activities involving high risks, e.g. when operating electrical equipment and certain classes of machinery, and when using chemicals.

When an accident occurs at work, an employee must inform his employer immediately and complete a report (*denuncia*). If recovery takes longer than three days, employers must inform the INAIL within two days; in the case of death, INAIL must be informed by telegram within 24 hours.

There are various kinds of compensation to which employees (or their survivors in the case of death) are entitled, depending on whether an accident results in temporary or permanent disability (see **Disability Benefits** on page 277). If an employee or self-employed person dies as a result of an accident at work or an illness caused by work, a survivor's pension is paid to his family based on a percentage of the deceased's last annual salary (see **State Pensions** on page 279).

Salary Insurance

Salary insurance (*assicurazione di stipendio*) pays employees' salaries during periods of sickness or after accidents and is provided under social security. All workers are compulsorily enrolled with the relevant national institutions. After a certain number of consecutive sick days (the number varies with the employer, although it's usually three), a percentage of your salary is paid by your employer and by social security, although employees in industry usually have their salary paid entirely by their employer. For information see **Sickness Benefit** on page 277.

RETIREMENT

Your employment conditions may be valid only until the official Italian retirement (*pensionamento*) age, which is 65 for men and 60 for women in most trades and professions (although some employees can retire on a full pension earlier). If you wish to continue working after you've reached retirement age, you may be required to negotiate a new employment contract.

All employees in Italy are obliged to contribute to a state old age pension fund (*pensione di vecchiaia*), to which payments are made in your monthly social security contributions. Almost every trade or occupation has its own pension scheme. Managerial staff usually make additional contributions to a supplementary managerial company pension fund run by National Security for Managers of Commercial Concerns (INPADAC) or National Social Security for Managers of Industrial Concerns (INPDAI). For further information see **State Pensions** on page 279.

UNION MEMBERSHIP

The Italian constitution establishes the right to organise trade unions (*sindacale*), which are active (some 30 per cent of the Italian workforce is unionised) and powerful. In fact, one of the main reasons why many employers are tempted to employ workers illegally is that legal employees are heavily protected by unions and employers often find it almost impossible to sack them, even for poor time keeping, theft and other offences. The right to strike is also guaranteed by the constitution, and it remains a potent weapon in the hands of the trade unions. Nevertheless, union membership isn't obligatory.

There are three major unions in Italy, each with different political or religious alignments. The Confederazione Generale Italiano del Lavoro (CGIL) is closest to the left and was formerly dominated by the Italian Communist Party; the Confederazione Italiana Sindicati Lavoratori (CISL) is closest to the Catholic church with links to the Italian Popular Party (Partito Popolare Italiano); and the Unione Italiana del Lavoro (UIL) is closest to the secular parties and associated with the Socialists. A number of independent unions are also active, particularly in the public-service sector; these are quite militant and increasingly challenge the monopoly of the three confederations on national contractual negotiations.

Collective bargaining contracts between the unions and employers regulate employees' employment conditions, and employment contracts are reviewed and new minimum wages fixed every few years. Unions also negotiate with the government on policies concerning the economy and welfare.

In addition to trade unions, Italy has numerous workers' associations (*ordine*) for different professions, which have branches in major Italian cities; you can obtain a list of associations from your local town hall or chamber of commerce.

In companies with over 40 employees, employee delegates must be elected to the board of directors and a labour management committee formed. In addition to dealing with matters relating to the terms and conditions of employment, major changes relating to the operation, organisation and management of a company must be discussed with the committee before they can be initiated. However, a company isn't usually required to act on the opinion of the labour management committee.

OTHER CONDITIONS

Acceptance Of Gifts

Employees are usually forbidden to accept gifts of more than a certain value from customers or suppliers. Many suppliers give bottles of wine or small gifts at Christmas, and businessmen often exchange small gifts (e.g.a watch or pen) when they close a deal or sign a contract. These don't breach the rules, but providing a 'sweetener' (e.g. cash) to oil the wheels of bureaucracy, obtain a contract or receive better treatment in a hospital is illegal, although part of everyday life in Italy.

Changing Jobs & Confidentiality

Companies in a high-tech or highly confidential business may have restrictions on employees moving to a competitor in Italy or elsewhere within a certain period of resigning, or restrictions regarding starting a company in the same line of business. You should be aware of these restrictions, as they're enforceable under Italian law, although it's a complicated subject and disputes often need to be resolved by a court. Italian laws regarding industrial secrets and general employer confidentiality are strict. If you breach this confidentiality you may be dismissed and could be unable to find further employment in Italy.

Probationary & Notice Periods

For most jobs in Italy there's a probationary period (*perioda di prova*) of one to three months, depending on the type of work, the employer and your contract (three months is usual for permanent positions). A probationary period isn't required by law, although there's no law forbidding it. The length of a probationary period is usually stated in collective agreements, which impose restrictions on the maximum period. During the probationary period, either party may terminate the employment contract without notice or any financial penalty, unless otherwise stated in a collective agreement.

Notice periods (*periodo di preavviso*) usually vary with length of service and are governed by law and collective agreements. The minimum notice period is usually a month for clerical and manual workers, two months for foremen and supervisors, and three months for managerial and senior technical staff. The minimum notice period for employees with over two years' service is two months. If you resign, your employer can decide whether you should work to the end of your notice period or be paid in lieu of notice (*indennità di mancato preavviso*), while if you've been dismissed, you can choose to be paid in lieu of notice. Compensation must also be paid for any outstanding annual holiday entitlement up to the end of the notice period. See also **Dismissal** on page 66.

Dismissal & Redundancy

Employees are entitled to a severance payment on the termination of their employment, for whatever reason, depending on their salary and number of years service. Dismissal (*licenziamento*) is permitted only if it's given in writing for a 'just cause' (*giusta causa*) or a 'justifiable reason' (*giustificato motivo*). Just cause includes any event that renders the continuation of employment impossible, such as a serious non-performance of contractual obligations, a repeated failure to turn up for work, violence against a colleague or employer, or theft from your employer; dismissal is immediate and requires no notice. Justifiable reason, which includes redundancy due to a general reduction of the workforce or an employee's position being abolished, must be negotiated with a trade union and requires an employer to give notice. If no cause or reason for a dismissal is given, an employee is entitled to compensation and to be reinstated if the unit from which he was dismissed employed over 15 people or the employer has over 60 employees in Italy. If you're fired or made redundant, you have two months in which to lodge an appeal and, if you've been dismissed unfairly, you can reclaim your old job with compensation for any lost wages. If you lose a contracted position, you're also entitled to state unemployment benefits (see page 278).

Uniquely, if you're made redundant, fired (for any reason!) or resign voluntarily from a job in Italy, you're entitled to a termination payment (*trattamento di fine rapporto/TFR* or *liquidazione*) based on your average salary and calculated according to your length of service. (Your average monthly salary is reckoned to be a twelfth of 13.5 month's wages.) You also receive any compensation payments agreed under trade union rules and any holiday pay due. This termination payment is yours by right and isn't a voluntary payment on the part of the employer; any severance incentives, e.g. for taking voluntary redundancy, are paid in addition to this. Employees can even obtain an advance of up to 70 per cent of their termination payment to buy a home or pay for urgent medical expenses, provided they've worked for a company for at least seven years. Part of your termination payment can be converted into securities and lodged with a private pension fund.

Medical Examination

Many Italian employers require prospective employees to have a pre-employment medical examination (*esame medica*) performed by a doctor nominated by the employer. An offer of employment is usually subject to a prospective employee being given a clean bill of health. However, this may be required only for employees over a certain age (e.g. 40) or for employees in certain jobs, e.g. where good health is of paramount importance for safety reasons. Thereafter a medical examination may be required periodically, e.g. every one or two years, or may be requested at any time by your employer. A medical examination may be necessary as a condition of membership of a company health, pension or life insurance scheme. Some companies insist on certain employees having regular health screening, particularly executives and senior managers.

Part-Time Job Restrictions

Restrictions regarding part-time work (*lavoro a tempo parziale* or *lavoro part-time*) may be detailed in your contract or general terms and conditions. It's common for people to have second or even third jobs, although most Italian companies don't allow full-time employees to moonlight for another employer in the same line of business. Much part-time employment is done illegally (i.e. without declaration to the authorities), particularly as part-time employment involves complying with more stringent requirements and formalities with regard to contracts.

CHECKLISTS

When negotiating your conditions of employment, you will find the checklists on the following pages useful.

The points listed under **General Positions** (below) apply to most jobs, while those listed under **Executive Positions** (on page 70) usually apply to executive and senior managerial appointments only.

General Positions

Salary

- Is the salary adequate, taking into account the cost of living (see page 321)? Is it index-linked?
- Is the total salary (including expenses) paid in euros or is it paid in another country in a different currency, with expenses for living in Italy?
- When and how often is the salary reviewed?
- Does the salary include a 13th (or more) month's salary and annual or end-of-contract bonuses?
- Is overtime paid or time off given in lieu of extra hours worked?

Relocation Expenses

- Are removal expenses or a relocation allowance paid?
- Does the allowance include travelling expenses for all family members? Is there a limit and is it adequate?
- Are you required to repay relocation expenses (or a percentage) if you resign before a certain period has elapsed?
- Are you required to pay for your relocation in advance? This can run to several thousand euros for normal house contents.
- If employment is for a short period only, will your relocation costs be paid by the employer when you leave Italy?
- If you aren't shipping household goods and furniture to Italy, is there an allowance for buying furnishings locally?
- Do relocation expenses include the legal and agent's fees incurred when moving home?
- Does the employer use the services of a relocation consultant (see page 98)?

Accommodation

- Does the employer pay for a hotel or pay a lodging allowance until you find permanent accommodation?
- Is subsidised or free, temporary or permanent accommodation provided? If so, is it furnished or unfurnished?
- Must you pay for utilities such as electricity, gas and water?
- If an employer doesn't provide accommodation, is assistance given to find a home? If so, what sort of assistance?
- What will accommodation cost?
- Are your expenses paid while looking for accommodation?

Working Hours

- What are the weekly working hours?
- Does the employer operate a flexi-time system? If so, what are the fixed working hours? How early must you start? Can you carry forward extra hours worked and take time off at a later date, or carry forward a deficit and make it up later?
- Are you required to clock in and out of work?
- Can you choose whether to take time off in lieu of overtime or be paid?

Leave

- What is the annual holiday entitlement? Does it increase with length of service?
- What are the paid public holidays? Is Monday or Friday a free day when a public holiday falls on a Tuesday or Thursday respectively?
- Is free air travel to your home country or elsewhere provided for you and your family, and if so, how often?

Insurance

- Is extra insurance cover provided besides obligatory insurance (see **Chapter 13**)?
- Is free life insurance provided?
- Is free health insurance provided for you **and** your family (see page 282)?
- For how long will your salary be paid if you're sick or have an accident?

Company Or Supplementary Pension

- What percentage of your salary must you pay into a pension fund (see page 281)?
- Are you required or able to pay a lump sum into the fund in order to receive a full or higher pension?
- Is the pension transferable to another employer?

Employer

- What are the employer's prospects?
- Does he have a good reputation?
- Does he have a high staff turnover?

Other Terms

- Are free or subsidised Italian lessons provided for you and your spouse?
- Is a travelling allowance (or public transportation) paid from your Italian residence to your place of work?
- Is free or subsidised parking provided at your place of work?
- Is a free or subsidised company restaurant provided? If not, is an allowance paid or are luncheon vouchers provided? (Some companies provide excellent staff restaurants that save employees both money and time.)
- Will the employer provide or pay for professional training or education, if necessary abroad?
- Are free work clothes or overalls provided? Does the employer pay for the cleaning of work clothes?
- Does the employer provide any fringe benefits, such as subsidised banking services, low interest loans, inexpensive petrol, employees' shop or product discounts, sports and social facilities, and subsidised tickets?
- Do you have a written list of your job responsibilities?
- Have your employment conditions been confirmed in writing?
- If a dispute arises over your salary or working conditions, under the law of which country will your employment contract be interpreted?

Executive & Managerial Positions

The following generally apply to executive and top managerial positions only:

- Is private schooling for your children financed or subsidised? Will the employer pay for a boarding school in Italy or abroad?

- Is the salary index-linked and protected against devaluation? This is particularly important if you're paid in a foreign currency that fluctuates wildly or could be devalued. Are you paid an overseas allowance for working in Italy?

- Is there a non-contributory pension fund besides the supplementary company scheme? Is it transferable and, if so, what are the conditions?

- Are the costs incurred by a move to Italy (e.g. the cost of selling your home, employing an agent to let it for you and storing household effects) reimbursed?

- Will the employer pay for domestic help or contribute to the cost of a servant or cook?

- Is a car provided? With a chauffeur?

- Are you entitled to any miscellaneous benefits, such as membership of a social or sports club or free credit cards?

- Is there an entertainment allowance?

- Is there a clothing allowance? For example, if you arrive in Italy in the winter from the tropics, you will probably need to buy new winter clothes.

- Is extra compensation paid if you're made redundant or fired? Redundancy or severance payments (see page 66) are compulsory for employees in Italy (subject to length of service), but executives often receive a generous 'golden handshake' if they're made redundant, e.g. after a take-over.

3.

PERMITS & VISAS

Before visiting or moving to Italy, you must ensure that you have the necessary documents and permits. These will depend on your country of origin, the length of your intended stay and the purpose of your visit or stay.

While in Italy, you should always carry your passport, permit to stay or residence permit (as applicable), which serves as an identity card (*carta d'identità*) that all Italians must carry by law. A passport or other identity card is also required to check into a hotel. **Keep photocopies of these documents in a safe place, because if the originals are lost or stolen they will save you time in obtaining replacements.** You can be asked to produce your identification papers at any time by the Italian police or other officials and if you don't have them you can be taken to a police station and interrogated.

Immigration is a sensitive issue and in recent years Italy has been flooded with refugees and illegal immigrants (*clandestini*) from Africa, Eastern Europe (particularly Albania, Turkey and the former Yugoslavia) and Asia (particularly China). Italian immigration laws change frequently and new legislation may alter some of the information contained in this chapter. You shouldn't base any decisions or actions on the information contained herein without confirming it with an official and reliable source, such as an Italian consulate. Permit infringements are taken seriously by the authorities and there are penalties for breaches of regulations, including fines or even deportation for flagrant abuses.

If you understand Italian, there's a useful (if heavy-going) book, *La Condizione Giuridica Del Cittadino Extracomunitario – Lineamenti E Guida Pratica* by Paolo Bonetti (Maggioli Editori), which explains Italy's immigration laws, although it may not be up-to-date unless a new edition has just been published.

Bureaucracy

Although Dante didn't know it at the time, he perfectly described the labyrinth of Italian government offices and bureaucracy when he wrote 'Abandon hope all who enter here'. Italian bureaucrats would appear to love red tape and have invented official papers and stamps for every possible occasion and purpose. Just finding the right office is a challenge and when you finally locate it, it's invariably closed (many offices open on a few days per week for a couple of hours only). You even need documents to obtain other documents and the laws governing the issue and use of these documents are frequently incomprehensible. For example, in what other country can your birth certificate be printed with varying information, on two kinds of official paper, have varying costs, and expire if you fail to renew it? Once you have the correct documents, they must be officially translated and numerous copies made. Wander into any post office, police headquarters or government office and you hear a chorus of stamping and banging while long lines of confused Italians pray that they're in the right place and the right line for the document required. If all this bureaucracy is bewildering for Italians, just imagine how it is to foreigners!

The situation isn't helped by the fact that the Italian judicial system is based upon a simple law: *La Legge non ammette l'ignoranza* – The Law doesn't admit ignorance. Laws have been created to govern everything under the Italian sun, but there's no official process of communicating or explaining them to the general public. This leaves the responsibility of gathering information entirely to the individual with little or no help from the state. A plethora of documentation is necessary to obtain a visa, stay, residence or work permit. Unfortunately, not all the official information explaining how to obtain this documentation is readily available or interpreted in the same way, making the tortured road to obtaining visas and permits fraught with dead ends and U-turns. Due to the difficulties in conforming to Italian laws and documentation, there are official 'document agencies' which can obtain documents and make applications on your behalf (listed in the yellow pages under *certificati, agenzie*).

When dealing with Italian bureaucracy, try to remain composed and polite (even when you feel like strangling the person behind the counter) and if your Italian isn't excellent take someone with you who's fluent (most officials speak only Italian). Never take anything for granted where Italian civil servants (*servitori civili*) are concerned, and make sure that you understand all communications. If in doubt have someone translate them for you.

Since February 1999, many official documents have been abolished and substituted by a simple auto-certification, usually written on a printed form (*modulo*) available in public offices. However, local officials may not be aware of this and you may be asked to provide documents that are no longer required. The good news is that the government is trying to reduce bureaucracy and provide more access to information, particularly via the Internet, e.g. ⌨ www.governo.it.

VISITORS

European Union (EU) nationals don't require a visa for stays of up to 90 days. Citizens of the following countries don't require a visa for stays of between 30 and 90 days depending on the country (check with your local Italian embassy or consulate): Andorra, Argentina, Australia, Benin, Bolivia, Bosnia-Herzegovina, Brazil, Burkina Faso, Canada, Chile, Colombia, Costa Rica, Croatia, Cyprus, Czech Republic, Ecuador, El Salvador, Estonia, Fiji, Guatemala, Guyana, Honduras, Hungary, Iceland, Israel, Ivory Coast, Japan, Kenya, (South) Korea, Latvia, Liechtenstein, Lithuania, Macedonia, Malaysia, Maldives, Malta, Mexico, Monaco, New Zealand, Nicaragua, Niger, Norway, Paraguay, Poland, Samoa, San Christopher and Nevis, San Marino, Singapore, Slovakia, Slovenia, Switzerland, Togo, Trinidad and Tobago, Uruguay, USA and Venezuela. **All other nationalities require a visa to visit Italy for any period.**

Citizens of many EU countries can visit Italy with a national identity card, while all others require a full passport. However, while identity cards are accepted at all points of entry to Italy, the Italian authorities may not accept them when applying for a permit to stay. If you're an EU national and wish to remain in Italy for longer than 90 days, it's therefore highly recommended to enter with a full passport.

Since 1st August 1998, Italy, along with a number of other EU member states, has issued a new kind of visa for visitors called the 'Schengen visa' (see page 90). This allows the holder to move freely between Schengen countries (Austria, Belgium, France, Germany, Greece, Italy, Luxembourg, the Netherlands, Portugal and Spain). To obtain a Schengen visa, you must hold a passport or travel document recognised by all the Schengen member states and valid for at least three months beyond the validity of the visa. You can apply for a Schengen visa, which is valid for 90 days within a six-month period, from the consulate of the country that's your main destination or the one you intend to visit first.

A Schengen visa isn't the appropriate visa if you wish to remain in a member state, including Italy, for longer than 90 days, study, take up employment or establish a trade or profession (see Visas below). If you wish to stay longer than 90 days, you must obtain an extension of your visa from the local police headquarters, although this isn't a right and cannot be taken for granted (you need a good reason and proof of financial resources) and must obtain a permit to stay (see page 79). However, if your passport hasn't been stamped (which is likely, particularly for EU nationals), the authorities have no way of knowing when you entered the country, so the system is 'flexible'.

The Italian immigration authorities may require non-EU visitors to produce a return ticket and proof of accommodation, health insurance and financial resources.

When you stay with friends in Italy (rather than, for example, at a hotel or campsite) for longer than three days, you're officially required to register with the local police, although in practice few short-stay visitors comply with this. **Failure to register is punishable by a fine of up to around €220.**

EU nationals who visit Italy to seek employment or start a business have 90 days in which to find a job or apply for permit to stay (see page 79), although if you haven't found employment or have insufficient funds, your application will be refused. If you're a non-EU national, it isn't possible to enter Italy as a tourist and change your status to that of an employee, student or resident, and you must return to your country of residence and apply for the appropriate visa.

VISAS

EU nationals don't require visas for visits to Italy but require a permit to stay (see page 79) if they plan to remain longer than 90 days. Non-EU nationals need a 'residence visa' (*visto per ragioni di dimora*) to enter Italy with a view to staying more than 90 days and may need one for a visit of a shorter duration (see **Visitors** above). Application should be made at an Italian consulate abroad well in advance of your planned departure date. Visas may be valid for a single entry only or for multiple entries within a limited period. A visa is in the form of an adhesive sticker (not a stamp) inserted in your passport, which must be valid until at least three months **after** the visa expires.

Visas are issued for many reasons, each of which has its own abbreviation (*sigla*). These include tourism (A), business (B), religion (C), diplomatic service

(D), domicile (DM), joining family (F), dependent work (L-1), self-employment (L-2), artistic work (L-3), medical care (M), mission (MS), study (S), sporting activity (SP), re-entry (R), transit (T), airport transit (TA) and visiting family (V).

The type of visa issued depends on the purpose of your visit and the length of your stay, and determines the type of permit to stay that's issued after you arrive in Italy. **If you plan to stay in Italy for longer than six months, you must ensure that you obtain a visa that's valid for at least a year; otherwise you will be able to obtain a permit to stay (see page 79) for only six months and won't be able to renew it.**

Some of the documentation you may need to apply for a visa, mainly concerning permission to work, must be obtained in Italy. Although your prospective employer normally handles this on your behalf, your presence in Italy can help to speed up the process. If you plan to start a business or work freelance, you must also register at the local tax office (*intendenza di finanza*) and chamber of commerce (*camera di commercio*) or professional registrar (*albo dei professionisti*), and present the documents from these agencies together with your visa application. This can be a costly and time-consuming process, as once the documentation is obtained you must return to your country of residence to apply for the visa. Nevertheless, it may be worthwhile.

Another reason you may decide to visit Italy to obtain documents in connection with a visa application is simply to obtain proof that you've been in Italy. This evidence may be important, as the Italian government is continually changing the immigration laws. For example, a law passed by the Italian government in October 1998 included a remedy clause (*sanatoria*) stating that all non-EU citizens who could prove their presence in Italy before 27th March 1998 could apply for a permit to stay without having to obtain a visa from their country of residence. This wasn't the first time a new immigration law included this kind of clause, nor will it be the last.

Having obtained the necessary paperwork, an application for a visa must be made to your local Italian consulate with jurisdiction over your place of residence. It may be possible to make an application by post, but in other cases you're required to attend in person. If you decide to apply in person (or have no choice), bear in mind that there are invariably long queues at consulates in major cities (take a thick book). The documentation required for a visa application depends on the purpose of your visit to Italy. All applicants require:

- a passport valid for at least three months beyond the validity of the requested visa with a blank page to affix the visa sticker;
- a number of black and white, passport-size photographs on a white background.

Depending on the urpose of your visit, you may require some of the following (note that some consulates may require both originals and photocopies):

- Proof of residence in the country from which you're applying;

- Proof or travel arrangements showing your name and exact dates of entry into and exit from Italy (if applicable);
- Proof of financial resources (see below);
- A health insurance certificate if you aren't eligible for health treatment under Italian social security or through your employer;
- Employees require an authorisation to work in Italy issued by the Italian Department of Labour (see below);
- Students require proof of admission from an approved educational establishment (see below);
- A non-EU national married to an Italian citizen or to a foreigner who's resident in Italy, requires a marriage certificate;
- Applicants under 18 need written authorisation from a parent or guardian.

Many of the above documents must be translated into Italian. All translations must be done by a translator approved by your local consulate, a list of whom (*elenco di traduttori*) is provided by Italian consulates on request. Many documents need tax stamps (*marche da bollo*) affixed to them, and in many cases requests for official documents must be made on special lined paper (*carta da bollo*), to which a tax stamp must be attached. The standard stamp (*bollo*) for administrative documents (*atti civili*) costs €10.33 and can be purchased from a tobacconist (*tabacchi*).

Proof Of Financial Resources: Proof of financial resources or financial support may take the form of bank statements, letters from banks confirming arrangements for the regular transfer of funds from abroad, or letters from family or friends guaranteeing regular support. Letters should be notarised. Students may submit a letter from an organisation or institution guaranteeing accommodation or evidence of a scholarship or grant. Retired people should take their pension book or copies of recent pension cheques. Proof of financial resources isn't required by someone coming to Italy to take up paid employment.

Authorisation To Work: A non-EU national wishing to work in Italy requires an authorisation to work issued by the local Department of Labour office (Ispettorato Provinciale del Lavoro) where the business is registered. This must in turn be authorised by the local police headquarters who stamp it *nulla osta* (literally 'nothing hinders') on the back. This document must be obtained by your prospective employer in Italy and be sent to you in your country of residence for presentation at an Italian consulate with your other documents. **Be warned, however, that for non-EU nationals, obtaining authorisation to work is a highly bureaucratic and time-consuming process.** It can take a year or more, and unless you're employed by an Italian company in your own country or are living in Italy already, it's rare to find an employer in Italy who's willing to go to the trouble involved.

Proof Of Admission: Students require proof of admission from an approved school or university in Italy indicating when their studies start and end. The letter must either have the seal of the school or be notarised. If your studies are sponsored by an educational institution in your home country (or country of residence), you should also have a letter from the institution concerned confirming this. This must also contain the seal of the school or be notarised.

There's a fee for a visa, which can vary considerably. It can take up to a month to obtain a routine visa or up to 90 days in 'difficult' cases. A visa is usually valid for a first entry within 60 days. If you require a visa to enter Italy and attempt to enter without one, you will be refused entry. If you're in doubt as to whether you require a visa to enter Italy, enquire at an Italian consulate abroad before making travel plans. **If you required a visa to enter Italy and have entered the country and obtained a permit to stay (see below), you may still require a re-entry visa to return to Italy after a trip abroad.** This must be obtained from your local police headquarters before leaving Italy.

PERMITS TO STAY

All foreigners (*extracomunitari*) planning to remain in Italy for longer than 90 days must apply for a 'permit to stay' (*permesso di soggiorno* or *carta di soggiorno*) at the local police headquarters (*questura*) within eight days of their arrival.

The latest immigration law (passed in October 1998) changed the name of permits to stay for EU citizens from *permesso di soggiorno* to *carta di soggiorno*, even though the substance of the permit has remained the same. However, this isn't common knowledge and not all local police headquarters are aware of the change in name. Don't be surprised, therefore, if you apply for a *permesso di soggiorno* and receive a *carta di soggiorno* or vice versa. To avoid confusion, the more commonly used term, *permesso di soggiorno*, is used throughout this chapter to refer to all types of permits to stay.

A permit to stay *isn't* a residence permit (see page 86), which must be applied for after you have your permit to stay, if you wish to become a formal resident.

It can take up to three months to obtain a permit, which can be issued only for the purpose stated on your visa. There are many types of permit to stay, the most common of which include the following:

- *Permesso di soggiorno per turismo* – for tourists. Technically anyone visiting Italy for over a week who isn't staying in a hotel, boarding house or an official campsite should apply for one, although in practice this rarely happens;

- *Permesso di soggiorno per coesione familiare* – for the foreign spouse and children of an Italian citizen when they move to Italy together;

- *Permesso di soggiorno per lavoro* – a work permit for an employee (see **Employees** below);

- *Permesso di soggiorno per lavoro autonomo/indipendente* – for independent or freelance workers (see **Self-Employed** below);

- *Permesso di soggiorno per studio* – for students (see **Students** below);
- *Permesso di soggiorno per ricongiungimento familiare* – for the spouse, children (under 18) and dependent parents of foreigners married to Italian citizens and also for family members from overseas who come to join others already in Italy (see **Family Members** below);
- *Permesso di soggiorno per dimora* – for foreigners establishing residence in Italy who don't intend to work or study (see **Non-Employed Residents** below).

There are also permits to stay for various other special classes, including refugees and employees of religious missions. If you're a non-EU citizen and haven't obtained a specific visa, the local police headquarters normally issue you with a permit for tourism (*permesso di soggiorno per turismo*). This is valid for three months only and isn't renewable, nor may it be modified for any other purpose. You may not apply for residence with this permit or study, take up employment or establish a business, trade or profession.

Employees

If you're a national of an EU member country (your passport must show that you have the right of abode in an EU country), you don't require official approval to live or work in Italy, although you still require a permit to stay (*permesso di soggiorno per lavoro*). If you're unemployed, you have the right to live in Italy for a 'reasonable period' of time in order to look for a job. However, no matter how long you take to find a job, you cannot be asked to leave the country if you can prove that you're still seriously looking for employment and have a real chance of finding work (for example, you still have interviews to attend or tests to undergo). In certain circumstances, if you're receiving unemployment benefit in one EU country, you may continue to receive that benefit for up to three months in Italy. To do so, you must apply to the authorities in the country that pays your unemployment benefit.

EU nationals who visit Italy with the intention of finding a job should apply at the foreigners' office (*ufficio stranieri*) at the local police headquarters for a permit (*ricevuta di segnalazione di siggiorno*) within eight days, which entitles them to remain in Italy for three months while looking for a job. When you've found work, you take the *ricevuta* together with a letter from your employer confirming your employment to the police headquarters to obtain a permit to stay. You must also apply for a work permit (*permesso di lavoro* – see page 80), which is valid only for as long as you're employed and is available to both residents and non-residents.

Non-EU nationals require an 'entry visa for reasons of work' (*visto d'ingresso per motivi di lavoro*), which they must obtain in their home country or country of residence. All employees except managers and executives (*dirigenti*) require a workers' registration card (*libretto di lavoro*) from the Provincial Inspectorate of

Work (*Inspettorato Provinciale del Lavoro*), which is valid for ten years. It's a booklet that employees (whether Italian citizens or foreigners) require in order to be legally employed, which serves as an employment record (the start and end dates of all periods of employment are entered in it).

Italy has restrictions on the employment of non-EU nationals, which have been strengthened in recent years due to the high unemployment rate (around 8.9 per cent). The 1998 Immigration Law introduced a quota system that restricts the number of freelance people of any nationality and category allowed into the country each year. Uncertainty in the interpretation of the new rules, especially in consulates abroad, is making it difficult and long-winded for foreigners to work in Italy legally. However, thousands of non-EU nationals are being employed due to a severe shortage of semi-skilled and skilled workers in the north (the north-east in particular). Employers are putting pressure on the government for immigration quotas to be handled by the regions, according to local employment needs, while the politicians would prefer to create jobs for southern Italians.

Work permits for non-EU nationals must be obtained outside Italy, where an application for work authorisation (*autorizzazione al lavoro*) must be made at your local Italian embassy. The employment of non-EU nationals must be approved by the Italian labour authorities, who can propose the employment of an EU national in place of a foreigner (although this is rare). **Note that it's impossible to convert a tourist visa into a work visa and therefore if you're a non-EU national and need a visa to work in Italy, you must obtain it before your arrival in the country.** There's nothing to stop you visiting Italy as a tourist in order to find a job, but you cannot work without going home and applying for a work visa (which can take months to obtain).

Self-Employed

If you're an EU-national or a permanent resident with a *certificato di residenza* you can work as self-employed (*lavora in proprio*) or as a sole trader (*commerciante in proprio*) in Italy. If you wish to work as self-employed in a profession or start a freelance business in Italy, you must meet certain legal requirements and register with the appropriate organisations, e.g. the local chamber of commerce (*camera di commercio*). Note that a standard permit to stay doesn't automatically allow you to work as self-employed and needs to be changed to a *permesso di soggiorno per lavoro autonomo*, which depends on your nationality and status.

Under Italian law, a self-employed person must have an official status and it's illegal to simply hang up a sign and start business. People setting up in a self-employed capacity must provide evidence of their status, such as membership of a professional or trade body, a VAT number, or registration on a trade register. Members of some professions and trades must have certain qualifications and certificates recognised in Italy (see page 23). You should never be tempted to start work before you're registered as there are harsh penalties, which may include a large fine, confiscation of machinery or tools, deportation and a ban from entering Italy for a number of years.

EU nationals are entitled to work as a self-employed person (or an employee) without waiting for a residence permit to be issued. This document is merely a means of proof and not a condition of your entitlement to live in the country. If you're an EU national and obtained a residence permit as an employee, this doesn't prevent you from changing status during its period of validity and setting up in a self-employed capacity.

Students

Non-EU nationals wishing to study in Italy must prove that they're enrolled (or have been accepted) at an approved educational establishment for the principal purpose of following a course of education or vocational training. You must also prove that you're covered by health insurance and provide a declaration in writing that you have sufficient resources to pay for your studies and for living expenses for yourself and any members of your family accompanying you.

Foreign students wishing to attend university in Italy should apply to the Italian consulate in their country of residence. They will send you a list of the documents required, which include an application form where you're required to select four universities in order of preference and, for EU students, a form E111 (certificate of entitlement to health treatment). Once they've received your completed application, the consulate sends EU citizens an identity card stamped with a consul's visa, while non-EU students receive a student visa. You must present these documents to the police headquarters within eight days of arriving in Italy in order to obtain a student's permit to stay (*permesso di soggiorno per studio*) which is valid for a maximum of one year only.

Au pairs (see page 46) wishing to work in Italy are generally advised to obtain a study rather than a work visa if they're planning to stay in the country for longer than 90 days. Because the 'pocket money' they receive isn't considered a salary, the au pair agencies say that technically there's no need for them to obtain a work visa.

Family Members

Family members of Italian citizens or EU nationals don't require a visa to enter Italy if they're also Italian citizens or EU nationals. If you're an EU national, members of your family, whatever their nationality, may go with you and take advantage of their right to live in Italy. Your family is defined as your spouse, children under 21 (or dependent on you), as well as your parents and your spouse's parents, if they're also dependent on you. If you're a student, the right of residence is limited to your spouse and dependent children.

If members of your family aren't EU nationals, they may, however, require an entry visa, which should be granted free of charge and without undue formalities. There are two main types: the *visto per coesione familiare* and the *visto per ricongiungimento familiare*. The former is required when all family members are currently living outside Italy, while the latter is necessary when some family members are already living in the country. In the latter case, those living outside Italy must apply for a visa at an Italian consulate in their country of residence as usual, and their Italian relatives in Italy must also visit their local police headquarters to file an application for their relatives to join them. For both visas, in addition to the usual documents you also need documents proving your family connections, e.g. a marriage licence (*dispensa matrimoniale*). **Non-EU family members don't have the right to work in Italy unless they have their own work visa.**

The right to travel enjoyed by non-EU members of your family under EU law isn't an independent right, and it applies only when they're accompanied by an Italian or EU national. Accordingly, they aren't entitled to the visa facilities available under EU legislation when they're travelling alone. On the other hand, non-EU members of your family don't require an entry visa if they wish to travel to another country, provided they're in possession of their identity document and residence permit (see page 86).

Non-Employed Residents

Retired and non-active EU nationals don't require a visa before moving to Italy, but an application for a permit to stay (*permesso di soggiorno per dimora*) must be made within eight days of your arrival. Non-EU nationals require a residence visa to live in Italy for longer than 90 days (see page 86). All non-employed residents must prove that they have an adequate income (*reddito*) or financial resources to live in Italy without working. You're usually considered to have adequate resources if your income is at least equal to the basic Italian state pension of around €7,740 per year (see page 279) for each adult member of a family (although you're unlikely to be able to live on it!). This can be a regular income such as a salary or pension, or funds held in a bank account.

All foreign residents (including EU residents) who don't qualify for medical treatment under the Italian national health service (*servizio sanitario nazionale/SSN* – see page 254) must have private health insurance and be able to support themselves without resorting to state funds. EU nationals in receipt of a state pension are usually eligible for medical treatment under the *SSN*, but require form E-121 from their home country's social security administration as evidence.

If you're an EU national and have lived and worked in Italy for over three years, you're entitled to remain there after you've reached retirement or re-retirement age, although if you retire before the official retirement age you won't be entitled to a state pension.

Frontier Workers

Frontier workers are defined as people working in Italy but residing outside the country and returning there at least once a week. Frontier workers don't require a permit to stay but must apply for a frontier worker's card at the police headquarters nearest to their place of employment and produce evidence of their employment status and residence abroad. EU rules on social security contain certain specific provisions for cross-border workers who are covered by EU social security legislation in the same way as all the other categories of people. You're entitled to receive sickness benefits in kind in either your country of residence or your country of employment, but if you're registered as unemployed you're only entitled to claim unemployment benefit in your country of residence.

Applications

All applications for permits to stay must be made at the local police headquarters (*questura*). The validity of permits varies from a minimum of six months to indefinite and they may or may not be renewable, depending on the original purpose. An initial permit to stay for an EU national should be valid for five years. The documents required vary according to your particular circumstances and nationality, therefore you should check in advance and obtain a list – don't believe anything you're told unless it's written down (and even then it may be wrong)!

All applicants require the following:

- A valid passport, with a visa if necessary, and a photocopy of the information pages, including a visa if applicable;
- A completed application form – IPS 209 (blue) for first time applications or IPS 210 (green) for a renewal – available from the local police headquarters;
- Your previous permit (*permesso*) if you're renewing one;
- Two or three black and white (white background) passport-size photographs;
- A tax stamp (*marca da bollo*) to the value of €30 (non-EU nationals only);

The following are required for certain people, depending on their status (or at the whim of your local *questura*!):

- A birth certificate (*estratto di nascita dell'Anagrafe*) for each minor child under 18 to be included on a permit;
- Proof of residence, which may consist of a copy of a lease or purchase contract or an electricity bill. If you're a lodger, the owner must provide an attestation (*attestazione*) that you're living in his home.
- A photocopy of spouse's permit if he is a foreigner or a photocopy of spouse's identity documents if he is Italian;
- Health insurance or a medical certificate (e.g. students), if you aren't covered by Italian social security (or another country's social security system);
- Students require an admission letter to an educational institution;

- Non-employed or retired persons need proof of their financial resources.

- A family-status certificate (*stato di famiglia*), available from your town hall (*comune*) in Italy or your marriage (*certificato di matrimonio*) or divorce certificate (*sentenza di divorzio*) or other papers relating to your marital status. If you were married abroad you also need a consular declaration (translated and authenticated) to the effect that you're married;

- A criminal record (*fedina penale*) certificate – many countries don't issue these, although you should be able to get the police or a government bureau in your home country to issue a 'statement of good conduct', which may satisfy the Italian authorities;

- Employees require a declaration from a prospective employer stating his intention to hire you (or that you've started work, if permitted) and describing your professional capacity, and a *nulla osta* for work (see **Authorisation To Work** on page 78);

- Autonomous workers require a VAT number (*partita IVA*) or a letter of exemption and a chamber of commerce registration certificate (*iscrizione all camera di commercio*) or a letter from the company where they're accredited;

If you don't have all the required documents you're sent away to obtain them. Certain documents must be translated by a notarised translator (*traduttore autenticato*) and authenticated (*vidimato*). It isn't recommended to have documents translated in advance as it's expensive and the requirements often vary according to the area or office and your nationality. Certain documents must be notarised by a public notary (*notaio*) and all copies should be stamped 'official copy' (*copia ufficiale*) at the town hall or *questura*. **Original documents must always be presented with official copies.**

Renewals

An application for the renewal of a permit to stay (made on a green form) must be made well before its expiry date. When you renew your permit to stay, you must reconfirm your status and provide the same documentary evidence as for the original application. If you're self-employed, you need a photocopy of your latest tax return and the receipt for payment. If you're working in Italy, a renewal may be valid for one, two or four years, or even indefinitely (a so-called permanent permit to stay – *tempo indeterminato*), depending on how long you've been working there and other factors. There's a fee for the renewal of a permit to stay and fines for late renewal or failing to renew your permit to stay.

Moving House

When you move house, you must inform the *questura* with jurisdiction over your new place of residence and produce proof of your new address. Your permit to stay is updated with your new address. This is particularly important if you're in the process of renewing your permit to stay, as the change of address must be recorded before a new permit can be issued.

RESIDENCE PERMITS

Obtaining your permit to stay (see above) doesn't constitute residence. To obtain registration as a resident (*residenza anagrafica*) you must apply to the registry office (*ufficio anagrafe*) at your local town hall (*comune*). To obtain a residence permit (*certificato di residenza*) you require a 'suitable' address. **Although all addresses are potentially suitable for residence, some rental contracts forbid you to use an apartment's address for this purpose.** Such rental contracts are mainly used with foreigners, so that landlords can regain possession of their property more easily should they wish to do so. Eviction of any person from their legal residence is almost impossible in Italy and landlords don't want to take any unnecessary risks with foreigners.

To apply for a residence permit you require the following documents:

- A valid passport;
- A valid permit to stay (see above);
- A completed declaration of residence (*dichiarazione di residenza*) form, which is available from your town hall (*comune*);
- A consular declaration (*dichiarazione consolare*) from your country's consulate in Italy containing your name and surname, father's name, mother's name, place and date of birth, civil status (with name of spouse if married), along with the date and place of the wedding, or the date of your spouse's death if you're a widow(er), nationality, and details of other members of your family.

Once your application has been received, you're given a certificate stating that you've applied, which is valid for three months and can be renewed if necessary. A decision on whether to grant your first residence permit must be taken within six months of your application. A city police officer (*vigile urbano*) will visit the address that you've given as your habitual residence (*dimora abituale*) to ensure that you actually live there. When your permit has been granted you receive a notification that it's ready for collection from the *ufficio anagrafe*.

A residence permit for an EU national is valid for at least five years and is automatically renewable, while a student's permit is valid for one year only but is renewable. Members of your family are issued with a residence permit for the same period as the principal applicant. A residence permit remains valid even if you're absent from Italy for up to six months or if you're doing military service in your country of origin. If you change residence within Italy, you must declare it at the police headquarters of your new residence within 15 days of moving home. Your new address is entered on your residence permit.

Despite the hassles, having the right of residence (*il diritto di soggiorno*) entitles you to ship your personal effects from abroad without paying duty or VAT, buy land or property, buy and register a car, open a resident bank account, apply for an Italian driving licence, obtain an identity card (*carta di identità*), obtain health care from the local health authority (see **National Health Service** on page 254), and send your children to a state school.

When you've been granted resident status, you're entitled to most of the rights and privileges accorded to Italian citizens, apart from the right to vote in Italian parliamentary elections. For anyone planning to stay in Italy for more than a few months, applying for residence is likely to be highly desirable. Unlike most other EU countries, anyone staying in Italy for longer than 183 days per year *isn't* legally required to apply for residence. When you're resident in Italy (with a resident permit) you need to provide a 'certificate of residence' for certain transactions such as converting your driving licence and obtaining a residential electricity contract.

Foreigners who have obtained residence can, if they wish, obtain an Italian identity card from their local registry office.

Renewals, Rejections & Cancellations

All foreigners must renew their residence status within 60 days of renewing their permit to stay and may be subjected each time to a visit from the *vigile urbano*. You may renew your residence permit by carrying out the same formalities as when you first applied (indicating any change in status), except that this time you don't need to produce a visa, medical certificate or proof of your ascendants'/ descendants' relationship to you if you've already provided it. If, at the time of renewal, you've been involuntarily unemployed for more than 12 months in succession, your residence permit may be renewed for a limited period, which may not be less than 12 months. The authorities may refuse to renew your permit again if you're still unemployed when it next expires. The fee for the issue or renewal of a residence permit is the same as that for the identity card issued to Italian nationals (currently €5).

If your application for the issue or renewal of a residence permit is rejected or if a deportation order is served on you, you must be notified of the relevant decision and the reasons, except where considerations of state security prevent this. You cannot be refused a residence permit purely on the grounds that the identity documents with which you entered the country have expired.

If you're leaving Italy permanently, you must cancel your residence permit at the *sala dei certificati* section at the local police headquarters and receive confirmation. This permits you to export your personal effects from Italy without problems with customs or paying taxes.

4.

ARRIVAL

On arrival in Italy, your first task is to negotiate immigration and customs. Fortunately this presents few problems for most people, particularly European Union (EU) nationals after the establishment of 'open' EU borders on 1st January 1993. However, visitors from most other countries require a visa (see page 76). Italy has some 300 frontier crossing points, although entry for non-EU nationals with a visa is restricted to certain road/rail crossings and major airports only (as stated in a visa). A list is available from Italian consulates and embassies. All foreigners planning to remain in the country for longer than 90 days must apply for a permit to stay within eight days of their arrival (see page 79).

IMMIGRATION

Italy is a signatory to the Schengen agreement (named after a Luxembourg village on the Moselle River where it was signed), which came into effect on 26th March 1995 and introduced an open-border policy between member countries. Other Schengen members are Austria, Belgium, France, Germany, Greece, Luxembourg, the Netherlands, Portugal and Spain. Under the agreement, immigration checks and passport controls take place when you first arrive in a member country, after which you can travel freely between other Schengen countries (see also **Visitors** on page 91).

If you're a non-EU national and arrive in Italy by air or sea from outside the EU, you must go through immigration (*immigrazione*) for non-EU citizens. Officially, Italian immigration officials should check your passport, although this doesn't always happen. If you have a single-entry visa, it will be cancelled by the immigration official – if you require a visa to enter Italy and attempt to enter without one you will be refused entry. Some people may wish to get a stamp in their passport as confirmation of their date of entry into Italy.

If you're a non-EU national coming to Italy to work, study or live, you may be asked to show documentary evidence, e.g. a return ticket, proof of accommodation, health insurance and financial resources, including cash, travellers' cheques and credit cards. The onus is on you to prove that you're genuine and won't violate Italy's immigration laws. Immigration officials aren't required to prove that you will break the immigration laws and can refuse you entry on the grounds of suspicion only. Young people may be liable to interrogation, particularly long-haired youths with 'strange' attire.

Italian immigration officials are usually polite and efficient, although they're occasionally a little over-zealous in their attempts to exclude illegal immigrants, and certain nationalities or racial groups (e.g. Africans and Albanians) may experience harassment or persecution.

CUSTOMS

The Single European Act, which came into effect on 1st January 1993, created a single trading market and changed the rules regarding customs (*dogana*) for EU nationals. The shipment of personal (household) effects to Italy from another EU country is no longer subject to customs formalities, although an inventory must be provided. **All people arriving in Italy from outside the EU (including EU citizens) are still subject to customs checks and limitations on what may be imported duty-free.** You may import or export up to €10,330 in any combination of foreign or Italian currency and travellers' cheques without formality. Amounts over €10,330 (e.g. to buy a home) must be declared in order to prevent money laundering and provide statistical data for the Banca d'Italia. Information about duty-free allowances can be found on page 399 and pets on page 419.

Visitors

Your belongings aren't subject to duty or valued added tax (VAT) when you visit Italy for up to six months (183 days). This applies to the import of private cars, camping vehicles (including trailers or caravans), motorcycles, aircraft, boats and personal effects. Goods may be imported without formality, provided their nature and quantity doesn't imply any commercial aim (there may be limits on some items for non-EU nationals). All means of transport and personal effects imported duty-free mustn't be sold or given away in Italy, and must be re-exported when you leave the country. If you enter Italy by road, you may drive through a border post without stopping (most are now unmanned anyway). However, any goods and pets that you're carrying mustn't be subject to any prohibitions or restrictions. Customs officials can still stop anyone for a spot check, e.g. to check for drugs or illegal immigrants, anywhere in Italy.

If you arrive at a seaport by private boat there are no particular customs formalities, although you must show the boat's registration papers on request. A vessel registered outside the EU may remain in Italy for a maximum of six months in any calendar year, after which it must be exported or imported (when duty and tax must be paid). Foreign-registered vehicles and boats mustn't be lent or rented to anyone while in Italy.

Non-EU Residents

If you're a non-EU resident planning to take up permanent or temporary residence in Italy, you're permitted to import your furniture and personal effects free of duty. These include vehicles, mobile homes, pleasure boats and aircraft. However, to qualify for duty-free importation, articles must have been owned and used for at least six months. VAT (*IVA*) must be paid on all items owned for less than six months that weren't purchased in the EU. If goods were purchased in the EU, a VAT receipt must be produced.

All belongings should be imported within six months of the date of your change of residence, although they may be imported in a number of consignments (but it's best to have only one). A complete inventory (in English and Italian) of all items to be imported must be approved by your local Italian consulate abroad (it will be stamped and a copy returned to you), together with proof of residence in your former country and proof of settlement in Italy (i.e. a permit to stay – see page 79). If there's more than one shipment, subsequent consignments should be cleared through the same customs office. If you fail to follow the correct procedure, you may encounter problems and delays. If you use a removal company to transport your belongings to Italy, they usually provide all the necessary forms and take care of the paperwork. Always keep a copy of all forms and communications with customs officials, both in Italy and in your previous country of residence. You should have an official record of the export of valuables from any country in case you wish to re-import them later.

Prohibited & Restricted Goods

Certain goods are subject to special regulations and in some cases their import and export is prohibited or restricted. This applies in particular to animal products, plants, wild fauna and flora and products derived from them, live animals, medicines and medical products (except for prescribed drugs and medicines), firearms and ammunition, certain goods and technologies with a dual civil/military purpose, and works of art and collectors' items. If you're unsure whether any goods that you're planning to import fall into the above categories, you should check with Italian customs. Visitors arriving in Italy from 'exotic' regions, e.g. Africa, South America, and the Middle and Far East, may find themselves under close scrutiny from customs and security officials looking for illegal drugs.

EMBASSY REGISTRATION

Nationals of some countries are required to register with their local embassy or consulate after taking up residence in Italy. For other foreigners, registration isn't usually mandatory, although most embassies like to keep a record of their country's citizens resident in Italy (it helps to justify their existence). From your point of view, it makes it easier for them to find you in an emergency. For a list of embassies see **Appendix A**.

FINDING HELP

One of the most important tasks facing new arrivals in Italy is how and where to obtain help with essential everyday tasks such as buying a car, obtaining medical help and insurance requirements. This book was written in response to this need. However, in addition to the comprehensive information provided herein, you will also require detailed local information. How successful you are at finding local help depends on your employer (if applicable), the town or area where you live (those who live in major cities are usually better served than those who inhabit small towns), your nationality, Italian proficiency and sex (women are usually better served than men, through numerous women's clubs). Some companies may have a department or staff whose job is to help new arrivals settle in, or they may contract this task out to a relocation company. Unfortunately, many employers in Italy seem totally unaware of (or uninterested in) the problems and difficulties faced by their foreign employees.

There's an abundance of information available in Italian, but little in English and other foreign languages. An additional problem is that much of the available information isn't intended for foreigners and their particular needs. You may find that your friends and colleagues can help, as they can often offer advice based on their own experiences and mistakes. **But take care!** Although they mean well, you're likely to receive as much false and conflicting information as accurate (it may not necessarily be wrong, but may be invalid for your particular situation). Your local community is usually an excellent source of reliable information, but you need to speak Italian to benefit from it.

If a woman lives in or near a major town, she is able to turn to many English-speaking women's clubs and organisations for help. The single foreign male must usually fend for himself, although there are men's expatriate clubs in some areas and mixed social clubs throughout the country. Among the best sources of information and help for women are the American Women's Clubs (AWC) located in major cities. AWC provide comprehensive information in English about both local matters and topics of more general interest, and many provide data sheets, booklets and orientation programmes for newcomers to the area. Membership of the organisations is sometimes limited to Americans or those with active links to the US, e.g. through study, work or a spouse who works for a US company or the US government, but most publications and orientation programmes are available to others for a small fee. AWC are part of the Federation of American Women's Clubs Overseas (FAWCO), which can be contacted through their website (⌨ www.fawco.org).

In addition to the above, there are many social clubs and expatriate organisations for foreigners in Italy, whose members can help you find your way around. They may, however, be difficult to locate, as most clubs are run by volunteers and operate out of the president's or secretary's house, and they rarely bother to advertise or take out a phone listing. If you ask around among your neighbours or colleagues, it's possible to find various Anglo-Italian 'friendship' clubs or English-speaking organisations. Finally, don't neglect to check the Internet, where local newspapers, government offices, clubs and organisations often have their own websites. Contacts can also be found through expatriate magazines and newspapers such as *Wanted in Rome* and *The Informer* (Milan), an Internet magazine (see **Appendix A** for a list).

Many businesses (particularly large multi-national companies) produce booklets and leaflets containing useful information about clubs or activities in the area. Bookshops may have some interesting publications about the local region, and tourist and information offices are also useful sources of information. Most embassies (see page 442) and consulates in Italy also provide their nationals with local information, including the names of lawyers, interpreters, doctors, dentists, schools, and social and expatriate organisations.

CHECKLISTS

Before Arrival

The following checklist contains a summary of the tasks that should (if possible) be completed before your arrival in Italy:

- Check that your family's passports are valid!
- Obtain a visa, if necessary, for you and all your family members (see **Chapter 3**). Obviously this **must** be done **before** your arrival in Italy.
- If possible, visit Italy prior to your move to compare communities and schools, and arrange for schooling for your children (see **Chapter 9**).
- Find temporary or permanent accommodation and buy a car if you will need one. If you purchase a car in Italy, you need to register it and arrange insurance (see **Chapter 11**).
- Arrange the shipment of your personal effects to Italy.
- Arrange health (and travel) insurance for your family. This is essential if you aren't already covered by a private insurance policy and won't be covered by the Italian national health service.
- Open a bank account in Italy and transfer funds – you can open an account with some Italian banks from abroad or even via the Internet. You may also find it more convenient to obtain some euros before you arrive, which will save you having to change money immediately on arrival.
- Obtain an international driver's licence, if necessary.
- Obtain an international credit or charge card, which will prove invaluable during your first few months in Italy.
- Obtain as many credit references as possible, for example, from banks, mortgage companies, credit card companies, credit agencies, companies with which you've had accounts, and references from professionals such as lawyers and accountants. These will help you establish a credit rating in Italy.

If you're planning to become a permanent resident, you should also take all your family's official documents with you. These may include birth certificates, driving licences, marriage certificate, divorce papers or death certificate (if a widow or widower), educational diplomas and professional certificates, employment references and curricula vitae, school records and student ID cards, medical and dental records, bank account and credit card details, insurance policies (plus records of no-claims' allowances), and receipts for any valuables. You also need the documents necessary to obtain a residence permit plus certified copies, official translations and numerous passport-size photographs (students should take around a dozen).

After Arrival

The following checklist contains a summary of the tasks to be completed after arrival in Italy (if not done before arrival):

- On arrival at an Italian airport, port or border post, have your visa cancelled and your passport stamped, as applicable.

- If you aren't taking a car with you, you may wish to rent (see page 246) or buy one locally. **Note that it's practically impossible to get around in rural areas without a vehicle.**

- In the few days after your arrival complete the following (if not done before arrival):

  - Apply for a permit to stay (see page 79) within eight days of your arrival;

  - Register with your local social security office (see page 274);

  - Apply for a fiscal code (*codice fiscale*) from your local tax office (*intendenza di finanza*);

  - Register with your local embassy or consulate (see page 92);

  - Open a post office or bank account (see pages 134 and 299 respectively) and give the details to your employer and any companies that you plan to pay by direct debit or standing order (such as utility companies);

  - Register with a local doctor (see page 256);

  - Arrange schooling for your children (see **Chapter 9**);

  - Arrange whatever insurance is necessary (see **Chapter 13**), including health insurance (see page 282), household insurance (see page 285), car insurance (see page 226) and third party liability insurance (see page 288).

5.

ACCOMMODATION

In most areas of Italy, finding accommodation to rent or buy isn't difficult, provided your requirements aren't too unusual. There are, however, a few exceptions. For example, in major cities such as Rome and Milan, rented accommodation is in high demand and short supply, and rents can be high. Accommodation accounts for around 25 per cent of the average Italian family's budget, but can be up to 50 per cent in the major cities. Property prices and rents vary considerably according to the region and city, and have increased steadily in all major cities in recent years. For example, an apartment renting for €550 per month in Naples would cost up to €1,650 per month in Milan or Rome. In cities and large towns, apartments are much more common than detached houses, which are rare and prohibitively expensive.

The average Italian lives with his parents until the age of around 30, including some 50 per cent of those aged between 25 and 30. However, around 70 per cent of Italians own their own homes, around the same as in Britain, compared with some 80 per cent in Spain, 55 per cent in France and just 40 per cent in Germany and Switzerland. Many Italians also own second homes in the country (perhaps in their home village) or in a mountain or coastal resort.

TEMPORARY ACCOMMODATION

On arrival in Italy, you may find it necessary to stay in temporary accommodation for a few weeks or months, e.g. before moving into permanent accommodation or while waiting for your furniture to arrive. Some employers provide rooms, self-contained apartments or hostels for employees and their families, although this is rare and usually for a limited period only. Many hotels and bed and breakfast establishments cater for long-term guests and offer reduced weekly or monthly rates. In most areas, particularly in Rome and other main cities, service and holiday apartments are available. These are fully self-contained, furnished apartments with their own bathrooms and kitchens, which are cheaper and more convenient than a hotel, particularly for families. Service apartments are usually rented on a weekly basis. In most provincial regions, self-catering holiday accommodation (see page 333) is available, although this is very expensive during the main holiday season (June-August).

For information about hotels, budget accommodation and self-catering, see **Chapter 15**.

RELOCATION CONSULTANTS

If you're fortunate enough to have your move to Italy paid for by your employer, it's likely that he will arrange for a relocation consultant to handle the details. There are fewer relocation consultants in Italy than in some other European countries and they usually deal exclusively with corporate clients with plenty of money to pay their fees. Fees depend on the services required, with packages usually ranging from around €1,700 to €8,000. The main service provided by relocation consultants is finding accommodation (either to rent or purchase) and arranging viewings.

Other housing services include conducting negotiations, drawing up contracts, arranging mortgages, organising surveys and insurance, and handling the move. Consultants also provide reports on local schools, health services, public transport, sports and social facilities, and other amenities and services. Some companies provide daily advice and help, and assistance in dealing with Italian officials, e.g. residence procedures. Finding rental accommodation for single people or couples without children can usually be accomplished in a few weeks, while locating family homes may take up to four weeks, depending on the location and requirements. You should usually allow two to three months between your initial visit and moving into a purchased property.

ITALIAN HOMES

Italian homes and living standards used to be fairly basic, particularly in rural areas, where many homes had no bathroom or toilet. However, with the huge rise in the standard (and cost) of living in the last few decades, Italian homes have been transformed and today's average Italian is better housed than many other Europeans. In cities, people generally live in apartments, houses being rare and prohibitively expensive. Italian apartments are usually surprisingly small and it's unusual to find apartments with four or more bedrooms and even three-bedroom apartments aren't easy to find. Most do, however, have two bathrooms. New detached homes (called villas) are generally luxurious internally, but often have bland or even ugly exteriors. In contrast to modern homes, old buildings are an architectural delight and contain a wealth of attractive period features. Whether old or new, Italians take great pride in their homes and no expense is spared to make them comfortable and beautiful.

Homes are as varied as the climate and people, but one thing they all have in common is sturdy building materials. The exterior may be made of wood, stone, brick or other (usually fire resistant) materials. Interior walls are usually white *stucco* plaster (*intonaco*), which may be painted in pastel colours and makes a perfect backdrop for paintings and tapestries, while bedroom walls are often covered with wallpaper. Wood floors (*parquet*) are common in northern Italian homes, but are considered a luxury in the rest of Italy and therefore generally reserved for the master bedroom. Marble or *travertino* is often used in entrance halls (*ingressi*), corridors (*corridoi*) and living rooms (*saloni*), while kitchens (*cucine*) and baths (*bagni*) are generally enhanced by beautiful ceramic tiles (for which Italy is famous). Bathrooms are fitted with a toilet (*gabinetto*), washbasin (*lavandino*), bidet (*bidé*) and a shower (*doccia*) or bath (*vasca*), or perhaps a bath with a shower attachment. Luxury homes often sport a Jacuzzi (*idromassaggio*). When there's no separate utility or laundry room (*lavanderia*), the hot-water heater (*scaldabagno*) and washing machine (*lavatrice*) are usually stored in the main 'service' (*servizio*) bathroom.

Italian homes are completely empty when purchased, except perhaps for the bathroom porcelain and the kitchen sink. All furnishings and appliances are chosen and bought by the new owner, who can have the kitchen fitted by a local carpenter-artisan or buy factory-produced kitchen cabinets. Ovens can be electric or mains gas (which is available in most urban areas) and country properties may also have an outside pizza/bread oven (*forno a legna*) and sometimes a *tinello* or *taverna* that acts as a family room or a summer kitchen/dining room. Very few Italians use clothes dryers (the sun and wind suffice), but washing machines are as common as televisions. If you live in a rural area, you may find a public washhouse (*lavatoio*), which is good for washing voluminous things such as curtains, in addition to being a good place to catch up on local gossip.

Country properties that haven't been restored rarely have any kind of heating ('What you don't spend in wood, you spend in wool' is an old Italian saying), except for numerous fireplaces, which mean lots of atmosphere and a well-stacked wood pile. The thick stone walls (which in old buildings may be over one metre) of older homes keep out the cold in winter thus reducing heating (*riscaldamento*) costs, while in summer they act as insulation against the heat. In northern Italy and mountainous areas, double-glazing is necessary. Heating systems may consist of an oil fired furnace, mains gas or gas bottles in rural areas. In apartments (*condominio*), hot water and heating are centralised and paid for along with other *condominio* fees that may include the cleaning of common areas (*pulizia scale*), a porter (*portiere*) and gardener (*giardiniere*).

In old rural homes, the fireplace (*camino*) plays an important role, being used for heating and cooking as well as for atmosphere. (Most city dwellers dream of having a fireplace, while many country homeowners would like to have central heating!). Sometimes the fireplace surround is missing, as old buildings are often 'stripped' of architectural detail, although replacements can be bought from architectural salvage dealers. However, an old fireplace surround in marble or *peperino* costs between €1,500 to €5,500, although a local artisan can make a new one to order for much less. If you suspect that a room once had a fireplace, you can 'sound' the walls to find the flue, which can then be reopened. Windows are usually protected with shutters (*persiane*), which are usually closed at night to keep heat in and prying eyes out. In city apartments they're known as *tapparelle* or *avvolgenti* (rolling shutters) and are made of metal, wood or plastic slats. They're raised and lowered manually with cords (that break frequently) or with an electric motor.

BUYING PROPERTY

Buying property in Italy is usually a good long-term investment and is preferable to renting. However, if you're staying only for a relatively short term, say less than five years, you may be better off renting. For those staying longer than this, buying is usually the better option, particularly as buying a house or apartment is generally no more expensive than renting in the long term and could yield a handsome profit (or a loss!). Provided you avoid the most expensive areas, property is relatively inexpensive compared with many other European countries, although the fees associated with a purchase add an average of around 12 per cent to the cost.

Italians aren't very mobile and move house much less frequently than the Americans and British, which is reflected in the fairly stable property market. More Italians own their own homes than the inhabitants of most other EU countries, although they don't generally buy property as an investment, but as a home for life. It generally isn't worth buying a home in Italy unless you plan to stay for the medium to long term, say a minimum of five years and preferably 10 to 15 and you shouldn't expect to make a quick profit, although there has been no capital gains tax (see page 318) on property since 1993. Property values are currently increasing at around 8 per cent per year, meaning you must own a home for over two years simply to recover the high fees associated with buying. Property prices rise faster than average in some fashionable areas, although this is generally reflected in higher purchase prices (in recent years, prices have risen sharply in the most popular major cities such as Rome, Milan and Florence).

As when buying property anywhere, it's never wise to be in too much of a hurry. Have a good look around in your preferred area(s) and make sure that you have a clear picture of the relative prices and the kinds of properties available. There's a huge variety of properties in Italy, ranging from derelict farmhouses requiring complete restoration to new luxury apartments and villas with all modern conveniences. Some people set themselves impossible deadlines in which to buy a property or business (e.g. a few days or a week) and often end up bitterly regretting their impulsive decision. Although it's a common practice, mixing a holiday with a property purchase isn't recommended, as most people are inclined to make poor business decisions when their mind is on play rather than work.

It's a wise or lucky person who gets his choice absolutely right first time, which is why most experts recommend that you rent before buying unless you're absolutely sure what you want, how much you wish to pay and where you want to live. To reduce the chances of making an expensive error when buying in an unfamiliar region, it's often prudent to rent for 6 to 12 months, taking in the worst part of the year (weather-wise). This allows you to become familiar with the region and the weather, and gives you plenty of time to look around for a permanent home at your leisure. There's no shortage of properties for sale in Italy and whatever kind of property you're looking for, you will have an abundance from which to choose. Wait until you find your 'dream' home and then think about it for another week or two before signing a contract.

To get an idea of property prices in different regions, check the prices of properties advertised in English-language property magazines and Italian newspapers, magazines and property journals (see **Appendix A**). Property price indexes for various regions are published by some Italian property magazines (e.g. *Ville & Casali*), although these should be taken as a rough guide only. Before deciding on the price, make sure you know **exactly** what's included, as it isn't unusual for Italians to strip a house or apartment bare when selling and remove the kitchen sink, toilets, light fittings and even the light switches! If applicable, have fixtures and fittings listed in the contract.

When you buy a home in Italy, you should go to the town hall (*municipio*) to register your ownership. After this date all bills for local services are sent automatically and are payable at a post office or local bank (or by direct debit).

For anyone planning to buy a home in Italy, our sister publication, *Buying a Home in Italy* by David Hampshire is essential reading (see page 472). A comprehensive list of other books is contained in **Appendix B**.

RENTED ACCOMMODATION

If you're planning to stay in Italy for only a few years (say less than five), then renting is usually the best solution. It's also the answer for those who don't want the trouble, expense and restrictions associated with buying a property. **In fact, it's prudent for anyone looking for a permanent home in Italy to rent for a period until you know exactly what you want, how much you wish to pay and where you want to live.** This is particularly important for retirees who don't know Italy well, when renting allows you to become familiar with an area, its weather, amenities and the local people, to meet other foreigners who have made their homes in Italy and share their experiences, and not least, to discover the cost of living at first hand. This section is concerned with long-term rentals and **not** short-term holiday rentals (for information about holiday rentals see **Self-Catering** on page 333).

Italy has a strong rental market and it's possible to rent every kind of property, from a tiny studio apartment (bedsitter) to a huge rambling castle (*castello*). Rental properties are mostly privately owned, but include properties owned by companies and public housing owned by local councils. If you're looking for a home for less than a year, you're better off looking for a furnished apartment or house. Most rental properties are let unfurnished (*non-ammobiliato*), particularly for lets longer than one year, and long-term furnished (*ammobiliato*) properties are difficult to find. Bear in mind that in Italy, unfurnished means a property is completely empty, except perhaps for the bathroom porcelain and possibly a kitchen sink. There will be no kitchen cupboards, appliances, light fittings, curtains or carpets, although you may be able to buy these from the departing tenant. Semi-furnished apartments usually have kitchen cupboards and bathroom fixtures, and possibly a few pieces of furniture, while furnished properties tend to be fully equipped, including crockery, bedding and possibly towels (similar to renting a self-catering apartment).

Finding A Rental Property

Your success in finding a suitable rental property depends on many factors, not least the kind of rental you're seeking (a one-bedroom apartment is easier to find than a four-bedroom detached house), how much you want to pay and the area where you wish to live. There are a number of ways of finding a property to rent, including the following:

- Ask your friends, relatives and acquaintances to help spread the word, particularly if you're looking in the area where you already live. A lot of rental properties are found by word of mouth, particularly in major cities, where it's almost impossible to find somewhere with a reasonable rent unless you have connections.
- Check the small advertisements in local newspapers and magazines (see below).
- Look for properties with a 'to rent' sign (*affittasi* or *da affitare*) in the window.
- Visit accommodation and letting agents. Most cities and large towns have estate agents (*agenzie immobiliari*) who also act as letting agents for owners. Look under *Agenzie Immobiliare* in the yellow pages. It's often better to deal with an agent than directly with owners, particularly with regard to contracts and legal matters.
- Look for advertisements in shop windows and on bulletin boards in shopping centres, supermarkets, universities and colleges, and company offices.
- Check newsletters published by churches, clubs and expatriate organisations, and their notice boards.

To find accommodation through small advertisements (*piccola pubblicità – affittasi appartamento*) in local newspapers you must usually be quick off the mark. Buy newspapers as soon as they're published and start phoning straight away. You can also view rental advertisements on the Internet, and all major newspapers have websites (see **Newspapers, Magazines & Books** on page 392). Other sources include expatriate publications published in major cities such as *Wanted in Rome* (see **Appendix A**) and small newspapers such as *Porta Portese* (Wednesdays and Saturdays) in Rome, *La Pulce* (Florence) and *Secondamano* (Milan) – there are equivalents in most cities. Some estate agents also provide apartment listings in their real estate magazines, such as *Solo Casa* in Rome.

You must be available to inspect properties immediately or at any time. Even if you start phoning at the crack of dawn, you're still likely to find a queue when you arrive to view a property in Rome or Milan. The best days for advertisements are usually Fridays and Saturdays. Advertisers may be private owners, real-estate managers or letting agencies (particularly in major cities). You can insert a 'rental wanted' (*cercasi appartamento* or *cercasi in affitto*) advertisement in many newspapers and on notice boards, but don't count on success using this method. Finding a property to rent in Rome is similar to the situation in London and New York, where the best properties are usually found through personal contacts. The worst time to look is during September and October when Italians return from their summer holidays and students are looking for accommodation.

Rental Costs

Rental costs vary considerably according to the size (number of bedrooms) and quality of a property, its age and the facilities provided. However, the most significant factor affecting rents is the region of Italy, the city and the particular neighbourhood. Until recently, Italy had a fair rent (*equo canone*) law that limited rents to those set by the local authorities rather than market levels. This resulted in a shortage of rental properties in some areas and owners are now permitted to set market level rents, which has encouraged more owners to let properties. Most rents are negotiable and you should try to obtain a reduction. Sometimes an agent will suggest offering a reduced rent and even tell you what to offer. **Rental payments are tax deductible for residents.** The table below is a guide to current rents:

Size of Property	Monthly Rental (€)
Studio (bedsitter)	300 – 900
1 bedroom	450 – 1,100
2 bedrooms	650 – 1,500
3 bedrooms	800 – 2,000

The above rents are for unfurnished, good quality, new or renovated properties in most rural and suburban areas. They don't include properties in major city centres and popular resorts (such as the Alps, Italian lakes and resorts), exclusive residential areas or furnished accommodation, for which the sky's the limit.

If you rent a property through an agent, you must pay the agent's fee, typically around 10 per cent of a year's rent or one month's rental. Provided rent isn't paid in advance at more than two-monthly intervals, the landlord can ask for a deposit equal to one to three months' rent. The deposit must be returned with interest within two months of the termination of the lease, less the amount due to the landlord for damages, redecoration, etc. Although it's illegal, many tenants don't pay their last few months' rent and forfeit their deposit. Rent is normally paid one month in advance and you cannot be required to pay your rent by direct bank deposit.

In addition to rent, tenants in an apartment must have compulsory insurance and pay service charges. There will also be a set of house rules and regulations (*regolamento*), of which you should obtain a copy. Service charges usually include such things as heating, hot water, rubbish removal, upkeep of grounds and gardens, use of lift, communal lighting and maintenance, and possibly a caretaker's services. Other utilities such as gas, electricity and water are usually paid separately by tenants. Always check whether rent is inclusive or exclusive of charges, which is usually stated in advertisements. Service charges are calculated monthly (payable with the rent) and are usually higher in a new building than an old one. They can vary considerably from as little as €20 to €200 or more per month. Ask to see a copy of the bills from the previous year.

You should also ask to see the bills for telephone and utilities (electricity, gas and water) and check that the previous tenant has paid the bills up-to-date, otherwise you could be liable for any debts.

Rental Contracts

New rental regulations were introduced in 1999, since when there have been two kinds of rental contract: a free market contract (*contratto a libero mercato*) and a 'convention' contract (*contratto convenzionati*) containing pre-determined conditions. A free market contract is for four years renewable for an additional four-year period, in which the tenant and landlord agree the conditions between themselves. A *contratto convenzionato* is a three-year contract with a two-year renewal option, although the initial period can be increased to five years with no renewal option. These new contracts replace the old rent control (*equo canone*) and long-term (*patti in deroga*) contracts, although these contracts remain valid until their expiry date, when they're replaced by one of the new contracts. Luxury apartments (*di lusso*), public housing and tourist apartments are exempt from free market contracts. If applicable, a 'tenants and owners' association must usually approve contracts for apartments. A contract should be registered with the local *ufficio del registro* to be valid.

If a landlord needs to reclaim a property before the expiration of a free market contract, he can do so by giving the tenant six months' notice (*disdetta*) in writing, but only under certain conditions. These include requiring the property for his own use, for a child who's getting married, for an elderly parent or in-law, or to make improvements or repairs prior to selling it. However, if within a year the property isn't used for the purpose stated in the notification, the landlord must renew the original rental contract with the same tenant or pay an amount equal to three years' rent as compensation. Otherwise a landlord can reclaim a property only by giving a tenant six months' notice prior to the end of the contract expiry date. If a landlord wishes to sell a property, a tenant has the first option to buy it.

A convention contract includes properties rented under national agreements between property associations and renters' unions, who establish the rent. It's possible to terminate the contract prior to the first expiration date, while the landlord must give a tenant six months' notice prior to the end of the contract expiry date. A convention contract can also include short-term leases for university students and transitory workers.

The new regulations provide tax breaks for landlords and also established a national fund to help low-income families who are eligible for public housing, but because of a lack of public housing are required to rent apartments on the open market.

Although all addresses are potentially suitable for residence, some rental contracts forbid you to use an apartment's address for this purpose. Such rental contracts are mainly used with foreigners, so that a landlord can regain possession of his property more easily should he wish to do so. Eviction of a person from his legal residence is almost impossible in Italy and landlords don't want to take any unnecessary risks with foreigners.

Inventory

One of the most important tasks to perform after moving into a new home is to make an inventory of the fixtures and fittings and, if applicable, the furniture and furnishings. When you've purchased a property, you should check that the previous owner hasn't absconded with any fixtures and fittings included in the price or anything which you specifically paid for, e.g. carpets, light fittings, curtains, furniture, kitchen cupboards and appliances, garden ornaments, plants or doors. It's common to do a final check or inventory when buying a new property, which is usually done a few weeks before completion.

When moving into a long-term rental property, it's necessary to complete an inventory (*inventario*) of its contents and a report on its condition. This includes the condition of fixtures and fittings, the state of furniture and furnishings, the cleanliness and state of the decoration, and anything that's damaged, missing or in need of repair. An inventory should be provided by your landlord or agent and may include every single item in a furnished property (down to the number of teaspoons). The inventory check should be carried out in your presence, both when taking over and when terminating a rental agreement. If an inventory isn't provided, you should insist on one being prepared and annexed to the lease. If you find a serious fault after signing the inventory, send a registered letter to your landlord and ask for it to be attached to the inventory.

An inventory should be drawn up both when moving in and when vacating a rented property. If the two inventories don't correspond, you must make good any damages or deficiencies or the landlord can do so and deduct the cost from your deposit. Although Italian landlords are generally no worse than those in most other countries, some do almost anything to avoid repaying a deposit. **Note the reading on your utility meters (e.g. electricity, gas and water) and check that you aren't overcharged on your first bill.** Meters should be read by utility companies before you move in, although you may need to organise this.

It's wise to obtain written instructions from the previous owner regarding the operation of appliances and heating and air-conditioning systems, maintenance of grounds, gardens and lawns, care of special surfaces such as wooden, marble or tiled floors, and the names of reliable local maintenance men who know a property and are familiar with its quirks. Check with your local town hall regarding local regulations about such things as rubbish collection, recycling and on-road parking.

HOME SECURITY

When moving into a new home, it's often wise to replace the locks (or lock barrels) as soon as possible, as you have no idea how many keys are in circulation for the existing locks. This is true even for new homes, as builders often give keys to sub-contractors. In any case it's recommended to change the external locks or lock barrels periodically, particularly if you let a home. If not already fitted, it's best to fit high security (double cylinder or dead bolt) locks. Modern properties may already be fitted with high security locks that are individually numbered. Extra keys for these locks cannot be cut at a local hardware store and you need to obtain details from the previous owner or your landlord. Many modern developments have security gates and caretakers.

In areas with a high risk of theft (e.g. most major cities and resorts), your insurance company will insist on extra security measures such as two locks on all external doors, internal locking shutters, security bars on windows less than 10m (33ft) from the ground and grilles on patio doors. An external door must usually be of the armoured (*porta blindata*) variety with a steel rod locking mechanism. An insurance policy may specify that all forms of protection must be employed when a property is unoccupied. If security precautions aren't adhered to, a claim may be reduced. It's usually necessary to have a safe for any insured valuables, which must be approved by your insurance company.

You may wish to have a security alarm fitted, which is usually the best way to deter thieves and may also reduce your household insurance (see page 285). It should include all external doors and windows, internal infra-red security beams, and may also include a coded entry keypad (which can be frequently changed and is useful for clients if you let a home) and 24-hour monitoring (with some systems it's even possible to monitor properties remotely from another country). With a monitored system, when a sensor (e.g. smoke or forced entry) detects an emergency or a panic button is pushed, a signal is sent automatically to a 24-hour monitoring station. The duty monitor will telephone to check whether it's a genuine alarm and if he cannot contact you someone will be sent to investigate.

You can deter thieves by ensuring that your house is well lit and not conspicuously unoccupied. External security 'motion detector' lights (that switch on automatically when someone approaches), random timed switches for internal lights, radios and televisions, dummy security cameras, and tapes that play barking dogs triggered by a light or heat detector may all help deter burglars. In remote areas, it's common for owners to fit two or three locks on external doors, alarm systems, grills on doors and windows, window locks, security shutters and a safe for valuables. The advantage of grills is that they allow you to leave windows open without inviting criminals in (unless they're *very* slim). You can fit UPVC (toughened clear plastic) security windows and doors, which can survive an attack with a sledge-hammer without damage, and external steel security blinds (which can be electrically operated), although these are expensive.

A dog can be useful to deter intruders, although he should be kept inside where he cannot be given poisoned food. Irrespective of whether you actually have a dog, a warning sign with a picture of a fierce dog may act as a deterrent. If not already present, you should have the front door of an apartment fitted with a spy-hole and chain so that you can check the identity of a visitor before opening the door. **Remember, prevention is better than cure, as stolen property is rarely recovered.**

Holiday homes are particularly vulnerable to thieves and in some areas they're regularly ransacked. No matter how secure your door and window locks, a thief can usually obtain entry if he is sufficiently determined, often by simply smashing a window or even breaking in through the roof or by knocking a hole in a wall! In isolated areas, thieves can strip a house bare at their leisure and an unmonitored alarm won't be a deterrent if there's no-one around to hear it. If you have a holiday home in Italy, it isn't wise to leave anything of real value (monetary or sentimental) there.

If you vacate your home for an extended period, it may be obligatory to notify your caretaker, landlord or insurance company, and to leave a key with the caretaker or landlord in case of emergencies. If you have a robbery, you should report it immediately to your local police station, where you must make a statement (*denuncia*). You receive a copy, which is required by your insurance company if you make a claim.

Another important aspect of home security is ensuring that you have early warning of a fire, which is easily accomplished by installing smoke detectors. Battery-operated smoke detectors can be purchased from around €8 and should be tested weekly to ensure that the batteries aren't exhausted. You can also fit an electric-powered gas detector that activates an alarm when a gas leak is detected.

MOVING HOUSE

After finding a home in Italy, it usually takes only a few weeks to have your belongings shipped from within continental Europe. From anywhere else it varies considerably, e.g. around four weeks from the east coast of America, six weeks from the US west coast and the Far East, and around eight weeks from Australasia. Customs clearance is no longer necessary when shipping your household effects from one European Union (EU) country to another. However, when shipping your effects from a non-EU country to Italy, you should enquire about customs formalities in advance.

If you're moving to Italy from a non-EU country you must present an inventory (in English and Italian) of the items that you're planning to import at your local Italian consulate, which must be officially stamped. You also need a 'permit to stay' (see page 79) from the local police station (*questura*). If you fail to follow the correct procedure you can encounter problems and delays, and may be charged duty or fined. The relevant forms to be completed by non-EU citizens depend on whether your Italian home will be your main residence or a second home. Shipping companies usually take care of the paperwork and ensure that the correct documents are completed (see **Customs** on page 90).

It's wise to use a major shipping company with a good reputation. For international moves it's best to use a company that's a member of the

International Federation of Furniture Removers (FIDI) or the Overseas Moving Network International (OMNI), with experience in Italy. Members of FIDI and OMNI usually subscribe to an advance payment scheme providing a guarantee. If a member company fails to fulfil its commitments to a client, the move is completed at the agreed cost by another company or your money is refunded. Some shipping companies have subsidiaries or affiliates in Italy, which may be more convenient if you encounter problems or need to make an insurance claim.

You should obtain at least three written quotations before choosing a company, as costs vary considerably. Moving companies should send a representative to provide a detailed quotation. Most companies pack your belongings and provide packing cases and special containers, although this is naturally more expensive than packing them yourself. Ask a company how they pack fragile and valuable items, and whether the cost of packing cases, materials and insurance (see below) is included in a quotation. If you're doing your own packing, most shipping companies provide packing crates and boxes. Shipments are charged by volume, e.g. the square metre in Europe and the square foot in North America. You should expect to pay from €3,200 to €6,400 to move the contents of a three to four-bedroom house within Western Europe, e.g. from London to the north of Italy. If you're flexible about the delivery date, shipping companies will quote a lower fee based on a 'part load', where the cost is shared with other deliveries, which can result in savings of 50 per cent or more compared with an individual delivery. Whether you have an individual or shared delivery, obtain the maximum transit period in writing, otherwise you may need to wait months for delivery!

Be sure to fully insure your belongings during the move with a well-established insurance company. **Don't insure with a shipping company that carries its own insurance as they usually fight every 'penny' of a claim.** Insurance premiums are usually 1 to 2 per cent of the declared value of your goods, depending on the kind of cover chosen. It's prudent to make a photographic or video record of valuables for insurance purposes. Most insurance policies cover for 'all-risks' on a replacement value basis. Note that china, glass and other breakables are usually only included in an 'all-risks' policy when they're packed by the shipping company. Insurance usually covers total loss or loss of a particular crate only, rather than individual items (unless they were packed by the shipping company). If there are any breakages or damaged items, they should be noted and listed before you sign the delivery bill (although it's obviously impractical to check everything on delivery). If you need to make a claim, be sure to read the small print as some companies require customers to make a claim within a few days, although seven is usual. Send a claim by registered post. Some insurance companies apply an 'excess' of around 1 per cent of the total shipment value when assessing claims. This means that if your shipment is valued at €25,000 and you make a claim for less than €250, you won't receive anything.

If you're unable to ship your belongings directly to Italy, most shipping companies will put them into storage and some allow a limited free storage period prior to shipment, e.g. 14 days. **If you need to put your household effects into storage, it's important to have them fully insured as warehouses have been known to burn down!** Make a complete list of everything to be moved and give a copy to the shipping company. Don't include anything illegal (e.g. guns, bombs, drugs or pornographic videos) with your belongings as customs checks can be rigorous and penalties severe. Provide the shipping company with **detailed** instructions how to find your Italian home from the nearest motorway (or main road) and a telephone number where you can be contacted.

After considering the shipping costs, you may decide to ship only selected items of furniture and personal effects, and buy new furniture in Italy. If you're importing household goods from another European country, it's possible to rent a self-drive van or truck. **If you rent a vehicle outside Italy you need to return it to the country where it was hired.** If you plan to transport your belongings to Italy personally, check the customs' requirements in the countries you must pass through. Most people find it isn't wise to do their own move unless it's a simple job, e.g. a few items of furniture and personal effects only. It's no fun heaving beds and wardrobes up stairs and squeezing them into impossible spaces. If you're taking pets with you, you may need to ask your vet to tranquillise them, as many pets are frightened (even more than people) by the chaos and stress of moving house.

Bear in mind when moving home that everything that can go wrong often does, therefore you should allow plenty of time and try not to arrange your move from your old home on the same day as the new owner is moving in. That's just asking for fate to intervene! **Last but not least, if your Italian home has poor or impossible access for a large truck, you must inform the shipping company (the ground must also be firm enough to support a heavy vehicle).** Note also that if furniture needs to be taken in through an upstairs window, you may need to pay extra. See also **Customs** on page 90 and the **Checklists** on page 438.

ELECTRICITY

Most electricity in Italy is supplied by Ente Nazionale per l'Energia Elettrica (ENEL, 🖳 www.enel.it), which had a monopoly on providing electricity before being privatised in 1998, although there's still little competition. Most electricity is generated by burning oil, none of the country's four nuclear power plants having been in operation since a public vote against the use of nuclear power in a referendum in 1987. Italy imports around 15 per cent of its electricity from France and Switzerland. In major cities, electricity may be controlled by a local municipal energy board, e.g. the Azienda Energetica Municipale (AEM) in Milan. Electricity and other utility offices are listed in telephone directories under *Numeri di Pubblica Utilità*.

After buying or renting a property (unless utilities are included in the rent), you must sign a new contract (*volturazione delle utenze*) at the local office of your electricity company. You need to take with you some identification (passport or residence permit), a copy of the deeds or rental contract, the registration number of the meter (*contatore*), the previous tenant's electricity contract or a bill paid by the previous owner (and a good book as queues can be long). If you've purchased a home in Italy, the real estate agent may arrange for the utilities to be transferred to your name or go with you to the office (no charge should be made for this service). Make sure all previous bills have been paid and that the contract is transferred to your name from the day you take over. If you're a non-resident owner, you should also give your foreign address or the address of a representative in Italy, in case there are any problems requiring your attention such as your bank refusing to pay the bills. You need to cancel (*disdire*) the contract when you move house.

Power Supply

The electricity supply in Italy is generally 220 volts AC with a frequency of 50 hertz (cycles) and either two or three phase, although in some areas older buildings may still use 125 volts. Not all appliances, e.g. TVs made for 240 volts, will function with a power supply of 220 volts. Power cuts are frequent in many areas of Italy (many lasting just a few micro-seconds or just long enough to crash a computer), particularly in rural areas, and the electricity supply is also unstable, with power surges commonplace. If you use a computer you should have an uninterrupted power supply (UPS) with a battery backup, which allows you time to shut down your computer and save your work after a power failure. If you live in an area where cuts are frequent and rely on electricity for your livelihood, e.g. for operating a computer, fax machine and other equipment, you may need to install a backup generator. **Even more important than a battery backup is a power surge protector for appliances such as TVs, computers and fax machines, without which you risk equipment being damaged or destroyed.** In remote areas you must install a generator or solar power system if you want electricity, as there's no mains electricity, although some people make do with gas and oil lamps (and without TV and other modern conveniences).

Wiring Standards & Connection

Most modern properties (e.g. less than 20 years old) in Italy have decent electrical installations. However, old rural homes may have no electricity or may need totally rewiring. You should ensure that the electricity installations are in good condition well in advance of moving house, as it can take some time to have a new meter installed or get the electricity reconnected. The wiring in a new or renovated house (that has been rewired) must be inspected and approved by an ENEL inspector before a contract is issued and connection (*allacciato*) is made. If you have any electrical work done in your home you should ensure that you employ an electrician (*electtricista*) who's registered at the local chamber of commerce or a member of an official body such as Uane, who works to ENEL's standards. There are safety regulations for all domestic electrical and gas systems and appliances, which must be inspected annually. Householders must have a certificate of inspection and there are fines of up to €5,200 for offenders who break the law.

If you buy a rural property without electricity that's over 500 metres from the nearest electricity pylon, you must pay to have the service extended to the property. The cost of connecting a rural property to mains electricity can be prohibitively expensive or even be impossible, in which case you can install a generator or solar power system (see page 121). In this case, wiring doesn't need to be installed to the high standard required by ENEL. **A generator should be powered by diesel and secured against theft.**

Meters

In an old apartment block there may be a common meter, with the bill shared among the apartment owners according to the size of their apartments. However, all new properties have their own meters, which for an apartment block or townhouse development may be installed in a basement in a special room or be housed in a meter 'cupboard' in a stairwell or outside a group of properties. A meter should be located outside a home so that it can be read by electricity company staff when you aren't at home.

Plugs

Depending on the country you've come from, you will need new plugs (*spine*) or a lot of adapters. Plug adapters for most foreign electrical apparatus can be purchased in Italy, although it's wise to bring some adapters with you, plus extension cords and multi-plug extensions that can be fitted with Italian plugs. There's often a shortage of electricity points in Italian homes, with perhaps just one per room (including the kitchen), so multi-plug adapters may be essential. Electricity points don't usually have their own switches. Most Italian plugs have two or three round pins (when present, the middle pin of three is for the earth or ground) and come in various sizes depending on the power consumption of the appliance. Small low-wattage electrical appliances such as table lamps and small TVs don't require an earth. However, plugs with an earth must be used for high-wattage appliances such as fires, kettles, washing machines and refrigerators, and must be used with earthed sockets. Electrical appliances that are earthed have a three-core wire and must never be used with a two-pin plug without an earth socket. **Always make sure that a plug is correctly and securely wired, as bad wiring can be fatal.**

Fuses

In modern properties, fuses (*fusibili*) are of the earth trip type. When there's a short circuit or the system has been overloaded, a circuit breaker is tripped and the power supply is cut. If your electricity fails, you should suspect a fuse of tripping off, particularly if you've just switched on an electrical appliance (usually you will hear the power switch off). Before reconnecting the power, switch off any high-power appliances such as a cooker, washing machine or heater.

Make sure you know where the trip switches are located and keep a torch handy so you can find them in the dark (see also **Power Rating** below).

Bulbs

Electric light bulbs in Italy are of the Edison type with a screw fitting. If you have lamps requiring bayonet bulbs you should bring some with you, as they cannot be readily purchased in Italy. You can, however, buy adapters to convert from bayonet to screw fitting (or vice versa). Bulbs for non-standard electrical appliances (i.e. appliances that aren't made for the Italian market) such as refrigerators and sewing machines may not be available in Italy, therefore bring some spares with you.

Power Rating

If the power keeps tripping off when you attempt to use a number of high-power appliances simultaneously, e.g. an electric kettle, heater and cooker, it means that the power rating of your property is too low. This is a common problem in Italy. If this is the case, you may need to contact your electricity company and ask them to upgrade the power supply to your property (it can also be downgraded if the power supply is higher than you require). Bear in mind that it can take some time to get your power rating changed. The power rating to a private dwelling in Italy can be 1.5kw, 3kw or 6kw (the maximum). The minimum rating is 1.5kw, which is sufficient for a few lights only and even with a 3kw rating you're unable to run more than two or three high-powered appliances simultaneously. Consequently many people are now switching to 6kw. The maximum is generally unrestricted, although in some remote areas (e.g. mountainous areas) you may be limited to just 3kw and to increase it you need to take out another contract for another 3kw (making a maximum of 6kw). If you have a low supply, you can install a generator to increase it and use timers to ensure that no more than one high-powered apparatus is in operation at one time.

Your standing charge depends on the power rating of your supply, which is why owners tend to keep it as low as possible. A higher power rating also increases the cost per unit of consumption. For example, changing from 3kw to 6kw can cost €500 or more per year! Of the over 22 million electrical service contracts in Italy, over 18 million are for 3kw, including most apartments. The basic service cost depends on your power rating and whether your usage is low, medium or high, with current costs (subject to change) as shown in the table below:

Power Rating	Basic Service Cost (€)		
	Low Use	Medium Use	High Use
1.5kw	3.5	9	15
3kw	7	18	30
6kw	14	36	60

Converters & Transformers

If you have electrical equipment rated at 110 volts AC (for example, from the USA) you will require a converter or a step-down transformer to convert it to 220 volts. However, some electrical appliances are fitted with a 110/220 volt switch. Check for the switch, which may be inside the casing, and make sure it's switched to 220 volts **before** connecting it to the power supply. Converters can be used for heating appliances, but transformers are required for motorised appliances. Total the wattage of the devices you intend to connect to a transformer and make sure that its power rating **exceeds** this sum. Generally all small, high-wattage, electrical appliances such as kettles, toasters, heaters and irons need large transformers. Motors in large appliances such as cookers, refrigerators, washing machines, dryers and dishwashers, need replacing or fitting with a large transformer. In most cases it's simpler to buy new appliances in Italy, which are of good quality and reasonably priced (and sell them when you leave if you cannot take them with you). **The dimensions of cookers, microwave ovens, refrigerators, washing machines, dryers and dishwashers purchased abroad may differ from those in Italy (and therefore may not fit into an Italian kitchen).**

An additional problem with some electrical equipment is the frequency rating, which in some countries, e.g. the USA, is designed to run at 60Hertz (Hz) and not Europe's 50Hz. Electrical equipment **without** a motor is generally unaffected by the drop in frequency to 50Hz (except TVs). Equipment with a motor may run okay with a 20 per cent drop in speed; however, automatic washing machines, cookers, electric clocks, record players and tape recorders must be converted from the US 60Hz cycle to Italy's 50Hz cycle. To find out, look at the label on the back of the equipment. If it says 50/60Hz it should be okay; if it says 60Hz you can try it, **but first ensure that the voltage is correct as outlined above.** Bear in mind that the transformers and motors of electrical devices designed to run at 60Hz run hotter at 50Hz, so make sure that apparatus has sufficient space around it to allow for cooling.

Tariffs

The cost of electricity in Italy is relatively high compared with many other EU countries. The tariff depends on your usage and power rating (see above), which is used to calculate your monthly standing charge, which is payable irrespective of whether you use any electricity during the billing period. Your actual consumption is charged per KwH and the cost depends on the amount of usage: around €0.16 per kWh for low usage,€0.11 for medium usage and €0.09 for high usage. In other words, the basic cost (standing charge) increases with the power rating, but the actual cost of electricity consumption is reduced the more you use. **ENEL charges non-residents a higher rate and a residence permit (*certificato di residenza*) is necessary to obtain a resident's contract.** You can also buy energy-friendly appliances that consume less energy than average and energy saving devices can be installed in appliances such as washing machines, dishwashers and dryers.

Bills

You're billed for electricity every two months. Bills (*conti* or *bolleta*) are based on estimated consumption and adjusted twice per year when meters have been read. Consumption is usually estimated for four months (two bills) and then adjusted (*conguaglio*) when a meter reading is taken. This may result in a larger than expected bill, and therefore if you're a non-resident, you should ensure that you have sufficient funds in your bank account. If you've overpaid, you receive a refund in the form of a postal order, which can be cashed at a post office. Half the bill contains account information and how to pay the bill, and the other half a payment slip and a receipt for your records. Bills show the account number (*numero utente*), amount payable (*importo*), due date (*scadenza*) and the utility company's account number (*conto corrente*). Bills may be paid at banks, post offices and electricity company offices, although ENEL prefers to be paid by direct debit (*domiciliazione*) from a bank account (for which there's a small surcharge). Italian utility companies are notorious for over-charging, although customers rarely, if ever, receive a refund. It's recommended to check that your meters remain static when services are turned off and to learn to read your electricity bill and meter, and check your consumption to ensure that you aren't being overcharged.

GAS

Mains gas (*gas di città* or *mettano città*) in Italy is supplied by the *Societa Italiana per il Gas* (*ITALGAS* or *SIG*, 🖥 www.italgas.it). The country has the third-largest gas market in Europe (behind Germany and the UK) and gas provides some 30 per cent of Italy's total energy requirements. It's widely available in cities and large towns in the north of the country, but isn't available in the south or in rural areas (e.g. in Tuscany and Umbria). When moving into a property with mains gas, you must contact *SIG* to have the gas switched on and the meter read, and have the account put into your name. You need to give the gas company the registration number of the meter and (if known) the name of the previous tenant. As with electricity, there are different contracts for residents and non-residents. The cost of mains gas is around €35 per megacalorie (MCAL) plus a standing charge of around €2 per month. You're billed every two months and bills can be paid at banks, post offices and *SIG* offices, or by direct debit (*domiciliazione*) from a bank account.

Mains gas is mostly used for central heating and cooking. All gas appliances must be approved by *SIG* and installed by your local gas company. **Gas water heaters cannot be installed in bathrooms for safety reasons (although many people do so, often with fatal consequences).** Old gas water heaters can leak carbon monoxide and have been the cause of a number of deaths in Italy and other countries, although this is unlikely with a modern installation. Gas water heaters must be regularly serviced and descaled annually. You can have a combined gas hot water and heating system installed (providing background heat), which is relatively inexpensive to install and cheap to run.

Bottled

Bottled gas is mostly used for cooking, but can also be used to provide hot water and heating. The use of gas bottles (*bombole*) is common in rural areas and they're also frequently used for portable gas fires in cities. Cooking by bottled gas is cheaper than electricity and there's no standing charge (as with mains gas). Cookers often have a combination of electric and (bottled) gas rings (you can choose the mix). If your gas rings are sparked by electricity, keep some matches handy for use during power cuts.

You must pay a deposit on the first bottle and thereafter can exchange an empty bottle for a full one. The most common bottle size is 10 or 15kg, which cost around €11 and €16 respectively, plus €3 for delivery. Check when moving into a property that the gas bottle isn't empty. Keep a spare bottle or two handy and make sure you know how to change bottles (if necessary ask the previous owner or your estate agent to show you). Bottles are delivered in many areas and you can also buy them from agents and supermarkets. A bottle used just for cooking lasts an average family around six weeks. Some people keep their gas bottles outside, often under a lean-to. If you do, you must buy propane gas rather than butane, as it can withstand a greater range of temperatures than butane, which is for internal use only. Although bottled gas is very safe, if you use it you must inform your household insurance company as there's an extra premium to pay.

If you live in a rural area, you can have a gas tank (*bombolone*) installed. Tanks come in various sizes and can be installed by gas companies. It isn't necessary to buy the tank as it remains the property of the gas company who make their money through the sale of gas (although you can also buy your own tank and buy gas from whichever supplier is cheapest). When a tank is installed free, you must sign a contract to purchase a minimum amount of gas per year, e.g. to the value of €500 to €1,000. Gas can officially be used only for heating and hot water, although many people also use it for cooking and gas fires. A gas tank usually holds between 750 and 1,500 litres of liquid gas (1,000 litres is the most common size) and bulk gas costs around €0.50 per m³ . The installation of gas tanks is strictly controlled and they must be at least 25m (82ft) from a house or road. If you have a gas tank installed on your property you must inform your insurance company, as it increases your home insurance premium.

WATER

Water is supplied by local companies, e.g. a *Società d'Acquedotto* (*SADA*) or *Azienda Comunale Energia e Ambiente* (*ACEA*), and each commune has its own rules concerning the use of water, which vary from area to area. Water, or rather the lack of it, is a major concern in many areas of Italy and the price paid for those long, hot summers. There's generally sufficient water in the north, but central and southern areas (and the islands) often experience acute shortages in the summer. Water shortages are exacerbated by poor infrastructure (up to 50 per cent is lost due to leaking pipes in some areas) and wastage due to poor irrigation methods.

Water is usually metered, with the meter installed at the householder's expense. If water is metered, as in most of northern Italy, it's usual to have a contract for a limited number of cubic metres per household, per year (e.g. 300m³, irrespective of the number of occupants. You're charged a higher rate for consumption above this limit. **You cannot use this water for a garden or swimming pool, for which you need a special contract (called *uso vario*) and a separate meter.** In rural areas, you may have access to 'agricultural' water for garden use. A *uso vario* contract can cost €500 to €1,000 per year. In some regions, the cost is prohibitive and therefore few residents have swimming pools, although you can recycle water for the garden and also have a pool filled by tanker (*autobotte*). In some areas, homeowners build an artificial water basin (*vasca*) that fills with rainwater during the winter and can also be fed by a spring or well. With a lining and filtering system, a *vasca* can even double as a swimming pool in summer.

Cost

The price of water varies considerably within each region according to its availability, and is among the most expensive in Europe. In central Italy, water costs around €0.40 per m³. When moving into a new home, ask the local water company to read your meter. Where no water meter is installed, water is calculated on the size of a home. You receive a bill (*acquedotto comunale*) every six months after your meter has been read. Like other utility bills, water bills may be paid by direct debit (*domiciliazione*) from a bank account (unlike in some other countries, your water is unlikely to be cut off if you're late paying a bill). Most apartment blocks (*condominios*) have a single meter for the whole block, where the cost is shared equally between the owners and included in the fees or expenses (*spese*), which isn't recommended if you have a holiday home in Italy.

Shortages

Water shortages are rare in towns, although they do occur occasionally, but are common in rural areas during the summer, when the water is periodically switched off. In areas with prolonged droughts, water may be switched off from 6pm to 6am daily to conserve supplies. Water shortages are exacerbated in resort areas in summer, when the local population may swell tenfold and coincides with the hottest and driest period of the year. The use of sprinklers and hose-pipes is banned in many areas in summer. If you plan to maintain a garden in a region with low rainfall, you need a reserve supply for dry periods (you can also use waste water). In some areas, water shortages create low water pressure, resulting in insufficient water to take a bath or shower. If you live in an area where cuts are common, you can have a storage tank (*cassone*) installed, which is topped up automatically when the water is switched on. A 500 litre tank is usually large enough for a family living in an apartment in a city or in a rural area that doesn't suffer water shortages. In a rural area without mains water, it may be necessary to install an underground tank of 500,000 or one million litres (1,000m³) which is large enough to supply a family for up to six months. This is filled by tanker and is expensive.

Wells

Beware of the quaint well (*pozzo*) or spring (*sorgente*) as they can dry up, particularly in parts of central and southern Italy. Always confirm that a property has a reliable water source. If a property gets its water from a spring or well (possibly on a neighbour's land), make sure that there's no dispute over its ownership and your rights to use it, e.g. that it cannot be stopped or drained away by your neighbours. However, well water is usually excellent (and free), although you may need a pump (manual or electric) to bring it to the surface. You can also create your own well if land has water. Dowsing (finding water by holding a piece of forked wood) is as accurate as anything devised by modern science and has an 80 per cent success rate. A good dowser or water diviner (*rabdomante*) can estimate the water's yield and purity to within 10 or 20 per cent accuracy. Before buying rural land without a water supply, engage an experienced dowser with a successful track record to check it. Rural homes with their own well or spring are at a premium in Italy.

Mains Connection

If you own a property in or near a town or village, you can usually be connected to a mains water system. **However, connection can be expensive as you must pay for digging the channels required for pipes.** Obtain a quotation (*preventivo*) from the local water company for the connection of the supply and the installation of a water meter. Expect the connection to cost at least €800 and possibly much more, depending on the type of terrain and soil (or rock!) which must be excavated to lay pipes. If you're thinking about buying a property and installing a mains water supply, obtain a quotation before signing the contract.

Water Heaters

If you need to install a hot water boiler or immersion heater, ensure that it's large enough for the size of property, e.g. one room studio (100 litres), two rooms (150 litres), three to four rooms (200 litres) and five to seven rooms or two bathrooms (300 litres). Many holiday homes have quite small water boilers that are often inadequate for more than two people. If you need to install a water heater or a larger water heater, you should consider the merits of both electric and bottled gas heaters. An electric water boiler with a capacity of 75 litres (sufficient for two people) usually takes between 75 to 125 minutes (in winter) to heat water to 40°C (104°F).

A (bottle) gas flow-through water heater is more expensive to purchase and install than an electric water boiler, but you get unlimited hot water immediately whenever you want it and there are no standing charges. A gas heater should have a capacity of 10 to 16 litres per minute if it's to be used for a shower. There's usually little difference in quality between different priced heaters, although a gas water heater with a permanent flame may use up to 50 per cent more gas than one without. A resident family with a constant consumption is usually better off with an electric heater, while non-residents using a property for short periods will find a self-igniting gas heater more economical. A solar power system can also be used to provide hot water (see page 121).

Security Measures

Before moving into a new home you should check where the main stop-valve or stopcock is located, so that you can turn off the water supply in an emergency. If the water stops flowing for any reason, you should ensure that all the taps are turned off to prevent flooding when the supply starts again. **In community (*condominio*) properties, the tap to turn the water on or off is usually located outside the building.** Note that water damage caused by burst pipes due to old age or freezing may be excluded from insurance policies and that under Italian law you're required to turn off the water at the mains if a property is left empty for more than 24 hours. When leaving a property empty for an extended period, particularly during the winter when there's the possibility of freezing, you should turn off the main stopcock, switch off the system's controls and drain the pipes, toilets (you can leave salt in the toilet bowls to prevent freezing) and radiators. It's also recommended to have your cold water tank and the tank's ball valves checked periodically for corrosion, and to check the hosing on appliances such as washing machines and dishwashers. **It can be expensive if a pipe bursts and the leak goes undiscovered for a long time!**

Quality

When water isn't drinkable it's usually marked 'non-drinking' (*acqua non potabile*). **Water from wells and springs isn't always safe to drink.** You can have well or spring water analysed by the public health department or the local water authority. It's possible to install filtering, cleansing and softening equipment to improve water quality, but you should obtain independent advice before installing a system as not all equipment is equally effective. While boiling water kills any bacteria, it won't remove any toxic substances contained in it. Although mains water in Italy is usually drinkable, it may be contaminated by industrial chemicals and nitrates, although supposedly not enough to harm your health. However, many Italians consider it undrinkable and drink bottled water (when not drinking wine!). In general, water is hard with a high calcium content. In some areas the iron, calcium and other minerals stain sinks and porcelain, which can be removed only by rubbing regularly with a soft pumice stone. You can use a water softener to soften hard water and a filter to prevent the furring of pipes, radiators and appliances. Water may be fluoridated, depending on the area.

HEATING & AIR-CONDITIONING

Central heating systems in Italy may be powered by oil, gas, electricity, solid fuel (usually wood) or even solar power. Whatever form of heating you use, it's essential to have good insulation, without which up to 60 per cent of heating is lost through the walls and roof. Over half of Italian homes have central heating, which is essential in northern Italy if you plan to spend any time there outside the summer months. Many people keep their central heating on a low setting during short absences in winter (which can be controlled via a master thermostat) to prevent freezing. Heating requirements in winter vary from six hours per day for around 14 weeks per year in the south to over 14 hours per day for six months or longer in the north.

Apartment blocks (*condominios*) usually have central heating (*riscaldamento*), which can be either autonomous (*autonomo*) or central (*centrale*). With *riscaldamento autonomo* you can control the heating independently and are billed according to use. With *riscaldamento centrale* the heating is turned on in autumn (October) and off in spring (March) and you have no control and must pay the same as other residents, even if you're a non-resident in winter. Aluminium radiators are preferable to cast-iron as they withstand extreme cold better and are less likely to leak or burst; **more importantly, Italian insurance companies won't cover you for burst cast-iron radiators and the subsequent water damage.**

Solid Fuel

Many people rely solely on wood-burning stoves or fireplaces for their heating and hot water, particularly in rural areas. Stoves come in a huge variety of sizes and styles, and may also heat radiators throughout a house and provide hot water. Most people burn wood (which should have been seasoned for at least two years), which is relatively inexpensive in Italy, rather than coal or coke. You can have it delivered cut and dried or can also collect it free if you live in the country. The main disadvantages are the chores of collecting and chopping wood, cleaning the grate and lighting fires. Smoke can also be a problem. **Note that an open fireplace can be wasteful of heat and fuel.** An enclosed hearth with a glass door is more effective and often has the advantage of a hot-air chamber that warms other parts of a home, plus less heat wastage, a reduced fire hazard, and less ash and dust.

Electric

Electric central heating isn't common in Italy, as it's too expensive. However, many people with modern homes with good insulation and a permanent system of ventilation, use storage heaters. Electric central heating isn't recommended for old properties with poor insulation. If you install an electric central heating system you may need to increase your electricity rating (see **Power Rating** on page 113) to cope with the extra demand. Stand-alone electric (e.g. halogen) heaters are relatively expensive to run and are best suited to holiday homes.

Gas

Mains gas central heating is popular, relatively cheap to run and widely used in the north of Italy. Gas is clean, economical and efficient, and the boiler is usually fairly small and can be wall-mounted. In rural areas where there's no mains gas, you can have a gas tank (*bombolone*) installed on your property (see page 116). The cost of heating with methane (*metano*) gas is between €0.50 and €0.70 per m³.

Oil

Oil-fired central heating isn't common in Italy due to the high cost of heating oil and the problems associated with storage and deliveries. Heating oil costs around €1.10 per litre and is among the most expensive in Europe (the price fluctuates with the price of crude oil). An average family of four can expect to use around 1,700 litres per year over some 120 days at a cost of around €1,900. You also need space to install the storage tank. If you have a tank with a 2,000-litre capacity or larger it must be buried in your garden or stored in a separate location sheltered from frost and away from the house. A smaller tank can be located in or near your home, but needs to be refilled more often.

Solar Power

A solar power system can be used to supply all your energy needs, although it's usually combined with an electric or gas heating system, as solar power cannot be relied upon year-round for lighting, heating and hot water. The main drawback is the high cost of installation, which varies considerably according to the region and how much energy you require. A solar power system must be installed by an expert. The advantages are no running costs, silent operation, maintenance free and no electricity bills. A system should last 30 years (it's usually guaranteed for ten years) and can be upgraded to provide more power in the future. Solar power can also be used to heat a swimming pool. Continuous advances in solar cell and battery technology are expected to dramatically increase the efficiency and reduce the cost of solar power, which is forecast to become the main source of energy world-wide in the 21st century. A solar power system can also be used to provide electricity in a remote rural home, where the cost of extending electricity is prohibitive.

Costs

The cost of heating a property varies according to a number of factors, not least the fuel used, the size of your home, and the length of time your heating is switched on. You can have your home inspected by a heating engineer who assesses its heating requirements and cost, taking into account the insulation and equipment installed. The engineer produces a report detailing the most effective means of insulating and heating your home, and a number of cost estimates.

Humidifiers

Central heating dries the air and may cause your family to develop coughs; those who find the dry air a problem or unpleasant can purchase a humidifier to add moisture to the air. Humidifiers that don't generate steam should be disinfected occasionally with a special liquid available from pharmacies, (to prevent nasty diseases). Humidifiers may range from simple water containers hanging from radiators to expensive electric or battery-operated devices.

Air-Conditioning

Few homes in Italy have air-conditioning (*condizionamento d'aria*), despite the fact that summer temperatures often reach over 40°C (104°F) in some areas. Although properties are built to withstand the heat, you may find it beneficial to install air-conditioning, although there can be negative effects if you suffer from asthma or respiratory problems. You can choose between a huge variety of air-conditioners, fixed or moveable, indoor or outdoor installation, and high or low power. Air-conditioning units cost from around €800 (plus installation) for a unit that's sufficient to cool an average sized room. An air-conditioning system with a heat pump provides cooling in summer and heating in winter. Many people fit ceiling fans for extra cooling in the summer (costing from around €80), which are standard fixtures in some new homes.

6.

POST OFFICE SERVICES

Italy has a long history of organised postal systems dating back to the *cursus publicus* of the Romans, although a national postal system wasn't established until 1862 after the unification of the country. Today, the Italian post office (Poste Italiane S.p.A.) is currently undergoing its first radical restructuring since the 19th century and is making strenuous efforts to shed its reputation as the slowest and most inefficient postal service in western Europe. For many years it was part of the state-run post and telecommunications monopoly Poste, Telegrafi e Telefoni (PTT), but it has recently become a limited company, although 75 per cent of its shares are still owned by the government. In December 2000, the post office introduced a four-year plan of investment in automated sorting, post office improvements and further computerisation.

While not all of the promised improvements have been fully implemented, the introduction of a two-tier letter post service has done much to improve standards. Other innovations include an increasing range of online services. However, while the ordinary postal service is acceptable for everyday items, many people in Italy prefer to send important letters and parcels by registered post (*posta raccomandata*) or use a private courier service, as stories of post disappearing are legion. The (independent) Vatican City post office in Rome is the most efficient and reliable, as it sends all its international post via Switzerland (with colourful Vatican stamps!). Many companies and courier services in Italy also use the Swiss and other foreign post offices to deliver their international post, e.g. Deutsche Poste World Net (🖳 www.dpwn.com). The American company, Mailboxes, Inc., has franchises in Rome and other major cities.

There's a post office (*ufficio postale*) in most towns and villages in Italy, a total of over 14,000, providing a wide range of services. In addition to the standard postal services, post offices offer facilities for telegram, fax and telex transmissions, exchange of foreign currency, domestic and international cash transfers, and payment of utility bills, road tax and TV licences. A range of financial and banking services is available, including cheque and savings accounts, investment plans, tax-paying facilities, and the sale of post office shares and bonds. Telephone cards, lottery tickets, train and bus tickets, and pre-paid toll cards for Italian motorways are sold at post offices. The post office also acts as an agency for the payment of social security benefits such as state pensions. There are public telephones in main post offices.

Main post offices have separate counters (*sportelli*) for different services, which are divided between those dealing with post and those handling financial services, with sometimes a third counter for telegrams, faxes and telexes. New layouts in main post offices include a single-queue system with an electronic board showing the number of the next available window. When this system isn't in operation, you must ensure that you join the correct queue (shown by a sign above the window), or you will need to start queuing all over again. If you require different services, you may need to queue at different counters at a main post office, although in rural towns and villages one or two counters usually provide all services.

The identifying colour of the Italian post office is currently red, although new documentation and office layouts use sky blue. Post vans may be red, white or brown, and the post office logo is a rhomboid-shaped envelope made up of horizontal lines with a diagonal flap. The sign above post offices is *Poste e Telecomunicazioni* or sometimes just the initials *PT*, while in phone books they're listed under *Poste Italiane*. In main towns and cities there's a central post office for each district, as well as some smaller post offices (*agenzie*). The yellow pages list all post offices in a province. Post offices in Italy are always operated by post office employees and there are (as yet) no post offices run by private businesses or located in shops.

Information (in Italian only) about all postal services is available from the post office's website (🖳 www.poste.it). For information about telegrams, fax and telex, see page 154.

OPENING HOURS

Post offices in towns and cities are generally open from around 8.15am to 6 or 7pm, Mondays to Fridays, and from around 8.15am to 12.30 or 1pm on Saturdays and the last day of the month (when they may close at noon). Main post offices in major cities often remain open until 8pm for postal transactions, although counters dealing with financial services are likely to close at around 5 or 6pm. Unlike post offices in some other European countries, Italian post offices don't usually close for lunch. Opening hours in rural towns and villages are limited, with post offices usually open from 8am until 1.30 or 2pm, Mondays to Fridays and from 8 to 11.45am on Saturdays. There may be shorter hours on the last day of the month.

LETTER POST

There are two categories of letter post in Italy: the ordinary postal service (*posta ordinaria*) and the recently introduced and much-publicised priority postal service (*posta prioritaria*). Envelopes for both priority and ordinary letter services may be up to 5mm thick and should be a maximum size of 12cm x 23.5cm (*standard* or *normalizzato*); otherwise, they're charged at the next higher postal rate. There's a maximum weight limit of 2kg for all letter post, unless it's registered or insured (see **Registered Post** on page 131).

Ordinary Post

Ordinary post for letters and postcards takes three to seven days for inland post (letters posted in Milan, for example, are sorted in Sicily!) and anything from four to ten days for the rest of Europe – in theory! Airmail letters to the USA take on average a week to arrive, and those to Australia and New Zealand up to two weeks. Tariffs for ordinary post within Italy and to all other countries in the EU, Norway and Switzerland are the same and are as follows:

| Weight | Ordinary Tariff (€) | |
	EU Countries*	Other Countries
Up to 20g	0.41	0.52
21g–100g	0.77	1.24
101g–349g	1.55	2.58
350g–1kg	3.62	4.13

* Plus Norway and Switzerland.

The rates for Other Countries are for surface post. Airmail rates are as follows:

| Weight | Airmail Tariff (€) | | | |
	Rest of Europe*	Africa*	America & Asia	Australasia
Up to 20g	0.57	0.65	0.67	1.03
21g–100g	1.34	1.42	1.44	1.50
101g–349g	2.68	2.76	2.78	2.84
350g–1kg	4.23	4.31	4.33	4.39

* The Rest of Europe rates apply to Algeria, Cyprus, Egypt, Jordan, Israel, Libya, Lebanon, Morocco, Syria, Tunisia and Turkey; the Africa rates apply to all other African countries.

For airmail you should affix a blue airmail sticker (*per via aerea*), available free from post offices and tobacconists, although writing *Per Via Aerea* in the top left corner of the envelope is also acceptable. Even though post within Europe is automatically sent by air, it's wise to indicate this so that your post isn't mistakenly sent via the domestic surface post sytem. You should write your name and address on the back of all airmail letters.

Priority Post

The priority service (equivalent to first class post in other countries) provides next working day delivery for letter post within Italy (although this isn't guaranteed), and two to three days for letters to all other EU countries, plus Norway and Switzerland, although the tariff is the same. The priority service isn't available to other European countries and the rest of the world. You must obtain a gold *prioritaria* stamp (which is affixed to the top right corner) and a blue airmail sticker (*per via aerea*) for the top left corner for foreign destinations.

Ordinary stamps cannot be used for priority post. The cost increases according to weight, as follows:

Weight	Priority Tariff (€)
Up to 20g	0.62
20g–100g	1.24
101g–349g	1.86
350g–1kg	4.96
1–2kg	8.06

Express Post

There's an express post service (*Postacelere*) for important documents. Delivery is guaranteed the next working day within Italy (except some small islands), in one to three days for the rest of Europe, and in two to five days for the rest of the world. Prices start at €8 for items weighing up to 3kg (plus €2.58 for compensation for loss or damage up to €1,032.91) and all express post has a barcode to allow it to be computer tracked to its destination. This service doesn't operate from every post office and you may be required to go to a special counter. To check where this service is available, you can call the free phone number ☎ 800-009966 or you can check the *Postacelere* website (🖳 www.post acelere.it). *Postacelere* can also be used for parcels (see page 132).

General Information

Note the following when posting letters in Italy:

- Allow plenty of time if you need to visit the post office, as there are often **very** long queues, particularly in urban areas. One reason for this is that banknotes are regularly checked to see if they're forged. Also make sure that you have the correct window for the service you require; there may be sign near the entrance indicating the services provided at each window.

- Stamps (*francobolli*) are available from post offices, tobacconists' (*tabaccheria*), which are distinguished by a large black 'T' sign outside, and licensed bars (*bar tabacchi*). They're currently available only loose (not in booklets), and you must ask for them over the counter. It's generally much simpler and quicker to buy stamps at a tobacconist's or small post office than at a main post office. Pre-stamped domestic letter cards (*biglietti postali*) are also available. Fiscal stamps (*marche da bollo*) used for paying government taxes can be purchased at some post offices, but official document paper (*carta bollata*) used for legal communications is available only from tobacconists (see page 398).

- Post boxes are red and either free-standing on a metal pole or attached to a wall. They're located outside tobacconists' and post offices, as well as on platforms at main railway stations. It's recommended to post urgent letters at a main post office or railway station, as collections are more frequent. In cities and at main post offices there are often two boxes, one for local (*per la città*) post and one for all other destinations (*per tutte le altre destinazioni*), including abroad. There may also be a separate box for priority (*prioritaria*) post. Latest collection times at main post offices are generally 5pm for ordinary post and 6pm for priority post, Mondays to Fridays, and noon for all post on Saturdays. At smaller post offices, collections are usually made at noon on all six days.

- There's one post delivery per day, in the morning from Monday to Saturday. If the postman is delivering to an apartment block, he presses the intercom of one of the apartments to gain access to the post boxes (*casette postali*), which are situated in the entrance hall/foyer and accessible by key only. If a caretaker (*portiere*) lives in the block, he may be in charge of distributing post to individual boxes. In rural areas, a postman isn't obliged to deliver post to the front door unless it's located on a street. If it isn't, you must install a letterbox at the boundary of your property.

- On Italian letters, the surname often precedes the Christian name and the number of the house comes after the name of the street. It's no longer necessary to put a comma after the street name before the house number. **If the person to whom you're addressing post isn't normally resident at that address, you must address your post 'care of' (c/o or *presso*) the person named on the postbox or on the nameplate of the apartment itself. Otherwise you risk your letter being returned to the sender or simply not being delivered.** The post code is written before the town or city, which is followed by the abbreviation for the province in brackets (this isn't required for post addressed to Rome, as *Roma* isn't abbreviated – see the list of provinces and abbreviations in **Appendix E**).

  All letters to Italian addresses should bear a 5-digit post code (*codice di avviamento postale* or *CAP*) which indicates the town and province. All provincial capitals use a different code for each street, the first two numbers indicating the town or city and the last three the street. If the first two numbers of the code are correct, your post will generally be delivered. All post codes with their corresponding towns, cities and provinces are listed in a *CAP* booklet, available free from post offices and can also be downloaded from the post office website (🖥 www.poste.it).

  A typical Italian address is shown below:

  > Bianchi Mario
  > Via Cavour 41
  > I-10123 Torino (TO)
  > Italy

- Aerogrammes (*aerogrammi*) are available from both tobacconists and post offices and cost €0.47 for EU countries, Norway and Switzerland.

- Stamps, commemorative issues (*prodotti filatelici*) and specially minted coins are produced for collectors and can be ordered from special windows at some 280 main post offices. For information about philatelic services, you can write to Poste Italiane S.p.A., Divisione Filatelica, Piazza Dante, 25, 00185 Rome, or to the person in charge of philatelic services (*sportelli filatelici*) at the central post office in your provincial capital.

- If a letter is identified at the sorting office as having insufficient postage, it's usually returned to the sender. If it isn't, the postman insists on the addressee paying the postage due. If a letter isn't stamped, it's destroyed unless the sender's name is written on the envelope, in which case it's returned. You won't need to pay a fee in the latter case – merely face the postman's disapproval!

- Although the reliability of Italy's postal service has increased considerably in recent years, registering items with proof of delivery is recommended for all important documents and items of value, including cheques. When cancelling contracts and subscriptions, some companies and organisations make it a requirement that letters are registered (see below).

REGISTERED POST

You can register post (*posta raccomandata*) with proof of delivery (*avviso di ricevimento*) or without (*semplice*) by completing a *raccomandata* form. The bottom half of the form, which is stamped by the post office clerk, is your receipt (*ricevuta*). The charge for registering a letter weighing up to 20g both within Italy and abroad is €2.58, in addition to the cost of postage. Fees then rise on a weight scale up to €8.37 for within Italy and €9.40 for abroad, for weights of between 1 and 2kg. Proof of delivery costs an extra €0.62 and, in addition to the standard form, you must complete a yellow postcard, which is signed by the addressee and returned to you. For certain types of official correspondence (for example, judicial and tax correspondence and writing to the President of the Republic), you must use the same form but with red lettering (*raccomandata descritta*). Parcel post (see below) cannot be registered, although it can be insured.

Insurance

Registered letters can be insured (*assicurata*) using either of two services (which have names meaning the same thing!):

- *Assicurazione convenzionale* ('standard' insurance) costs a flat rate of €0.82 and provides compensation for loss or damage up to €5.16 for letters and €25.83 for parcels.

> ● *Assicurazione ordinaria* ('ordinary' insurance) costs €3.10 plus €2.06 for each €51.67 (or fraction of €51.67) of an item's declared value. This provides compensation of up to €1,033.60 for all post.

An *assicurata* form with green lettering must be completed in addition to the *raccomandata* form. A computer tracking and tracing facility is available.

PARCEL POST

Parcels may be sent either by air or by surface post, as well as via the express service, called *Postacelere* (see below). You may need to go to a separate parcel section of the post office (*ufficio pacchi*). A parcel weighing up to 3kg (6.6lb) costs €8 to send within Italy and takes anything from 5 to 15 days to arrive, depending on whether its destination is a major city or a remote rural area. You can pay an extra €4.40 and send a parcel as urgent, which takes two or three days to most regions, three or four to Sicily and other islands. Parcels weighing up to 500g, however, are cheaper and more likely to arrive when sent via the *Postacelere* service (see below). If you send a parcel nationally, it's worth telephoning the recipient to let them know it's on its way, as it may not be delivered with normal letter post and a collection form may be left instead (see **Post Collection** below).

Parcels sent abroad via airmail take on average a week to ten days to arrive in Europe and two to four weeks to the USA and Australia, while surface post can take as long as two months to the USA or Australia. The cost of sending a parcel varies according to the weight and destination. For example, a parcel weighing 3kg sent to a non-EU country costs between €18 and €23. (It's often cheaper as well as faster to use the 'Quickpack' service – see **Express Post** below). Airmail parcels weighing up to 3kg cost €28.50 to the US and €44 to Australia, while overland the fee is €17.57 to both countries. Parcels weighing up to 2kg are cheaper to send as letter post provided their combined length, width and thickness don't exceed 90cm (35.43in).

There are further charges for parcels if they're bulky or fragile. For parcels sent within Italy using the ordinary postal service, you must complete a form (*bollettino di spedizione*) costing €0.10, one part of which is your receipt. For non-EU international parcels, you must complete a white customs declaration form (*dichiarazione doganale*) declaring its content and value, plus the details of the sender (*mittente*) and the addressee (*destinatario*). **If you insert a letter inside a parcel it should be declared and the relevant postage added. Otherwise, if your parcel is opened, you risk it being returned to you and you can even be fined.** Parcel post cannot be registered, but it can be insured – see **Insurance** above.

Express Post

To send a parcel more quickly inland or abroad, you can also use Quickpack, part of the *Postacelere* service (see also page 129). Parcels up to 500g cost €6.20 to send nationally and, as with letters, are guaranteed to be delivered the next working day. International parcels can be sent via the post office's EMS service, which accepts parcels weighing up to 20kg (44lb). Parcels up to 500g cost €15.50 to send within Europe, €23.77 to the USA and Canada, and €35.14 to Australia and New Zealand. A parcel weighing 3kg to the rest of Europe costs a flat rate of €20.67 compared with up to €23 using the standard airmail service (see above). Self-sealing parcel boxes (called *postpacks*) can be purchased in four sizes from main post offices but don't include string or packing paper, which can be obtained from a tobacconist or stationer (*cartolibreria*).

Express post and courier services are also provided by the Italian railways and airlines, and international courier companies such as DHL, TNT (also called *Traco* in Italy) and UPS, as well as the cheaper Italian company, Bartolini. These are the services to use if you need express local deliveries (within an hour in major cities) or 24-hour delivery to any country in the world. For express and courier services in your area, look under *Corrieri* or *Recapito pacchi, plichi e lettere* in the yellow pages. The latter are privately operated delivery services within a particular area, e.g. a city.

POST COLLECTION

If the postman calls with post requiring a signature, payment of import duty or excess postage when you aren't at home, he will leave a yellow collection form. Go to the address of the office stamped on the front of the form within the hours shown and present it, together with some identification (e.g. passport, identity card, residence permit or driving licence). If you cannot go in person, another person may go on your behalf provided you enter their name in the appropriate box on the back of the form and sign it. They must produce identification at the post office or at the relevant collection office if the item has been sent using the *Postacelere* service (see pages 129 and 132). The post office will hold any item that needs collecting free of charge for three days, after which there's a daily charge of €0.26 for a maximum period of one month. This is a good reason to inform the post office if you're going to be away from home for more than a few days (see **Change Of Address** below), as they will hold your post for you.

You can receive post at any post office in Italy via the *poste restante* (*fermo posta*) service. Letters should be addressed to your nearest main post office, as follows:

> Smith, Marmaduke Cecil
> Fermo Posta
> I-65100 P.T. Pescara Centro
> Italy

If you use one of the smaller post offices, you must specify the number of the post office (e.g. *agenzia numero 2*), **not** its street address. There's a charge of around €0.20 for each letter received and you must produce an identity card, passport or driving licence as identification when collecting post. If you want to remain anonymous, you can have post addressed to you via a document number, e.g. a passport or driving licence. The document in question must be produced as proof of identity when collecting post. Post is kept at the post office for a maximum of 30 days, after which it's returned to the sender.

Another widely used service for receiving post if you don't want it delivered to your home address, is to rent a post office box (*casella postale*), which are available at main post offices. There are two kinds of box: open (*aperta*) and closed (*chiusa*). Open boxes are free but are allocated only to companies that receive large amounts of post and prefer to use a post office box address. With this kind of box, post is collected from the appropriate post office window (usually *poste restante*) by a representative of the company. Smaller companies and private individuals are offered a closed box, for which there's a deposit of around €25. You're issued with a key to access your box, which is located inside the post office. **The post office doesn't advise you of the arrival of any registered or express post in your box, so if you have a closed box it's wise to check it frequently.**

CHANGE OF ADDRESS

If you move house, your post can be redirected to your new address (*cambio indirizzo*) by making a written request to your local post office at least two days beforehand on plain paper (not *carta bollata*). The service is available for a maximum period of 90 days and costs €0.77 for post redirected within the same city or postal district and €1.30 for redirection within the rest of Italy or to an address abroad. There's no service for parcels to be redirected abroad (they're returned to the sender) and you're liable for any extra postage for letters redirected abroad. Note that responsibility for redirecting your post falls to your local postman and therefore this service cannot be relied upon. If possible, it's recommended to ask a neighbour or friend to visit your old home periodically to collect any post and forward it to your new address.

FINANCIAL SERVICES

The Italian post office offers a number of financial services. It's the largest single banking facility in Italy and provides a variety of cheque and savings accounts. In rural areas, where the nearest bank is often many kilometres away, many people use the post office as their local bank.

Post Office Accounts

Post office accounts (*conto bancoposta*) provide most of the same services as bank accounts (see below). In addition to the longer opening hours of post offices, one of the main advantages of a post office account over a bank account is that bills are debited free (with a bank, you normally pay a €0.62 charge) and other costs are generally lower. The standard account is a postcheque account (*conto corrente postale* or *c/c postale*), which can be opened by any resident aged over 18. A postcheque account offers the following services:

* Automatic bill payment;
* Direct debits;
* A cheque book;
* Unlimited withdrawals (provided you have the money in your account!);
* Confirmation of every transaction with a receipt sent through the post;
* An annual interest rate (currently 2 per cent) on your credit balance;
* Money transfers;
* Credit card facilities.

Charges for the first 60 transactions are €0.52 per transaction, or an annual maximum of €30.99, with all additional transactions free. You can choose to receive monthly, quarterly or annual statements. There's no limit to the amount you can withdraw from your account using a cheque, but for every withdrawal of €51.67 (or fraction) there's a fee of €0.10. For withdrawals above €15,500, a day's notice is required. An overdraft on a postcheque account isn't permitted. Postcheques may be used to pay for goods in shops but, like bank cheques, it's up to shopkeepers whether they accept cheques (or **your** cheques). If you're known to a shopkeeper he will probably accept your cheque, but if you're new to the area (or the shop) you shouldn't rely on it. **There are no cheque guarantee cards in Italy.** See page 303 for information about writing cheques in Italy.

For every payment into your account you must complete a paying-in slip (*bollettino di conto corrente*); your account is usually credited within three to four days. If you want your account to be credited the day after the deposit, you can insert a cross in the appropriate box on the slip and pay a fee of €0.10.

A 'Postcard' (*carta postamat*) is currently available to all account-holders for paying bills and withdrawing cash. This is being replaced by a post office credit card (*carta bancoposta*), which holders will be able to use in stores and other businesses accepting Cirrus, Maestro and MasterCard cards. The card costs €15.50 annually and holders can withdraw cash via post office cash dispensers as well as from automated teller machines (ATMs).

Savings accounts (*libretto di risparmio postale*) are also available.

Bill Paying

The post office provides a service for paying bills (*pagamento delle bollette*) for telephone, gas and electricity, as well as road tax, television licence fees, university entrance fees and property rent. Most people in Italy pay their bills in cash at a post office, using the payment form included with every bill received by post. If the form is pre-printed (*bollettino premarcato*), it includes all the necessary payment details, including your name and address, and the payee's name and account number. If it isn't pre-printed, you must enter these details and must also state the reason for the payment (*causale*) on the reverse of the form. Post office payment forms must be completed in black or blue-black ink – if you make a mistake you must complete a new form, as you aren't permitted to make corrections.

Payment forms generally come in two parts. The larger, left-hand part is retained by the post office and sent to the company or individual being paid. The remaining part is your receipt (*ricevuta*), which is stamped and returned by the post office clerk (check that it has been stamped). If you need more than one receipt, you can complete a payment form in three or four parts, or photocopy your original receipt (the photocopy must, however, be used only for your records, as some organisations don't accept this as proof of payment).

You must complete a separate form for each bill that you're paying and take them to the payments window (*bancoposta*). Payments may be made through a postcheque account, in which case a cheque, Postcard or post office credit card can be used. If you don't have a postcheque account, payment must be made either in cash or by ATM (using a Bancomat card – see page 303) and each bill is subject to a charge of €0.62. It's wise to add up the total in advance so that you can confirm it (write it down if you don't speak Italian). Other forms of credit card and bank cheques aren't accepted.

Bill payments may also be made through a bank account, by post (by cheque), or, in certain cases, at the local office or agent of the company concerned. If you choose to pay them at a post office, it's wise to do so early in the morning, e.g. on your way to work. The deadline (*scadenza*) for paying many bills in Italy falls at the same time for everyone and therefore long queues are likely – even longer than usual!

Other Services

Other financial products available at the post office include state bonds (*titoli di stato*), post office pension schemes (*postevita*) and post office bonds (*buoni ordinari*). Bonds pay from 2.25 per cent for the first year to 5.5 per cent from 15 to 20 years, but if you cash the bonds within the first year, you receive no interest.

Money transfers (*vaglia*) up to the value of €2,585 can be made within Italy and internationally. A blue form must be completed for money transfers within Italy (*richiesta vaglia nazionale*) and a green-blue form for transfers abroad (*richiesta di trasferimento fondi verso l'estero*). Transfers up to €51.67 cost €2.58 and transfers above this amount €5.16. They can be made in cash or by postcheque (if you have an account) and take a day to arrive at another Italian post office. International money transfers take 15 days or more depending on the destination and aren't possible to all countries. In order to cash a money transfer, you must produce an official form of identification.

Foreign currency exchange facilities (*cambiavalute*) are provided at some main post offices, although only major currencies are exchanged. There's a fee of €2.58 (less than that charged by banks) for each transaction. Certain types of travellers' cheque (*assegni turistici*), e.g. American Express, can be cashed at post offices in Italy.

You can also collect your pension, arrange for your salary to be paid into your postcheque account and pay your tax bills at a post office.

7.

TELEPHONE

Until recently, the use of telephones in Italy was hampered by two serious drawbacks: the first was that holding a phone interfered with the Italians' predilection for speaking with both hands and the second obstacle was the unavailability of phone numbers. The latter was due to an old-fashioned system that couldn't accommodate the number of lines that were needed. As a result, people in some areas had to wait literally for years for a phone line to be installed! However, Italians gradually learned to gesticulate with one hand and a major modernisation of the telephone system in the early 1990s saw the introduction of fibre optics and electronic switching that greatly increased the availability of phone lines. By around 1995, Telecom Italia had completed the conversion, although some remote areas still have mechanical switchboards. Nowadays tone dialling is the rule rather than the exception.

Telecom Italia (formerly SIP) was privatised in 1997 and used to be the only provider of telephone lines and fixed-line (non-mobile) telephones in Italy. Towards the end of the 1990s, Tiscali, Wind and a number of other companies provided some much-needed competition for long-distance domestic calls and international calls, and (surprise, surprise) calls charges started to fall dramatically. Telecom Italia used to have a monopoly on local calls from fixed-line phones, but since 2002 the company Infostrada (part of Wind) has offered it some competition. Three separate companies provide mobile phone services.

INSTALLATION & REGISTRATION

To have a fixed-line phone installed – at least for the first time – you must visit your local Telecom Italia office (there's one in most large towns and cities and all provincial capitals). The employees there can provide information about the equipment and services available, and help you to complete the application form. However, staff usually speak only Italian, so if you don't you need to take along an interpreter, plus your passport (and a photocopy) for identification purposes.

The fee for installing a line in a property where one wasn't previously installed is €250. Transfer of a telephone number to another location within the same code area is free of charge, as it's to change the name of the user of an existing telephone line. Additional charges apply depending on the distance involved if a phone is to be installed in a remote area that isn't considered 'inhabited' (*oltre perimetro abitato*). Nowadays, it usually takes just a few working days to have a line installed.

You're expected to lease or buy a telephone from Telecom Italia, but you can also replace it with another phone purchased elsewhere. Telecom Italia's 'INSIP' shops sell phones that have been approved by themselves (marked *omologato*), although it isn't illegal to sell non-approved phones and most electronics shops stock a wide variety. The contractual requirement that the subscriber must use equipment provided by Telecom Italia or approved by them is seldom enforced. In principle, Telecom Italia could confiscate a phone connected to its network that isn't *omologato*, but this is highly unlikely unless it's a cordless phone that uses frequencies allocated to the emergency services.

For ordinary analogue lines, Telecom Italia usually installs a standard three-prong connector with a standard receiver. It's up to the user to change the connector or use adapters for the equipment that will be used. Digital ISDN lines are growing in popularity and are usually marketed as a package with two lines. The cost (excluding VAT) of a new ISDN installation is around €103, and switching from an analogue line costs the same. The monthly fixed cost for two lines is €16.50 for private users and €25.85 for business users. There are three categories of subscriber (*abbonati*) in Italy.

- **Category A** – All subscribers that aren't included in categories B and C. In practice, this means all business enterprises and professional offices.

- **Category B** – The first installation made in a private home where there's no business or professional activity and it's in the name of a private person.

- **Category C** – Subsequent installations made after the first installation in category B, with the same user characteristics and the same subscriber.

Categories B and C can be installed as single user lines or as duplex lines when they will carry low traffic. Having a duplex line means you share a line (but not the phone number – so you cannot hear what is being said on the other line) with another party. This has the drawback that you won't be able to use your phone if the person with whom you're sharing is using the line. Otherwise it works like a normal phone line, with exactly the same costs for installation and calls. The difference is in the line rental for each two-month period (see **Charges** on page 144).

Infostrada does not charge a fee for telephone installation, and offers a wide, ever-changing range of different customer packages – for private use, business use and internet access – detailed on its website (🖳 www.infostrada.it).

USING THE TELEPHONE

Using the telephone in Italy is much the same as in any other country, with a few Italian eccentricities thrown in for good measure. **One unusual feature of the Italian phone system is that you must include the area code (*prefissi*) when making local calls, not just when making calls outside your local code area.** If you leave out the area code when making a call, you hear a recorded message telling you to dial it before the number. However, this message is (naturally) given in Italian, so visiting friends or relatives who try to call you from within the country (who leave out the code) may not understand why they cannot get through. If you don't know the area code you can get it from the operator (dial 12 for domestic codes). A booklet listing area codes (and postcodes) is published by Telecom Italia and available from bookshops and stationers.

Since 1998 you've also had to include the '0' of the area code when calling from abroad, unlike when making calls to almost every other country (Italy doesn't care much for international standards). If you omit the zero when calling from abroad you hear an engaged tone, with no further explanation, which has caused a lot of confusion and upset many people who have often tried for days on end to call someone in Italy! When dialling a number in Italy from abroad, you dial the international access code of the country from which you're calling (e.g. 00), followed by Italy's international code (39), the area code *with* the first 0 (e.g. 02) and the subscriber's number (e.g. 12345678). Therefore using the previous example you would dial 00-39-02-12345678. Telephone numbers in Italy are often written with a dash or forward slash (as in this book) after the area code and a space after each two or three digits, e.g. Milan 12345678 should be shown as 02-123 456 78 or 02-123 456 78. However, there may only be a space after the area code, or the code and number may be written with no spaces at all, e.g. 0212345678. Italian phone numbers vary in length; for example, Rome numbers may be between five and eight digits. Mobile phone (see page 148) numbers start with 03 and are more expensive to call than ordinary fixed lines.

Answering The Phone

Italians usually answer their phones with '*pronto*' (ready), with the exception of companies and office switchboards. Sometimes the caller asks *Chi parla?* (Who's talking/there?). However, this is generally considered bad manners and the answer is usually *Con chi vuole parlare?* (With whom do you wish to talk?). You may prefer not to give your name to someone who may have dialled a wrong number, particularly if you're a woman. If the caller has the wrong number, you can say *Ha sbagliato numero* (wrong number). Once it has been established that the correct contact is made, the caller states his name and asks for the person he wants to speak to.

Nuisance Calls

Nuisance calls are no more frequent in Italy than elsewhere, but they happen. The best advice is to hang up as soon as you realise the nature of the call; most telephone pests soon lose interest if they fail to receive a response. If the calls continue, you could blow a piercing whistle down the line the next time they call to discourage them. You should also report the problem to the police. If you have an ISDN line you can buy a phone that shows the caller's number (Caller ID), which allows you to screen calls before answering them.

Answering Machines

The standard phrase used on answering machines in Italy is 'We are momentarily out', even if you're away for three months in another country. Burglars are a serious problem in Italy and they often monitor people's movements, sometimes by phone. A message such as, 'We have left for England for two weeks and will be back on 15th October' is an invitation no burglar is likely to resist. Most answering machines are built into the phone, but they can also be purchased separately from electronic and phone stores. Prices start at under €50, rising to €100 or more for top-of-the-range models. The latter may provide a wide range of special features, including automatic dial-back, call forwarding, remote playback of messages (only accessible by special code), and recording of the date and time of incoming calls.

Useful Phrases

Listed below are some useful everyday phrases when using the phone:

English	Italian
I would like to speak to ___ .	*Vorrei parlare con ___ .*
Could you connect me with ___ ?	*Mi potrebbe collegare con ___ ?*
Please wait, I will connect you.	*Un attimo, prego, faccio il collegamento.*
___ is not in.	*___ è fuori* or *___ non c'è.*
I will try again later.	*Chiamo di nuovo più tardi.*
You've reached the wrong number.	*Lei ha sbagliato il nùmero.*
I'd like to leave a message for ___ .	*Vorrei lasciare un messaggio per ___ .*
Could you ask ___ to call me back?	*Mi farebbe richiamare ___ ?*

Phonetic Alphabet

When spelling names on the telephone, you should use the following words:

A	Ancona	J	Jolly	S	Savona
B	Bologna	K	Kennedy	T	Torino
C	Como	L	Livorno	U	Udine
D	Domodossola	M	Milano	V	Venezia
E	Empoli	N	Napoli	W	Washington
F	Firenze	O	Otranto	X	Icks
G	Genova	P	Palermo	Y	York
H	Hotel	Q	Quaderno	Z	Zara
I	Imola	R	Roma		

ALTERNATIVE PROVIDERS

In addition to Telecom Italia, there are a number of other providers of national and international long-distance phone calls, the largest of which include Tiscali and Wind, who also operate a mobile phone network. To access these you must dial a company's code (prefix) before dialling a number, e.g. 10030 for Tiscali and 1088 for Wind. Both require pre-registration and a minimum advance payment of around €50. This isn't a deposit but an advance payment of calls, which must be renewed when it's exhausted by having it charged automatically to a credit card or by obtaining a re-chargeable card from the carrier (the companies aren't taking any chances on you absconding without paying your bill). Calls can only be made from the phone numbers specified in the contract with the carrier and you can use the service from your home phone plus one additional number (e.g. your office) only, but not from anywhere else. The same access prefix can be used to call mobile phones at a lower cost than charged by Telecom Italia. Additional information about the tariffs and conditions of Tiscali and Wind is available on the Internet (🖳 www.tiscali.it and www.wind.it).

There are also numerous other companies offering long-distance services in Italy, including AT&T (🖳 www.att.com), MCI Worldcom (🖳 www.mci.com) and Lyra (🖳 www.lyratel.it), who reportedly offer the cheapest rates for international calls. Approximate rates (per minute) levied by Lyratel in 2002 included the following:

Country	Rate Per Minute (€)
United Kingdom	0.13
France, Germany, USA	0.14
Canada, Spain, Switzerland	0.15
Iceland, Luxembourg	0.18
Australia, Hong Kong, New Zealand	0.23
Morocco, Singapore, Tunisia	0.41

CHARGES

Line rental and call charges in Italy are among the highest in Europe, although they've fallen considerably recently due to increased competition. Telephone charges from Telecom Italia include line rental, telephone and other equipment rentals, special services such as call transfer and three-way conversation, credit card calls, and general call charges. If you have a standard category B private line the bimonthly line rental is €29.14 for a single line. If you have a line installed or reconnected, the charge appears on your first bill. **The charges and tariffs listed below apply only to calls made via Telecom Italia, and when**

making long-distance or international calls you should compare Telecom's rates with those of alternative carriers, which are sometimes cheaper.

Until November 1999, the cost of phone calls was based on 'pulses', a number of which made up one time unit (*scatto*), which varied according to the type of phone call. However, charges are now based on the duration of the phone call in seconds, plus an initial 'connection' fee of around €0.06 for local calls and €0.06 for national long-distance calls. The charges for calls via analogue and ISDN (digital) lines are the same. The tariff per minute depends on the time of the day and the distance of the call.

For local calls there are two charging periods from Mondays to Fridays. During the peak period (8am to 6.30pm) the charge for local calls is around €0.19 per minute for up to 15 minutes, after which it falls to €0.17 per minute. A cheaper rate of €0.10 for the first 15 minutes and €0.09 thereafter applies on weekdays outside the peak period, after 1pm on Saturdays, and all day on Sundays and public holidays. For long-distance domestic calls, the cost depends on the distance, with tariffs increasing in steps for calls (a) within the local district, (b) up to 15km, (c) between 15 and 30km, and (d) beyond 30km. The cost also depends on the time of day, as noted above. International calls can be particularly expensive via Telecom Italia and there is no longer an off peak time. The charges for international calls also depend on the country – the world is divided into 12 zones. Generally, the 'connection' fee is around €3.09, plus the fee per minute, e.g. a call to the UK costs €1.81 per minute.

Telecom Italia's charges for calls from a fixed-line phone to a mobile phone depend on the type of mobile phone owners' contract, which is indicated by the number's prefix. Cheaper rates usually apply on Saturdays and Sundays, but still vary according to the phone number prefix – there are up to six different periods in a single day! For some prefixes there's also a higher charge between 8am and 1pm on Saturdays. This complex system is expected to be simplified in future in line with the billing method used by independent long-distance carriers.

Telecom Italia has an extensive website with an English-language version (⌨ www.telecomitalia.it/perte/index.uk.shtml) containing an explanation of tariffs and the range of discount schemes available.

PHONE BILLS

Your phone bill (*bolletta*) is issued monthly for ISDN lines, and bimonthly for standard fixed-line and mobile phones. The standard phone bill contains the following information:

Italian	English
Giorno entro il quale deve essere effettuato il pagamento. Periodo al quale si riferiscono I canoni.	Date of deadline for payment of the bill and the period covered.

Nome ed indirizzo del intestato.	Name and address of the subscriber.
Codice fiscale.	The fiscal code of the subscriber.
Prefisso e numero di telefono.	Area code and phone number.
Ubicazione del telefono.	Location of the phone.
Numero totale degli scatti/secondi addebitati tra le date di relvazioni delle letture.	Number of pulses during the two-month period (will probably change to number of seconds), based on readings made at the beginning and end of the period.
Costo unitario e totale degli scatti.	Cost of pulses, units and total.

Description of charges and credits during the period for items such as:

Costo fisso per la linea urbana e la categoria installata.	Fixed costs for urban line and category installed.
Eventuali canoni di noleggio per impianti interni speciali.	Cost of the lease of deregulated . accessories
Canone per noleggio dell' apparecchio.	Cost of lease of phone.
Canone per la documentazione dell' traffico, se ricchiesta.	Charges for an itemised bill (if requested).
Servizi telefonici supplementari.	Supplementary telephone services.
Costo totale delle chiamate.	Total cost of phone calls.
Spese di spedizione bolletta.	Cost of invoicing.
Arrotondamento precedente.	Previous rounding-off.
Arrondotamento attuale.	Present rounding-off.
Saldo imponibile.	Total debit subject to VAT.
IVA totale.	Total VAT.
Totale bolletta.	Total invoice and amount to pay.

Bills should be paid by the deadline shown on them. If a bill is unpaid 45 days after the deadline, Telecom Italia can suspend outgoing calls and a penalty must be paid for re-activating the line. Bills can be paid at any post office or bank, by automatic bank payment (direct debit) or at a Telecom Italia office using an autobank (*bancobol*). Some banks also have machines that accept payment of bills from their clients, including phone bills. Receipts should be kept for five years.

Cancellation

You must provide 15 days' notice of cancellation of a phone line in writing and pay the final bill when it arrives. This is best done in person at a Telecom Italia office, where you can obtain a receipt, rather than entrust a letter to the Italian post office.

PUBLIC TELEPHONES

Public telephones (*telefono pubblico* or *cabina telefonica*) are located in bus depots, railway stations and airports, bars, cafés and restaurants, motorway rest areas, various business premises, main post offices, and in streets in cities and towns. All payphones allow International Direct Dialling (IDD) and international calls can also be made via the operator. Some public phones are coin operated but these are now being phased out and are being replaced by phones that only accept phone cards (*scheda telefonica prepagata*) or Telecom debit cards. Telecom Italia also provide pre-paid international phone cards and credit cards.

Phone cards are available from bars, news kiosks, tobacconists, post offices, shops and dispensing machines in various small denominations, most commonly €2.58, €5.16 and €7.75. To activate a phone card, you tear off the perforated tab at the corner and insert it in the slot provided. The outstanding credit on the card is displayed when it's inserted and used cards can be replaced mid-way through a call. Units are recorded on the card and subtracted automatically after each call. Don't expect to be able to use your international credit cards in Italian public phones, although airports, railway stations and hotels may have a few phones providing this service.

You can usually make both national and international calls from public phones, provided you have sufficient credit on your phone card. Bear in mind that calling a mobile phone from a public phone involves a special charge for connection of around €0.50. Normally the minimum amount accepted by payphones is €0.10, although if you phone a mobile you must insert over €0.50 to cover the additional cost.

Throughout the country there are *posto telefonico* offices, usually situated in small towns, where you can obtain assistance when making calls, and automatic telecommunication centres (*centri di telecomunicazione automatici*) offering self-service automatic calls (no assistance) in major cities and resorts. In cities and many towns in Italy there are also private telephone offices operated by a range of companies, including AT&T, Infostrada, Italia Blu, MCI, Teledue and Wind Telecom, from where you can make international calls.

TELEPHONE DIRECTORIES

Telecom Italia issues white (*pagina bianche*) and yellow pages (*pagina gialle*) for the major cities annually, while provincial towns usually get a new directory every three years or so. Directories provide an alphabetical list of subscribers, tariffs, international and national direct dialling codes, plus yellow pages, useful phone numbers and a map of the city concerned. All Telecom Italia subscribers are entitled to a free copy of the white and yellow pages, which are delivered to your door (the old ones must usually be returned for recycling), and extra copies can be purchased from local Telecom offices. The yellow and white pages can be accessed via the Internet (💻 http://paginegialle.virgilio.it or www.pagine gialle.it and 💻 www.paginebianche.it). Telecom Italia also issue a free booklet entitled *Tutta Città* in major cities containing maps, useful phone numbers and addresses, and postcodes for local streets, which is delivered annually with the white and yellow pages.

English-speaking residents will find the English yellow pages (EYP) useful, which is a directory of English-speaking professionals, organisations and services in Bologna, Catania, Florence, Genoa, Milan, Naples and Rome, and their surrounding areas. Unlike ordinary telephone directories, the listings contain full postal addresses with postcodes, telephone and fax numbers, and email and website addresses. For more information contact EYP, Via Belisario, 4/b, 00187 Rome (☎ 06-4740 861, 💻 www.englishyellowpages.it or http://eyp.alfanet.it).

Directory Enquiries

To find the phone number of a subscriber in Italy, you can call directory enquiries on 12. The system is now fully automated and if you don't know sufficient Italian it's difficult to use; however, if you stay on the line a human operator will assist you. **You can request only one number per call and each call costs around €0.50.** Some information is free, however, such as information about dialling codes and the numbers of new subscribers who aren't yet listed in directories.

MOBILE PHONES

At Sunday lunch-times in Italy in the mid-1980s, it was common to see a group of Italians in a restaurant with one brandishing a mobile phone and calling his friends to tell them what the group had eaten. The phone was then handed round, so that everybody in turn could tell their absent friends the same thing and emphasise that they were using Giorgio's mobile phone. Giorgio was obviously deeply proud of his new toy. Today, mobile phones are everywhere in Italy. The country ranks around third in the world in mobile phone ownership, with well over 20 million users and cover extending to some 99 per cent of the population (the other 1 per cent live on remote islands or on the top of mountains). The inexperienced newcomer to Italy may think many Italians suffer from intense toothache, walking around all day with one hand clasped to their cheek – until you realise they're only speaking into their mobile phones!

Before buying a mobile phone, you should be aware that in recent years there has been widespread (and conflicting) publicity regarding a possible health risk to users from the micro-wave radiation emitted by phones.

There are four mobile phone networks in Italy: Omnitel (🖳 www.neomnitel.it/vodafone), TIM (🖳 www.tim.it), Wind (🖳 www.wind.it) and Blu (🖳 www.blu.it). TIM (Telecom Italia Mobile) is a subsidiary of Telecom Italia, while Omnitel was founded in 1990 and is principally owned by Olivetti, Bell Atlantic International, Cellul Communication International, Telia International and Lehman Brothers. Wind was formed jointly by the Italian company Ente Nazionale della Energia Elettrica (ENEL), France Telecom and Deutsche Telekom. TIM provides two mobile phone networks: The Global System for Mobile Communication (GSM) and the Extended Total Access Communication System (ETACS), while Omnitel and Wind provide access only to GSM. ETACS is an old analogue network, which although still quite popular, is being phased out.

The best national cover is provided by TIM, although this is countered by a reluctance to provide access to international calls on a **rechargeable phone** (phones with a contract can be used to make international calls in Italy and world-wide). Omnitel and Wind don't cover the whole of Italy, although they're more generous with international access, which they provide through the TIM network. **When you're considering which company to sign up with, you must ensure that its network covers your home area and any other areas where you travel frequently or do business.**

All the mobile phone companies provide the option of either having a contract for access or using a rechargeable card. A rechargeable card usually costs €55, half of which is for the card itself and half credit for calls. Cards can usually be recharged with up to €250 of credit, but most people recharge for €25 or €50, which is valid for 12 months. Many shops offer recharging, which can also be done via some cash-dispensing machines (ATMs) or through your mobile phone if your contract provides it. There's usually a separate fee for the actual recharging, the cost of which depends on the network provider.

With contract phones (as opposed to rechargeable cards), providers offer a range of tariffs, with terms to suit light, medium and heavy users. In all cases there's a fixed monthly network charge and sometimes also a monthly minimum call charge. The cost of calls varies considerably according to the provider, the tariff, and the day of the week and/or time of day a call is made. Due to increasing competition, the terms and conditions change frequently, with extras such as 'voicemail' frequently included free of charge. Before signing up with a provider, you should obtain the latest information on tariffs and special offers for the main providers from phone shops, who are agents for the mobile phone companies. You can then compare these and calculate which is likely to be the most cost-effective, bearing in mind your anticipated usage. If you make a lot of calls, you should select a tariff with low call charges. Conversely, if you make few calls or need a phone mostly for incoming calls, you should choose a tariff with low monthly costs.

Payment terms vary according to how you plan to pay your mobile phone bills. No deposit is required if bills will be charged to a credit card, but if they will be charged directly to a bank account (direct debit) there's usually a deposit of up to €50. If you will be paying on receipt of your monthly bill, the deposit may be as high as €100. There's also a fixed charge for the initial connection to the network of around €25. Connection is often made within a few hours of signing a contract, although contracts usually state that connection will be made 'within 24 hours'.

The cost of mobile phones themselves, affectionately called 'little phones' (*telefonini*), is quite high in Italy. Unlike countries such as Germany and the UK, where mobile phones are often provided 'free' (although they remain the property of the provider) on signing a contract with a provider, Italians must buy their phones at the market price. However, the cost of a 'free' phone and a one-year contract in the UK is equal to around the same as the price of a mobile phone in Italy. The cost of a phone varies according to the manufacturer and its level of sophistication, and ranges from around €100 to €800, with most costing around €175. Mobile phone retailers advertise in newspapers and magazines, where a wide range of special offers is promoted. There's also an active market in second-hand mobile phones. Good places to look are the classified advertisements in newspapers such as *Porta Portese* (Rome – named after the city's famous flea market), *La Pulce* (Florence) and *Secondamano* (Milan) – there are equivalents in most cities. There are a number of 'bazaars' on the Internet offering used mobile phones at competitive prices – search on *cellulari usati* or *di seconda mano*. Bear in mind, however, that as well as buying a phone you must negotiate a contract with a service provider (or buy rechargeable cards).

Before buying a mobile phone you should compare battery life (lithium battery packs last the longest), memory number capacity, weight (now down to 100g or less for the lightest models), size and features. The latter may include alphanumeric store, automatic call-back, unanswered call store, call timer, minute minder, lock facility, call barring, mailbox, messaging services, Internet web-surfing and email. However, bear in mind that the last two items may require a special contract with a service provider and additional equipment, which may cost as much as the mobile phone. This usually isn't mentioned when a shop tries to sell you a more expensive *telefonino*.

Mobile phone companies will continue to bill you, even if you leave Italy during your contract period, and will pursue you until the money is paid (if necessary, by engaging debt collectors in other countries). Most mobile phone companies don't include a cancellation clause in their contracts, as many foreigners have discovered, and customers are stuck with monthly payments for the full term of the contract. Short-term phone rentals aren't common but are possible for visiting business people with generous expense accounts (suffice to say, they don't come cheap).

Each mobile phone company is assigned different numbers starting with 03, including Blu (0380, 0388-9), Omnitel (0340, 0347-9) Tim (0330, 0333-0339, 0360, 0366, 0368) and Wind (0328, 0329).

Security

The theft of mobile phones used to be a huge problem, with stolen phones usually reprogrammed (cloned) to make free international calls. The risk remains for phones used on the ETACS network (TACS phones), although less so with GSM phones as their signals are less easily intercepted. Obviously you shouldn't leave your phone lying around in public (or in your car) where it can be stolen. If your phone is stolen, you're held responsible for the cost of any calls a thief makes prior to you reporting the theft to your phone company. Phones are provided with a unique serial number that allows their use to be blocked if they're stolen and they can also be programmed to bar users from making certain calls, e.g. international calls.

INTERNET

Perhaps due to the relatively high cost of telecommunications, Italy has been slower than many other European countries to adapt to the Internet. However, this is changing and most large and medium-sized companies now quote an email address and often a website in their advertising. Private consumers are also joining up in droves, lured by the recent arrival of a number of free Internet service providers (ISPs). The most popular ISP is Tin (🖳 http://tin.virgilio.it), a subsidiary of Telecom Italia, which offers two services, one of which, ClubNet, is free. This provides you with one email address, 20 MB of home page space and access to the Internet via a local phone number. The other Tin service, Premium, is similar to CompuServe and AOL, in that it provides special content for subscribers only and you're charged a monthly subscription fee. Like CompuServe and AOL (although unlike ClubNet), Premium gives you international access to the Internet from places outside Italy, with some 400 nodes world-wide. CompuServe and AOL also have local access in Milan and Rome, although unless you live in one of these two cities your access will be through long-distance calls (which can be very expensive). The long-distance phone company, Wind, also provides free Internet access (☎ 159 or 🖳 www.inwind.it).

Telecom Italia offers four different Internet tariffs. The most basic costs €12.95 per month, plus €0.15 per minute, or you can have unrestricted Internet access for €35.75 per month (which is much more cost-effective). Tiscalinet (🖳 www.tiscali.it) is a free access provider, with local access numbers in most areas. They give you one free e-mail address and 30 MB of homepage space and, unlike some free services, your email can be accessed directly using third party software such as Microsoft Outlook. One drawback with free services is that there can be a lot of traffic on the networks, particularly during the evenings and weekends. This can slow things down considerably and sometimes means you cannot connect at all. Furthermore, the telephone support available is of variable quality and availability, and may be charged at extortionate rates (even by Italian standards). You may therefore be better off choosing a subscription service.

Most computer shops have agreements with local ISPs and act as agents for them. They will sell you a software kit, access numbers and so on, and the service is usually activated within a few hours. The cost is quite reasonable at around €100 per year, which usually includes one email address and unlimited access to the Internet. The actual provider depends on where you live, with some areas well covered by local ISPs and others not at all.

If you already have Internet access (e.g. at work) and don't want to pay for an email account of your own, you can sign up with one of the free web-based email services such as Yahoo Mail (🖥 www.yahoo.com) or Micro-soft Network's Hotmail (🖥 www.hotmail.com). One advantage of these services is that you can access your email from any computer with Internet access, e.g. at a library or cybercafe. Note, however, that mail sent to and from such services isn't necessarily secure.

Modems

At one time Telecom Italia insisted that you buy an enormous 300bps modem from them at a cost of about three times the normal price for a much faster modem on the free market. Of course, being practical people, Italians soon found ways around this regulation and completely ignored it. Today you can use your own modem without restrictions, but you should note that a modem imported from abroad may not work in Italy without modification. You must ensure that your modem accepts a four-wire cable where the two wires in the middle are active (the UK system, for example, uses the two outer wires). Therefore, in order to avoid problems it may be better to purchase a new modem in Italy. Modern 56k (V90) internal and external modems can be obtained for around €50 and €75 respectively. You may also need a telephone plug adapter, which are available from any hardware store (*ferramenta*).

EMERGENCY & USEFUL NUMBERS

The general emergency number in Italy is 113. However, people are discouraged from using this except in cases where there's a real, serious danger for the caller or other persons, or in the event of a serious accident. Otherwise, the preferred emergency procedure is to call the relevant organisation directly. People witnessing someone being beaten up at night and calling 113 on their mobile phones have been told to call 112 (the number for the *Carabinieri* – see below) instead. Even calling 112 may not produce the expected result. Some youngsters once called this number when they saw a car being stolen in the early morning hours. The reply was, 'We only have two cars and they're not for that sort of thing', from which you may conclude that car theft isn't a particularly high priority for the Italian police. The most important emergency numbers are:

112	Paramilitary police (*carabinieri*) for crimes and traffic accidents;
113	General emergency number for serious emergencies only (*soccorso pubblico di emergenza*);
115	Fire brigade (*vigili del fuoco*);
118	Ambulance or first aid (*emergenza sanitaria*).

Calling the above numbers from public phones is usually free of charge. Other useful numbers include:

110	Information (*informazioni*);
12	Directory enquiries (*informazioni elenco abbonati* – see page 148);
114	Alarm call (*sveglia automatica*);
116	Vehicle breakdown assistance (*soccorso stradale*) – Automobile Club d'Italia (ACI);
161	Time signal (*ora esatta*);
172	Reverse charge or collect calls – for international calls 172 must be followed by the international code of the country you wish to call (an operator will answer in the language of the country you're calling);
176	International operator (*informazioni internazionali*), who can provide general information in English;
197	For urgent phone calls (*chiamate urgenti*) – if a number is busy you can get the operator to interrupt an ongoing call.

Local telephone operators usually speak only Italian, although a translation service (in Arabic, English, French or German) is available on 170.

There's a range of special numbers in Italy that are assigned different colours. Green numbers (*numeri verdi*) are 'freephone' numbers with a prefix such as 147 or 800 – although you're charged one or more units for each freephone call you make! Free numbers are often shown with a *numero verde* phone logo in green with a box enclosing the number. Blue numbers (*numeri azzurri*) are to report child abuse, pink numbers (*numeri rosa*) to report abuse of women, and violet numbers (*numeri viola*) to report any other kind of abuse. Red numbers (*numeri rossi*) are to obtain prenatal advice, while orange numbers (*numeri arancioni*) are for general psychiatric counselling.

TELEGRAMS, TELEX & FAX

Telegrams (*telegrammi*), both national and international, can be sent from post offices or by phone (186). Telegrams are sent either from the main counter in smaller post offices or from a separate *telegrafo* section at main post offices. Domestic telegrams not exceeding twenty words (excluding the address) cost €4.39. The cost of sending telegrams internationally varies according to the destination. For most countries within Europe there's an initial fee of €7.11, plus a fee of €0.26 for each word excluding the address. For the USA, Canada and Australia there's no base fee, but each word costs around €0.67. For telegrams sent via the phone, there's a surcharge of €0.50 within your local area and €0.62 for telegrams outside this area. The account-holder of the phone from which the telegram is dictated is considered to be the sender and the cost is added to the bill. The phone number of a digital (ISDN) line is transmitted to the operator using the keypad of the phone, although with analogue lines the phone number must be dictated to the operator. This service is available throughout Italy 24 hours per day, seven days per week.

Fax is widely available in Italy, where messages can be sent and received from post offices and many private offices offering business services. Faxes sent nationally and internationally from a post office cost around €1.30 per page. Tobacconists, stationery shops and other establishments also send and receive faxes (and may also provide photocopying services), and many petrol stations on motorways also provide access to fax machines. Unlike the post office (which charges by the page), private businesses charge according to the number of telephone units used and therefore the price may be lower.

There are no special rules for fax machines except that they should conform to the international G3 standard. The cost of a fax machine varies according to the make, the kind of paper used (e.g. fax rolls or plain paper), the features (such as an answer phone) and multiple-use features. For example, some fax machines can be used as a scanner and colour printer when connected to a computer. An average price for a standard, middle-of-the-range machine is around €250. If you bring your own fax machine to Italy it should work without any problems, provided it operates on a 220v power supply, although some machines will need modifying.

Telexes can be sent from most main post offices, and many hotels offer telex facilities for their clients. The use of telexes has to a large extent been superseded by fax and email, although the telex network still has over two million subscribers in over 200 countries.

8.

TELEVISION & RADIO

Italy's pride in its cultural heritage is by no means evident in its television (TV) programmes – you could be excused for thinking that Italians invented junk TV – although they aren't (much) worse than the fare dished up in many other European countries. Italian radio (including expatriate stations) is generally excellent and the equal of that in most other European countries.

TELEVISION

Italians are avid TV viewers (over 90 per cent of homes have at least one TV) and according to some surveys, rate third in Europe (after the Portuguese and British) in average viewing time per day, per head (around four hours). There's usually a TV in the kitchen/dining room, which seems to be permanently switched on, and conversation often has to be pitched several decibels higher than normal to be heard over the blaring of a passionate lunchtime soap. Some 90 per cent of Italians over the age of 14 watch TV every day and most receive their news from the TV (relatively few Italians buy newspapers).

The choice of programmes is vast, although it's a disappointing hotchpotch of mind-numbing game shows, boring cabarets, bizarre dubbed soaps (where sound and mouth movements are rarely synchronised), trashy films and relentless repeats. Some local TV stations broadcast programmes on a continuous loop that they change at their leisure, which can give a distinctly 'Groundhog Day' feel to channel-hopping, knitted together with endless advertising, most of which is of equally poor quality.

After a campaign in 1996 by parents worried about the influence that certain programmes could have on their children, programmes with a sexual or violent content aren't shown between the hours of 7am and 10.30pm. If an image of a child in red is shown on the screen at the start of a film, it indicates that it should be viewed in the presence of an adult. Italians also pioneered the 'violence chip', which is an electronic device designed to filter out violent programmes on TV when children are watching.

There's no cable TV in Italy; some cables were installed, but it became too expensive and was abandoned in favour of satellite TV. TV reception (both terrestrial and satellite) is good in most of Italy.

Many TV magazines are available, including *TV Sorrisi & Canzoni*, *Guida TV*, *Onda TV*, *Radio Corriere* and *Film TV*, all of which are sold by newsagents and include radio programmes. There are separate magazines for satellite TV such as *Tele +*, *Tele 7*, and *TV Sat*. TV magazines are also provided free each week with the major daily newspapers.

Standards

The standards for television reception in Italy aren't the same as in some other countries. Due to the differences in transmission standards, TVs and video recorders operating on the British (PAL-I), French (SECAM) or North American

(NTSC) systems won't function in Italy, which, along with most other continental European countries, uses the PAL-BG standard. It's possible to buy a multi-standard European TV (and VCR) containing automatic circuitry that switches between different systems. Some multi-standard TVs also offer the NTSC standard and have a jack plug connection allowing you to play back American videos. A standard British, French or US TV won't work in Italy, although British TVs can be modified. The same applies to foreign video recorders, which won't operate with an Italian TV unless the VCR is dual-standard. Some expatriates opt for two TVs, one to receive Italian programmes and another (e.g. SECAM or NTSC) to play their favourite videos.

A portable 36cm (14in) colour TV can be purchased in Italy for around €160, a 55cm (21in) TV costs from around €235 and a 71cm (28in) model from around €470. Many TVs feature Nicam stereo sound, and high-quality, digital sound is available in most of Italy. Digital wide-screen TVs are also widely available and, although still relatively high, prices are falling. Most new TVs offer a teletext system, which apart from allowing you to display programme schedules, also provides a wealth of useful and interesting information. Teletext information is called *Televideo* on RAI stations and *Mediavideo* on Italia Uno, Rete 4 and Canale 5 stations.

Terrestrial TV

Italian TV changed dramatically after deregulation of the Television Board in 1976, up to which time it had been totally state-owned and censored by the Catholic Church. Today, Italy has six main terrestrial stations, RAI 1, 2 and 3, Italia 1, Rete 4 and Canale 5 (see below), plus hundreds of local stations. The country has the highest density of independent broadcasting companies in the world, exceeding even Japan and the USA. The number of stations increased from around 70 in 1976 to almost 1,000 by the early 1990s, and the hours of programmes broadcast per year leapt from 6,000 to more than one million in just a decade.

RAI: There are three state-owned RAI channels, which generally offer the best quality programmes and command the highest viewing figures. These are RAI UNO (RAI1), RAI DUE (RAI2) and RAI TRE (RAI3). RAI3 is the most 'cultural' of the three, although they're all subject to political patronage, which can inject a little bias into certain topics. The three RAI stations attract around 40 per cent of viewers. For further information, visit the RAI website (🖳 www. rai.it), which has an English-language version.

- **RAI 1** is the most popular RAI station among older viewers and shows major events, popular series (usually about the mafia) made by RAI, quiz/game shows, film premieres and news. At the weekend, it broadcasts children's programmes in the early morning. On Sundays, it shows a popular soap called *DomenicaIn* (now surpassed in popularity by Italia Uno's *Buona*

Domenica), which accompanies Sunday lunch in many households and lasts most of the afternoon.

- **RAI 2** has more films and 'tele-films' (films made for TV, usually American) and soaps such as the American *Friends*. During the day, it shows its own programmes. Children's programmes are shown late on Sunday morning and at 4pm on weekdays.

- **RAI 3** features more sport than the other RAI stations and regional news programmes and shows a film at around 8.40pm most days. Children's programmes are shown just before lunchtime on Sunday.

Independent Stations: The most important independent TV stations in Italy are Italia 1, Rete 4 and Canale 5, which are owned by media magnate and prime minister Silvio Berlusconi through his Fininvest company. They're most famous for their mildly pornographic shows which may involve contestants stripping to win bonus prizes. These channels collectively attract over 50 per cent of Italian viewers.

- **Italia 1** is similar to Canale 5 (see below) and has excellent news reports and good entertainment programmes in the evening, including a film at 8.45pm. It shows a surfeit of cartoons from morning until early evening and *Buona Domenica*, a popular soap.

- **RETE 4** mainly broadcasts a series of tele-films interrupted by three feature films at 4pm, 8.35pm and 11pm. It's supposed to be the most highbrow of the three Berlusconi stations but there isn't much difference between them.

- **Canale 5** shows a mixture of tele-films, soaps and sitcoms (some Italian), news and weather, with a film at 9pm each day.

Other significant stations include Telemontecarlo, TMC and TMC2, Italia 7/Telecity and Odeon/Quadrifoglio TV. There are many local TV stations and in northern Italy you can also receive terrestrial broadcasts from Austria, France and Switzerland (the most popular include the French station Antenne 2 and Telemontecarlo). Over 900 local channels 'share' around 10 per cent of viewers; with little money and resources, programming is dominated by the most appalling amateurism, film repeats, abysmal, locally-produced advertising and soft porn (especially late at night).

Satellite Television

Domestic

Over 1 million people subscribe to pay TV in Italy, where there are currently two main pay TV providers: Stream and Telepiu. As in most countries, the mainstay of pay TV is sport, particularly soccer, and films. Many films are broadcast with a double audio track (*doppio audio*) allowing you to switch from Italian to the original (usually English) soundtrack. Sport includes all matches live from *Serie A*, Italy's premier football league (you can sign up for all 34 of a team's matches or just their 17 away games).

You must rent or buy a decoder and pay a monthly or annual subscription to receive programmes. You can sign up by phone, via the Internet or at a TV store. Charges are €8 per month for the hire of the decoder (plus a deposit of around €100) or you can buy one. Costs vary from zero to €500, as some companies offer decoders 'free' and claw back the cost in installation and subscription charges. In recent years many broadcasters have changed their decoders in an effort to thwart pirates, although so far they've had little success. Until the situation is resolved, you would be better off renting a decoder than buying an expensive one. For example, Stream have announced that they intend to abandon the Irdeto system completely and move to Mediaguard. The broadcasting authority decreed that by June 2001, Stream must agree on a decoder and stick with it long enough for customers to obtain good value from their systems. However, to date they haven't agreed on anything (and as a result have been fined around €150,000!).

Subscription costs vary according to the channel package. Telepiu offers four packages, ranging in price from €19 to €45 per month, while Stream offers seven packages, costing from €24 to €57 per month.

In addition to pay stations, a number of free-to-air stations are broadcast via satellite, including Sat 2000 (religious), Nuvolari (sport), Video Italia (music videos) and the three RAI channels (see **Terrestrial TV** above). Information about satellite TV is available on the Internet (🖳 www.satellite.it).

International

There are a number of satellites positioned over Europe carrying over 200 stations broadcasting in a variety of languages. Satellite TV has been growing apace in Europe in recent years, particularly in Italy, which has no cable TV. TV addicts (easily recognised by their antennae and square eyes) are offered a huge choice of English and foreign-language stations, which can be received via the Astra satellites throughout Italy with an 85cm dish. A bonus is the availability of radio stations, including the major BBC stations (see **English-Language Radio** on page 165).

Among the many English-language stations available on Astra are Sky One, Movimax, Sky Premier, Sky Cinema, Film Four, Sky News, Sky Sports (three channels), UK Gold, Channel 5, Granada Plus, TNT, Eurosport, CNN, CNBC Europe, UK Style, UK Horizons, the Disney Channel and the Discovery Channel. Other stations broadcast in Dutch, German, Japanese, Swedish and various Indian languages. The signal from many stations is scrambled (the decoder is usually built into the receiver) and viewers must pay a monthly subscription fee to receive programmes. You can buy pirate decoders for some channels. The best served by clear (unscrambled) stations are German-speakers (most German stations on Astra are clear).

Sky: You must buy a receiver with a Videocrypt decoder and pay a monthly subscription to receive Sky stations except Sky News (which isn't scrambled). Various packages are available costing from around GB£12 to around GB£35 per month for the premium package offering all movie channels plus Sky Sports. To receive scrambled channels such as Movimax and Sky Sports, you need an address in Britain. Subscribers are sent a coded 'smart' card (similar to a credit card), which must be inserted in the decoder to activate it (cards are periodically updated to thwart counterfeiters). Sky won't send smart cards to overseas viewers, as they have the copyright for a British-based audience only (overseas homeowners need to obtain a card through a friend or relative in Britain). However, a number of satellite companies in Italy (some of which advertise in the expatriate press) supply genuine Sky cards – at a premium.

Digital Television: Digital TV was launched on 1st October 1998 by Sky in Britain. The benefits include a superior picture, better (CD) quality sound, wide-screen cinema format and access to many more stations. To watch digital TV you require a Digibox and a (digital) Minidish, which in 2003 could be purchased at a subsidised price by existing Sky customers in Britain. Customers must sign up for a 12-month subscription and agree to have the connection via a phone line (to allow for future interactive services). In addition to the usual analogue channels (see above), digital TV offers BBC1, BBC2, ITV, Channel 4 and Channel 5, plus many digital channels (a total of 200, with up to 500 possible later). Digital satellite equipment is offered by a number of satellite companies throughout Italy.

Eutelsat: Most of Eutelsat's channels are non-English. The English-language stations on Eutelsat include Eurosport, BBC World and CNBC Superchannel. Other stations broadcast in Arabic, French, German, Hungarian, Italian (RAI 1, 2 and 3), Polish, Portuguese, Spanish and Turkish.

BBC Worldwide Television: The BBC's commercial subsidiary, BBC Worldwide Television, broadcasts two 24-hour channels: BBC Prime (general entertainment) and BBC World (24-hour news and information). BBC World is free-to-air and is transmitted via the Eutelsat Hot Bird satellite, while BBC Prime is encrypted and requires a D2-MAC decoder and a smartcard, available on subscription from BBC Prime, PO Box 5054, London W12 0ZY, UK (☎ 020-8433 2221, ✉ bbcprime@bbc.co.uk). For more information and a programming guide, contact BBC Worldwide Television, Woodlands, 80 Wood Lane, London W12 0TT, UK (☎ 020-8576 2555). A programme guide is available on the Internet (🖳 www.bbc.co.uk/schedules) and both BBC World and BBC Prime have their own websites (🖳 www.bbcworld.com and www.bbcprime.com). When accessing them, you need to enter the name of the country (e.g. Italy), so that schedules are displayed in local time.

Equipment: A satellite receiver should have a built-in Videocrypt decoder (and others such as Eurocrypt, Syster or SECAM if required) and be capable of receiving satellite stereo radio. A system with an 85cm dish (to receive Astra stations) costs from around €310 plus the cost of installation, which may be included in the price. Shop around, as prices can vary considerably. With a 1.2 or 1.5 metre motorised dish, you can receive hundreds of stations in a multitude of languages from around the world. If you wish to receive satellite TV on two or more TVs, you can buy a satellite system with two or more receivers. To receive stations from two or more satellites simultaneously, you need a motorised dish or a dish with a double feed antenna (dual LNBs). There are many satellite sales and installation companies in Italy, some of which advertise in the expatriate press. Alternatively, you can import your own satellite dish and receiver and install it yourself. **Before buying a system, ensure that it can receive programmes from all existing and planned satellites.**

Location: To receive programmes from any satellite, there must be no obstacles between the satellite and your dish, i.e. no trees, buildings or mountains must obstruct the signal, so check before renting or buying a home. Before buying or erecting a satellite dish, check whether you need permission from your landlord or the local municipality. Some towns and buildings (such as apartment blocks) have laws or regulations regarding the positioning of antennae, although generally owners can mount a dish almost anywhere without attracting any complaints. Dishes can usually be mounted in a variety of unobtrusive positions and can also be painted or patterned to blend in with the background. Individual dishes will be soon removed in apartment buildings (*palazzine*) and substituted with a single communal antenna with a cable connection to apartments.

Programme Guides: Many satellite stations provide teletext information and most broadcast in stereo. Sky satellite programme listings are provided in a number of British publications such as *What Satellite, Satellite Times* and *Satellite TV Europe* (the best), which are available on subscription and from some newsagents in Italy. Satellite TV programmes are also listed in a number of expatriate newspapers and magazines in Italy. The annual *World Radio and TV Handbook* edited by David G. Bobbett (Watson-Guptil Publications) contains over 600 pages of information and the frequencies of all radio and TV stations world-wide.

TV Licence

A TV tax (*canone*) is payable in Italy of €97.10 per year for a colour TV; it can be paid quarterly, half-yearly or annually (at a post office). A single licence covers any number of TVs in a household. When you buy a TV in Italy, your name is automatically registered with the authorities, although many people avoid tax by buying a second-hand TV or making an 'arrangement' with the vendor. The tax must be paid to customs if you personally import a TV. The authorities have powerful detector vans to identify homes where people are watching TV and then check whether they've paid the tax. There are fines for non-payment, but the **maximum** fine is just 50 per cent of the licence fee (which makes it unsurprising that many people avoid paying).

Videos & DVDs

Videos are widely available to rent (*noleggiare*) or buy from video shops in all main towns and cities, which are listed in yellow pages under *Audiovisivi*. To rent videos you usually need to join a club and pay an annual fee and you can then rent videos from €2 per night (for an old 'classic') up to €5 to €7.5 per night for the latest Hollywood blockbuster. Many shops also sell videos from €10 to €50. The American video rental company Blockbuster has stores in major towns with a wide selection of films (both VCR and DVD) in the original language (you can also rent a VCR or DVD player). In some places you may also be offered pirate videos of new films that haven't yet been released on video, which should be avoided as the quality is usually terrible; they're also illegal!

You may be able to buy or swap English-language videos with other foreigners through expatriate clubs, and you can buy English-language videos via the Internet and through mail-order video catalogues. Choices Direct, 19-24 Manasty Road, Orton Southgate, Peterborough, PE2 6UP, UK (☎ 01733-236800, 🖳 www.choicesdirect.co.uk), who are licensed by the BBC to sell their videos, will search for anything you request if you don't find it in their catalogue; if you order from their website, you don't pay postage. BBC Television produces three-hour videos of its best programmes (including entertainment, humour, sport, natural history, news and current affairs) available on subscription from Video World, Subscription Dept, 680 Romford Road, London E12, UK.

DVDs are becoming increasingly popular in Italy. Although they're still considerably more expensive than videos, they often offer additional features such as extra scenes, multiple language soundtracks and subtitling. Be particularly careful, however, to buy DVDs for the correct 'zone', as films intended for an American audience (Zone 1) won't play back in a European (Zone 2) DVD player unless it has been modified, and Zone 1 versions often don't contain the alternate soundtracks and subtitling. There are multi-zone DVD players available and it's also possible to modify many single-zone players to read multiple-zone DVDs.

RADIO

Radio is popular in Italy with an estimated audience of some 35 million people, over a third of whom listen exclusively to popular music stations. Radio was deregulated in Italy in 1976, at the same time as television. Since then there has been an explosion in the number of stations available; there are now some 2,500, from large national stations to small local stations with just a 'handful' of listeners. The three main channels are Radio 1, 2 and 3 operated by the state controlled company RAI. Radios 1 and 2 are split into light (dance) music and general entertainment on one wavelength and popular music on another, while Radio 3 broadcasts serious discussion programmes and classical music.

The favourite station among young listeners is Radio DJ, which also features famous club disc jockeys (mostly on Friday and Saturday nights), while Radio Italia offers a selection of Italian singers and bands, and Radio Globo plays mostly dance music.

English-Language Stations

During the summer, RAI broadcasts daily news in English, and Vatican Radio also broadcasts news in English at various times. There are also expatriate English-language radio stations in the major cities.

The BBC World Service is broadcast on short wave on several frequencies (e.g. short wave 12095, 9760, 9410, 7325, 6195, 5975 and 3955 KhZ) simultaneously and you can usually receive a good signal on one of them. The signal strength varies according to where you live in Italy, the time of day and year, the power and positioning of your receiver, and atmospheric conditions. The BBC World Service plus BBC Radio 1, 2, 3, 4 and 5 are also available on the Astra (Sky) satellite. For a free BBC World Service programme guide and frequency information write to BBC World Service, BBC Worldwide, PO Box 76, Bush House, Strand, London WC2B 4PH, UK (☎ 020-8752 5040). The BBC publishes a monthly magazine, *BBC On Air*, containing comprehensive programme listing for BBC World Service radio, BBC Prime TV and BBC World TV. It's available on subscription from the BBC, On Air Magazine, Room 207 NW, Bush House, Strand, London WC2B 4PH, UK (☎ 020-7240 4899, ✉ on.air.magazine@bbc.co.uk) and from some newsagents in Italy.

Many other foreign stations can be received in Italy, including Radio Australia, Radio Canada, Denmark Radio, Radio Nederland, Radio Sweden International and the Voice of America. Schedules can be found via the Internet, and you can often download broadcast material.

If you have satellite TV, you can receive many radio stations via your satellite link. For example, BBC Radio 1, 2, 3, 4 and 5, BBC World Service, Sky Radio, Virgin 1215 and many foreign-language stations are broadcast via the Astra satellites. Satellite radio stations are listed in British satellite TV magazines such as *Satellite Times*. If you're interested in receiving radio stations from further afield, you should obtain a copy of the *World Radio TV Handbook* (Watson-Guptil Publications).

9.

EDUCATION

The foundations for Italy's current education system were established in 1946, when the country became a parliamentary republic. Since then, the state has provided free education for all, from nursery school to university. The state sector is the backbone of the Italian education system and most students attend state schools and universities; private schools are generally seen as an alternative, rather than a better form of education. Compulsory education (*scuola dell'obbligo*) applies from the ages of 6 to 15 (an increase to 16 is planned), although 90 per cent of young people in Italy continue their education beyond the age of 15. The adult illiteracy rate is officially around 3 per cent, although unofficially it's much higher (almost exclusively limited to the south). State education is also free for the children of foreigners living in Italy, irrespective of whether they're registered residents (in 2003, some 150,000 foreign children were enrolled in Italian state schools).

After the age of 15, tuition remains free, although enrolment taxes are payable (see **Provisions** on page 176); these are minimal for secondary school education but increase considerably for university students (although still relatively low). University education is free for foreign students and there are no quotas for EU nationals (non-EU students require a student visa). Most young people are acutely aware of the value of qualifications and, as a result, very few school-leavers go directly into employment without studying for a diploma, degree or a professional qualification, and Italy boasts one of the largest numbers of university students in the world. Despite this, the percentage of students who graduate from university or even obtain secondary school qualifications is relatively low compared with other EU countries. Two reasons for this are the traditional (and rigorous) nature of education in Italy and the number of years (seven or eight) most students require to complete a degree. There's a high dropout rate among university students, only one in three who enrol graduating. However, due to its demanding curricula, Italy considers its school and university qualifications to be of a higher standard than those of many other countries, with the consequence that educational qualifications gained abroad aren't necessarily recognised in Italy or given equal status.

Both the curricula and examinations in state schools are set by the Ministry of Education (Ministero della Pubblica Istruzione), in consultation with an advisory body, the National Education Council. The Ministry is represented at regional level by school 'superintendencies' (*sovrintendenze scolastiche*). Italy is divided into scholastic districts (*distretti*) administered by provincial local education offices. In theory, this centralised system should ensure the same standard of education throughout the country, although in practice there's a considerable disparity between the quality of education in northern and the southern schools, the former being regarded as far superior. Recent years have seen a progressive devolvement of responsibility to regional education authorities and schools, one effect of which has been to give schools a (limited) degree of freedom in setting their own curricula. Since September 2000, state schools have also been responsible for managing their own finances.

The education system is divided into a number of distinct stages: pre-school, primary school, lower and upper secondary school, and higher and further education. Students are required to make specialist subject choices on entry into upper secondary school, and a number of options are available at this stage. Admission to Italian secondary schools isn't selective and, provided students obtain their lower secondary school-leaving certificate, they may go to the upper secondary school of their choice.

A child's progress is based on annual evaluations, which in turn are based on tests and continuous assessment. Written tests are held each term and oral tests (*interrogazioni*) at the discretion of the teacher. This can come as something of a shock to foreign children who aren't used to responding orally and who come from a system where greater emphasis is given to written work and exams. At university, the emphasis on oral examinations, as opposed to written ones, is even more marked, the majority of exams being conducted orally.

Pupils gain admission (*promosso*) to the next year's class only after attaining a satisfactory level in all subjects at the end of the academic year. Pupils who fail (*bocciare*) to reach the required standard in a particular subject carry forward an educational debit (*debito formativo*), which must be made up either through extra tuition during the summer holidays or by attending extra classes during the following academic year. If pupils fail in a number of subjects (usually over half the total), they may be refused admission into the next year's class and must repeat the entire year (*respinto*). All schools have regular parent-teacher meetings, where every attempt is made to prevent this happening.

As educational courses at school and university are largely determined by the Ministry of Education, they aren't tailored to the needs of individual students. At university a certain amount of choice can be exercised through a student's individual study plan, but a frequent criticism is that the structure of courses does little to encourage self-expression and personal development. Teaching methods at all levels are also often criticised as old-fashioned, with over-emphasis on learning by rote. The rigid adherence to a core curriculum (with textbooks often standardised) in state schools helps to ensure uniform standards but can be hard on slow learners. The need to introduce more flexible study programmes in schools has long been a subject of debate in Italy, and the last ten years have seen a gradual broadening of the school curriculum, partly through the introduction of experimental classes (*classi sperimentali*) based on students' own choices and needs.

The need to obtain a satisfactory level in all subjects each year, as well as passing exams at the end of each school cycle, means that Italian children must study hard from an early age. From primary school onwards, children are expected to do regular homework (*compiti*), the amount increasing with the age of the child (parents often set aside a considerable amount of time to help children with their homework).

Information about Italian schools and universities can be obtained from Italian embassies and consulates abroad, from foreign embassies and from educational departments within the Ministry of Education, Ministero della Pubblica Istruzione, Viale Trastevere, 76/a, 00153 Rome (☎ 06-58491, 🖥 www. istruzione.it). Local school information can be obtained from town halls (*comune*) and from local education offices (*provveditorati*), as well as from the Ministry's website which lists the names and addresses of all state schools and many private schools by province (click on *Anagrafe Scolastica*). The Italy Schools page of the Worldwide Classroom's online directory (🖥 www.world wide.edu/ci/italy/index.html) lists many educational institutions accepting both Italian and foreign students, including language schools, universities, private institutes and international schools.

CHOOSING A SCHOOL

If you're able to choose between state and private education and between Italian and foreign-language schooling, the following information will help you to decide.

Language

Choosing the language of study is one probably the most important decision to be made when selecting the best type of school for your children. How do you and your children view the thought of their studying in Italian? What language is best from a long-term point of view? Is schooling available in Italy in your children's mother tongue?

The only schools in Italy using English as the teaching language are a few private foreign and international schools. If your children attend any other school, they must study all subjects in Italian. For most children, studying in Italian isn't the handicap it may at first appear, particularly for young children who adapt easily. The watershed age for learning a foreign language is between 10 and 12 years of age, after which children tend to learn languages more slowly. In recent years, Italian state schools have made a great effort to integrate foreign children and provide intensive Italian-language lessons, remedial classes and cultural activities. Nevertheless, some children have great difficulty learning Italian and many foreign parents arrange private Italian lessons, often with the children of other foreign parents in their area, or send their children to a international school, where lessons are taught in English and they can learn Italian at a more leisurely pace without the pressure.

English is generally the second language taught in state schools in Italy, where it's introduced as a compulsory subject in primary school and continued throughout secondary school. However, the level of instruction will do little to maintain your child's ability to read and write in English, particularly as Italian students are rarely fluent by the time they leave school.

In some areas of Italy, the languages most commonly spoken are French and German, with Italian the second language (see **Language** on page 49). Schools in the Val d'Aosta (French) and the Trentino-Alto Adige region (German) teach school syllabi in two languages and bi-lingualism is often a prerequisite for future employment. Other minority languages, including Slovenian, Albanian and Greek, may be included in the school curriculum if there's sufficient demand from parents.

Other Considerations

You should also take into account the following:

- State education is perceived to be of an equal or higher standard than private education, and Italian parents generally send their children to private schools only for religious reasons or to obtain extra help that's unavailable in a state school.

- Due to language (see above) and other integration problems, enrolling a child in an Italian state school is recommended only if you're planning to stay for a minimum of a year, particularly for teenage children who aren't fluent in Italian. If you're uncertain how long you will be staying in Italy, it's probably best to assume a medium to long stay.

- The area where you choose to live may affect your choice of school. For example, state schools may give preference to children living locally, and international schools (where the curriculum is taught in English) tend to be situated in or near the major cities. Children usually attend local nursery and primary schools, although Italy's falling birth rate has led to many school closures in rural areas, with the result that children may need to travel some distance to the nearest large town or city to attend school, particularly at secondary level.

- Do you know where you're going after Italy? This may be an important consideration with regard to your children's language of tuition and system of education in Italy. How old are your children and what age will they be when you plan to leave Italy? What plans do you have for their education and in which country?

- What educational level are your children at now and how will they fit into a private school or the Italian state school system? The younger they are, the easier it will be to place them in a suitable school.

- Will your children require your help with their studies and, more importantly, will you be able to help them, particularly with their Italian? Is special or extra tutoring available in Italian and other subjects, if required?

- What are the school hours? What are the school holiday periods? State schools generally have compulsory Saturday morning classes. How will the school holidays and hours affect your family's work and leisure activities?

- Is religion an important aspect in your choice of school? There are very few denominational schools in Italy, where most Catholic private schools accept non-Catholic students.
- Do you want your children to go to a co-educational or single-sex school? All Italian state schools are co-educational.
- Should you send your children to a boarding school? If so, in which country?
- What are the secondary and further education prospects in Italy or another country?
- Are Italian examinations recognised in your home country or the country where you plan to live after leaving Italy?
- Does the school have a good academic record?
- How large are the classes? What is the pupil-teacher ratio? State schools have a maximum of 25 children in a class.

Obtain the opinions and advice of others who have been faced with the same decisions and problems, and collect as much information from as many different sources as possible before making a decision. Speak to teachers and the parents of children attending the schools on your shortlist. Finally, most parents find it pays to discuss the alternatives with their children before making a decision. See also **Choosing A Private School** on page 184

STATE SCHOOLS

State-funded schools in Italy are termed both state schools (*scuole statali*) and public schools (*scuole pubbliche*), although the term 'state' has been used in preference to 'public' in this book to prevent confusion with the British term 'public school', which refers to a private, fee-paying school. The state school system in Italy differs considerably from school systems in, for example, Britain and the US, particularly regarding secondary and university education. Schooling is divided into four educational cycles, as follows:

- Nursery school – a three-year cycle from three to six years of age;
- Primary school – a five-year cycle from 6 to 11;
- Lower secondary school – a three-year cycle from 11 to 14;
- Upper secondary school – a three, four or five-year cycle from 14 to 17, 18 or 19.

Attendance at a state nursery school isn't compulsory and there are a number of other private pre-school options for children aged under six. Compulsory schooling begins with primary school and continues until the age of 15 or the first year of upper secondary school, provided a year's schooling hasn't been repeated. At the end of the upper secondary cycle, pupils take a state examination; if they pass, they receive a leaving certificate that allows them to progress to higher education.

Some years ago, it was proposed that from September 2001 the primary cycle be increased to seven years, from 6 to 13 years of age, and the secondary cycle begin at 13 (one year earlier than at present), with a nationally-controlled curriculum for the first two years. The result would have been the amalgamation of primary and lower secondary schools and one year's less schooling for students who completed their secondary education, who would leave school at age 18. In addition, the number of state exams would have fallen from three to two. The new system was due to have been introduced gradually, to start affecting children at primary and secondary entry level (aged 6 and 13 or 14) from 2001. In spring 2003, however, these changes hadn't been implemented. Therefore, for the purposes of this chapter, the term 'primary' is used to refer to the five-year cycle and 'secondary' for the combined cycles of lower and upper secondary school.

In small towns and villages, nursery, primary and lower secondary schools often form one unified school (*istituto comprensivo*), and state nursery and primary schools are also sometimes grouped together within one teaching circle (*circolo didattico*).

Each school has a principal (*dirigente scolastico* in primary schools and *preside* in secondary schools), who's responsible for day-to-day management, co-ordinating school activities and establishing disciplinary sanctions. An important role is played by the school's consultative committee (*consiglio d'istituto*), made up of the principal, teaching and non-teaching staff, and (in secondary schools only) parents and pupils, who make decisions about the school's budget as well as organising teaching and extra-curricular activities. A teaching committee (*collegio dei docenti*) prepares a school's educational plans, including timetables and the choice of textbooks. There's also a class council (*consiglio di classe*) consisting of a panel of teachers, whose main task is to assess pupils' progress at the end of each term and decide on their promotion to the following year's class.

An hour of religious studies per week is part of the curriculum of all Italian schools, although this isn't obligatory and parents may ask for their children to be exempted. The presence of disabled children in a class, provided they aren't too seriously disabled (mentally or physically), is considered a source of general enrichment. Disabled children are entitled to up to 12 hours' tuition per week with a specially qualified teacher (*maestro di sostegno*) and, where applicable, schools must provide lifts.

A general criticism of Italian state schools often made by foreigners is the lack of extra-curricular activities such as sport, music, drama, arts and crafts. Although these subjects all form part of the school curriculum, they're limited to a small number of hours per week; inter-school sports competitions, for example, are rare. Extra-curricular activities offered by Italian schools generally take place during afternoons and operate on a much more limited scale than, for example, in Britain and the US. To play in a sports team, a child must usually join a private (and therefore fee-paying) association, which entails parents ferrying him back and forth after school hours. Similarly, for music lessons it may be necessary to find a local teacher or enrol at a private music school.

Classes (grades) in Italian schools differ considerably from those in the American and British systems. Classes at each level are numbered from one upwards. Thus, the first class in primary school is the *prima elementare*, followed by the *seconda elementare* and so on, until the fifth and final class (*quinta elementare*). In lower secondary school, the classes are *prima media, seconda media* and *terza media*. In both upper secondary school and university, the numbering refers to the year: *primo anno, secondo anno* and so on.

Italian schools don't provide transport for children who live in outlying districts, although local councils are obliged to provide transport for state nursery schools, together with an adult chaperone. School buses are provided for primary and secondary schools only if there's no school within a distance of 3km (2mi), when a small contribution towards the cost of transport (usually between €12 and €24 per month) is usually payable.

Enrolment

Information about schools in a particular area can be obtained from the local education office (*provveditorato*) or the town hall (*comune*). This may simply be a list of schools with addresses and phone numbers, and it's up to parents to apply to schools directly. If your child has already attended school in another country, a translation of his qualifications and previous school experience is required for enrolment in the Italian school system, together with a letter from the previous school's principal. You also need to contact the Italian consulate before arriving in Italy and obtain an evaluation certificate (*dichiarazione di valore*). Once this has been done, getting started in an Italian school is relatively straightforward, as schools are generally flexible about accommodating foreign students. However, it's difficult or impossible to organise state education in advance from your country of origin. A visit to Italy before your arrival is recommended, particularly as places may be limited, and you may end up ferrying children long distances to school if the one nearest to your home has no vacancies. Bear in mind that all schools and many public offices are closed during August.

Enrolment in an Italian state school doesn't depend on your living within its catchment area, as is the case, for example, in France and the UK. You can make an application to the school of your choice and, provided a place is available, your child will be admitted, although when places are limited, priority is given to those who live in the local area. Schools have a deadline (around 25th January of the previous school year) by which they need to know the number of students who will be attending school the following September. Most schools have a flexible attitude to pupils who need to start school or change schools during the academic year. Provided you have a good reason, it's possible for a child to change schools within the same area or to another part of the country; a request must be in writing and be signed and approved by the principal of your child's previous school.

To enrol a child in an Italian school, you need to complete an application form and provide the following documents:

* Certificate of family status (*certificato di stato di famiglia* – see page 277);

* Your child's birth certificate (*certificato di nascita*) and proof of immunisation against hepatitis B, polio, diphtheria and tetanus (with relevant translations, if necessary);

* A photograph of your child and your permit to stay (*permesso di soggiorno*) or residence certificate (*certificato di residenza*). Alternatively, written proof of your intention to move permanently to Italy (if you haven't already done so) is acceptable.

Parents can declare that they possess the necessary documents without actually producing them (a process called *autodichiarazione*). However, you can be prosecuted if details on an application form are subsequently found to be incorrect.

School Hours

School hours vary considerably according to the kind of school. Nursery school hours are usually from 8am to 4pm, with an hour's break for lunch, five or six days per week. Primary and lower secondary schools generally schedule classes for 30 hours per week, Mondays to Saturdays. Most primary schools start at 8am and finish at 1pm, although attendance may be required for afternoon lessons on a few days per week. Some primary schools operate from Mondays to Fridays, when lessons end at 4 or 4.30pm, with an hour's break for lunch. Lessons at most lower secondary schools start at 8.15am and end at 1.15pm. Upper secondary school classes usually finish at 1.30pm.

Lessons in both primary and secondary schools traditionally last an hour, although schools now have the option of introducing 50-minute lessons. In primary schools, there's usually a mid-morning break of 30 minutes, while in secondary schools it's typically just ten minutes. Extra-curricular activities or afternoon lessons (if scheduled) generally commence at around 2.30pm.

School Holidays

Children attend school for 200 days in the school year, which runs from mid-September to mid-June and is divided into three terms (*trimestri*). The regional school superintendency sets the school calendar (*calendario scolastico*) for all state schools in the region. School holiday dates vary little between regions in Italy, although schools in Sicily start a few days later in September due to the hotter weather. Typical holiday periods for a school year (all dates inclusive) are shown below:

Holiday	Dates
Christmas	23rd December to 6th January
Easter	Around six days, between mid-March and mid-April
Summer	9th June to 14th September

State exams are held after 9th June. Schools are closed on public holidays (see page 60) when they fall within term time. In addition, schools in some regions are closed for one or two days in March. However, schools don't have half-term holidays.

Absence from school is normally permitted only for a visit to a doctor or dentist, or for reasons of illness. In primary school, a note to the child's teacher is sufficient, while in secondary school students have an official booklet (*libretto della giustificazioni*) that must be signed by both a parent and a teacher if a child is absent for any reason. A medical certificate must be produced after five days' absence from school.

Provisions

State education is free until the end of primary school, after which an enrolment tax (*tasse d'iscrizione*) of around €17 is payable at the beginning of each school year. However, pens, stationery and sports clothing must be provided by parents. Textbooks are free only until the end of primary school. Parents can expect to pay an average of around €160 per year for books for a child at lower secondary school and up to €320 for a child at upper secondary school, depending on the subjects studied. Up to the end of compulsory schooling, families on low incomes receive a contribution from regional authorities to buy textbooks, and books can be purchased secondhand (but you must make sure that they're still current). Italian schoolchildren usually carry their schoolbooks to and from school in a small rucksack (*zaino*).

Nursery and primary schools usually require children to wear school aprons (*grembiule*), which have a distinguishing pattern of little squares at nursery school and a plain colour (usually blue) at primary school. These can be purchased from most clothing stores and supermarkets.

State schools don't generally provide meals during the day. Where there are canteen facilities (*mensa*), a small contribution is generally required. Otherwise, children with afternoon lessons who don't have time to go home for lunch must make their own arrangements by either bringing a packed lunch or going to a local *pizzeria* or snack bar near the school. There may be somewhere for children to buy snacks to eat during the mid-morning break.

Pre-School

Pre-school education isn't compulsory in Italy. However, around 95 per cent of children attend some form of nursery or pre-primary school and the country's pre-school education is internationally recognised as one of the best in the world. Pre-school comprises two levels: day nursery or kindergarten (*asilo nido*, literally 'infant nest') and nursery school proper (*scuola materna*).

Asilo nurseries take children from as young as three months. They're primarily a facility for working parents who are unable to look after their children during the day. Costs vary according to the number of hours children attend and the particular nursery, but they're generally lower when facilities are run by the local council (*comune*). Places in such nurseries are consequently in huge demand and priority is usually given to parents who are unemployed or with a low income (applicants must complete a form at the town hall stating their family income).

Materna schools are also both state and privately run (communal, religious and private establishments account for over 40 per cent of *materna* schools) and take children from the ages of three to six, before entry to primary school. Attendance at state nurseries is free, although a contribution is requested from families for transport and meals provided by the local council. Places are usually limited and you must submit an application well in advance to be sure of a place. For private *materna* schools, parents pay enrolment fees at the beginning of the year plus further monthly contributions. In the Rome area you can pay as little as €40 for enrolment at a private nursery school, with monthly fees of between €90 and €150 depending on whether your child attends for a half or full day. For extra-curricular activities, such as physical education and music, where specialist teachers may be required, an extra monthly fee may be payable. It's therefore worthwhile checking the fees and extra expenses likely to be incurred at different nursery schools before enrolling your child (see also **Private Schools** on page 182).

Asilo nursery school hours are usually from 8.30am to 12.30pm, but parents have the option of leaving their children later. At *materna* schools, activities last a minimum of seven hours per day – four hours in the morning and three in the afternoon – and may be held on five or six days per week. Parents can often leave their children under the supervision of a qualified help after school (*doposcuola*) until 5 or 5.30pm, during which time activities are less structured and non-educational. State nurseries generally have the same holiday periods as state schools, so working parents must find alternative provision for their children during these periods. Schools may also organise summer activity programmes for children whose parents are working, and some local councils organise educational and recreational courses during July and August.

Materna schools are organised into groups (*sezioni*) according to age, with a minimum of 14 children and a maximum of 28. In schools in less populous areas, however, a school may have only one group comprising children of different ages. Each group must have two teachers (generally female), who usually remain with the same group for three years. The minimum number of children required to establish a school is 16, and they must all live within 2km (1.3mi) of the school.

In *materna* schools, the emphasis is on learning through play, rather than the day-care facility provided by the *asilo nido*. Teaching at these schools can take a variety of forms, although reforms passed in 1991 laid down a number of educational aims. These stipulate certain 'fields of experience' to be included in educational activity: body and movement, speech and words, space, order and measure, time and nature, messages, forms and media, and the self and others.

Music, physical activity, and arts and crafts all form part of the nursery curriculum, although children don't usually begin to learn the rudiments of reading and writing until they begin state primary school at the age of six. Therefore you may wish to consider a private school if you want your children to get a head start, particularly if your mother tongue isn't Italian. Children are assessed by teachers on entry into nursery school and several times during the course of the school year, a final report on their capabilities being made before their transfer to primary school.

Primary School

Primary schools (*scuole elementare*) have traditionally figured highly in international educational studies. Attendance is compulsory and children must be aged six by 31st December of the year in question to enrol in primary school, which they attend for five years. The school timetable usually involves 27 hours' tuition per week, increasing to 30 hours in the second year to accommodate learning a foreign language (usually English). Provision is made for pupils with special educational needs. Attendance is generally mornings only, with one or two afternoon classes per week. The five-year primary cycle is divided in two parts, the first two years concentrating on basic skills and the final three years introducing pupils to broader concepts.

A recent innovation has been the introduction of team teaching for some subjects, which has helped to increase the number of teachers at primary level, although it has also contributed indirectly to the closure of some smaller primary schools. There are typically three teachers for every two classes or four teachers for every three classes.

Subjects are grouped into areas, which are taught by the same teacher or teachers for the whole five years, as follows:

- **Area A** – Italian, art and a foreign language;
- **Area B** – Mathematics, sciences and physical education;
- **Area C** – History, geography, social studies and music.

There's also usually a specialist teacher for religion.

Around 15 per cent of primary schools are full-time school (*scuola a tempo pieno*), where children attend both mornings and afternoons for five days per week. The timetable usually includes one and a half hours' rest in the middle of the day, during which lunch is provided in a school canteen. There are typically two teachers per class, one taking the morning session and one the afternoon session, with all subjects divided between them. This kind of school generally appeals to working parents, who find it more convenient to collect their children later in the day.

Most primary schools use a system of assessment based on teacher observations made throughout the school year. Assessments are recorded on each child's report card (*scheda*), which is designed to provide a detailed profile of the pupil's academic ability and personality. The record card is passed to a pupil's next school when he leaves. In the fifth year of primary school, pupils must usually obtain their primary school leaving certificate (*diploma della licenza elementare*) to progress to lower secondary school; those who are unsuccessful may need to repeat their final year.

Lower Secondary School

Attendance at lower secondary school (*scuola media*, literally 'middle school' and equivalent to a junior high school in the US) is compulsory for all children between the ages of 11 and 14. As with primary school, there's a national curriculum that must be studied by all children. In addition, the numbers of hours each subject must be taught each week is stipulated by the Ministry of Education. For the first and second years, the weekly requirements include:

- seven hours of Italian (including lessons in literature, grammar and writing);
- six hours of mathematics, physics, chemistry and natural sciences;
- four hours of history, geography and social studies;
- three hours each of a foreign language (usually English) and technical drawing;
- two hours each of physical education, music and art/design;
- one hour of religion.

In the third year, pupils lose one hour of Italian in favour of an extra hour of history, geography and social studies. Each subject is taught by a different specialist teacher, with the exception of Italian, history, geography and social studies, which are generally divided between two teachers.

The timetable totals 30 hours per week, schools having the option of extending this to up to 40 hours for extra-curricular or subsidiary study activities if there's sufficient demand from parents (e.g. computer studies or learning a second foreign language). In recent years, schools have introduced a number of optional, experimental classes. These classes, which are generally financed from a school's own budget, take place in the afternoons and may include sports, music lessons (instruments must usually be purchased by parents), film, computer and chess clubs, and foreign language conversation classes.

As at primary school, a report is completed by teachers each term on all subjects, which provides an overview of the aptitude, behaviour and achievement of each pupil. A separate, shorter report is produced for a student's performance in religious instruction. Assessments include excellent (*ottimo*), very good (*distinto*), good (*buono*), satisfactory (*sufficiente*), and unsatisfactory (*non sufficiente*). At the end of the third year, pupils sit a state examination comprising written papers in Italian, a foreign language and mathematics and science, followed by an oral exam in all subjects except religion. Successful students are awarded their lower secondary school diploma (*diploma di licenza media*) and graduate to upper secondary school.

Upper Secondary School

At the age of 14, students must make a choice as to the kind of upper secondary school (*scuola superiore*, equivalent to a senior high school in the US) they want to attend, according to which subjects they would like to specialise in and what they would like to do when they leave school. There are essentially two categories of upper secondary school: a *liceo* (similar to a British grammar school), which provides a more academic training, and an *istituto*, where more practical and technical disciplines are taught. Within these two categories, there are several types of school, as explained below.

The following types of upper secondary school are present in every school district: a classics school, a science school and a technical or a vocational school. In larger districts and provincial towns, there's also a teacher training school and an artistic school, and there may be a number of vocational schools, which often reflect the needs of local industries.

Entry to upper secondary school isn't competitive and, provided there are sufficient places available, students may attend the school of their choice.

Since 2001, all pupils have had the same core curriculum for the first two years of upper secondary school; this comprises Italian language and literature, mathematics, at least one foreign language (usually English), science, history, geography and social studies, religion and physical education. Their specialised courses (*indirizzi*) start in the third year.

In all schools a considerable amount of homework is set for each subject, which may take the form of memorising information or writing an essay. As in lower secondary school, teachers test a student's knowledge (and the extent to which he has done his homework) through regular oral and written tests (*prove scritte*), which, together with a more general evaluation of a student's performance, form the basis of a student's report (*pagella*). Marks (*voti*) for all work are given out of ten, six being the minimum necessary to proceed to the next year.

All students can enter university, provided they complete a five-year course at secondary school and acquire their upper secondary school diploma, and it's now common for students who have attended technical and vocational schools to go on to university. In schools where the duration of the diploma course is four years only (e.g. artistic schools), students must stay on for an extra year to qualify for university entrance.

Before deciding upon the correct kind of school for your child, it's important carefully to study the curriculum offered by each. **This is particularly important if a child is planning to attend a university outside Italy.** In many countries (including the US and UK), university admission is based on competitive entry, and therefore the choice of secondary school and curriculum should reflect a specialisation in the subjects the student plans to study at university.

Classics School (*liceo classico*)**:** Latin, Greek and Italian literature form a large part of the demanding academic curriculum. Philosophy and history of art are also studied in the last three years.

Science School (*liceo scientifico*)**:** This school is traditionally for students planning to study science and medicine at university, with the emphasis on physics, chemistry and natural sciences. Latin and one modern language (usually English) are also studied to a high level.

Artistic Schools (*liceo artistico* or *istituto d'arte*)**:** These provide a four-year foundation course for students wishing to enrol at arts academies, study art or architecture at university, enter a career in the arts or teach art subjects at school.

Language School (*liceo linguistico*)**:** Students study three foreign languages.

Teacher Training Schools (*scuola magistrale* or *istituto magistrale*)**:** These schools provide a four-year training course for primary school teachers (*istituto magistrale*) and a three-year training course for nursery school teachers (*scuola magistrale*). A nursery school teaching diploma doesn't qualify you to enrol at a university.

Technical School (*istituto tecnico*)**:** By far the greatest number of upper secondary school students enrol in technical school, which prepares students to work in a technical or administrative capacity in agriculture, industry or commerce. Technical schools have responded to Italy's fast-growing economy by offering an ever-widening range of courses tailored to meet the needs of today's employers, with courses in computer skills in particular seeing tremendous growth in recent years. All technical schools share a common curriculum for the first two years, with some practical training carried out in workshops and businesses. In the last three years, the number of hours of practical training increases.

The main kinds of technical schools are agricultural, commercial (with specialisations in business administration, accountancy, commerce, foreign languages and computer programming), surveying, tourism, nautical, aeronautical and industrial (including many specialisations such as mining, electronics, engineering, industrial physics, computer science and food processing). There are also 'feminine technical schools' (*istituti tecnichi femminile*), which were originally for the study of subjects traditionally associated with women, such as home economics, but now cater for both sexes and include the study of dietetics, social work and child care.

Vocational School (*istituto professionale*): Vocational schools are the least academic of upper secondary schools. They aim to train people in a variety of craft and industrial skills, such as cabinet-making, carpentry, mechanics and engineering, building and construction, food and catering, secretarial and office work. The timetable varies between 35 and 40 hours per week, and for the first two years includes 14 hours per week of practical training relevant to a pupil's chosen area of specialisation. In the third year, the number of hours of specialist practical training increases to between 21 and 24 hours per week. After three years, students gain a diploma in their specialist subject (*diploma di qualifica*), after which they may take a two-year course in order to earn their upper secondary school diploma, either at the vocational school or at a technical school.

Diploma

At the end of the upper secondary school cycle, students study for the upper secondary school diploma (*diploma di maturità*), which automatically qualifies them for enrolment at a university. The exam consists of three written exams (*esame*) plus an oral test (*colloquio*). The first exam involves writing an essay or newspaper article in Italian on a historical, social, scientific or literary subject. The second is a test of one subject from a number of options relating to a student's specialisation; the subject of the exam is given to students two months in advance. The third exam, which was introduced in 1999, is an inter-disciplinary exam that includes questions on cultural and social issues and tests the knowledge of a foreign language.

The oral test follows the written exams and is conducted by a board of six teachers, who question students on all the subjects they've studied in their final year. Out of a possible total of 100 marks, a maximum of 45 is awarded for the written exams, 35 for the oral and 20 for scholastic credits, which are earned from students' school reports during their last three years of study. To pass the *maturità*, a minimum of 60 marks are necessary.

The full title of the diploma depends on the kind of school students have attended, e.g. *diploma di maturità classica* for students who have attended a classics school and a *diploma di maturità scientifica* for students who have attended a science school. Diplomas gained at technical school are further qualified by the specialisation students have followed. The *maturità* is recognised throughout the world as a university entrance qualification, although it isn't accepted by all institutions.

PRIVATE SCHOOLS

Private schools (*scuole private*) educate less than 10 per cent of schoolchildren. They include schools run by religious organisations (the majority by the Jesuits), schools following unorthodox teaching methods such as Montessori and Rudolf Steiner, and a number of foreign and international schools, including American and British schools. The majority of private schools are co-educational, non-denominational day schools (Catholic private schools usually admit non-Catholic students), many of which operate a Monday to Friday timetable. There are very few boarding schools in Italy.

Most private schools in Italy are either authorised or given legal recognition by the state and many receive state funding and must therefore adhere strictly to central government directives on syllabi and curricula. Teachers' qualifications must also be recognised. As a result, there's little difference between the quality of education in the state and private sectors, and many people consider standards in private schools to be inferior. The majority of private schools duplicate the curriculum offered in state schools, with perhaps the inclusion of a few extra courses.

One advantage of most private schools is that they offer a more caring and protective atmosphere, and the opportunity of additional or intensive lessons, which some parents believe to be more conducive to learning. Parents in some of the wealthier areas of the major cities may also send their children to a private school simply for its exclusivity.

Private schools usually have fewer pupils than state schools, but class sizes aren't necessarily any smaller. Private schools often cater for a wide age range (from 6 to 19) and some also offer nursery facilities. At secondary level there's a bias toward classics, scientific and linguistic schools, few private schools offering technical or vocational training. There's sometimes a stricter regime in private schools, particularly as many are run by religious orders, and uniforms may be compulsory.

Private school fees vary according to the kind of school and the variety of services that are offered. Most require parents to pay an initial enrolment fee followed by either annual or monthly fees. For private primary and secondary schools, you can pay between €275 and €430 in enrolment fees, plus monthly fees of between €135 and €275.

There are also a number of international schools in Italy, whose main language of instruction is English. These tend to offer the best alternative for expatriates who want their children to continue their education in the American or British system. International schools are invariably situated in the major urban centres, including Florence, Genoa, Milan, Naples, Padua, Rome, Treviso, Trieste and Turin, and range from pre-schools and kindergartens through to secondary schools, with pupils aged from 3 to 19 years.

They teach a variety of syllabi, including the British GCSE and A-level examinations (including key stages in the National Curriculum SATS tests), American High School Diploma and college entrance examinations (e.g. ACT, SAT and AP exams), and the International Baccalaureate (IB), which is recognised world-wide as a university entrance qualification.

Class sizes tend to be small, with students drawn from a wide range of nationalities, and schools pride themselves on the variety of sports and extra-curricular activities on offer, some even boasting campus sites of several acres. Many international schools offer bi-lingual programmes, enabling students to sit Italian state exams (for reintegration into the Italian state system), as well as English as a Foreign Language (EFL) exams if their first language isn't English. Fees for international schools range from €3,700 to €10,700 per year; only a few offer boarding facilities. Admission is usually based on previous school reports and sometimes personal interview.

Among the most prestigious international schools is the United World College of the Adriatic near Trieste. Pupils are selected on academic ability and 20 scholarships are offered annually via the National Commission for United World Colleges, Ufficio Selezioni, Palazzo Altemps, Via dei Gigli d'Oro, 21, 00186 Rome (☎ 06-689 2201, 💻 www.uwcad.it). Students who aren't resident in Italy must apply via the sister college in their home country.

A list of American and British schools can be obtained from the cultural sections of Italian embassies abroad and from the European Council of International Schools (💻 www.ecis.org). The American Embassy in Italy lists many English-speaking schools on its website (💻 www.usembassy.it). There are also French lycées in Rome and Milan, and a number of private schools that teach in other foreign languages.

Among the private schools that aren't state supported are schools known as scuole di recupero (literally 'schools of recovery'), designed to meet the needs of students who, for various reasons, must repeat one or more years' schooling in order to gain their upper secondary school diploma. Fees are generally high, particularly if you want to cover the maturità syllabus. These schools don't function as exam centres and pupils must usually take their examinations at a recognised centre and pay an additional fee. Ricupero schools usually also offer exam preparation at university level.

Choosing A Private School

The following checklist is designed to help you choose an appropriate private school in Italy:

- Does the school have a good reputation? How long has it been established? If it's an international school, does it belong to a recognised association?

- Does the school have a decent academic record? For example, what percentage of pupils obtain good examination passes or go on to university? All schools should provide exam pass rate statistics.

- How large are the classes and what is the student/teacher ratio? Does the stated class size tally with the number of desks in the classrooms?

- What are the classrooms like? For example, their size, space, cleanliness, lighting, furniture and furnishings. Are there signs of creative teaching, e.g. wall charts, maps, posters and students' work on display?

- What are the qualification requirements for teachers? What nationality are the majority of teachers? Ask for a list of the teaching staff and their qualifications.

- What is the teacher turnover? A high teacher turnover is a bad sign and usually suggests under-paid teachers and poor working conditions.

- What extras must you pay for? For example, art supplies, sports equipment, outings, clothing, health and accident insurance, meals, private bus transport, text books and stationery. Some schools charge parents for every little thing.

- Which countries do most students come from?

- Is religion an important consideration in your choice of school?

- Are special English classes provided for children whose English doesn't meet the required standard?

- What standard and type of accommodation is provided in a boarding school?

- What is the quality and variety of food provided? What is the dining room like? Does the school have a dietician?

- What languages does the school teach as obligatory or optional subjects?

- What is the student turnover?

- What are the school terms and holiday periods? Private school holidays are usually longer than those of state schools, e.g. four weeks at Easter and Christmas and ten weeks in the summer, and often don't coincide with state school holiday periods.

- What are the school hours?

- What are the withdrawal conditions, should you need or wish to remove your child? A term's notice is usual.

- What does the curriculum include? What examinations are set? Are examinations recognised both in Italy and internationally? Do they fit in with your education plans? Ask to see a typical pupil timetable to check the ratio of academic to non-academic subjects. Check the number of free study periods and whether they're supervised.

- What sports instruction and facilities are provided? Where are the sports facilities located?

- What facilities are provided for art and science subjects, e.g. arts and crafts, music, computer studies, biology, science, hobbies, drama, cookery and photography? Ask to see the classrooms, facilities, equipment and students' projects.

- What sort of outings and holidays does the school organise?

- What reports are provided for parents and how often?

- What medical facilities does the school provide, e.g. infirmary, resident doctor or nurse? Is medical and accident insurance included in the fees?
- What punishments are applied and for what offences?
- Last but not least, unless someone else is paying, what are the fees?

Before making a choice, it's important to visit the schools on your shortlist during term time and talk to teachers, students and, if possible, former students and their parents. Where possible, check the answers to the above questions in person and don't rely on a school's prospectus to provide the information. If you're unhappy with the answers you get, look elsewhere.

Having made your choice, keep a check on your child's progress and listen to his or her complaints. Compare notes with other parents. If something doesn't seem right, try to establish whether a complaint is founded or not and, if it is, take action to have the problem resolved. Don't forget that you or your employer are paying a lot of money for your child's education and you should demand value. See also **Choosing A School** on page 170.

APPRENTICESHIPS

Many young people in Italy look forward to starting work and learning a trade, and the majority who don't go on to higher education enter an apprenticeship (*apprendistato*) or vocational training. Over half a million young people in Italy are involved in apprenticeship schemes each year. An apprenticeship aims to give people between the ages of 16 and 26 a combination of on-the-job training and further education, with around four hours per day spent on practical training and three-and-a-half in theoretical training at an apprentice training centre. Apprenticeships last from 18 months to four years and cover a huge range of occupations, including waitresses, cooks, plumbers, carpenters, hairdressers, car mechanics and agricultural workers. Employers pay apprentices 80 per cent of the salary of a fully-qualified worker, which increases with age and experience. They also pay for schooling and sometimes the cost of travel to and from school. Apprentices are entitled to the same holiday periods as fully qualified staff (see **Holidays & Leave** on page 59).

Another kind of vocational training is a combined training and work contract (*contratto di formazione lavorativa/CFL*) for those aged between 16 and 23, whereby employers provide a training programme for a specific professional qualification as part of a fixed-period employment contract. Contracts last either one or two years and include an initial trial period. The state pays insurance contributions but employment isn't guaranteed at the end of the training period. See also **Further Education** on page 190.

Careers advice for young people is available via the nationwide network of Informagiovani offices.

HIGHER EDUCATION

Over a million students attend institutes of higher education in Italy, although the country produces a smaller percentage of graduates than most other western countries. The country has around 90 institutes of higher education, including 47 state universities, several private universities and over 20 institutes of physical education. There are also two universities of Italian language and culture. There's a university in every major city in Italy, some with a number of branches situated in different towns throughout a region. The University of Bologna (11th century) is the world's oldest and highly regarded, while Rome has three universities, the oldest being La Sapienza. Other higher education facilities include the University Naval Institute in Naples and the College of Education in Pisa.

Higher education is controlled by the Ministry for Universities (Ministero dell'Università e della Ricerca Scientifica e Tecnologica/MURST). Universities are organised into faculties for different teaching subjects and departments, which are in charge of research. Most degree subjects are offered by all universities (apart from a few specialised fields, such as music, which is taught in academies or *conservatoires*) and anyone with an upper secondary school diploma can apply to study any subject provided there are places available. However, for degree courses that are heavily over-subscribed (which include architecture, dentistry, medicine and veterinary science), universities set entrance examinations (*esame di ammissione*) to select the best candidates. Non-EU students are required to take an Italian-language exam unless they possess a *CILS* certificate (see **Language Schools** on page 191).

There's no central clearing system for enrolment in Italian universities and you must apply to each university separately. There are enrolment fees (*tasse di iscrizione*) which are payable at the beginning of each year or in instalments throughout the year, plus regional taxes of around €80. Each faculty sets its own course fees, average fees for first-year students being around €550 (for the year). Students from families with medium to low incomes are entitled to grants, information about which is available from the student welfare office (Diritto allo Studio Universitario/DSU). Foreign applicants must provide a translation of their qualifications (obtainable through Italian consulates), which must usually be equivalent to a high school diploma or 12 years' education. Applications must be made to Italian consulates by May for enrolment the following September; non-EU students must apply through an Italian consulate in their home country.

Italian universities are frequently criticised for the academic nature of their courses. Although students have some choice over their study programme (*piano di studi*), the curriculum for each subject is fairly standardised (there's little variation between courses offered by different universities) and there's generally little room for self-expression. As in schools, students are expected to study set texts (sometimes written by the professors) and are examined on their knowledge. The emphasis is firmly on self-motivation and determination, particularly in view of the drawn-out nature of university degrees.

Overcrowding in lecture-halls for popular courses is common, resulting in a more distant relationship between students and professors than in some other countries, and the student drop-out rate is high.

Many students live with their parents and attend the nearest university to their home, particularly in large cities such as Rome, where student accommodation is prohibitively expensive. Others enrol at a university in the north or in Rome, particularly students from the south of Italy, and look for part-time work to support themselves during their study (even part-time work is difficult to find in the south) as well as to have better employment prospects when they graduate.

The average student must pass over 20 exams to obtain a degree (some subjects, such as medicine, require students to take around 50 exams), most of which are oral rather than written. Of these, a certain number are obligatory and common to all study programmes, while the rest are in subjects chosen by students. Courses, each of which is followed by an exam, can be pursued in any order and, if you fail an exam, you're permitted to retake it any number of times. Attendance at lectures is mostly voluntary, leaving students free to pursue their studies at home if they prefer, although some professors insist on attendance at lectures. The regular submission of essays throughout a course isn't generally required, although students must write a thesis (usually of between 50,000 and 60,000 words) at the end of their course in order to earn their degree.

The structure of the Italian university system allows students to take a longer time to complete their degrees than is usual in the UK and the US. The number of years necessary to complete a degree (*corso di laurea*) at an Italian university is laid down by law. Most degree courses are for a minimum of four years but some (e.g. medicine and architecture) are for six. However, few students manage to complete their degrees in the minimum period and it's usual for students to take seven or eight years, with the result that many are in their mid to late 20s by the time they graduate.

The traditional qualifications awarded at Italian universities are a university degree (*diploma di laurea*), a specialised diploma (*diploma di specializzazione*) and a research doctorate (*dottorato di ricerca*). Universities have recently introduced a university diploma (*diploma universitario*) or short degree course lasting two or three years. These are currently in specialised fields of engineering, physical education, auxiliary medicine (e.g. nursing and physiotherapy) and languages, with admission for the limited number of places available by competitive examination. Foreign students who wish to accumulate credits at an Italian university without completing a degree course may apply to do individual subject courses (*corsi singoli*).

Student accommodation isn't usually provided by Italian universities, although some subsidised student housing (*casa dello studente*) may be available through the DSU. The majority of students make their own arrangements and there's usually a university notice board where rooms and apartments are advertised for rent. Students should expect to pay anything between €200 (central and southern regions) and €280 (Rome and northern cities) per month for a room in a shared apartment. In addition to rent, students must usually pay utility bills plus maintenance for items such as cookers, refrigerators and washing machines. Italian universities offer little in the way of extra-curricular sports and social activities (there's no 'campus' feel as in American universities), although most have a refectory (*mensa*) where inexpensive, wholesome food is available.

In addition to Italian institutions of higher education, there are a number of American colleges and universities in Italy offering an American degree programme, e.g. Johns Hopkins University in Bologna (🖳 www.jhu.edu) and John Cabot University in Rome (🖳 www.johncabot.edu). John Cabot University offers four-year BA degrees on a rolling admission basis in art history, business administration, English literature, international affairs and political science, as well as associate degrees and credit transfers on a semester basis for students wishing to do part of their study in Italy. Fees are around €10,500 per year, but there are various financial aid and scholarship packages available. Students come from around 40 countries and universities offer many extra-curricular activities. A list of American institutions of higher education in Italy and information about American study programmes at Italian institutions can be obtained from the American embassy in Italy (🖳 www.usembassy.it) and from the cultural sections of Italian embassies abroad.

EU nationals who wish to complete part of their studies at an Italian university may be interested in the Erasmus programme, part of the EU Socrates programme funded by the European Commission. Under this programme, students don't pay fees for attending an Italian university (although you may need to continue to pay fees at your own university) and grants are available to cover the costs of moving, language training and a higher cost of living (if applicable). For further information, contact the Erasmus Bureau, Rue Montoyer 70, B-1040 Brussels, Belgium (☎ +32-2-233 011), your country's national Erasmus agency or your university's Erasmus representative. The Italian Ministry of Foreign Affairs also allocates a number of scholarships to foreign students attending courses at Italian universities. Information is available from Italian embassies abroad.

For further information about universities in Italy, contact the Dipartimento per l'Autonomia Universitaria e gli Studenti, Ministero dell'Università e della Ricerca Scientifica e Tecnologica, Piazzale J. F. Kennedy, 20, 00144 Rome (☎ 06 59911). The Ministry of Foreign Affairs provides information about applying to universities on its website (🖳 www.esteri.it), and Campus Web (🖳 www. campusweb.it) provides a wealth of information about Italian universities. The publication, *Higher Education in Italy: A Guide for Foreigners*, contains comprehensive information about all aspects of higher education and is available free from MURST at the above address (☎ 06-5991 2319). Requests must be made in writing, by post or fax. DSU offices provide free guides to student services. and some universities have an office that provides advice to foreign students.

FURTHER EDUCATION

Italy has many private schools and university-level institutions (some affiliated to American universities), including business and commercial colleges, hotel and catering schools, and language schools, which offer a range of further education courses for school-leavers, university graduates, workers and the unemployed. They include post-degree courses (specialist diplomas, masters and doctorates) and a wide range of vocational training courses. Courses vary in length from a few months to two or three years and may be either full or part-time.

Many further education courses are vocational (*corsi di formazione professionale*) and aim to facilitate access to employment through a mixture of practical and theoretical training. Courses are either first level (aimed at school-leavers who haven't attained a secondary school diploma) or second level (for holders of specific qualifications such as a secondary school diploma or a university degree). Many courses are targeted at job-seekers and employees wishing to specialise or re-qualify in order to obtain a new position. Applicants usually outnumber available places and you may be required to sit an admission test. Courses for secondary school diploma holders normally consist of between 400 and 1,200 hours' tuition for five hours per day and usually include placement periods in industry.

Free courses are available in some deprived regions (funded in association with the European Social Fund) for certain categories of people, including the unemployed, graduates seeking work, young people who have failed to complete compulsory schooling and the disabled. Details can be obtained from regional education offices, vocational training centres, the information sections of trade union offices, local newspapers or by browsing through regional websites. Information about further education can also be obtained from regional Centro di Informazione e Orientamento (CIO) offices.

A number of educational institutions in Italy offer an American MBA degree, e.g. St John's University in Rome and the Bocconi University in Milan. Subjects include banking, business administration, communications, economics, information systems, management, marketing, public relations, and social and political studies. Tuition costs are high and study periods strictly organised, most courses being taught in English. Another institution offering further education courses in English is the European University Institute in Florence. Founded in 1972, the Institute offers postgraduate courses and research opportunities in the field of human and social sciences. Admission is merit-based and courses are open to students from all EU and some other European countries with a high mark in a first degree. The British Open University, The Open University, CP 1141, 20101 Milan (☎ 02-8138 048) offers distance learning degree courses (from BA to MBA – a choice of over 150 courses) to residents of the EU and Switzerland.

LANGUAGE SCHOOLS

If you don't speak Italian fluently, you may wish to enrol in a language course. If you want to make the most of your time, it's **essential** to learn Italian as soon as possible. For people living in Italy permanently, learning Italian isn't an option, particularly as in many areas little or no English is spoken. Although it isn't easy, even the most non-linguistic (and oldest) person can acquire a working knowledge of Italian. All that's required is a little hard work and some help and perseverance. You won't just 'pick it up' (apart from a few words), but must make an effort to learn. **Your business and social enjoyment and success in Italy will be directly related to the degree to which you master Italian.**

Teaching Italian is a huge business in Italy, with classes offered by language schools, Italian colleges and universities, private and international schools, foreign and international organisations, town councils, cultural associations, vocational training centres, clubs and private teachers. Tuition ranges from introductory courses for beginners to specialised business or cultural courses and university-level courses leading to recognised diplomas.

There are many language schools (*scuole di lingua*) throughout Italy offering a wide range of classes to suit your language ability, how many hours you wish to study a week, how much money you want to spend and how quickly you wish to learn. Language classes roughly fall into the following categories:

Category	No. Of Hours Per Week
Standard	Up to 20
Intensive	20 to 30
Total immersion	40+

The cost of a one-week (40 hour) total immersion course is around €140 depending on the school. Courses vary in length from four months to a year and can be attended either in small groups or individually.

Many language schools offer a variety of other courses, ranging from translation and interpreters' courses to business, cooking, literature and history of art. Schools offer a variety of language diplomas (including their own internal qualifications) but only a few offer the *Certificato d'Italiano come Lingua Straniera* (*CILS*), which is recognised as an entry-level qualification for non-EU students wishing to study at Italian universities.

One of the longest-established language associations in Italy is Dante Alighieri, which has schools throughout the country (not to be confused with schools that use *Dante Alighieri* in their title but don't belong to the society) and promotes the Italian language and culture through a network of world-wide committees. The British Institute has a number of schools in major cities, where it teaches both Italian to foreigners and English to Italians. Many universities in

Italy have language centres (*Centri Linguistici Atenei/CLA*) offering a variety of courses; these are generally held only in the summer and are cheaper than most private schools. The Universities for Foreigners (Università per Stranieri) in Sienna and Perugia (not strictly universities but large language schools) offer year-round, Italian-language courses at various levels.

As with all private schools, it pays to shop around and compare fees, as there's a considerable variation in standards and facilities, and famous international schools don't necessarily offer the best value or the best tuition.

A quicker, although more expensive, way to learn Italian is to have private lessons. Because Italian teachers also among the worst paid in Europe, there's no shortage of people prepared to give private lessons. Rates vary widely according to where you live, from around €12 per hour in some central and southern regions to €30 per hour in Rome and Milan with a qualified teacher. Some good places to look for a suitable teacher or to place an advertisement include local newspapers, and university and public notice boards. Friends, neighbours and work colleagues may be able to recommend a good teacher. In some areas, the local youth advisory service (Informagiovani) provides free conversation classes for foreign students.

Families planning to move to Italy may be interested in Intercultura, the Italian branch of the American Field Service (🖥 www.afs.org) organisation – an international, voluntary, non-profit organisation offering world-wide educational and cultural exchanges for young people. Exchanges with Intercultura are for students of 15 or over wishing to stay with an Italian family for between two weeks and a year. For more information, contact Intercultura, Via Gracco del Secco, 100-53034 Colle Val d'Elsa (SI) (☎ 0577-900 011, 🖥 www.intercultura.it).

A number of scholarships and grants are available from the Universities for Foreigners at Sienna and Perugia. For information, contact the cultural sections of Italian embassies abroad.

A guide to many language schools, institutions and organisations offering Italian-language tuition is provided by the Associazione Scuole di Italiano come Lingua Seconda/ASILS (☎ 09-422 3441, 🖥 www.asils.it) and from the Italian Cultural Institute, 39 Belgrave Square, London SW1X 8NX, UK (☎ 020-7235 1461, 🖥 www.italcultur.org.uk). A good directory of Italian-language schools is available on the Internet (🖥 www.it-schools.com), covering most regions of the country and offering links to a number of schools.

10.

PUBLIC TRANSPORT

The standard of public transport (*mezzi pubblici*) services in Italy can best be described as mixed; at its best it can be excellent, but sometimes it's simply dire. Like many other aspects of Italian life, it's marked by excessive complication and a lack of co-operation and co-ordination between companies, regions and modes of transport. There's a huge difference between services in (and connecting) the major cities and those in rural areas. Most cities have an efficient, inexpensive and reliable transport system, consisting of underground trains or trams in some cities, buses and suburban trains. However, in rural areas you're dependent on a few, generally very slow buses, and services vary from infrequent to non-existent on Sundays and holidays. If you're going to be living for any length of time in a rural area, there's really no alternative to having your own transport.

The railway system in particular reflects two other aspects of the Italian character: on the one hand the zest for speed, manifested in the super-fast ETR trains (the equivalent of France's *TGV*), and on the other hand, the easygoing, unhurried approach to life, as depicted by local trains. All modes of public transport are susceptible to strikes, although they've been less frequent in recent years. Strikes are usually short, lasting 12 or 24 hours only, but they can be extremely disruptive as it takes much longer before services return to normal. The problem for foreigners is knowing when strikes are about to take place. If you don't have Italian friends, who complain vociferously about the latest *sciopero* (strike), or watch the TV news avidly, they can easily catch you unawares. On the positive side, most forms of public transport in Italy are good value.

Long journeys often require advance planning, particularly in the high season. As far as holidays are concerned, Italians are creatures of habit, and almost all inhabitants of the major cities take their holidays in August. Consequently, public transport (not to mention the roads) is very crowded and booking months in advance is recommended.

Few Italian public transport companies make concessions for the disabled or provide discounts, although things are slowly improving. Railways now offer assistance for disabled passengers and have welcome centres in major towns and cities, and some trains allow wheelchair access. **Enquire in advance if you require special assistance when travelling.**

A wealth of information about travelling to and within Italy is available on the Internet from a multitude of websites, including 🖳 www.initaly.com, 🖳 www.itwg.com, 🖳 www.italytour.com and 🖳 www.informare.it, a website devoted to transportation. Most cities and regions also have websites dedicated to them such as 🖳 www.romeguide.it, 🖳 www.florence.ala.it and 🖳 www. doge.it (Venice).

TRAINS

Trains are operated by the national company, Ferrovie dello Stato, usually referred to by the initials FS, although you may sometimes see FFSS. Italy's rail network is one of the most extensive in Europe, running to around 16,000km (circa 10,000mi) of lines, some two-thirds of which are electrified, and over 3,000 stations. There are also a number of private lines. FS was the first railway in Europe to be nationalised (or re-nationalised, as it was originally government owned), in 1908, but is now officially privatised, although the majority of shares remain in the hands of the government. After years of mismanagement and neglect, all aspects of Italian railways are currently being modernised with huge investments in infrastructure and rolling stock, particularly in new high-speed trains, although the system still has a way to go to compete with Europe's best.

The rail network is well distributed throughout the country, although there's a significant difference between services in the northern and southern parts of the country, with the north enjoying more frequent and faster trains, and more electrified and double track lines than the south. In an effort to reduce state subsidies, fares have risen in the last few years, although rail travel is still good value and cheaper than in most other European countries.

Trains can be crowded, particularly at weekends and in high summer, when southern Italians working in the north return home to their families. On the faster trains, seats should usually be reserved – look for the sign reservations (*Prenotazioni*) at stations. Reservations can be made between two months and three or four hours before a train's departure (except for Eurostar Italia/ES trains, when booking can be made right up to departure time). If you have a reservation, it's wise to locate your carriage while you're on the platform, rather than struggling up and down the corridors with your luggage. Most locomotives and rolling stock are fairly modern and well maintained, although some of the slower, local services use old equipment. A surprisingly large number of carriages are covered in graffiti, often very artistically, but unless you're into Italian youth culture the message is unfortunately (or maybe fortunately) impossible to interpret.

It's possible to travel between virtually any two points in the country by train, with the exception of some of Italy's more isolated mountainous regions, although incredible feats of engineering in the form of tunnels and viaducts have made inroads even into these seemingly inaccessible areas. In the broad river plains and coastal towns, the main railway station is usually situated in the city centre, for example, in Rome and Florence you can walk from the station to the historic centres in just a few minutes. However, in hilly regions, such as Tuscany and Umbria, many towns and cities were built on hilltops for defensive reasons and stations are situated on the plain. Fortunately, there are (usually) regular bus services, co-ordinated with train arrivals and departures, to whisk you to and from town centres. It's as well to check on the situation in advance, particularly if you're going to arrive loaded down with luggage.

General Information

- If the station isn't equipped with airport-style arrival (*arrivo*) and departure (*partenza*) boards, don't rely on the printed timetables to tell you the platform number where your train will arrive. Timetables are usually changed twice per year (around the 30th May and the 26th September) when the schedules change and therefore may not be wholly accurate. There's usually an indicator board on each platform listing (fairly well in advance) the trains arriving or departing there.

● Main stations such as Rome and Milan still have a uniquely Italian institution, a 'daytime hotel' (*albergo diurno*), open daily between 6am and midnight. It has no beds but provides services such as showers, hairdressers, cleaning and laundry facilities, and a place to relax and read the newspapers.

● There are official porters at main stations in Bologna, Florence, Milan, Naples, Padua, Rome and Venice, who charge a fee of around €1.75 per bag. In the same cities, passengers can also have their baggage delivered to their home or to the main station. Main stations have left luggage lockers and offices.

● A number of seats are reserved on high-speed ETR services for handicapped travellers and their travelling companions (where applicable). A service is provided for transporting disabled passengers to and from main stations in Bologna, Florence, Milan, Naples, Padua, Rome and Venice (a fee is payable).

● When travelling at night, take good care of your belongings (particularly your money and credit cards) and be wary of thieves. If you have a sleeping compartment, always lock the door and open it only for railway staff. Be careful about accepting food or drink from strangers, as there have been cases of thieves giving drugged food and drinks to travellers and stealing their belongings.

Types of Trains

Italian railways operate a variety of trains (painted in attractive red and white designs) from slow electric and diesel commuter trains to the high-speed ETR 450, 460 and 480 *Pendolino*, and ETR 500 trains on major routes. *Pendolino* trains are so-called because they lean to the centre of their path, thus compensating for centrifugal acceleration, which allows them to travel at speeds of up to 35 per cent faster than standard Intercity (IC) trains. Like France's *TGV* trains, ETR trains were designed to compete with air services and travel at speeds up to 300kph (186mph). ETR trains offer air-conditioning, a hostess service, video screens, hi-fi system with earphones, card-operated telephones, meals at your seat, dining car and minibar, free welcome drink, free newspaper (first class) and other benefits. Business lounges are provided on ETR 500 trains, which can be reserved for a fee of around €10.

FS operates many different classes of train with a wide range of supplements, obligatory reservations, classes (some trains have only first class carriages, some just second class, some both) and other variables, which make it important to check the kind of train you're planning to take. If you board a first class train with a second class ticket the ticket inspector may just charge you the difference, and you may need to pay a fine.

The categories of Italian trains, from the fastest to the slowest, are as follows:

- **Eurostar (ES) Italia** – International ultra-high-speed trains that make few stops and can whisk you from Rome to Milan in around four hours. They operate on three main routes taking in Milan, Bologna, Florence, Rome and Naples. ES trains are first and second class, and (free) reservations are obligatory on Fridays and Sundays, and on certain other days plus the Easter and Christmas periods (contact FS for exact dates).

- **Eurocity (EC)** – Fast, limited-stop international expresses operating between major cities in Italy and Europe. Sometimes first class only and seat reservations may be obligatory.

- **Intercity (IC)** – As EC above, but operating solely within Italy, with similar conditions to EC trains.

- **Express** (*espresso*) – Express (not coffee!) trains that stop in main towns along their routes. Both first and second class.

- **Direct** (*diretto*) – Slower than an *espresso*, making stops at most towns.

- **Local** (*locale/regionale*) – The real 'snails' of the system, which stop absolutely everywhere, often with no station in sight! These are the trains that serve rural areas and small towns, so if you're touring rather than on business, they can be a relaxing way to see the countryside, especially as the rolling stock is often quite ancient and interesting, particularly for train buffs.

- **Car Trains** (*auto al seguito*) – These operate on a number of international routes, including Bolzano to Dusseldorf, Bologna to Calais, Milan to Cologne and Düsseldorf, Milan to Amiens, Boulogne and Paris, Milan to Calais, Rimini to Munich, Rimini to Paris, Rome to Calais, Venice to Vienna and Verona to Hanover.

Long-distance and international night trains often have sleeping accommodation in the form of first and second class cabins (one to three berths), and couchettes or 'sleeperettes' (reclining seats – first class only). **It's recommended to avoid couchettes in the school holiday season (roughly June to September) if you wish to sleep!**

There are diagrams in stations showing the carriages that make up different types of train, e.g. number of first and second class carriages, buffet/restaurant cars and sleeping cars. Most long-distance trains have a trolley service for drinks and snacks, and some fast trains have a restaurant car or buffet, although these are few and far between. When on a long journey, it's wise to follow the Italians' example and take your own snacks and packed lunch/dinner.

Italy has direct rail connections with many other European countries, including Austria, France, Germany, the Netherlands, Spain and Switzerland. Italy's railways are connected with those in neighbouring countries by a number of mountain routes, linking Milan with Switzerland via the Milan-Simplon Tunnel, Turin with Fréjus in France, Venice to eastern Europe via Tarvisio, and Verona to Austria and Germany via the Brenner Pass.

Buying Tickets

You need to buy a single/one-way ticket (*solo andata*) or return/round trip (*andata e ritorno*) ticket before commencing your journey. Tickets can be purchased at ticket offices at most railway stations, although it's recommended to buy your ticket in advance at a travel agency, which saves you a lot of time queuing. If you plan to buy a ticket at a main station, you should allow plenty of time (at least 30 minutes). There is usually a special ticket window for Eurostar tickets. It's possible to avoid queuing by paying on a train, but you must usually pay a surcharge. However, surcharges aren't payable by passengers who board at a station without a ticket office or with non-operational ticket offices. If you need to board a train without a ticket, you should seek out the ticket inspector and buy a ticket as soon as possible.

Many stations are equipped with ticket machines on which instructions can be displayed in English. They're similar in operation to the timetable on the FS website (🖳 www.fs-on-line.com), except that you can choose the class of ticket and pay for it immediately using a credit card or by stuffing wads of banknotes into the machine. In the cities of Bologna, Florence, Milan, Naples, Padua, Rome and Venice, you can telephone the Welcome Centre and arrange for tickets to be delivered to your home. Most tickets are valid for two months and passengers can make unlimited stops within the period of validity. Seats on Intercity services can be booked in advance, for which there may be a fee.

Before boarding a train you must validate your ticket by inserting it in a small yellow validation (*convalida*) machine (*macchine obliteratici*), where it's punched to indicate that it has been used. If there's no machine, you can write the date and time by hand on the back of the ticket and seek out the ticket inspector after you've boarded a train, otherwise you can be fined for travelling without a ticket. Once punched, a ticket is valid for six hours on journeys of up to 200km (124mi) and 24 hours for journeys over 200km.

Fares

Rail fares are good value compared with most other European countries, although ticket (*biglietto*) prices are rising along with the investment in improved services. There are, however, a wide range of concessionary fares, season tickets and special offers, many of which are listed below under **Special Tickets**. All children under four automatically travel free (but shouldn't occupy a seat) and those aged from 4 to 12 travel for half fare. First class tickets cost almost double the price of a second class ticket.

Fares on local trains on journeys of up to 100km (62mi) are calculated on the distance travelled. For all other trains, including Eurostar, Eurocity, Intercity and Intercity Night trains, from 16th January 2000 fares have been set by FS based on 'market values', and supplements (*supplemento*) will eventually no longer apply. However, if you wish to upgrade to a train in a superior category or from second to first class, you must pay a 'change of service' fee, or, in the case of a downgrade, you can claim a refund. If a ticket is unused (through no fault of FS), a refund will be made within two months of the date of issue and is subject to a fee of 20 per cent of the fare or a minimum of €5.

If an Intercity train arrives over 30 minutes late you receive a 'bonus' equal to 30 per cent of the fare and booking charge. For Eurostar trains the bonus is increased to 50 per cent. Take note of the train's number, point of departure/arrival, and its scheduled and actual arrival times, and complete a *richiesta di bonus* form available at stations. You can do this at any FS station up to 15 days after the journey, and aren't required to make a claim on arrival at your destination. Your reimbursement is sent by post in the form of a discount coupon that you can use to buy future train tickets.

To give you an idea of fares, the cost of a single (one-way) journey from Rome's Termini Station to Florence's Santa Maria Novella, a distance of around 240km (145mi), is shown below, including supplements where applicable:

Type of Train	Fare (single/one-way)		Journey Time*
	First Class	Second Class	
Eurostar	€70	€52	1hr 34m – 2hrs 2m
Intercity	€58	€41	1hr 52m – 2hrs 25m

* The journey time depends on the particular train you choose and the number of stops it makes.

Special Tickets

FS offers a range of reduced and concessionary fares, which, if you're planning to do a lot of travelling, are worth looking into. Special tickets include the following (although they change frequently):

● **Season Card** (*tessera d'abbonnamento*) – Monthly season ticket for IC or ES trains that provides unlimited return journeys on the same route up to 1,000km (621mi). Example: Rome–Milan, IC trains, first class (€400), second class (€295). You can order and pay for monthly season tickets online from 🖳 www.abbonamenti.fs-on-line.it, although you must order the ticket at least four working days (weekdays) prior to the starting date and pay by credit card (Visa or Mastercard). The ticket is sent to you by priority post (*posta prioritaria*).

- **Silver Card** (*carta d'argento*) – Residents who are aged over 60 can obtain fare reductions by buying a Silver Card for €25.82. It's valid for one year and provides a discount of 40 per cent on first class fares and 30 per cent on second class fares for all journeys, including Eurostar Italia and Eurocity on national and regional lines. It's valid only for the named holder and isn't transferable.

- **Green Card** (*carte verde*) – For young people aged 12 to 26, it costs €25.82 and provides15 per cent reductions on first and second class fares . Cardholders can also obtain reductions at Gardaland, Countdown International and the Italian Youth Hostel Association.

- **Blue Card** (*carta blu*) – Allows a physically or mentally handicapped person and an accompanying person to travel for the price of one ticket. It costs €5 and is valid for five years.

- **Club Eurostar Card** (*carta club Eurostar*) – Provides a 20 per cent discount on first class fares, including IC and Eurocity (EC) trains, throughout Europe. Valid for one year, it costs €77.47.

- **Friends Of The Train Card** (*carta amico treno*) – Provides a 50 per cent discount on selected regional (local) trains and 10 per cent discount on first and second class fares. Benefits apply to the cardholder and one other named person when travelling together. The *amico treno* card costs €50.

- **Kilometre Ticket** (*biglietto chilometrico*) – The holder can travel a total of 3,000km (1,864mi) over a maximum of 20 journeys, first or second class. It's valid for up to five named people, travelling together or separately (children aged between 4 and 12 are charged half the km travelled). The ticket isn't accepted in all regions and a supplement is payable on ES, IC and EC trains. The kilometre ticket costs €180.76 for first class and €116.72 for second class, and is valid for two months. It's due to be cancelled towards the end of 2003.

- **Families** (*famiglie*) – A discount of 30 per cent for families travelling together, including children aged 4 to 12. The offer is valid for first and second class travel on all domestic journeys, including Eurostar Italia, EC and IC trains. This concession isn't available from the Friday preceding Palm Sunday to the Sunday after Easter, or for the peak periods of 1st July to the 31st August and 15th December to the 10th January.

- **Group Ticket** (*biglietto di gruppo*) – Groups of at least six people receive a discount of 20 per cent (first and second class) or 10 per cent on Eurostar Italia and couchettes; you must reserve tickets, at a cost of €1.5. Groups of over 50 people receive discounts and details (which vary) are available at main stations, which give you a quote. Certain periods are excluded, as shown above for families.

If you find all the different tickets and discounts bewildering, it's hardly surprising. With such an abundance of season and special tickets available, the only thing you can be sure of is that unless you're travelling free, you may be paying too much. The solution is simply to tell the ticket office clerk where you want to go, when and how often you want to travel, and whether first or second class. However, you may not be able to rely on him to provide you with the cheapest ticket available, as he may be just as confused as you are!

Visitors' Tickets

A range of visitors' tickets is available for travel in Italy and other European countries, including the following:

- **Italy Rail Card** – A personal card (first or second class) for non-residents only, which allows unlimited travel throughout Italy. It can purchased for 8, 15, 21 or 30 days and there are no supplements for EC or IC trains (although supplements are payable for Eurostar trains). Tickets can be purchased from travel agents abroad and at main stations in Italy on production of a passport.

- **Italy Flexi-Rail Card** – A personal card (first or second class) for non-residents only, which allows unlimited travel throughout Italy. It can be purchased for 4, 8 or 12 days travel during a one-month period. Other conditions are the same as for the Italy Rail Card above.

- **Rail Europe S Card** – Senior citizens travelling outside Italy can buy a Rail Europe S Card for one year for €20. It's valid for the named holder only and provides a 30 per cent discount on international direct tickets on the networks of 28 participating countries (including all EU countries).

In addition to the above, a range of European Inter Rail, Euro Domino and BIJ tickets also allow train travel in Italy, but must usually be purchased abroad.

Information

Information about rail services is available from FS Informa (☎ 147-888 088), although it can be difficult to get through and you need to speak Italian. Timetables can also be displayed via the TV televideo (RAI page 159) and Mediavideo 'teletext' services. If you have access to the Internet, FS has an excellent website (🖳 www.fs-on-line.com) that includes the following information, most of which can be displayed in English (plus Italian, French, German and Spanish):

- A do-it-yourself timetable. This is in English but you must enter the town or city names in Italian, e.g. Firenze not Florence, Venezia not Venice. You enter your departure station, arrival station, date of journey and earliest starting time, and all scheduled trains are displayed for that day (for long journeys it may also include trains departing on the following day), including journey times, connecting stations, on-board facilities, whether reservations are necessary and wheelchair access.

● Information about the main Italian railway stations, such as the facilities available (restaurant, news kiosk, change office, etc.), telephone numbers, and opening hours for information and reservation services.

● A list of FS agencies (the best place to buy tickets) for all major towns in Italy.

● Special offers such as reductions, monthly tickets and special excursion tickets (many of which are listed above under **Special Tickets**). Bear in mind, however, that these change frequently and the website may not show the latest information, therefore it's recommended to check with an FS agent or main railway station information office.

● Detailed information about Eurostar services.

● Telephone numbers for tourist hotels and car hire companies.

BUSES, TRAMS & UNDERGROUND TRAINS

Italy has no national bus (*autobus*) or coach (*pullman*, or sometimes *pulman*) companies, but has more buses and operators than any other European country. Buses are more expensive than trains, although they're often quicker for short journeys. Companies usually operate at a fairly local level and although some of the larger companies provide long-distance, inter-city services, these are limited. Because of the lack of national services, it's difficult to obtain detailed information on fares and there's little published on the Internet. Timetables, route maps and fares are available from local bus and railway stations, tourist information offices, bookshops and newsagents. As with rail travel, there's a bewildering range of concessionary fares for frequent travellers; obtain the latest information direct from bus companies.

An example may help illustrate how the system works. Florence has several bus companies, most with their headquarters at or near S. Maria Novella railway station in the centre. The most important companies are Lazzi (which has a useful website, 🖳 www.lazzi.it, some of it in English) and Sita, either of which will get you to most of Tuscany's major destinations, albeit in their own good time. Lazzi also operates long-distance coaches to Rome and other major cities. Timetables for all routes can be obtained from an information booth outside the railway station. A single ticket (*biglietto*) from Florence to Pisa (100km/62mi) costs €6.10 with Lazzi and takes around 2hrs 40m. Sienna is particularly geared to bus travellers and has a huge complex to the west of the city at Piazza San Domenico (from where a shuttle service operates to the city centre), equipped with tourist and hotel information offices, destination boards and ticket offices. In addition to serving the local area, long-distance coaches also go to Rome, Pisa and other destinations.

At the local and rural level, because of the large number of independent companies, you will find many different systems operating. Tickets, for both long-distance and local services must usually be purchased from tobacconists, bars, news kiosks or bus company offices – **you cannot buy them on buses!** You may be given a number of tickets when a journey involves using a number of bus companies. If you live in a rural area, you just arm yourself with a sheaf of tickets of different values and, as you get to know the fares, use them as necessary. Many bus companies in rural areas operate on the request stop (*fermata a richiesta*) system, whereby they stop to pick you up or let you off only if you request it by signalling the driver or ringing a bell. A bus's route and destination is shown by a sign in the front window. Major bus companies usually offer a variety of tickets, including single/one-way (valid for the day of issue only), return/round trip (valid for a number of days), which is usually cheaper than two single tickets, a weekly ticket (valid for five or six return trips), and a monthly season ticket, which may be valid only for a limited number of return journeys.

A final word of caution: because of the large number of bus companies operating in most areas, all with their own rules and schedules, journeys in rural areas need careful planning and a good deal of local knowledge. Services can be infrequent or even non-existent on Sundays and public holidays.

City Services

This is where Italy often excels in the field of public transport, with bus and other city transport generally comprehensive, frequent, inexpensive and fairly rapid. This is particularly true as more cities are closing streets around historic centres to private cars and introducing more bus lanes. However, Italians have an enduring love affair with their cars and sometimes drive into city centres when it's forbidden, and often treat bus lanes with total contempt. Although there are a few variations, most cities use the same system for buses. There's a flat fare, usually around €0.80, that entitles you to make as many journeys as you like within an hour. Single tickets and blocks of five or ten can be purchased from tobacconists, bars, news kiosks and sometimes ticket machines located near bus stops. Local information offices provide route maps and timetables. Some cities (e.g. Rome) have introduced buses specially adapted for disabled passengers on certain routes. Many modern buses and trams, mercifully, are now air-conditioned. If possible, it's wise to avoid the 'school run' between around 1 and 2.30pm, when schoolchildren crowd buses.

City buses and trams usually have three doors, where you board at either end and exit via the middle door. If you have a standard ticket, you usually enter the bus or tram at the back and insert it in the orange or yellow validation (*convalida*) machine that's generally situated to the right or driver's side, past the middle doors. Once stamped (it may also cut the corner off), the ticket is good for 60 or 75 minutes, including changing buses or trams. If you're changing buses/trams and have a stamped ticket or hold a pass, you can enter from the front door. Failure to validate your ticket can result in a fine of around €30 or up to 20 times the fare. Bus stops are called *fermata* or *fermata a richiesta* – request stops where you must hold out your arm to signal the driver to stop. If you wish to get off at a request stop (i.e. not a mandatory stop), you need to push an orange or red button prior to your stop to signal the driver to stop at the next stop.

Many cities in Italy's lower-lying regions, including Genoa, Milan, Naples, Rome, Trieste and Turin, operate tram or light rail networks. Turin has several enclosed tram routes, completely separated from other traffic, which transport you quickly around the outskirts of the city or from one side to the other. The ticket system is basically the same as for buses, but trams tend to be a bit quicker as they have absolute right of way. There are some streets in Turin, for example, where, because there are tram lines on either side of the road, cars park in a line in the middle!

Naples, Milan and Rome also have underground railways known as 'metros', but don't expect anything like London, New York or Paris. Rome has only two lines, in the form of a cross, based on Termini Station in the centre. Several stations on line B near the centre were upgraded for the year 2000 to be more user-friendly for disabled travellers. Line A hasn't been upgraded but the route is also served by bus route 590, which operates specially-adapted buses for disabled passengers.

Most city transport operates from around 5.30 or 6.00am until 11.30pm or midnight, although you should check the times of the first and last services. Trams in Rome cease operation at 9pm, although most bus services continue until around midnight and there are night buses (*servizio notturno*) on some routes. Services are less frequent on Sundays and public holidays. In cities where there are two or more modes of public transport, it's usually possible to buy a ticket that can be used on all services. In Rome, for example, these tickets are known as *metrebus* and can be used on buses, trams, underground and over-ground FS trains, except the shuttle service to Fiumicino Airport. There are the usual concessions in nearly all cities. Both Rome and Milan issue an unlimited-travel, 24-hour ticket for €3.10, Milan offers a 48-hour ticket for € 4.65, and Rome provides monthly CIS passes, costing €25.80 for a personal pass (which contains personal details of the holder and which can only be used by him) or €36.10 for a non-personal pass, which can be used by anyone. Some cities provide discounts of up to 50 per cent for pensioners and students.

There are river buses in many cities, e.g. Rome, although these are usually strictly for tourists and aren't intended for residents.

TAXIS

Taxis in Italian cities are usually yellow, although sometimes white, while in smaller towns, white is the most common colour with a small number in other colours. They're usually found at official taxi ranks, for example at railway stations or near town centres, and aren't usually hailed in the street, although they may stop if they're returning from a fare. Taxis should have a meter, which you should ensure is switched on! If the driver claims that it's broken, you must agree the fare before starting a journey. If you're familiar with a town, it may be worthwhile mentioning that you wish to go via a particular landmark on the direct route to your destination, so that you aren't taken via the 'scenic route'. Taxi journeys in Italian cities aren't for the faint-hearted and can be hair-raising for the uninitiated, with drivers ignoring speed limits and any semblance of road rules, while roundly cursing other motorists.

Fares are set by the local authorities. In Milan, for example, they start at €3.10 and are then charged on a time and distance basis. There are also supplements for such sins as having luggage, wishing to travel at night and for journeys to local airports. It isn't necessary to tip taxi drivers, although most Italians round up the fare to the nearest euro or leave some small change. In rural areas, drivers will usually take you to small villages or isolated houses, and the fare is invariably reasonable, for example, from Chiusi Station to a farmhouse in deepest Umbria costs around €17 for an 8km (5mi) journey, including a few kilometres on dirt roads. Obviously the driver would have no chance of picking up a return passenger on this trip.

FERRIES

Italy has a well-developed network of ferry services, although services are usually severely curtailed during the winter months. Large ferries (*navi*) service the islands of Sardinia and Sicily, while smaller islands are served by small ferries (*traghetti*) and hydrofoils (*aliscafi*). Regular services connect the mainland with Italy's many islands, and ferries and hydrofoils also operate between towns on the lakes of Como, Garda, Maggiore and a number of smaller lakes. The most important domestic ferry routes include:

- Piombino – Elba
- Civitavecchia, Genoa, Livorno (Leghorn) and Naples – Sardinia
- Genoa, Naples, Reggio di Calabria and Villa San Giovanni – Sicily
- Naples – Lipari Islands (Stromboli, etc.)
- Naples – Pontine Islands (Capri, Ischia, Procida)

There are also connections from Sicily to Sardinia and international car and passenger ferry services between Italy and various countries, including Albania, Croatia, Egypt, France (Corsica), Greece, Israel, Malta, Spain (the Balearics), Tunisia, Turkey and parts of the former Yugoslavia. Ticket prices are usually reasonable but vary according to the time of year and are (naturally) most expensive during summer. **Some services operate during the summer only and services are severely curtailed during the winter on most routes or may be suspended altogether.**

To those more used to the Dover–Calais or Staten Island (New York) routes, some journeys seem very long. For example, the Genoa-Palermo boat takes 23 hours and Naples-Palermo departs at 8pm and arrives at 7am the next day (11 hours), although there's also a hydrofoil service taking just over five hours but operating only once per day, three days per week. On the other hand, boats leave from Villa San Giovanni for Messina (Sicily) every 15 minutes during peak hours; the trip takes half an hour and the service operates 24 hours per day.

Ships range from quite small, no-frills, no-services vessels on the shortest routes, to absolute leviathans carrying 1,800 passengers and 500 vehicles, with restaurants, bars, shops, discos and cinemas on the longer routes. Long-haul ferries also provide sleeping facilities in the form of reclining seats (*poltrona*) or couchettes, through to deluxe cabins with showers and toilets. Demand for these facilities is high at most times of year, so early booking is essential. You also need to book well in advance when travelling during peak holiday periods, particularly if you're taking a car. Bear in mind when planning a trip that services are infrequent on the longer routes, some of which have only one departure on three or four days per week. Information about times and fares is available on the Internet at 💻 www.traghetti.com, which has a link to the sites of several ferry companies, most with an English version.

The major companies serving the main destinations are as follows:

- **Adriatic Coast** – The Adriatic Company serves Ancona, Bari, Brindisi, Trieste and Venice (plus a number of international destinations);
- **Bay of Naples** (Naples, Capri, Ischia and Procida) – Caremar, Alilauro and SNAV;
- **Elba** – Nav.Ar.Mar and Toremar;
- **Lipari Islands** (Vulcano, Lipari, Stromboli, etc.) – Siremar and SNAV;
- **Sardinia** – Tirrenia, Sardinia Ferries, I Grandi Traghetti and FS (Italian Railways);
- **Sicily** – Tirrenia, I Grandi Traghetti, Aliscafi SNAV (Hydrofoil) and FS.

To give you some idea of fares, the average prices (mid-season, medium-sized car, etc.) on the Naples-Palermo route are deck passenger €32, deluxe cabin €64 and a car €70. In contrast, the short Villa San Giovanni–Messina trip costs €17 for a medium-sized car and €1.75 for a foot passenger.

Lake Services

Italy has many lakes, some very large. Most (Como, Garda, Iseo and Maggiore) are in the north, on the border with Switzerland, but there are some others, including Bracciano and Trasimeno. Ferries operate like a bus service on these lakes, carrying passengers (and often cars also) from one side to the other and, where applicable, calling at islands on the lakes. The car ferry service is usually convenient, as some of the northern lakes are long and narrow, and driving around them or trying to make the journey by bus or train takes hours, whereas the ferry gets you across in a much shorter time. Timetables are available from ferry companies and local tourist information offices. Companies serving the main lakes are shown below:

- **Lake Como** – Mostly operated by Navigazione Lago Como, ferries link Como, Cernobbio, Bellagio, Menaggio, Varenna, Bellano and other towns.

- **Lake Garda** – Ferries operated by Navigazione Lago Garda connect Riva, Torbole, Gargnano, Gardoe, Sirmione, Desenzano, Bardolino and other towns. There are also several hydrofoil services and a car ferry from Maderno to Torri del Benaco.

- **Lake Maggiore** – Mostly operated by Navigazione Lago Maggiore, frequent services connect Brissago, Cannobio, Verbania, Baveno, Stresa, Arona, Locarno and several other towns. Tickets are available from company offices at landing stages and some information offices. There's also a hydrofoil service between Arona, Stresa and Locarno, and a car ferry between Verbano, Intra and Laveno.

Venice

Venice is unique and, as such, merits a section to itself. Contrary to what some people may think, it isn't all canals and it's quite possible to see most of the city's major attractions on foot (and without getting wet). But that isn't as much fun as using the local transport system. Venice can be reached by boat from Mestre on the mainland or, more simply, by rail or road across the long causeway. This takes you to *Piazzale Roma*, which is a good starting-point for tours. There's also a ticket office here that sells tickets for the local ferries, *vaporetti* (literally 'little steamers'), Venice's equivalent of buses. *Vaporetti* cover most of the city and are used by locals and tourists alike.

Tickets cost €3.5 for any journey and you can buy them singly or in a book (*blocchetto*). There are also 24-hour (€10.50) and three-day (€22) tickets. Tickets are stamped on the boat in the same way as on buses and trams. If you don't have a ticket, perhaps because the ticket office was shut (after 9pm), you can pay on the boat – but if you don't do this immediately on boarding you can be fined.

The main route is line 1, which runs the full length of the Grand Canal from *Piazzale Roma* to St. Mark's Square, a journey of around 45 minutes. **A little care is required with routes.** You need to check the timetable at stops to ensure that a *vaporetto* is going in the direction you want, and look out for similar line numbers which cover slightly different routes (e.g. Lines 52 and 52/, which stop on different sides of the Giudecca Canal). If you want to cross the Grand Canal and you aren't near one of its three bridges, look out for the *traghetti* – little boats that take you across for a modest sum, usually less than a euro.

If you want to travel faster and in style, you can take a water taxi (*motoscafo*), which are handsome, fast launches – a bit like having your own personal powerboat. However, bear in mind that they're expensive and the fare system is arcane! You must agree the fare with the driver before starting a journey and be prepared to pay extra for luggage and late-night trips, as with city taxis.

Think of Venice and you naturally think of gondolas. They're unique and romantic, and not *too* expensive for a group of people. Try early evening before dinner, as prices increase after 8pm, although you may wish to take a glance at the water level in the canals, as low tide can produce some pretty awful smells. As with the *motoscafo*, agree a price before you start, and ask the gondolier to take you along some of the smaller, more intimate canals. A 50-minute trip should cost around €70 for up to five people – but who wants to share a gondola ride with more than one person?

AIR TRAVEL

There are direct international scheduled and charter flights to all major cities in Italy (e.g. there are direct flights from the UK to around 20 Italian cities) and many other towns are served by domestic flights. International airlines serving Italy (apart from the national carrier Alitalia) include Air Canada, Air France, American Airlines, British Airways, Continental Airlines, Delta Airlines, Iberia, Icelandair, KLM, Lufthansa, Northwest Airlines, Sabena, SAS, Swissair, TWA and US Airways. The major international gateways are Rome, Milan, Pisa, Venice and Naples, although more cities are becoming accessible by direct international flights, including Florence, Bologna and Perugia.

The Italian national airline, Alitalia, has its main hub at Rome's Fiumicino airport and flies to over 100 cities in six continents. For years it had a reputation as one of Europe's least efficient national carriers, plagued by strikes, over-manning and restrictive practices. However, in recent years modern business practices have been implemented to address these problems, and in 1997 the company's balance sheet finally moved into the black, although the company lost money again in 2002. Alitalia is currently partially state owned, with complete privatisation planned. Not surprisingly, it dominates the busy and lucrative Milan–Rome route.

International Services

There are usually several direct flights per day to/from London Heathrow to Bologna, Florence, Genoa, Milan, Naples, Pisa, Rome, Turin and Venice, and there are also scheduled and charter flights from London Gatwick and other UK airports to various Italian cities (including Palermo). Normal scheduled fares to Rome are around £300 single and £550 return. Apex and chartered fares are much cheaper and cost from around £150 return to Milan or Rome and an additional £20 to £30 to Pisa or Naples. **Fares vary considerably according to the time of the year, when you book and the airline.** The vast majority of flights go to Milan or Rome, although there's usually at least one per day to Bologna, Naples, Pisa and Turin. There are also flights from Manchester (UK) to Milan and Rome, and Meridiana fly from London to Olbia (Sardinia) and to Cagliari (Sardinia) via Florence.

Several airlines fly direct to Italy from the US, including Alitalia, Delta and American Airlines, although scheduled fares are expensive. Alitalia offer the widest choice of direct flights from the US, including daily flights from Boston, Chicago, Los Angeles, New York and Miami, to both Milan and Rome (usually with a stop over at Milan's Malpensa airport). Delta fly daily from Chicago, Los Angeles and New York to Rome, and American Airlines fly daily from Chicago and Los Angeles via New York to Milan and Rome. Most European airlines fly via their European base to Italy, rather than direct. The cheapest return fares from the USA are around US$500 from New York to Rome, rising to US$700 during the shoulder season and to US$900 during the peak season; add around US$100 for flights from Chicago and Miami, and US$200 from Los Angeles. Charter flights are available from the US to Italy, but aren't such good value as in Europe, as scheduled airlines can often beat the prices with special offers, and offer more convenience and fewer restrictions. Flights take around eight hours from New York to Milan or Rome. From Canada, both Alitalia and Air Canada have direct flights to Rome and Milan from Toronto and Montreal.

Domestic Services

A number of airlines provide domestic services within Italy, including Aero Transporti Italiani (a subsidiary of Alitalia), Aermediterranea, Air Dolomiti, Air One, Air Sicilia, Alitalia, Alisarda, Aligiulia, Alpi Eagles, Azurra, Meridiana, Minerva and Transavia. Some 40 Italian airports are served from Rome and most domestic flights take under an hour. However, travelling by air within Italy is expensive, although discounts are available, notably for evening and night flights. You can also buy APEX tickets that must be booked and paid for at least seven days prior to departure, and must include at least one Saturday and Sunday night between the outward and return journeys. Juniors (those aged under 22), students (up to 26), seniors (over 60) and families (consisting of a minimum of three persons) can purchase tickets immediately prior to departure. With the exception of seniors, these groups can also purchase one-way tickets for half the price of reduced tariffs. You should allow at least 20 minutes to check in for internal flights. Private air taxi services also operate from many airports.

Airports

Italy has international airports in Rome (Leonardo da Vinci, better know as Fiumicino, and Ciampino, which serves mainly charter flights), Milan (Linate for domestic and European flights, and Malpensa for intercontinental flights), Bologna, Catania (Sicily), Genoa, Olbia (Sardinia), Naples, Pisa, Palermo (Sicily), Turin and Venice. However, the dearth of major international airports in the north of the country sometimes forces travellers to take connecting flights to Italy from Zurich, Paris, Frankfurt or London. This was eased with the opening of Milan's Malpensa 2000 airport in 1998, although it has been plagued by controversy as the Italian government forced all foreign intercontinental flights to use the new airport, while the old Linate airport is mainly used by Alitalia and Air One (also Italian) domestic flights from Rome. For travellers (and airline companies), Malpensa suffers the disadvantage that it's 53km/33mi from Milan, compared with Linate, which is just 10km/6mi from the city centre. However, express trains operating every 30 minutes connect the airport with Milan's Cadorna railway station, taking around 40 minutes (which will eventually be reduced to 30 minutes). The service operates from 6am through to 1.30am and costs €7.8 single (one-way).

As mentioned above, Rome is served by two airports. The main one, and Italy's largest, is Fiumicino, around 25km (15mi) west of Rome, almost on the coast and just off the Rome–Ostia motorway. Depending on the wind direction, you sometimes get a wonderful bird's-eye view of the ruined Roman city of Ostia Antica as you come in to land. Fiumicino receives flights from around the world and has all the facilities you would expect, including car hire (all major companies), exchange bureaux, hotel booking agencies, shopping, and short and long-term car parking. Planes usually arrive directly at terminals where you're delivered straight to your arrival gate. The airport also has the advantage of being connected to Rome's Termini Station by a rail shuttle operating every 30 minutes. Most overseas travel agents can book not only your flight to Fiumicino, but also the shuttle and onward rail travel ticket if required, and provide you with connection times. If you've hired a car, a free shuttle bus takes you the relatively short distance to the hire company offices and pick-up point.

The second airport serving Rome is Ciampino. It's around the same distance from the city centre, but to the south-east. Used mainly for internal and charter flights, it's smaller and more intimate than Fiumicino, although planes must park on the apron from where you're taken by bus to the terminal. Trains run to the centre of Rome every 20 minutes from Ciampino town, not the airport, taking 15 minutes. It's a convenient airport if you're hiring a car, as it's close to *the Gran Raccordo Annulare (GRA)* – Rome's ring road. An excellent airport to arrive at if you aren't hiring a car is Pisa. It's small and easy to find your way around, and the railway station is situated inside the airport complex, providing direct access to the national rail network. A number of companies operate a minibus shuttle service from your home to major airports for a reasonable fee, e.g. ☎ 06-4201 4507 or 06-7759 0475 in Rome.

At the other end of the scale are the domestic airports. These can be tiny, for example Perugia, which basically comprises a check-in, a waiting area and a bar. Even here, however, there are two car hire company offices. You must walk from your aircraft to the terminal, but your luggage is taken. Alitalia has a website (🖳 www.alitalia.it) detailing special offers on internal flights (in Italian, but fairly comprehensible).

There are over 100 domestic airports in Italy, some of which also cater for international flights (particularly during summer), including Alghero, Ancona, Bari, Bergamo, Bologna, Brindisi, Cagliari, Catania, Florence, Genoa, Lamezia

Terme, Lampedusa, Olbia, Palermo, Pantelleria, Parma, Perugia, Pescara, Reggio di Calabria, Rimini, Sassari, Trapani, Trieste, Treviso, Turin and Verona.

All international airports have wheelchairs and ambulance staff on hand to assist handicapped travellers, although it's better to telephone in advance. Long and short-term parking is available at most airports, including all international airports, with reserved parking for the disabled. International airports have shopping centres, which are normally open for longer hours than city shops, seven days per week.

Airport authorities state that x-ray machines used for hand baggage at Italian international airports are safe for films. However, a hand-search is normally possible on request and is particularly recommended if you're carrying high-speed film (over 400 ASA). **Metal detectors may not be safe for magnetic storage media such as computer hard and floppy disks.**

For flight information telephone:

Airport	Telephone Number
Alghero	079-935 033
Ancona	071-2827 233
Bari	080-5382 370
Bergamo	035-326 323
Bologna	051-6479 615
Brindisi	0831-418 963
Cagliari Alitalia	147-865 643
Genoa	010-6015 410
Milan (Malpensa)	02-2680 0619
Milan (Linate)	02-2810 6310
Perugia	075-6929 447
Pescara	085-4324 200
Pisa	050-500 707
Rome (Ciampino)	06-794 941
Rome (Fiumicino)	06-6595 3640
Turin	011-567 6361
Venice	041-2606 111

11.

MOTORING

The love affair between Italians and their cars is well documented (most would rather lend you their wife for a weekend than their car), so it comes as no surprise to find that Italy has the highest number of cars per head of population of any country in Europe – around 600 for every 1,000 inhabitants. The problems caused by such a high rate of car ownership have been exacerbated by many Italians' refusal to dispose of their pride and joy for a newer and safer model. In 1997 and 1998 the Italian government introduced incentives to get old cars off the road by offering to pay an inflated price for the old car if it was sold (for scrap) in exchange for a new one. Until then you would still see large numbers of old Fiat 500s (*cinquecenti*) rattling around Italian towns, some with their bodies held together by little more than innumerable layers of paint. The subsidies for scrapping old cars coupled with more frequent technical inspections have significantly reduced the number of such 'death-traps' on the roads in recent years. Nevertheless, the accident rate remains one of the highest in Europe and there are some 7,000 deaths on Italian roads each year.

Italian roads are generally good, with an excellent motorway (*autostrada*) network covering some 6,000km (3,700mi), most of which are toll (*pedaggio*) roads. However, many town centres are based on medieval street plans and are unable to cope with today's levels of traffic, to say nothing of the pollution generated by motor vehicles. This has led several cities, including Rome and Milan, to introduce measures to reduce the number of cars entering the city centre during peak hours. Hundreds of cities and towns throughout Italy have also introduced 'car-free' Sundays once a month, on which motor vehicles are banned from city and town centres.

There's a general emergency number (113) for reporting accidents and breakdowns, but for a quicker response in an emergency you can call 112 for the *Carabinieri* or 118 for an ambulance. In the event of a breakdown, call 116 and the nearest Automobil Club d'Italia (ACI) office will be advised to come to your assistance. Road conditions can be checked 24 hours per day by calling the Automobile Club d'Italia (☎ 06-4477, ⌨ www.aci.it). You can also obtain motoring information on ISO Radio (FM 103.3), Jiaradio RTL (FM 102.5) and via the RAI Videotel teletext service.

IMPORTING A VEHICLE

It's usually cheaper to buy a vehicle abroad and import it into Italy, where cars are **very** expensive owing to high taxes. If you intend to bring a vehicle, either temporarily or permanently, ensure that you know the latest regulations. If you have a new private vehicle purchased in another EU country with an EU type-approval certificate, no formalities or checks on the technical specifications of the vehicle are necessary. However, if you plan to import a vehicle permanently from outside the EU, it may need expensive modifications. For information about type-approval (*omologazione*), contact the Ministry of Transport, Ministero dei Trasporti, Direzione Generale Motorizzazione Civile, IV Direzione Centrale, Via Caraci, 36, 00157 Rome (☎ 06-4158 6204).

The problem of finding spare parts and service facilities for foreign-made vehicles should also be taken into account. However, with the increase in the number of foreign-made cars in Italy in the last decade, service facilities now exist for practically all European-manufactured cars plus most Japanese and Korean models. Facilities for American-made cars, however, remain rare.

Foreigners staying temporarily in Italy are permitted to drive imported vehicles with foreign registrations for up to 12 months, provided the vehicle registration remains valid while in Italy. A registration document with an Italian translation may be required. The use of the vehicle is duty and tax-free for six months only, unless you're a diplomat. If you become a resident in Italy, your car must be imported within your first six months of residence.

If you will be in Italy for less than six months and won't be a resident, it may pay you to buy a car in another European country and re-sell it when you no longer need it. If you buy a car privately and strike a good deal, you could even make a profit! Some dealers will sell you a car and buy it back for an agreed price after six months.

Duty & Tax

A vehicle can be imported from another EU country without paying any taxes (e.g. VAT or import duty), provided tax was paid in the former EU country and it has been owned and used for at least six months in that country prior to importation. Note that this is a one-time concession.

Temporary residents may import a vehicle registered outside the EU for private use for a maximum of six months in any 12-month period without being liable for duty or tax provided they don't lend, rent or give the vehicle to an EU citizen. Vehicles (which are classed as household goods) can be imported duty and tax free when moving to Italy from a non-EU country and establishing residence, provided that:

- the vehicle has been in your possession, was registered abroad at least six months before your arrival in Italy **and** has covered more than 6,000km (3,728mi);
- you can supply proof of residence outside the EU for 12 months;
- the vehicle is for personal use only;
- you register as a resident in Italy;
- the vehicle is immediately registered in the *Pubblico Registro Automobilistico* (PRA) at the local motor vehicle office (Motorizzazione Civile) – see **Vehicle Registration** below;
- the vehicle isn't sold, lent or rented for one year after its importation.

After payment of any duty and tax due, you will receive a customs receipt or clearance certificate. If no duties are to be paid, a permit of customs exemption is issued. These documents are required when registering the vehicle.

For those who don't qualify for exemption under the above criteria, the following tariffs are levied:

- **Import duty** at 10 per cent of the purchase price plus freight costs to the place of destination in Italy plus freight insurance;
- **VAT** at 20 per cent of the purchase price, freight costs and import duty.

These rates apply irrespective of the type of vehicle being imported. The importer must present a dealer's invoice as evidence of the purchase price of the vehicle. If, however, customs officials don't consider this a fair and accurate representation of the vehicle's market value, they may calculate their own figure by reference to a dealer's car buying guide or obtain a certified appraisal. The Italian authorities recommend that private importers without a recent invoice or who ship an unusual model should have their vehicle appraised before declaring the value. Some shipping agencies will complete clearance and customs formalities on your behalf for a fee.

VEHICLE REGISTRATION

If you import a vehicle temporarily, you're given a customs receipt (*bolletta doganale*) and can drive it on foreign registration plates for up to a year if you're a non-resident. However, if you become a resident, the vehicle must be imported permanently and registered (*immatricolata*) in Italy. Registration must be applied for within ten days of taking up residence. In order to register a vehicle, you must produce your residence permit (it's illegal for non-residents to buy a car in Italy unless it's for export – see **Buying a Car** on page 222).

If you have provisional residence (while waiting for your residence permit), you will be given special 'tourist' registration plates with the letters 'EE' (*Escursionisti Esteri*) on them.

If you buy a car directly from the previous owner, you must pay a fee to transfer ownership (*passaggio di proprietà*), which is usually between €365 and €415. The registration plates remain with the car, but the car must be registered in the name of the new owner. To do this, you and the buyer must go to an ACI office or an agent (*agenzie pratiche auto*), who takes care of the paperwork. It isn't recommended to try to do it yourself.

Note also that you may need to wait months for your car registration papers to arrive, although you can obtain interim documents (*foglio sostitutivo*), which must be renewed every three months. If you buy a new or second-hand car from a dealer, he will take care of the registration for you.

Foreign Vehicles

Before a foreign car can be registered in Italy, it must pass an inspection (*collaudo*). The regulations surrounding this are complex and change constantly, so unless you enjoy getting to grips with Italian bureaucracy at its worst you're recommended to have the inspection and paperwork done by an specialist agent (*agenzie pratiche auto*). Most agents charge around €135 for this service, although you should make sure that you receive a written quotation beforehand.

Motor vehicles can normally be registered only if there's a general operating licence for that model issued by the motor vehicle authority (Motorizzazione Civile). Each new model made in or imported into Italy is subject to a general inspection, including safety and emissions tests (see below). This inspection is normally instigated by the manufacturer or importer when a new model is released and guarantees that the performance of the vehicle meets Italian technical, environmental and safety standards. After successful completion, an operating permit is granted. The vehicle authority issues a 'title' for each different model, listing its main technical features, a copy of which is issued to car buyers by the manufacturer or dealer. You're therefore recommended not to make any substantial modifications to an already licensed vehicle without obtaining expert advice, or you may lose the general operating licence and your insurance cover.

Foreign vehicles imported privately won't usually have the necessary Italian title among their papers. If the model in question has already been granted a general operating licence in Italy, a copy should be obtained at the beginning of the registration procedure from the local car registration office. If a licence hasn't previously been issued, it's the responsibility of the applicant to supply the necessary technical data. This applies particularly to American cars, as these aren't common in Italy. To avoid the time-consuming and expensive procedure of establishing the technical specifications of a car through a general inspection, you should contact the manufacturer of your vehicle before importing it for information on the vehicle identification number (VIN), year of manufacture, vehicle type and other technical data, including:

- engine type/displacement;
- power (DIN hp/kW);
- maximum speed;
- emissions results;
- admissible wheel and tyre sizes;
- admissible gross front/rear axle weight.

If the vehicle doesn't have any other valid registration plates, special temporary plates (*targa di prova*) must be obtained to drive it to an inspection station. You must request these from the local motor registry (Ufficio Motorizzazione).

The date of the vehicle's first registration, which you must provide, determines the legal standard that applies. **However, even when an overseas model has been granted a general operating licence, modifications may be necessary to meet Italian safety and environmental standards.** Most authorised garages can do the preliminary checks and carry out the modifications.

Registration Procedure

To register a motor vehicle you must apply at the local motor vehicle office in the town where you live and present:

- proof of identity and residence, i.e. your passport and residence permit. Only residents and resident companies may register a car – either themselves or through an authorised representative, who must have power of attorney;
- a customs clearance certificate stating payment of (or exemption from) import duty and VAT (see **Importing a Vehicle** on page 216);
- proof of ownership, e.g. a bill of sale or commercial invoice;
- vehicle documents, including the title if one has been issued; if no title has been issued, you will be given a blank title to be completed by a certified expert. You must also have the safety inspection and emissions test certificates (see below), or you're instructed how to obtain them.

You must pay a fee of around €55, which must be paid in cash, plus an additional amount of around €27.50 for registration plates (front and rear). After you've paid the fee and been given a receipt, your vehicle registration certificate (*libretto*) is issued. Be prepared to fit your plates before driving away.

Italian registration plates no longer carry provincial letters, which means that it's no longer necessary to change the number of a car to that of a new owner's province, although you must still register a change of ownership and/or address. Plates are valid as long as you own a car and they belong to the car not the owner, i.e. you cannot transfer them to another vehicle.

Under Italian law your vehicle registration certificate (and driving licence, receipt for your road tax payment, insurance certificate, and safety inspection and emissions test certificates) must be carried at all times when driving a vehicle (the last three must be displayed on the inside of your windscreen). If you're stopped by the police without one of these documents, you can be fined on the spot. It's wise to make copies of all your car papers (in case your car or documents are stolen) and keep them in a safe place.

SAFETY INSPECTION & EMISSIONS TEST

Until the 1980s, technical inspections were made only when a car was imported or new, after which there were no inspections at all, so Italian roads were filled with cars that were a danger to both the occupants and other road-users. Then regulations were introduced that required cars to be inspected 'regularly'. With the limited capacity of the motoring authority to achieve this, however, this usually meant once every ten years. With the recent delegation of the work to authorised garages, capacity has increased, and inspections are now due (and carried out) when a car is three years old and every two years thereafter.

Safety inspections are controlled by the motor vehicle authority (Motorizzazione), which licenses garages to carry out inspections. Vehicles can also be inspected at any office of the Motorizzazione. The process is usually straightforward: you don't require an appointment and can simply take your car to an inspection centre and ask for the inspection to be carried out; you hand over your car and the keys, and return the next day to collect it and the certificate (*bollino blu*). A mechanic checks your car for any operational defects (brakes, lights, exhaust, etc.) and repairs these if necessary. The basic fee is around €110 (excluding repairs).

If your vehicle doesn't pass the inspection, you're told what repairs or alterations are required. You're then obliged to have the repairs carried out and return it to the test centre for another inspection. If you don't want to take it yourself, you can pay a mechanic to do it for you.

In addition to the safety inspection, an exhaust emission test is required annually for both petrol and diesel-engine cars. This is also performed by authorised garages, who issue a special certificate (*bolletta blu*) on satisfactory completion of the test. The cost of the test and certificate is €8.

If you're unsure when your car is due for an inspection, check the sticker on the windscreen for the emissions inspection deadline and the sticker in your registration book for the date of the safety inspection. If the two dates coincide, they can be performed at the same time (which is recommended in any case).

If you're apprehended by the police with outdated stickers for either inspection, you're fined on the spot and are given a short period in which to take your car to a test centre – you aren't permitted to drive it until it passes.

ROAD TAX

Road or car tax (*tassa di circolazione*) is calculated according to the power of your car and whether it runs on petrol or diesel. For petrol-engine cars, you currently pay €2.60 per kW. Therefore, if your car has a power of 80kW (average engine power), you pay €208 per year. This means that the road tax bill for powerful cars is high. You can find out the cost of road tax from ACI offices, from charts posted in post offices and from the January edition of *Quattro Ruote* magazine.

The first payment must be within a month of registering a car. The local office of the ACI or a car dealer can advise you where it can be paid the first time. Subsequent annual payments are made at a post office. On payment, you receive a *bollo di circolazione* (commonly called a *bollo auto*), which no longer needs to be displayed behind your windscreen but should be carried by the driver. Road tax is required even when a car isn't being used and isn't parked on a public road. For most drivers it expires on 31st December, after which you have one month (until 31st January) to renew it.

Before buying a second-hand car in Italy, you should check that the road tax payments are up-to-date; otherwise you will be liable for any back payments when you renew it.

BUYING A CAR

You need a residence permit (*certificato di residenza*) and a tax number (*codice fiscale*) to buy a car in Italy. Non-residents can purchase a vehicle only from a manufacturer and must export it within a year. Homeowners who aren't residents but wish to keep a car in Italy for longer than a year must therefore either import a vehicle or register as a resident, then buy a car and register it and then cancel their residence application! Note that, before you can drive a car, you must have valid insurance cover (see **Car Insurance** on page 226).

Car manufacturers often want to sell this year's models before the end of the calendar year and consequently may offer special deals from October to December. The choice is somewhat limited regarding colour and options, but you can often get a new car with a discount of 20 per cent or more off the normal price.

Before buying a second-hand car, it's wise to consult the magazine *Quattro Ruote*, which lists the average prices for all new and second-hand cars in Italy. Prices vary according to how many kilometres a car has done, its general condition and where it's sold, but the prices quoted are usually a good guide.

SELLING A CAR

You can advertise a car for sale in local newspapers, on free local notice boards, in major newspapers (the Saturday editions are best) and in many motoring newspapers and magazines. A check of your local news kiosk will reveal a range of publications consisting entirely of used cars (and possibly other items) for sale. There's also a growing number of Internet-based advertising sites. If you belong to any clubs or organisations that publish a newsletter, they usually have a classified advertising section (even if you aren't a member, many accept advertisements for a small fee).

The best place to advertise a car depends on its make and value. Inexpensive cars are best sold in local newspapers, while expensive and collectors' cars are often advertised in the national motoring press. Buyers usually travel a long way to view a car that appears good value – if nobody phones, you know why! You can also put a 'for sale' (*vendesi*) sign (traditionally yellow or orange) in a car and park it in a prominent place, but make sure there are no parking restrictions.

The main points to note when selling a car are:

- To find the market value for a car sold in Italy, consult the magazine *Quattro Ruote* (see **Buying a Car** above).
- Insist on a cash deposit and full payment of the balance in cash on delivery.
- Inform your insurance company that the car has been sold.

> • Although the registration plates remain with the car when you sell it, the car must be registered in the name of the new owner (see **Vehicle Registration** on page 218).

DRIVING LICENCE

The minimum ages for driving in Italy are 18 for a motor car or for a motorcycle over 125cc, 16 for a motorcycle of between 50 and 125cc, and 14 for a moped (motorcycle up to 50cc). To ride a motorcycle over 50cc, you must have a motorcycle licence (Class A) and for a car a Class B licence. You must carry your licence (and other car papers) with you at all times when driving in Italy. If you wear spectacles or contact lenses, you're required to always wear them and carry a spare pair.

EU Licences

Since 1st July 1996, EU residents have enjoyed full recognition of their driving licences in other EU member countries for an unlimited period (officially, an old green UK driving licence is valid only with a translation). You aren't obliged to apply for a new licence, even when you transfers your permanent residence to Italy. A voluntary exchange is possible, in which case you must apply to the local ACI office and pay a small fee, but nothing further is required. However, an EU licence must be 'convalidated' at your local motor registry or an ACI office, where it's stamped to show that you're living in Italy.

If you have a driving licence of a class that allows you to drive professionally or in a larger vehicle than those allowed under Class B, you must reapply for such a licence in Italy. For example, if you were a bus driver and wish to drive a bus in Italy, you must obtain the appropriate Italian licence.

Non-EU Licences

Non-EU nationals resident in Italy can drive there for a year with a valid foreign licence but generally require a translation (or an international driving permit issued in their home country), which can be obtained from offices of the ACI. During this period, and before obtaining a residence permit, non-EU nationals must swap their foreign licence for an Italian licence (*patente*) or take an Italian driving test, according to whether the country in which their licence was issued has a 'reciprocity' agreement with Italy. If you live in Italy for a year without obtaining an Italian licence, you **must** take an Italian driving test (see below).

An Italian licence is valid for a maximum of ten years if you're aged under 50, five years above the age of 50 and three years if you're over 70. At the end of the licence validity period you must pass a medical examination and, if you're over 70, a medical certificate from your doctor may be required stating that you don't suffer from a medical condition that could affect your driving. If you're over 80, it can be difficult to obtain (or retain) a driving licence. The standard licence was changed in 1999 to a pink plastic credit card (*tessera*) format, which contains the EU logo in the top left-hand corner with an 'I' (for Italy) in the middle and the holder's photograph.

If you lose (i.e. mislay) an Italian licence, you must make a report (*denuncia*) to the police, where you complete a form and provide a photograph, and they will request a duplicate on your behalf. The police will issue you with a provisional licence, which is valid until you receive your new driving licence (by post), which should be within 90 days. The cost is around €40.

With Reciprocity: The following countries have reciprocity agreements with Italy, which means that driving licences from these countries are accepted for automatic conversion to an Italian licence: all EU countries, Algeria, Brazil, Bulgaria, Colombia, Costa Rica, Croatia, Cuba, Cyprus, Egypt, Haiti, Hungary, Honduras, Iran, Israel, Japan, Korea, Libya, Malaysia, Malta, Mauritius, Monaco, Morocco, Nicaragua, Norway, Oman, Panama, Philippines, San Marino, Saudi Arabia, Singapore, Slovenia, Sri Lanka, Sudan, Switzerland, Syria, Thailand, Tunisia, Turkey, United Arab Emirates and Vietnam.

If your licence was issued in any of the above countries, you aren't required to take an Italian theory or driving test, but you must apply to have your licence transcribed. To begin this process, you require:

- a valid passport or identity card and your residence permit;
- two passport photographs;
- a translation of your driving licence by an official translator with approval from the Italian courts or by one of the recognised automobile clubs in Italy;
- the original and a copy of your 'foreign' driving licence;
- an eye test certificate, not older than two years, stating that your eyesight is acceptable. Agencies for *pratiche auto* can give you the names of doctors who perform this test.

If your driving licence has been renewed since your arrival in Italy and the date it was first issued isn't noted, you need to prove that your driving history pre-dates your arrival in Italy – an expired licence or a letter from the licence issuing authority will suffice.

Conversion costs around €160 and takes around four months. You also require a medical certificate (*certificato medico*). Note that, as with anything to do with officialdom in Italy, the procedure is highly complicated and can take eons to complete. Don't attempt to handle the conversion procedures yourself unless you speak fluent Italian and have lots of spare time, but take the above documents to a *pratiche auto* agency and let them handle the application.

Without Reciprocity: If your driving licence was issued in any country other than those listed above, e.g. in Australia, Canada, New Zealand or the USA (unless you're a Canadian or US diplomat) . . . commiserations! You must take Italian written and road tests (see below).

When you've passed the tests, your driving school provides you with an Italian licence. Again you must present your passport to prove your identity and also your foreign driving licence, which is either returned with a stamp or retained. Once you have an Italian licence, your original licence is no longer valid and the Italian authorities may insist that you surrender it and, if you have one, your international driving permit (IDP). It's wise to take a photocopy of your licence or even obtain a duplicate before handing it over. Your original licence is usually returned to the authority that issued it with a note stating that you now have an Italian licence, although it may simply be stamped to that effect and returned to you. As your original licence is no longer deemed valid, neither is an IDP on which it's based. If you return to your home country, you may need to apply for an international licence based on your Italian licence, unless you can trace your old licence and have it returned in exchange for your Italian one!

Driving Test

The Italian driving test consists of a written examination and a road test. To take a driving test, you must go to a driving school, as only a licensed driving instructor can register you to take the test. Before registering for the driving test, you should decide whether you need driving lessons (e.g. if you've never driven on the right). Unfortunately, you cannot easily get objective feedback on your driving skills from a friend or neighbour, as it's illegal to drive on public roads in Italy without a licensed driving instructor or other qualified driver if you don't have a valid licence; and, as driving schools earn money every time you get behind the wheel with an instructor, some try to coerce you into additional hours by criticising your driving and saying that you aren't ready for the test. If you're an experienced driver you may need to be assertive and not allow your confidence to be undermined.

Whether or not you sign up for lessons, you must obtain a learner's licence (*foglio rosa*) before taking the driving test. A driving school will apply for this on your behalf.

If you have a foreign licence, you aren't obliged to attend the classroom sessions, as is the case for new drivers. You will, however, still need to take the written test, which must be taken in Italian. This can be difficult for foreigners (it's bad enough for Italians), many of whom fail a number of times. The written test has a multiple-choice format and any or all answers to each question can be right or wrong. Each time you answer incorrectly you lose the points allocated for that question, and to pass you cannot lose more than four points. The only way to be sure of answering correctly is to buy a complete set of all the questions and learn the answers by heart. The questions are available in book form with test sheets to practise on from driving schools and stationery shops. Don't even attempt to understand the logic of the questions and answers! You must take your passport when you go for the test, to prove your identity.

You can take your road test only after you've passed the written examination. Once again, don't forget to take your passport with you for identification. The road test is administered by an examiner who sits in the back seat and gives instructions. Your driving instructor will also be in the car (in the front seat) and the test is conducted on public roads and lasts from 10 to 15 minutes. It includes parking and performing some simple manoeuvres, e.g. a three-point turn and reversing around a corner. After you've finished, the examiner tells you whether you've passed and, if you haven't, why not. If you pass, the examiner stamps and signs the necessary documents and the driving school issues your driving licence immediately. For the first three years after passing your test, you aren't permitted to exceed 100kph (62mph) on motorways or 90kph (56mph) on main roads outside urban areas.

Learning To Drive

If you or a member of your family needs to learn to drive in Italy, you must do so through a driving school. When registering, you must provide:

- your tax code card (*codice fiscale* – see page 295);
- proof of identity such as your passport (it may be wise to take along your permit to stay or residence permit – see pages 79 and 86;
- two passport-sized photographs.

After one or two weeks you can pick up your learner's licence (*foglio rosa*) from the driving school, which you require before you can start your driving lessons. Once you have a learner's licence, you can also practise in the company of a close family member with at least five years' driving experience on all roads except motorways. In the meantime you can attend classes for the written examination, which you must pass before you can take your road test (see above).

CAR INSURANCE

All motor vehicles plus trailers and semi-trailers must be insured for third party liability when entering Italy. It isn't mandatory for cars insured in most European countries to have an international insurance 'green' card (British drivers are, however, recommended to obtain one). Vehicles insured in an EU country, the Czech Republic, Hungary, Liechtenstein, Norway, the Slovak Republic and Switzerland are usually automatically covered for third party liability in Italy when visiting the country. If you have comprehensive insurance in Italy and plan to drive abroad, however, you should obtain a green card (*carta verde*) from your insurance company, which is usually provided free of charge. A green card is compulsory for Andorra, Bulgaria, Poland and Romania and strongly recommended for Greece, Portugal, Spain and Turkey. Many insurers offer breakdown assistance (*assistenza e soccorso stradale*) as a supplement, which is useful if you aren't already covered, e.g. by a motoring organisation.

Insurance premiums are high in Italy, reflecting the high accident rate, the large number of stolen cars and the lack of competition; they can €1,000 per year, even with the maximum no-claims bonus. In theory, you aren't required to insure your car with an Italian insurance company or an insurance company in Italy and can insure it with any company in any EU member state, provided the company is licensed to do business in Italy. In practice, however, it may be difficult or impossible to persuade a foreign insurer to insure your car in Italy.

There are several levels of car insurance in Italy, including the following.

- **Third Party:** The basic category of car insurance is third party (*responsabilità civile* – commonly referred to as *RC auto*), which is the minimum required by law and compulsory for all motor vehicles. This covers you for the cost of third party damage or injury in accidents for which you're to blame. The compulsory minimum cover for private cars in Italy is €775,000 per accident, irrespective of the number of victims or the nature of the injury or damage. However, it's wise to take out a policy with a much higher level of cover than this – at least €2.5 million. Most insurance companies offer cover up to ten times the legal minimum, and there may be no maximum limit.

  Note that the car and not the driver is insured in Italy. Therefore, if you wish to have personal cover in an accident for which you're responsible, you must have additional cover called *infortunio del conducente*.

- **Third Party, Fire & Theft:** Third party, fire and theft insurance (*assicurazione contro terzi furto e incendio*), which is called part-comprehensive in some countries, can be added to your third party insurance for an additional fee.

- **Collision Cover:** This pays for damage to your car in the event of an accident for which you're responsible.

- **Comprehensive Cover:** Comprehensive insurance (*casco*) includes collision and non-collision damage to a vehicle, such as falling rocks or vandalism. Non-collision damage may also be included in third party, fire and theft cover, so check when you take out your policy. Comprehensive insurance doesn't provide the same level of cover as in many other countries and doesn't include injuries to passengers, although family members travelling as passengers can be included for an additional fee. Note that comprehensive cover is a separate policy from third party or collision insurance and doesn't need to be taken out with the same insurance company.

Insurance is available from many sources, including direct insurance companies and brokers. Shop around (you can do this via the Internet at 🖥 www. diagramma.it – see also **Insurance Agents & Companies** on page 273) as rates vary considerably; however, if you find a particularly low premium, it's wise to check that important benefits haven't been excluded. Premiums vary considerably according to a range of factors, including the type of insurance, a vehicle's horsepower, your age and driving (and accident) record, the province where you live, whether your car is garaged overnight and the maximum compensation to be paid out to a third party in the event of a claim. Premiums are based on a points system whereby points are allocated for the above factors. VAT at 20 per cent is payable on policies.

Italian insurance companies maintain tables showing the value of different models of various ages. Except for new cars, their values are around 20 per cent lower than the market value and they pay compensation only according to those values. It's therefore important to check that a vehicle isn't over-insured.

Car insurance policies are valid for a year and must usually be cancelled two months before the renewal date (in writing by registered post), or the policy is automatically extended for a further year. If you haven't paid your renewal premium within ten days of the expiry date, you're deemed to be driving without insurance. If you're changing insurance companies, the new company will be happy to cancel your old policy for you and will usually give you a standard letter to sign. It's important to shop around for the best deal each time your insurance comes up for renewal.

No-claims discounts apply only to third party and comprehensive cover. You're placed in a no-claims 'class' according to your number of years' insurance without a claim. For each claim-free year you're automatically moved into a higher class, although the maximum premium reduction is just 30 per cent. If you're involved in an accident for which you're deemed wholly or partly at fault, you may lose some or your entire no-claims bonus. If you're a young (e.g. under 25) or inexperienced driver or have a poor accident record, you may be required to pay a penalty (*malus*) or an excess (e.g. €250) on each claim.

Your insurance certificate must be displayed behind your vehicle's windscreen; while you're waiting for your official insurance documentation, you can display your receipt as proof of insurance.

There used to be a number of dubious companies providing car insurance in Italy; they charged low premiums but used delaying tactics to avoid paying claims – ever! Although these companies have mostly been weeded out, Italian insurers can still be **very** slow to pay in the event of accidents (especially serious ones) and a delay of six months or longer isn't uncommon.

If a car is repaired after a fire, vandalism or an accident, the insurer pays the labour cost in full (less any excess specified in the policy) but doesn't pay the full cost of any new parts because the parts replaced weren't new. Therefore it would be beneficial from an owner's point of view, for example, to have a dent in a door repaired rather than replace the door with a new one, even if the latter would actually cost less in labour! The catch is that the insurance company's assessor (*perito*) may make his estimate according to the cheaper suggestion anyway and he may not accept in full the bill or estimate you present. The difference between what he accepts and the cost of repairing a car may be as high as 20 per cent, even in a straightforward case. For this reason, most Italians don't claim for minor accidents (which would also affect their no-claims discount) or even bother to have the damage repaired.

If an accident is caused by an uninsured or unidentifiable car, under EU law you're entitled to compensation from the motor vehicle guarantee fund of the member state in which the accident occurred, in accordance with the rules in that country. The fund also covers motorists whose insurance company was being compulsorily wound up at the time of an accident or is put into compulsory liquidation some time thereafter.

Breakdown Insurance

Breakdown insurance in Italy and other European countries is provided by Italian car insurance companies and motoring organisations (see page 247). If you're motoring abroad or you live abroad and are motoring in Italy, it's important to have car breakdown insurance, which may be combined with holiday and travel insurance (see page 289), including repatriation for your family and your car in the event of an accident or breakdown. Most foreign breakdown companies provide multilingual, 24-hour centres where assistance is available for motoring, medical, legal or travel problems.

SPEED LIMITS

Speed limits in Italy change frequently. The general motorway (*autostrada*) speed limit is currently 130kph (81mph) for vehicles with an engine capacity of over 1,100cc. Vehicles with smaller engines and motorcycles with engines below 150cc are restricted to 110kph (68mph). Cars towing caravans or trailers are limited to 100kph (62mph) on motorways. There's a proposal to reduce maximum speeds on motorways at weekends and busy holiday periods such as Easter, Christmas and during the summer, but it has yet to be put into effect.

On regional highways the general speed limit is 110kph (68mph), although cars towing caravans or trailers are limited to 80kph (50mph); on secondary local roads it's 90kph (56mph), but it may be lower for certain stretches of road. In urban and populated areas the general speed limit is 50kph (31mph), which is sometimes reduced to 30kph (20mph), e.g. near schools or hospitals. Note that if you see a sign indicating 'end of speed limit', it doesn't mean that there's no speed limit, just that the general speed limit for the type of road now applies.

Speed limits are widely ignored in Italy, where people often drive at 150kph (93mph) or faster where the speed limit is just 90kph. However, the road police (*polizia stradale*) are introducing new electronic speed-testing equipment and plan to crack down on offenders; new regulations introduced in 2000 included fines of around €110 irrespective of how much your speed was above the limit. You can lose your licence if you're caught speeding three times or exceed the limit by more than 40kph (25mph).

ROAD SIGNS

Italy generally adheres to the international standard road signs. With some minor exceptions, most signs conform to these standard shapes and colours:

Colour/Shape	Function
Red triangle	Warning
Red circle	Restriction
Blue circle	Requirement
Square/rectangle	Guidance
Diamond	Priority
Octagon	Stop

Italian road signs generally use words sparingly. Some of those you're most likely to come across are shown below:

Italian	English
Accendere le luci/i fari (in galleria)	Use headlights (in tunnel)
Alt polizia	Halt – police checkpoint
Alt stazione	Halt – toll station on motorway
Area pedonale	Pedestrian area
Attenzione	Caution
Caduta massi	Falling rocks
Casello a *** Metri	Toll in *** metres
Curve	Bends ahead
Dare precendenza	Give way
Deviazione	Diversion (detour)
Divieto di accesso	No entry
Divieto di sorpasso	No overtaking
Divieto di sosta	No stopping
Divieto di transitio	No right of way
Entrata	Entrance
Incrocio	Crossroads
Lavori in corso	Road works ahead
Passagio a livello	Level crossing
Pedaggio	Toll

Pedoni	Pedestrians
Pericolo	Danger
Rallentare	Slow
Senso unico	One-way street
Senso vietato	No entry
Sosta autorizzata	Parking permitted
Sosta vietata	No parking
Strada ghiacciata	Icy road
Svolta	Bend
Tenere la destra	Keep to the right
Transito interrotto	No through road
Uscita (camion)	Exit (for trucks)
Veicoli al passo	Dead slow
Velocità controllata electtronicamente	Electronic speed checks
Vietato l'ingresso ai veicoli	No entry for vehicles
Zona di silenzio	Silence zone (i.e. use of horns forbidden)
Zona tutelata	Restricted parking zone (see **Parking** on page 240)

GENERAL ROAD RULES

The following general road rules may help you adjust to driving in Italy:

- When motoring outside the country where your car is registered, your vehicle must display either the new EU-style number-plates, which incorporate a letter or letters showing the country of registration and 12 yellow stars in a circle, or a separate nationality sticker alongside the rear number plate. You can be fined on the spot for not displaying this, although judging by the number of cars that fail to do so, this law is seldom enforced. Cars must show only the correct nationality sticker and not an assortment. Foreigners living in Italy often like to emphasise their nationality by displaying their nationality sticker (or maybe it's an attempt at self-protection), which is illegal but seems to be tolerated.

- All motorists must carry a red breakdown triangle (*triangolo*), which must be placed 50 to 200m (164 to 656ft) behind a stationary vehicle, depending on the type of road (see **Accidents** on page 242). It's recommended also to carry a spare set of bulbs/fuses, a fire extinguisher and a first-aid kit.

- If you need to wear spectacles or contact lenses when motoring, it will be noted on your Italian driving licence and you must always wear them **and** carry a spare pair.

- The wearing of seat-belts is compulsory in Italy and includes passengers in both front and rear seats. Children up to the age of 12 and less than 1.5m (4.92ft) tall must use an approved safety seat or a safety belt suitable for their age. You can be fined €32 on-the-spot for not wearing a seat belt. **If you have an accident and aren't wearing a seat belt, your insurance company can refuse to pay a claim for personal injury.**

- You may already have noticed that the Italians drive on the right (when not driving in the middle!). It saves confusion if you do likewise. If you aren't used to driving on the right, take it easy until you're accustomed to it. Be particularly alert when leaving lay-bys, T-junctions, one-way streets, petrol stations and car parks, as it's easy to lapse into driving on the left. It's helpful to display a reminder (e.g. 'Think Right!') on your car's dashboard.

- Most main roads are designated priority (*dare precedenza*) roads, indicated by a sign. The most common priority sign is a yellow diamond on a white background, in use throughout most of continental Europe. The end of priority is shown by the same sign with a black diagonal line through it. On secondary roads without priority signs and in built-up areas, you must give way to vehicles coming from your RIGHT. **Failure to observe this rule is the cause of many accidents.** The priority rule was fine when there was little traffic, but nowadays most countries (Italy included) realise the necessity of having 'stop' or 'give way' (*dare la precedenza*) signs at junctions. Most motorists no longer treat priority as a God-given right, although some still pull out without looking. The priority to the right rule usually also applies in car parks, but not when exiting from car parks or dirt tracks. If you're ever in doubt about who has priority, give way to trams, buses and all traffic coming from your RIGHT. Emergency (ambulance, fire, police) and public utility (electricity, gas and water) vehicles attending an emergency have priority on all roads.

- On roundabouts (traffic circles or rotaries), vehicles entering them usually have priority and not those already on it. However, this rule is changing to conform with other EU countries, where vehicles on roundabouts have priority and traffic entering is faced with a give way or stop sign. You're likely to encounter both types in Italy, so take care. Traffic flows anti-clockwise round roundabouts and not clockwise as in Britain and other countries where driving is on the left.

- The sequence of Italian traffic lights (*semaforo*) is red, green, yellow (amber) and back to red. There's no red-and-amber phase after red. Yellow means stop at the stop line; you may proceed only if the yellow light appears after you've crossed the stop line or when stopping may cause an accident. You can be fined around €60 for jumping (running) a red light (or get a ticket to the next life!), which nevertheless is a national sport in Italy. (It has been said that traffic lights in Italy are merely decorative and suggestive).

- At traffic lights, a yellow or green filter light – usually flashing and with a direction arrow – may be shown in addition to the main signal. This means that you may drive in the direction shown by the arrow, but must give priority to pedestrians or other traffic. If you get into the wrong lane by mistake, you will no doubt be informed by the irate honking of motorists behind you! Flashing yellow lights are a warning to proceed with caution and are often used at crossroads during periods when traffic is light (e.g. after midnight); you must give priority to traffic coming from your right.

- For left turns off a main road with traffic lights, there's often a marked filter lane or circle to the **right**, taking you to a junction where you cross the main road at right angles (indicated by a stop sign or traffic lights).

- Always come to a complete stop when required at junctions and ensure that you stop behind the white line – junctions are a favourite spot for police patrols waiting for motorists to put a wheel a few centimetres over the line.

- Don't drive in bus, taxi or cycle lanes (unless you're an Italian) as you can be fined for doing so, although it's permitted when necessary to avoid a stationary vehicle or an obstruction. Be sure to keep clear of tram lines and outside the restricted area, shown by lines on the road. Trams **always** have priority over other vehicles.

- The use of horns is forbidden in cities and areas indicated by a 'silence zone' (*zona di silenzio*) sign. However, it's tolerated by wedding parties, New Year's Eve revellers, football fans (e.g. when AC Milan have won the European Champions League, as they did in 2003), cars trapped by large vehicles or double/treble parked cars, to wake drowsy drivers at traffic lights, etc.. A car travelling at high speed with the horn permanently blaring and a white handkerchief or cloth waving from the window usually means that someone in the car is in need of urgent medical attention and drivers should clear the way as they would for an ambulance.

- Dipped (low beam) headlights must be used from half an hour after sunset to half an hour before sunrise. They're also required in tunnels, fog, snowstorms and heavy rain and when visibility is less than 200m (656ft). It's illegal to drive with only side (parking) lights at any time. Front fog or spotlights must be fitted in pairs at a regulation height and should be used only when visibility is less than 50m (164ft). Full beam can be used only outside cities and towns, and when no vehicles are approaching. When a stationary vehicle isn't clearly visible, side lights must be switched on.

- Headlight flashing, although strictly for warning purposes only, has different meanings in Italy according to the situation. It may mean 'After you, my friend', 'Get out of the ****** way!', 'Idiot!', 'I want to overtake you (but you're driving in the left-hand lane)', 'Your headlights are on in daylight', 'Your headlights aren't on at night', 'Hi babe!', 'There's a police checkpoint ahead', or any combination of these. Evaluate the situation before responding.

● White or yellow lines mark the separation of traffic lanes. A solid single line or two solid lines means no overtaking (*sorpassare*) in either direction. A solid line to the right of the centre line, i.e. on your side of the road, means that overtaking is prohibited in your direction. You may overtake only when there's a single broken line in the middle of the road or double lines with a broken line on your side of the road. No overtaking may also be shown by the international road sign of two cars side by side (one red and one black). Always check your rear view and wing mirrors carefully before overtaking, as Italian motorists often appear from nowhere and zoom past at a 'zillion' miles an hour, particularly on country roads. If you drive a right-hand drive (RHD) car, take extra care when overtaking – the most dangerous manoeuvre in motoring. It's wise to have a special 'overtaking mirror' fitted to an RHD car.

● Mopeds (*ciclomotore* or *motorini*) and scooters are extremely popular in Italy and are excellent for getting around cities but a menace if you're a motorist. You should be particularly wary of moped riders and cyclists, as it isn't always easy to see them, particularly when they're hidden by the blind spots of a car or are riding at night without lights. Many young moped riders seem to have a death wish and tragically hundreds lose their lives annually. They're constantly pulling out into traffic or turning without looking or signalling. **Follow the example set by Italian motorists, who when overtaking mopeds and cyclists, ALWAYS give them a wide ... WIDE berth.** If you knock them off their bikes, you may have a difficult time convincing the police that it wasn't your fault; far better to avoid them (and the police).

● When two vehicles meet on a narrow mountain road, the ascending vehicle has priority and the other must give way or reverse as necessary. On roads where passing is difficult or isn't allowed, slower traffic is required to pull over when possible to allow faster traffic to pass.

● On-the-spot fines can be imposed for traffic offences such as minor speeding, not being in possession of the required documents (i.e. vehicle registration certificate, driving licence, receipt for your road tax payment, insurance certificate, and safety inspection and emissions test certificates), not removing your ignition key when leaving a vehicle unattended, driving at night on side lights and parking infringements. If you wish to contest a fine, you must still deposit half the amount of a fine in cash.

● Anything hanging off the end of a vehicle (e.g. a bicycle) must be tagged with a reflective red-and-white striped plate 50cm (20in) square, which are available from motoring shops in Italy. You can be fined up to €55 if you fail to observe this law.

● It's illegal to use a mobile phone when driving except with a 'hands-free' system.

- The following rules apply to motorways (*autostrade*):

  - Vehicles with a maximum speed of less than 60kph (35mph) are prohibited from using motorways, as are bicycles, mopeds and pedestrians.

  - Overtaking on the right on a motorway is prohibited! The only exception is if you're entering a motorway faster than the traffic in the inside lane. Slower vehicles must move to the right to allow faster traffic to overtake (unless travelling at the speed limit). The left-hand lane is only for overtaking and, as soon as you have completed your manoeuvre, you must return to the right-hand lane. Unfortunately, overtaking on the right is common, so you should always ensure that nobody is overtaking you on the right before changing lanes.

  - Stopping (other than when broken down or in an emergency), parking, U-turns and reversing are prohibited, including on hard sliproads and hard shoulders. You can be fined €55 for doing so.

  - During traffic jams, motorists must leave the hard shoulder free for emergency vehicles.

- All motorists in Italy must be familiar with the Italian 'highway code', which is published as a guide (*guida pratica alla soluzione dei nuovi quiz ministeriali*) for each category of licence.

- Take particular care when crossing the road, even when using a pedestrian crossing, as drivers aren't required to stop, only to slow down – being hit by a 'slow' truck or bus can still kill you! Cross quickly when and where there's plenty of space for drivers to see you and reduce speed or stop as necessary.

ITALIAN ROADS

The Italian road network is subdivided into four categories: motorways (*autostrade*), national highways (*strade statali*), provincial roads (*strade provinciali*) and municipal roads (*strade comunali*).

Motorways

Italy has an excellent motorway (*autostrada*) network covering around 6,000km (3,700mi), most of which are toll (*pedaggio*) roads, although there are some 1,000km (620mi) of free 'expressways' (*superstrade*) around cities. Italy lays claim to having Europe's first motorway, which was built between Milan and Venice in the 1930s. Today, the main north-south route is the *Autostrada del Sole* from Milan to Reggio di Calabria (via Bologna, Florence, Rome and Naples), designated the A1 from Milan to Naples and the A3 from Naples to Reggio di Calabria (the latter stretch being toll-free). Given Italy's mountainous terrain, the country's motorways include many spectacular bridges and tunnels, especially in the Alps in the north of the country.

Motorway tolls depend on the official horsepower rating (*cavalli fiscali*) of your car (not necessarily its actual horsepower) or the wheelbase and number of axles and on the company operating the toll. The rate per kilometre varies but for a standard car is usually around 5 cents per km. On most motorways you collect a ticket when you start your journey and pay when you leave the motorway. On some stretches, however, there are fixed charges that are payable at the start of your journey. Tolls can be paid in euros and most major currencies, including pounds sterling, Swiss francs and US dollars. However, you usually receive a poor rate of exchange, so you're better off paying in euros. Credit cards are usually accepted, but don't take it for granted. When paying by credit card, look for a lane with a large sign showing a depiction of credit cards. Insert the toll ticket first (with the arrow pointing forward) followed by your credit card with the hologram outward. To obtain a receipt, push the red button after removing your credit card.

Some companies offer season tickets at reduced rates and you can also buy a Viacard (like a telephone smartcard) at some motorway tolls, bars, restaurants and certain banks (costing from € 30 to €50). This makes paying tolls easier and faster, as you can use reserved lanes. Alternatively you can obtain a Telepass that requires a sensor to be installed in your car, which records the distance you travel on toll roads when you pass through the Telepass gates. You're billed by direct debit from a bank account. Note that Viacards and Telepasses aren't available on all motorways.

If you plan to travel long distances on the motorway network, the Autostrade Spa website (🖳 www.autostrade.it) will prove invaluable. It provides information in English about routes, tolls and service stations, traffic forecasts and interactive maps.

Emergency phones are placed on yellow posts every 2km (1.25mi) on motorways, some of which have separate buttons for breakdowns (depicted by a spanner) and injuries (shown by a red cross). Simply press the appropriate button and wait for help to arrive. There are service stations at around 25km (15mi) intervals on motorways, where you can have minor repairs carried out.

Other Roads

State roads (*strade statali*) are major roads indicated by blue signs and shown on maps with the prefix 'SS' followed by a number. They're often multi-lane, dual-carriageway roads and although slower than motorways, have no tolls. Many *strade statali* follow the routes planned by the ancient Romans, including the famous consular routes, which have illustrious names such as the Via Appia, Via Pontina and Via Flaminia. Provincial roads (*strade provinciali*), also with blue signs, are shown on maps as 'SP' and vary considerably in quality; they may be little more than rough tracks in some areas. The lowest grade are 'community roads' (*strade comunali*) with white signs, which are maintained by the local communes they serve. Unlike motorways, state roads and most provincial roads community roads aren't numbered.

Most cities have a ring road (*cerchia dei navigli*), but access to the centre is often restricted to certain vehicles and there may also be a limited number of access routes and one-way systems where you can get lost for weeks. Road navigation in cities can be chaotic and traffic moves at a crawl – if it moves at all; you're recommended to park on the outskirts and use public transport to reach and get around city centres. In some cities, e.g. Milan, car parks are strategically placed on the edge of the city near major metro stations.

Driving in Italian cities, especially Naples, can be a nightmare and is best avoided. Traffic congestion and pollution in Italian cities are among the worst in Europe and consequently a pass is now required to enter many historic city centres (*centro storico*), which is available only to residents and local businesses. Some cities (such as Milan) have introduced a system whereby only vehicles whose registration number ends in an even digit may enter the city on even dates and vehicles with an odd number on odd dates. In some cities, only vehicles with a catalytic converter (*marmitta catalitica*) running on lead-free petrol are allowed to enter the city centre. Rome passed a 'blue band' (*fascia blu*) law in recent years banning most vehicles from the city centre, which has allowed local residents to breathe something resembling air once again. If the air pollution level in the centre of Rome rises above a certain limit, additional restrictions can be temporarily introduced for a few days at a time. Since January 2000, no cars without catalytic converters have been allowed to enter the ring formed by the main railway lines around Rome.

Italy has a number of toll tunnels, including Mont Blanc and Frejus between Italy and France, both around 11km (7mi) in length, and the Gran San Bernardino linking Italy and Switzerland. The fee is from around €15 one way for a small car (up to 2.3m/7.5ft between axles). Note that many mountain passes are closed in winter.

Road conditions can be checked 24-hours per day by calling the ACI (☎ 06-4477); motorway traffic conditions can be checked by dialling ☎ 055-2697.

WINTER DRIVING

If you drive in winter in northern Italy when snow, ice and fog are commonplace, take it easy! Fog is a common problem in northern Italy and is the cause of many multiple car accidents. In poor conditions, most Italian drivers slow down considerably and even the habitual tailgaters leave a larger gap than usual (at least a metre!). A light snowfall can be treacherous, particularly on an icy road. When road conditions are bad, you should allow two to three times longer than usual to reach your destination (if you're wise, you will stay at home). Note that many mountain passes are closed in winter (check with the ACI).

You may need to use snow chains (*catene da neve*) in winter in mountain areas – or in any area where there's heavy snow. (When it last snowed heavily in Rome, in 1985, shops sold out of snow chains and chaos reigned for around three days – but at least the Romans drove carefully for a while!) For the uninitiated, putting on snow chains can be an unpleasant task. Usually you lay the chains on the road (or snow or ice) and drive onto them. Then you kneel down and try to link the ends above the wheel. Your knees become cold and wet unless you have some sort of plastic sheet to kneel on, and feeling around for the bit of chain in ice and snow makes your fingers go numb, thus adding to the difficulty. Once you leave the area where snow chains are required, you can look forward to performing the process in reverse. Bear in mind that snow chains must be fitted on the wheels that are driven, depending on whether the vehicle is front or rear-wheel drive (on a four-wheel drive vehicle you can choose front or rear).

If you live in an area of Italy where snow is common in winter, e.g. in the mountains or in the north, you need to purchase snow tyres, which have tiny metal studs embedded in the rubber. With these you can drive all winter and you don't even need to fit them yourself, as any tyre supplier (*gommista*) will do it for you. The regulations regarding the use of snow tyres vary with the province, so check with a local garage or ACI office.

ITALIAN DRIVERS

Many newcomers to Italy, even those used to driving on the right, find the Italian way of driving frightening and undisciplined. If you have ever seen a demolition derby, you will have some idea of Italian driving, the main difference being that demo drivers are much more skilled and there are far fewer fatalities. The foreigner's first impression is that Italian drivers pay no attention to speed limits, have little or no concept of lane discipline, and stop at red lights or pedestrian crossings only in a dire emergency. However, although the 'rules' of the road (i.e. the conventions rather than the legal regulations – see **General Road Rules** on page 231) aren't always obvious or what you may be used to, they do exist. In fact, Italians are often alarmed at the way some foreigners drive.

Not surprisingly, Italy has one of the highest road accident rates in the European Union, although the death rate (around 7,000 per year) is relatively low considering the number of accidents. Poor discipline, lack of enforcement, inadequate road laws and the Italians' frenetic driving style all combine to create havoc. In this chaos, the only thing that saves the day is the Italian flexibility. Everyone tries to keep the traffic moving and accommodate other drivers and their intentions, however stupid. To show clearly what you want to do and then do it is the basic principle of city driving in Italy – even if it means driving the wrong way down a one-way street!

Driving in Italy is the survival of the fittest and it isn't a place for the faint-hearted. What makes driving in Italy even more of a lottery is that for many months of the year the roads are liberally sprinkled with foreigners whose driving habits vary from exemplary to suicidal and include many (such as the British) who don't even know which side of the road to drive on. The best way to introduce yourself to driving in major cities in Italy is to buy a second-hand car with a number of dents that show it has 'lived'; Italians will then give way more readily, as they respect veterans.

One quality most Italian drivers have in common is an inability to know when to slow down, and they're notorious for their impatience. (The shortest unit of time in Italy is said to be the period between traffic lights changing to green and the driver behind you honking his horn.) In Italy a red light is generally viewed as a sign to take care rather than stop, and some (colour blind?) drivers simply drive through them (particularly in Naples, the motoring anarchists' spiritual home).

When not overtaking, Italian drivers may sit a few metres from your bumper trying to push you along irrespective of traffic density, road and weather conditions, or the prevailing speed limit. Italians are among Europe's worst tailgaters and there's no solution, short of moving out of their way or stopping, which is often impossible. Always try to leave a large gap between your vehicle and the one in front. This isn't just to give you more time to stop should the vehicles in front decide to brake suddenly, but also to give the inevitable tailgater behind you more time to stop as well. The closer the car is behind you, the further you should be from the vehicle in front. On motorways and main roads, you must (by law) keep a safe distance from the vehicle in front and can be fined for not doing so. You should avoid the outside lane on motorways, unless you're prepared to drive at least 150kph (93mph).

Nevertheless, although many Italian drivers are reckless (or worse), in general they aren't as bad as their reputation may suggest, and many are actually good drivers.

MOTORCYCLES

To ride a motorcycle or moped (*motorino*) with an engine size of up to 50cc, you must be at least 14 years old. No licence is required, but a bike must be registered before it's permitted on public roads. The registration procedure is the same as for cars (see page 218) and, as with cars, moped licences are personal, so when selling a moped you must keep the registration plate. The rider must also carry proof of his age and the bike must be insured against third party claims. It has been suggested that a licence will be required in the future, so check this before buying a child a moped. Since January 2000, all riders of mopeds have had to wear a safety helmet (*casco*), and moped riders are prohibited from carrying passengers, although these are among many Italian laws which are flouted and it's common to see youths riding with a friend on board and no helmets, to which the police often turn a blind eye.

Many teenage moped riders are killed each year in Italy, where moped accidents are the number one cause of death for people under 24. If you have a child with a moped, it's important to impress upon him the need to take care (particularly in winter) and not take unnecessary risks, e.g. always observe traffic signals, signal before making manoeuvres and wear a crash helmet.

To ride a motorcycle over 50cc, you must have a motorcycle licence (Class A), for which the minimum age is 16. Up to the age of 18, you're limited to motorcycles with an engine capacity of under 125cc, after which there's no restriction. **As in other European countries, a standard car driving licence (Class B) no longer qualifies you to drive motorcycles as well.**

Like a car, a motorcycle must also pass a technical inspection every two years. If you're considering buying a motorcycle, bear in mind that there's likely to be an extra tax on those without catalytic converters in future. Motorcyclists and passengers must wear helmets and are required to use dipped (low beam) headlights at all times. You must also have at least third party insurance when driving a motorcycle and carry proof with you.

PARKING

Parking in Italy can be a challenge, particularly in large cities, where it's often so difficult to find a parking space that near anarchy rules (in cities, a car is a device used to create parking spaces). Cars are frequently parked in no parking areas, half or completely on the pavement and even double-parked, with the car owner usually in a shop nearby. The only place where a 'no parking' sign is usually respected is in front of busy exits and entrances, although even here someone may leave a car briefly while popping into a shop next door. Parking on pedestrian crossings or on corners, although prohibited, is commonplace in most Italian cities, although not in smaller towns. In most European countries you must park at least 5m (16ft) from a pedestrian crossing, but if such a regulation ever existed in Italy it has long since been forgotten and isn't enforced.

In Rome, the sign *zona tutelata* indicates that parking is prohibited from 7.30am until 6.30pm on weekdays and there are strict penalties for illegal parking. In Milan, entry to the city centre is restricted, and parking (even for residents) can be prohibitively expensive. In Florence, all vehicles are banned from the city centre between from 7.30am and 6.30pm on weekdays, apart from those loading or unloading. Parking in Naples and some other cities in southern Italy isn't recommended if you ever hope to see your car again and it's better to park some distance from the city and use public transport. (Driving in Naples is, in any case, an experience most motorists will never forget!)

Some cities have also introduced green zones (*zona verde*), where parking is prohibited between 8 and 9.30am and from 2.30 to 4pm on weekdays. You must usually park on the right-hand side of the road in a two-way street, but parking may be restricted to odd and even-numbered days on one side of a street, or it may be restricted to local residents. In some cities, parking and parking restrictions are indicated by coloured kerb stones, e.g. blue means parking is permitted (but you must pay), while yellow may mean parking is permitted for residents only or is prohibited.

In many cities there are blue zones (*zona a disco*) where you must display a parking disk behind your windscreen between 9am and 2.30pm and from 4 to 8pm from Mondays to Saturdays (except public holidays). Parking disks resemble a cardboard clock and are available free or for a nominal cost from petrol stations, motor accessory shops, tourist offices and motoring organisations. You must turn the dial to your time of arrival and are permitted to stay for up to an hour free of charge.

In recent years, some cities have introduced paid parking zones. In these areas, which are usually marked with blue lines, you must find a ticket machine where you buy a ticket (e.g. €1 per hour) and display it behind the dashboard. You must return and move your car when the period you've paid for has expired and aren't permitted to buy another ticket without moving your car. Note that ticket machines accept only coins, so you should carry a supply of euro coins. During the summer, some resorts provide parking areas close to the beach, usually marked with blue lines, where a youth on a moped drives around and collects the fixed parking fee. This varies but is usually a maximum of around €3 per day.

In cities and towns there are also multi-storey car parks and underground garages, although parking can be expensive. Some shopping arcades have free parking spaces for customers, as do certain shops, hotels and restaurants. There are reserved parking spaces for disabled motorists in major towns and cities, although they aren't common or always respected by other drivers. Parking permits for the disabled are issued by the local office for invalid permits (Ufficio Permessi Invalidi).

DRINKING & DRIVING

Although it may sometimes appear as if there are no laws against drinking and driving in Italy, this is definitely not the case! You're considered unfit to drive if you have more than 80mg of alcohol per 100ml of blood (there are calls to reduce it to 50mg, in line with most of the EU), which means that most people can drink no more than two or three small beers or glasses of wine. In recent years there has been a marked increase in serious accidents with drunken drivers late at night. These are often caused by youths who race each other after a night at a disco. As a result, the police have become more serious in their attitude towards drinking and driving. The police can stop and breathalyse drivers at random and, if you're involved in an accident and they suspect that you're under the influence of alcohol or drugs, they're authorised to carry out tests.

If you're found to be over the limit, you will be heavily fined (if you're unable to pay it, you may find yourself facing a jail sentence of up to five years) and your driving licence will be suspended for a period. Driving under the influence of drugs is also taken seriously and, if you're found driving with traces of marijuana, hashish or cocaine in your system, you lose your licence for at least a year. Penalty points are also allocated to your licence, a fine imposed and you need to undergo a psychological examination before you receive your licence back. (Licence penalty points are currently imposed only for drunken driving, although it's proposed to extend the system to other driving offences, as in France.)

Having an accident while under the influence of drink or drugs can also be expensive. Your insurance company isn't obliged to pay for damage to your car or any other vehicle that you damage, and you can be held personally liable for all medical expenses and property damage resulting from the accident.

If you want to enjoy a few drinks, it's therefore wise to have a driver who remains sober – or to take a taxi.

ACCIDENTS

Knowing the correct procedure in case of an accident (*incidente*) is important in Italy, where **motorists who see an accident are required by law to stop and render assistance.** This is as follows:

1. Stop and secure the scene of the accident.
2. Attend to the injured.
3. Call for help.

If your car is damaged or you're involved in an accident, stop immediately and pull over to the side of the road if possible. Place your red warning triangle (*triangolo*) at the edge of the road at least 50m (164ft) behind your car on secondary roads, 100m (328ft) on major roads, and 200m (656ft) on motorways. If necessary, e.g. when the road is partly or totally blocked, switch on your car's hazard warning lights and dipped (low beam) headlights, and direct traffic around the hazard.

If anyone is injured, call immediately for emergency help. The general number for the emergency services is 113, but for a quicker response call 112 for the police (*carabinieri*) or 118 for an ambulance. If someone is trapped, or oil or chemicals have been spilt, dial 115 for the fire brigade. If someone has been injured more than superficially, the police **must** be notified. Don't move an injured person unless absolutely necessary and don't leave him alone except to call for help. Cover him with a blanket or coat to keep warm.

If there are no injuries, and damage to vehicles or property is minor, it isn't essential to summon the police to an accident scene. (If you're involved in an accident with an Italian – a likely occurrence in Italy – you should wait ten minutes for him to calm down and stop berating you for denting his pride and joy, even if he was to blame.) However, it's usually recommended to call them and obtain an official report unless all parties have signed an accident declaration form (*costatazione amichevole di incidente/CID*) for your respective insurance companies. If you cannot agree, you should play safe and call the police. When the police arrive, under no circumstances should you admit guilt, even if you know you were in the wrong. Stick to telling what happened and let the police and insurance companies decide who was at fault. **If you admit responsibility, either verbally or in writing, it can absolve your insurance company from responsibility for paying a claim under your policy.** In any case, an Italian driver never admits that he is to blame – at least not straight away; even if he has hit driven into the back of your car while you're waiting in a queue, it's obviously your fault – you shouldn't have been there!

If the other driver has obviously been drinking or appears incapable of driving, call the police immediately! Don't sign any police statements unless you understand and agree with every word. The *carabinieri*'s report is usually available after a few days. They may fine one or all parties in varying proportions according to their deemed culpability. The insurance company then pays compensation according to the proportion of blame assigned to their client.

If either you or the other driver(s) involved decide to call the police, avoid moving the vehicles unless they present a traffic hazard. If they must be moved, record their positions before moving them by taking photographs, making drawings or marking their positions on the road. The accident form from your insurance company requires drawings of the positions of all vehicles involved, so it's recommended to have the situation clear on paper rather than just in your memory (which can go blank after an accident).

Check whether there are any witnesses to the accident and try to obtain their names and addresses, making a particular note of those who support your version of events. Note the registration numbers of all vehicles involved and their drivers' names, registration numbers, addresses and insurers. In return, you're expected to give the same information to any other drivers involved.

Use your insurance company form to report an accident involving your car, even if the other party is clearly at fault and agrees to pay the damages. If you don't report it and the other party later withdraws his admission or offer to pay damages, your insurance company can refuse your claim if you haven't previously filed a report with them. Don't forget to sign it and to obtain a new accident report form.

Note that minor scratches and dents are a way of life in Italy, where they aren't considered as 'accidents' but normal wear and tear. Inevitably you will accumulate them simply by parking your car in a street or a car park. Most Italians don't make a fuss over these and have them repaired when they've accumulated a reasonable number of them or need a major repair – or even ignore them altogether and wear them proudly as the scars of their daily battle on Italy's streets.

If you're the victim of a hit-and-run accident, report it to the local police immediately. If possible, summon them to the accident scene before moving your car. They will inspect your vehicle and take photographs and paint samples, which will assist with an insurance claim as well as help to find the culprit.

CAR CRIME

Most European countries have a problem with car crime, i.e. thefts of and from cars, and Italy is no exception. If you drive anything other than a worthless heap, you should have theft insurance, which includes your car stereo and belongings. New vehicles should be fitted with an alarm, an engine immobiliser of the rolling code variety (the best system) or another anti-theft device, plus a visible deterrent, such as a steering or gear stick lock. It's particularly important to protect your car if you own a model that's desirable to professional car thieves, e.g. most new sports and executive models, which are often stolen by crooks to order.

Few cars are fitted with deadlocks and most can be broken into in seconds by a competent thief; even the best security system won't usually prevent someone from breaking into your car and may not stop your car from being stolen, but it at least makes it more difficult and may persuade a thief to look for an easier target.

Windows are often broken to steal a car's contents (in Italy, BMW stands for 'break my window') and it happens so often that they can be replaced while you wait in major cities. When leaving your car unattended, store any valuables in the boot (trunk) or under a seat, or preferably take them with you. Note, however, that storing valuables in the boot isn't always safe, as a thief may be tempted to force open the boot with a crowbar. It isn't recommended to leave your original car papers in your car (which may help a thief to dispose of it).

Vehicles should also be garaged whenever possible. When parking at night, it's wise to use a secure car park or garage, or at least park in a well-lit area. If possible, you should avoid parking in long-term car parks (*parcheggi a lungo termine*), as they're favourite hunting grounds for car thieves. Motorway service stations are also favoured haunts for thieves, who can clean out your car in a few minutes and make a fast getaway; when stopping in a service station, you should park your car where you can keep an eye on it.

When driving in cities and large towns, it's wise to keep your doors locked and your windows partly or fully closed, and to store valuables and bags on the floor (not on seats). Some criminals specialise in robbing motorists at motorway toll booths.

Thieves in Italy operate various scams, including pretending that you have a flat tyre (they may even puncture your tyre in slow moving or stationary traffic) or that fuel is leaking from beneath your car. While one is pretending to help fix your car, another is stealing your belongings (women are popular targets). View any strangers offering to help you with suspicion. There has also been an increasing incidence of highway piracy, where gangs deliberately bump or ram cars to force drivers to stop (usually late at night when there's little traffic). Thieves may even pose as policemen and try to get you to stop by flashing a 'badge' or setting up a bogus road block. In the worst cases, thieves take not just the car and its contents but even the clothes their victims are wearing. Travelling at night in some areas (particularly in the far south of Italy) is hazardous due to armed highwaymen and should be avoided if possible. **Be on your guard!**

FUEL

Since January 2002, leaded petrol has been unavailable in Italy. Unleaded petrol (*benzina senza piombo*) is available in 95 octane (*EuroSuper*) and 98 octane (*super senza*). The price of petrol can vary from week to week according to the value of the US dollar and the world market price of crude oil (not to mention taxation). In spring 2003, ordinary unleaded cost around €1.07 per litre and super unleaded around €1.10. Prices on the motorway are a couple of cents higher per litre and there's also a surcharge of a couple of cents per litre for night service (unless a pump is automatic and accepts cash or credit cards). Diesel (*gasolio*) is widely available and costs around €0.87 per litre. LPG (known in Italy as *GPL* or *gas liquido*) is widely available in major cities in northern and central Italy – in petrol stations displaying a *GPL* or *Autogas* sign.

Petrol station opening hours in towns are usually from 7 or 8am until between noon and 1pm, when they close for lunch, and from around 3 or 3.30 until 7 or 7.30pm. On Sundays, most petrol stations are closed, but there's usually one in an area that's open on Sunday mornings (which is then usually closed on Mondays). When a petrol station is closed, there's usually a sign showing its opening hours and directing you to the next station. There are also 24-hour self-service filling stations in towns and on main roads, including all motorways. Credit cards are increasingly accepted by petrol stations, although it's wise to carry sufficient cash to fill your tank, particularly in rural areas and at weekends. Some petrol stations have automatic pumps that accept euro banknotes when the station is closed.

Note that it's illegal to carry a can of petrol in a car in Italy.

SERVICING & REPAIRS

Italian garages (service stations) are often highly specialised, although the range has diminished somewhat in recent years. You're likely to find the following specialists:

- *Autofficina* – handles most general jobs except bodywork and tyre changes and those that require a specialist.
- *Carrozziere* – repairs dents and scratches – a good business to be in in Italy!
- *Gommista* – sells and repairs tyres, and also does wheel-balancing.
- *Elettrauto* – fixes all electrical problems and installs car sound systems and alarms.

Two specialists that are slowly disappearing are the *carburatorista*, who tunes engines, and the *radiatorista*, who repairs and makes radiators.

The quality of work carried out by garages is usually good and they're generally well equipped to deal with any kind of problem. A garage will also check your car before the bi-annual safety inspection (see page 220) and, if required, take it for its inspection. Once a problem has been identified, always ask for an estimate, even an oral one (*preventivo*), which will save embarrassment and arguments later.

Garages are usually open from 8.30am to 1pm and from 3.30 to 8pm on weekdays, but are usually closed on Saturdays and always on Sundays and public holidays. If your car breaks down at a weekend, you can call 116 to get the ACI to tow you to a garage, where you can leave your car in a fenced area until it can be repaired. Some Italian insurance companies provide you with a card containing the phone number of a free towing service. If you use ACI, the service is free up to 30km (19mi) for members, while non-members must pay around €150. There may also be a storage charge for keeping the car in a garage's storage enclosure, unless it's repaired as soon as they open. Some manufacturers provide an emergency number in case of breakdown – check with a dealer whether this service applies to your car.

CAR RENTAL

To hire a car in Italy you must usually be aged at least 21, although it can be up to 25 or even as high as 30 for some vehicles. Drivers must have held a full licence for a minimum of a year and most companies have an upper age limit of 60 or 65. The rental is for specifically named drivers only and nobody else is permitted to drive the car – the licences of the drivers concerned must be shown to the rental agency. If payment isn't with a credit card, there's usually a cash deposit, and possibly the whole rental period must be paid in advance.

Car rental (*autonoleggio*) companies such as Avis, Europcar, Hertz and Maggiore have offices in most large towns and at major airports in Italy. If you're a visitor, it's wise to reserve a rental car before your arrival, which is generally cheaper. Fly-drive deals are available through most airlines and travel agents, and frequent flyer programmes also offer discounted car rentals from some agencies. Bookings can also be made at some main railway stations in Italy. Car rental in Italy is expensive compared with most other European countries, particularly for short periods, and includes VAT at 20 per cent. There's also a 14 per cent government tax if you pick up a car from a major airport.

Hertz, which has offices in 14 Italian cities, charges around €62 (including optional insurances and taxes) for a one-day rental of its cheapest models, e.g. a Fiat Punto. This is for limited mileage of 100km (62mi), after which there's a charge per kilometre. Rates reduce considerably over long periods, e.g. a week or a month. The weekly rate for a Fiat Punto is around €300 with the same daily limited mileage and €450 with unlimited mileage. Special rates are available for weekends, usually from noon on Fridays until 9am on Mondays, and there are also special offers outside periods of peak demand. Local rental companies are often cheaper than the multi-nationals, although cars must be returned to the pick-up point. Older cars can be rented from many garages at lower rates than those charged by the multi-national companies, although they aren't always in good condition and can even be unsafe.

Rates usually include collision damage waiver (CDW) and personal accident insurance (PAI), although you may need additional insurance (e.g. theft). When paying with a credit or charge card issued in the US, your card company may cover damage to a vehicle through its own insurance. Always ensure that you know what's included in (and excluded from) the price and what your liabilities are. If required, check in advance that you're permitted to take a car out of Italy, as it may be prohibited or you may be allowed to visit certain countries only.

Rental cars can be ordered with a luggage rack, and child seats can be fitted for an extra charge. In winter you can usually request snow chains and ski racks if you're heading for a winter sports destination. You can also hire a four-wheel-drive vehicle, station wagon, minibus, luxury saloon, armoured limousine or convertible, possibly with a choice of manual or automatic gearbox (although automatics are scarce, so you may need to book well in advance). There are also moped and motorcycle rental companies in the major cities. Minibuses accessible to wheelchairs can be hired, e.g. from Hertz, and vans and pick-ups are available from some major rental companies by the hour, half-day or day, and from smaller local companies (which, once again, are cheaper).

Note that cars can be rented from multi-national companies at a saving of up to 50 per cent on local rates by booking through their American offices, e.g. Alamo (☎ 1-800-462 5266), Avis (☎ 1-800-331 1212), Budget (☎ 1-800-527 0700), Dollar (☎ 1-800-800 4000), Hertz (☎ 1-800-654 3001) and National InterRent (☎ 1-800-227 7368), and paying by credit card. The toll-free (800) numbers of other US-based rental companies can be obtained from international directory enquiries, although you pay international rates when phoning from abroad. Car hire companies have no way of knowing where the calls were made and therefore are unable to prevent people from booking from outside the US.

Finally, if you want to rent a car but don't want to drive it yourself, some rental companies offer a chauffeur service and a 'welcome' service for visitors arriving at an airport of station. Private sightseeing tours are also available in chauffeured cars, which is a pleasant (expensive) way to take in a city's highlights.

MOTORING ORGANISATIONS

The main motoring organisations in Italy are the Automobile Club d'Italia (ACI), Via Marsala, 8, 00185 Rome (☎ 06-514 971, 💻 www.aci.it) and the smaller Touring Club Italiano (TCI), Corso Italia, 10, 20122 Milan (☎ 02-85261, 💻 www.touringclub.it). There are a number of local clubs, such as Automobile Club di Roma (ACR), which are affiliated to the ACO or TCI. Members benefit from:

- roadside emergency assistance;
- lock-out service;
- legal advice for motoring-related problems;
- car and travel insurance;
- translation of foreign licences;
- advice on local servicing facilities and spares suppliers;
- a wide range of driving and travel accessories.

Roadside emergency assistance (☎ 116) includes towing to a garage, hotel and travel expenses, and a courtesy car to replace your car for a period due to a mechanical fault, an accident or theft. The ACI offers two levels of cover: within Italy for €90 per year and throughout European for €150.

DRIVING ABROAD

You may be unfamiliar with the road rules and regulations in other European countries, particularly if you're a non-European, which often differ from those in Italy. The following hints and tips are designed to help you avoid a fine and survive a trip across the border:

- Don't forget your car registration and insurance papers, passports, identity cards, visas and inoculation certificates for pets. Make sure you have sufficient local currency for petrol, road tolls, food and fines!

- Ensure that you have valid insurance and a green card if necessary (see page 226).

- Breakdown insurance and travel insurance (see page 289) are also recommended. If you're a member of an Italian motoring organisation (see above), you're usually covered when travelling elsewhere in Europe through reciprocal agreements with local breakdown services. However, when motoring in some countries, it's wise to take out special legal protection insurance.

- Note that the procedure following an accident isn't the same in all European countries, although most western European countries use the standard European accident report form provided by insurance companies. **As a general rule, it's wise to call the police for anything other than a minor accident. In eastern European countries you should always call the police.**

- Check that your car complies with local laws and that you have the necessary equipment: for example, warning triangle (two may be required, e.g. in Spain), first-aid kit, fire extinguisher and headlight beam deflectors (Britain and Ireland). Check the latest regulations with an Italian motoring organisation.

- Ensure that you have sufficient spares such as bulbs, fan belt, fuses, and clutch and accelerator cables, particularly if you're driving a rare or 'exotic' model, e.g. most American and British cars.

- If your car doesn't have an alarm system fitted, use a visible lock, for example a lock for your steering wheel or gear stick. This may not deter a determined thief, but usually discourages a casual joy rider or opportunist. In some countries (especially Italy) car thieves queue up to steal your shiny new Ferrari, Lamborghini or Maserati (see **Car Crime** on page 243).

- A good map will come in handy, particularly when you're lost.

- If you're planning a long journey, a mechanical check-up for your car is recommended, particularly if it's a long time since its last service.

- In Britain and Ireland traffic drives on the left. Fortunately the majority of British and Irish motorists are quite civilised and most foreigners don't find it a problem (but you must adjust your brain and lights).

- Seatbelts must be worn in all European countries. In Finland, Norway and Sweden, dipped headlights (low beam) must be used at all times outside urban areas.

- The legal blood alcohol limit may be lower in some countries than in Italy, and you should check. **In some countries it's zero, which means that you aren't permitted to have any alcohol at all in your blood when motoring!**

- An international driving permit or a translation of your Italian or foreign driving licence is necessary in some countries, but usually isn't required within Western Europe (check with an Italian motoring organisation).

When driving anywhere, **never** assume that you know what another motorist is going to do next. Just because he is indicating left doesn't mean he is actually going to turn left or even move to the left – in some countries, he is more likely to be turning right, stopping or about to reverse, and in many countries motorists make turns without any indication at all! Don't be misled by any semblance of road discipline and clearly marked lanes. Try to be courteous, if only in self-defence, but don't expect others to reciprocate. The most dangerous European countries in which to drive vary according to the newspapers and magazines you read and whose statistics they use. What is indisputable is that the likelihood of having an accident is **much** higher in some countries (check the road accident statistics – which don't lie!). You should take extra care in winter, when ice and snow can make driving particularly hazardous. Driving in some European cities can be chaotic, a bit like a fun-fair dodgem ride without the fun, and nerve-racking at the best of times. If in doubt about your ability to cope with the stress or the risks involved, you'd be wiser to fly or take a train and use public transport on arrival.

12.

HEALTH

Italy's spending on health is only around 6 per cent of GDP, and expenditure per head is among the lowest in the EU. The quality of health care and of health care facilities varies from poor to excellent according to the region you live in and whether you use private facilities. Italian doctors and other medical staff are dedicated and well trained, the best Italian doctors being among the finest in the world (many pioneering operations are performed in Italy). The best private hospitals in Italy are also the equal of those in any country. However, state hospitals, particularly in the south of the country, are notoriously bad, a situation made worse by Mafia-inspired corruption and doctors fleeing to find work in better equipped (and run) hospitals in the north. Throughout Italy, nursing care and post-hospital assistance are also well below what most northern Europeans and Americans take for granted.

Italy has a national health service, which provides free or low-cost health care to all residents who contribute to social security and their families, plus university students and retirees, including those from other EU countries. It also provides emergency care to all visitors, irrespective of nationality. In addition to the state health service, Italy has many private doctors, specialists and clinics. Many Italians use these in addition to the national health service, e.g. to avoid long delays for operations, to obtain better hospital accommodation or simply to obtain treatment from a preferred specialist. Many Italians and most foreigners have private health insurance, which ensures that you receive the medical treatment you need, when you need it. **Whether you opt for state or private health care, it's important to have some form of health insurance, without which health care costs in Italy can be prohibitively expensive (see page 282).**

Non-EU citizens taking up residence in Italy should note that immigration officials may ask you for proof of health cover before issuing a permit to stay (see page 79).

Despite the shortcomings of the health service, Italians are generally healthy and have one of the highest life expectancies in Europe – around 82 for women and 76 for men – which is attributed in large part to their healthy Mediterranean diet of fresh fruit, vegetables, olive oil and red wine (in moderation). Infant mortality is around average for Europe, at six deaths per 1,000 live births. The generally mild Italian climate (at least in central and southern Italy) is therapeutic, particularly for sufferers from rheumatism and arthritis, and those who are susceptible to bronchitis, colds and pneumonia. The slower pace of life – outside the major cities, at least – is also beneficial to those susceptible to stress. However, the country has a high incidence of diseases of the circulatory system, as well as of cancer (often smoking-related) and liver-related illnesses (due to excess alcohol intake). Common health problems among expatriates include sunburn and sunstroke, stomach and bowel problems (due to the change of diet and, more often, water), and alcoholism. Italians' love of the motor car also gives rise to excessive air pollution in Italy's major cities, which is blamed for the increasing number of asthma and hay fever sufferers.

Consumption of alcohol per head is high (up to 90 per cent of Italian adults are reckoned to drink alcohol with every meal) and alcohol is responsible for a number of alcohol-related illnesses, e.g. cirrhosis of the liver and some forms of cancer. There's no official age for the legal consumption of alcohol (children tend to drink moderate amounts of wine from a young age), although young people under the age of 16 aren't permitted to buy alcohol. In common with other European countries, Italy has an increasing illegal drugs problem, particularly among young people (ecstasy and amphetamines have flourished in recent years). Drugs are comparatively cheap in Italy, but the law is strict on prohibition and the penalty for drug dealers can be life imprisonment. See **Social Services & Counselling** on page 265.

Otherwise, there are no special health risks in Italy and no vaccinations are required before visiting. Pollution levels in the sea are tested regularly (particularly during the tourist season) and swimming is generally safe unless there's a sign to the contrary, e.g. *divieto di balneazione* (bathing prohibited). On trains and other places where water isn't fit for drinking, you often see the sign *acqua non potabile*. However, you can safely drink most tap water in Italy, although many people prefer bottled water, and the wine tastes much better.

If you're planning to take up residence in Italy, even for part of the year, it's wise to have a health check before your arrival, particularly if you have a record of poor health or are elderly. If applicable, you should also bring a spare pair of spectacles, and contact lenses and spare dentures and a hearing aid with you.

EMERGENCIES

The action to take in a medical emergency depends on the degree of urgency. Keep a record of the telephone numbers of your doctor, local hospital and clinic, ambulance service, dentist and other emergency services (fire, police) next to your telephone. Emergency numbers are also displayed prominently at the front of all telephone directories. If you're unsure whom to call, dial the free national emergency number 113 and you will be put in touch with the relevant service. Note the following recommended courses of action:

- In a life-threatening emergency, such as a heart attack or serious accident, call the free public first-aid number 118. State clearly where you're calling from and the nature of the emergency, and give your name and the telephone number from where you're calling. Don't hang up until the operator asks you to. The appropriate emergency service is sent to you. Provided you call in response to a genuine emergency, you won't be charged for the use of the emergency services.

- If you need an ambulance (*ambulanza*), call the local ambulance service (*pronto soccorso ambulanza*). Most ambulances are equipped with cardiac equipment for emergency heart cases.

- If you're physically capable, go to a hospital emergency or casualty department (*pronto soccorso*). All foreigners in Italy have the right to be treated in an emergency, irrespective of whether they have insurance.

- If you need urgent medical treatment outside surgery hours and cannot get to your nearest casualty department, call the local duty doctor service (*guardia medica*). This service is usually available from 8pm to 8am on weekdays and from 2pm on Saturdays (and the day before a public holiday) until 8am on the Monday (or the day after a public holiday).

- If you need to see a doctor but are unable to visit a surgery, a doctor will visit you at home provided you call him during surgery hours. If he is away, his office will give you the name and number of a substitute doctor on call.

In Italy it's an offence to offer medical assistance in an emergency if you aren't a doctor or qualified in first aid, although it's also an offence **not** to assist someone in an emergency, e.g. by calling the appropriate emergency service or offering first aid when qualified to do so.

If you have an existing medical problem that cannot easily be seen or recognised, e.g. a heart condition, diabetes, a severe allergy or epilepsy, or you have a rare blood group, you may wish to join Medic-Alert. Medic-Alert members wear an internationally recognised identification bracelet or necklace, on the back of which is engraved details of your medical condition, your membership number and a 24-hour emergency phone number. When you're unable to speak for yourself, doctors, police or paramedics can obtain immediate, vital medical information from anywhere in the world by calling this number. Medic-Alert is a non-profit registered charity and members pay for the cost of the bracelet or necklace (from GB£20) plus an annual fee of GB£10. For more information contact the Medic-Alert Foundation, 1 Bridge Wharf, 156 Caledonian Road, London N1 9UU, UK (☎ 020-7833 3034, 🖳 www.medicalert.org.uk).

NATIONAL HEALTH SERVICE

Italy's national health service (*Servizio Sanitario Nazionale/SSN*) was established in 1978 and replaced the previous system of state insurance founded after the Second World War. The aim of the SSN was to create an efficient and uniform health system covering the entire population, irrespective of income or contributions, employment or pre-existing health conditions. The SSN provides free or low-cost health care to all residents and their families plus university students and retirees (including those from other EU countries) and emergency care to visitors, irrespective of their nationality.

In 1998 the SSN was separated from the INPS (see page 275) and funded directly by central government via the IRAP tax (*Imposta Regionale Sulle Attività Produttive*), which is paid by employers on behalf of employees; the self-employed pay for themselves through their taxes. You don't pay direct contributions and need only be a resident in Italy or a citizen of the EU to receive the same health benefits as an Italian. If you qualify for health care under the SSN, your dependants receive the same benefits and are listed on your card. Dependants include your spouse (if she isn't personally insured), children you support who are under the age of 16 (or under the age of 26 if they're students or unable to work through illness or invalidity), and ascendants, descendants and relatives by marriage supported by you and living in the same household.

If you aren't entitled to public health benefits through payment of Italian taxes or by receiving a state pension from another EU country, you must usually have private health insurance and must present proof of this when applying for a residence permit. If you're a retired EU national planning to live permanently in Italy, you need form E121. EU citizens who retire before qualifying for a state pension can receive free health cover for two years by obtaining form E106 from their country's social security department. If the temporary cover expires before you reach retirement age, you need to make voluntary social security contributions or take out private health insurance (see page 282).

The SSN is largely under the control of regional governments and is administered by local health authorities (Azienda di Sanità Locale/ASL – often referred to by their former name Unità Sanitaria Locale/USL). The SSN provides hospital accommodation and treatment (including tests, surgery and medication during hospitalisation), visits to family doctors (GPs), specialist medical assistance provided by paediatricians, obstetricians and other specialists, discounted medicines, laboratory services, appliances, ambulance services and free services at a local health unit (*consultorio*).

Those who are registered with the SSN are entitled to free or subsidised medicines (see page 258), a 75 per cent reduction on the cost of out-patient and after-care treatment, and some subsidised dental treatment (see page 264). All in-patient treatment, i.e. treatment requiring hospitalisation is free under the national health service. Many medical expenses can be totally or partially deducted for tax purposes, including the cost of spectacles, hearing aids and visits to medical specialists, so you should retain all medical receipts.

The Italian health service places the emphasis on cure rather than prevention and treats sickness rather than promoting good health. There's little preventative medicine in Italy such as regular health checks. The public health service has limited resources for out-patient treatment, nursing and post-operative care, geriatric assistance, or terminal illnesses and psychiatric treatment. Inadequate treatment due to staff shortages and long waiting lists as a result of a lack of hospital facilities are frequent complaints made against Italy's health service. Many problems are related to crippling bureaucracy, mismanagement, general disorganisation and spiralling costs. Despite the huge advances in medicine and the progress in health care in Italy in the last few decades, the public health service is facing enormous problems. Health service reform is a matter of intense public debate in Italy and it's likely that there will be major changes in the next decade.

Registration

You must register for membership of the SSN at your nearest local health authority (Azienda Sanità Locale/ASL), whose address you will find under ASL or USL (pronounced 'ahsle' and 'oosle') in your local telephone directory. You need to take the following documents with you, as applicable:

- Your permit to stay or residence permit (see pages 79 and 86);
- Your passport or other official identity document, such as an Italian driving licence;
- A family status certificate (*certificato di stato di famiglia*) if you want to claim benefits for your spouse or children (see **Applications** on page 84);
- Your fiscal code card (see page 295);
- A letter from your employer stating your employment start date (*dichiarazione de datore di lavoro*) and a statement from the INPS (see page 275) that you're regularly employed or a registration card (*attestato di iscrizione*) from the unemployment office (Ufficio di Collocamento) or proof of admission from an approved educational establishment.

Once you've completed the registration formalities, you're asked to choose a family doctor (see below) with a social security agreement (*convenzionato* or *con la mutua*) and, if you have children under six, a paediatrician (*pediatra*). You and each member of your family are issued with a national health number and receive a health card (*tessera sanitaria*) in which all medical occurrences, e.g. illnesses, general medical care and surgery, are recorded. Health cards are valid for a year and must be renewed (stamped) annually; if you lose your card or change your address, you must apply for a replacement.

There are certain health requirements for employees and schoolchildren in Italy. Employees who work in the food industry (bars, restaurants, food shops, factories producing food products, etc.) must obtain a health record book (*libretto sanitario*) from the public hygiene office at the town hall and undergo an annual medical examination. Schoolchildren at lower and upper secondary school are required to produce a medical certificate (*certificato di sana e robusta costituzione fisica*) from their school before participating in any sports activities. Participation in a competitive sport (*sport agonistico*) also requires a medical examination, which must be conducted by a specialist in sports medicine, usually at a local sports centre or your local health authority. Medical examinations for participation in sports activities are free under the national health scheme.

If you travel abroad frequently, a good way of keeping detailed health records for your family is to obtain an EU health passport (*passaporto sanitario*), which is printed in eight languages and available free from pharmacies.

DOCTORS

Italy has the highest number of doctors (*medici*) per head of any country in the world (one for every 160 inhabitants), and they're generally well trained and professional. Not surprisingly, however, it's difficult to find English-speaking doctors in some areas of Italy, although most cities and resorts have a medical service for tourists (*guardia medica turistica*) with English-speaking staff. Embassies and consulates in Italy keep lists of doctors and specialists in their area who speak English and other languages, and your employer, colleagues or neighbours may also be able to recommend someone. If you live in Milan, the International Health Center (☎ 02-720 040 80) has a number of English-speaking medical specialists.

General practitioners or family doctors (*medici generici*) are listed in yellow pages under *Medici Generici*, and specialists under *Specialisti* and their speciality e.g. *Ostetrica e Ginecologia* (obstetricians and gynaecologists). Note that the word *dottore* is a courtesy title used to address any university graduate.

If you wish to take advantage of the national health service, you must register with the Servizio Sanitario Nazionale (see **Registration** above). When registering, you're required to choose a family doctor with a social security agreement (*medico convenzionato*) and, if you have children aged under six, a paediatrician (*pediatra*) also. Local health authorities provide you with a list of doctors with whom you can register and you can choose any doctor who's willing to accept you (there's no requirement to register with a doctor within a certain distance of your home). Each member of your family is issued with a national health number and a health card (*tessera sanitaria*), which you must take with you when visiting a doctor or other health practitioner.

In addition to single private practices, family doctors also practise in group surgeries known as *poliambulatori*. Group practices can be either state, operating within an Azienda Sanità Locale (ASL) building, or private, and they offer a range of specialities usually unavailable at doctors' surgeries. These may include allergology, cardiology, dentistry, dermatology, gynaecology, ophthalmology, orthopaedic treatment, physiotherapy, psychotherapy, radiology, sports medicine, surgery, and urology. For a list of group surgeries and hospitals in your area, contact your local health authority.

You can make an appointment to see a private doctor, specialist or consultant at any time, provided you don't mind paying for their services. This means that you have total freedom of choice and can obtain a second opinion, should you so wish. In Italy, many family doctors who work for the national health service also work privately as specialists, and it's quite common for family doctors to suggest that you see them privately for specialist treatment; in this case, you will normally visit them at their private surgery (*studio medico*), which may be separate from their state practice. Unless you know exactly what the problem is, however, it's wise to see your family doctor first. To see a private doctor or specialist, you may need to pay an initial registration fee (around €12) plus a fee for each visit, which may be anything from €40 to €160. Note that you're normally expected to settle the bill in cash immediately after treatment, even if you have health insurance. (It's important to keep all medical receipts, as these can be offset against your income tax bill.)

Doctors' surgery hours vary, although surgeries are usually open from 8 to 10am and from 3 to 5pm, or there's one surgery only from 8am to 1pm, Mondays to Fridays only. Appointments aren't usually required and most surgeries operate on a first-come, first-served basis, so it's recommended to arrive early to avoid a long wait. Your family doctor will diagnose your problem and may write out a prescription (*ricetta*) for you to take to the chemist. He will arrange for you to have any necessary laboratory tests or X-rays at an authorised medical centre. If he thinks that you need to see a specialist, he will refer you to one who's registered with social security. He then writes a referral (*impegnativa*), which you must take with you if you wish to be claim social security benefits. If you want a doctor to visit you at home, you must telephone during surgery hours. House calls made by family doctors are free during normal working hours.

If you require specialist medical attention and want to take advantage of social security benefits, you must take your doctor's referral with you when you attend your appointment. Your family doctor may suggest a specialist, but you can also choose your own. Specialists registered with the SSN have their consulting rooms (*ambulatorio*) in state hospitals, local health authority buildings or other centres with an agreement with the SSN. Some private specialists, known as *privati accreditati*, also treat social security patients at their private surgeries. If you have X-rays or laboratory tests done, it's your responsibility to collect the results and take them to your family doctor or specialist, so you must find out when they will be ready.

If you're registered with social security, you must find the cashier (*cassa*) to pay the subsidised charge (*ticket*), so don't forget to take enough cash with you; you're then given a receipt, which you must hand to the specialist. The most you will pay for specialist treatment is €40 (some treatments, e.g. X-rays, cost less) and your doctor can request a maximum of six treatments for each referral. Certain categories of people pay a maximum of €3.50 per specialist treatment, including children under the age of six, those aged over 65 with a family income of less than around €37,000, those whose annual income is below €8,300, and anyone who suffers from a disability or a long-term, chronic illness such as rheumatoid arthritis, diabetes or epilepsy.

If you need the services of a medical auxiliary, e.g. a nurse, physiotherapist or chiropodist, you also need a referral from your family doctor in order to pay the reduced amount (*ticket*). If you don't, you must pay the full cost. Depending on where you live, home visits by nurses (for example, to administer injections) may not be covered by social security and you may need to pay the full cost.

If you're away from home and need the services of a doctor, provided you visit a doctor who's registered with the health service, you won't need to pay for his services. He will write a request (*richiesta*) on headed notepaper, which you can then take to your own doctor and exchange for a referral if medical treatment is required.

MEDICINES

Medicines (*medicine*) prescribed by a doctor are obtained from a chemist's (*farmacia*), denoted by the sign of a red or green cross on a white background.

Most chemists' are open from 8.30am until 12.30pm and from 3.30pm to 7.30pm. Outside these hours, at least one chemist's in all areas or towns is open until late (or 24 hours in major cities) for the emergency dispensing of drugs and medicines (a duty roster is posted on the door of chemists' and published in local newspapers). After midnight you may need to ring a bell to summon the chemist. Chemists' are privately owned in Italy, often passed from one generation to another within the same family, and the number is strictly controlled. There are no chain chemists' as in Britain and the USA.

Prices of medicines aren't controlled by the government and vary considerably according to the brand, and many medicines are available without a prescription in Italy that would require one in some other countries. Pills (*pillole*) are the most common prescriptions given by doctors, although you may also be prescribed a series of injections (*iniezioni*), suppositories (*supposta*) or, less commonly, powders (*polveri*). Some common medicines, e.g. vitamins and cough linctus, can be surprisingly expensive. If you're registered with social security, you pay a proportion of the cost of prescription medicines (known as the *ticket*) according to their 'group', as follows:

Group	Includes	Percentage Paid
A	Insulin, some painkillers (although not aspirin), antibiotics, cortisones, ulcer treatments & eye drops	10
B	Hormone treatments, antacids & some anti-inflammatory drugs	50
C	Aspirin, throat pastilles, vitamins, throat gargles & dermatological creams	100

In order to pay the *ticket* cost of Group A and B medicines, you must produce a doctor's prescription. Senior citizens with an annual income of less than €37,000, children under the age of six and those suffering from long-term chronic diseases pay a maximum of €3.50 for group A and B drugs. All Class C and non-prescription medicines, however, must be paid for at the full cost. Some medicines cost less than the *ticket* price, in which case you can save money by buying them **without** a prescription! If you need a small quantity of medicine, your doctor may provide it free from his own supplies. For certain medicines you can obtain one or more repeat doses (e.g. within a three-month period) without the need for another prescription.

Italian doctors commonly prescribe homeopathic medicines, which are popular in Italy and stocked by all chemists, some of which specialise in homeopathic medicine (look for the green *Omeopatia* sign). Note that the word *droga* means illegal drugs (narcotics).

Italian chemists stock a narrower range of goods than is the case in, for example, the US or the UK. Products are generally medically-related, although some cosmetics (usually skin creams) and toiletries are sold, as well as health and diabetic foods, and some orthopaedic items. Chemists also sell prescription spectacles and some can perform simple tests such as blood pressure. Chemists are often consulted for minor ailments and many Italians use them as their local clinic (often in order to avoid a long queue at a doctor's surgery).

Herbalist shops (*erboristerie*) selling herbal products and other 'alternative' medicines are found in many towns and cities. There are also shops known as *negozi sanitari*, which specialise in orthopaedic medical equipment and generally stock a wide range of products for handicapped and disabled people, including wheelchairs and bath aids, plus items such as prostheses, knee and arm supports, and orthopaedic shoes. Provided you have a clinical need, up to €36 of the cost of each item is paid by social security.

If you're visiting Italy and take a medicine regularly, you should ask your doctor for the generic name, as the brand names of medicines vary from country to country. If you wish to match a medicine prescribed abroad, you need a prescription with the medicine's trade name, the manufacturer's name, the chemical name and the dosage. Most medicines have an equivalent in Italy, although particular brands may be difficult or impossible to obtain. It's also possible to have medicines sent from abroad, for which no import duty or VAT should be payable. If you're visiting Italy for a short period, you should bring sufficient medicines to cover your stay. It's also recommended to bring your favourite non-prescription medicines (e.g. aspirin, cold and flu remedies, lotions, etc.), as they may be difficult or impossible to obtain in Italy or more expensive.

HOSPITALS & CLINICS

All Italian cities and large towns have at least one clinic (*clinica*) or hospital (*ospedale*), indicated by the international sign of a white 'H' on a blue background. Public hospitals are listed in the yellow pages under *Ospedali* and private hospitals under *Case di cura private*. If your Italian is poor or you prefer to be treated by English-speaking practitioners, the Salvator Mundi International Hospital, Viale Mura Gianicolensi, 67, Rome (☎ 06-588 961), the Rome American Hospital, Via E. Longoni, 69, Rome (☎ 06-0622 551) and the Milan Clinic, Via Cerva, 25, Milan (☎ 02-7601 6047) have English-speaking doctors and staff.

There's a wide discrepancy between public and private hospital facilities in Italy, although it's generally considered that there's little difference between the quality of medical treatment (e.g. surgery). The best hospitals are usually found in northern and central Italy, some of which, e.g. the Cancer Hospital (*Centro Tumori*) in Rome, have excellent reputations for specialist treatment. There are also a number of highly-regarded university hospitals. Private hospitals (*cliniche*), many run by the Roman Catholic Church, offer a pleasant alternative to the sometimes grim facilities of public hospitals, although they don't necessarily have the most sophisticated equipment. Some specialise in particular fields of medicine, such as obstetrics and surgery, rather than being full service hospitals. A number of private clinics have agreements with regional health authorities and provide beds that can be used by national health patients, although there may be long waiting lists. Public hospitals have a 24-hour accident and emergency (casualty) department (*pronto soccorso*).

Except in emergencies, you may be admitted or referred to a hospital or clinic for treatment only after consultation with a doctor. Normally you're admitted to a hospital in your own province, unless specialist surgery or treatment is unavailable there. In some regions, if a hospital cannot offer treatment within a reasonable period, patients may be referred to a private clinic without having to pay extra fees. Under the national health service, you can request that an operation be performed in a hospital in another city, although the best-equipped hospitals in the north of Italy often have long waiting lists. In an emergency outside your own city or province, you will obviously be treated in a local hospital.

Your choice of hospital and specialist depends on whether you choose a public or private hospital and the treatment required. A recent law banned private specialists from performing operations in state hospitals. If you're treated in a public hospital under the national health service, you must be operated on by the medical specialist on duty. If you request the services of a particular specialist or want to avoid a long waiting list for an operation, you must pay the full cost of treatment.

If you need to visit a hospital, don't expect to be able to find your way easily to the correct ward or consulting room, as few Italian hospitals have reception facilities and signs can be confusing or out-of-date. All patients have the right to an information booklet (*carta dei servizi*) containing details such as meal schedules, visiting hours, floor plans, doctors' names, hospital rules, and the location of telephones and toilets. However, the information may not be up-to-date or patient-friendly, and it may be quicker to simply ask the nearest person in a white coat.

Basic accommodation in public hospitals normally consists of wards with between three and six beds, although single bedrooms are usually available with an en suite bathroom for a supplement of between €60 and €75 per day. You can also usually rent a TV for a small daily fee if it isn't included. Patients normally need to bring everything they need with them, including towels, toiletries, pyjamas or night-dresses and dressing gowns, although meals are provided free of charge. Note, however, that the food may be inedible and you may need some outside assistance (food parcels) if you're to survive a stay in a public hospital! In contrast, in private clinics and hospitals, accommodation is generally of luxury hotel standard, with air-conditioned single rooms, TV and telephone, and an extra bed for a relative if required. Public hospitals usually have restricted visiting hours of around two or three hours per day, while private clinics generally have no restrictions.

In public hospitals, all in-patient treatment under the national health service is free. For out-patient treatment, e.g. consultations, tests and operations that don't require you to be hospitalised, you pay the *ticket* cost, which is a maximum of €36 for each treatment. As with other medical treatment, you must produce a doctor's referral.

The cost of hospitalisation in a private clinic can be extremely high, e.g. from €500 to €3,000 per day for hospital accommodation (including meals and medicines), plus the costs of medical treatment, e.g. over €5,000 for major surgery. Costs for private operations vary enormously according to the reputation of the specialists involved and the fees they command. Note that it can be much cheaper to have an operation abroad, particularly in France. The Ministry of Health sets minimum charges for all private operations, and specialist treatment information is available from local health authorities). If you have health insurance, be sure to check beforehand whether this covers you for the treatment planned.

If you aren't covered by the national health service, you must pay before you receive any treatment, irrespective of whether you have private health insurance, although some foreign insurance companies have arrangements with certain hospitals and pay bills directly.

If you're discharged from hospital and don't have transport to get home, you can usually pay for an ambulance to take you. Volunteer ambulance services such as the Red Cross (*Croce Rossa*) provide non-urgent ambulance transport services, for which a list of fees is usually available in hospitals.

CHILDBIRTH

Childbirth in Italy usually takes place in a hospital, where a stay of three days is normal, although it can be longer if complications arise. Maternity wards usually have two or three beds; mothers must provide clothing and accessories for their babies, although medical supplies are provided. Childbirth is supervised by a gynaecologist, an obstetrician, a nurse and a medical specialist who looks after babies during the first four weeks (*neonatologo*). Husbands usually attend births, although mothers can ask for any relative to do so. Italian women don't generally give birth at home and if you want to do so you must arrange (and pay) for a private obstetrician to attend the delivery.

A number of services relating to childbirth are provided by family planning centres (*consultori familiari*). These are staffed by qualified medical professionals and provide free advice and testing for all phases of childbirth, including ante-natal classes, gynaecological examinations and post-natal assistance by an obstetrician (including home visits). All services at family planning centres are free under the national health service, although preference may be given to low-income families and it may be quicker to pay for a private consultation. Family planning centres also provide free information and counselling on a range of other health issues, including contraception, abortion, parenting, and sexual and marital problems. See also **Social Services & Counselling** on page 265.

If you contribute to social security, the national health service pays for all treatment relating to pregnancy. To qualify, mothers must undergo a number of pre-natal examinations, including ultrasonography (*ecografia*) within the first, fourth, seventh and (if applicable) tenth months of pregnancy, where sound waves are used to check foetal growth, detect abnormalities, and test for hepatitis B and HIV. Where there's a risk of miscarriage, a baby is monitored throughout a pregnancy and women over the age of 35 undergo testing for Downs Syndrome. The public health service also pays for a number of pre-conception health tests, for both men and women, to determine whether any genetic malformations are present.

Giving birth in a private clinic in Italy can be very expensive; typical costs are between €3,000 and €3,750. You must also bear in mind that, although the surroundings are likely to be considerably more pleasant and less crowded than in a public hospital, private clinics may lack vital equipment in the event of an emergency. It's therefore important to check the level of equipment and facilities available, and obtain a complete list of fees in advance.

After you've given birth and left hospital, there's no specific post-natal provision, although a number of services relating to childbirth are provided by family planning centres (see above).

Abortion (*interruzione volontaria di gravidanza*) is legal in Italy and must normally be performed within 12 weeks of conception in a public hospital or private clinic (there are no specialist abortion clinics). The consent of the father isn't required, but the woman must sign a consent form. Girls under the age of 18 require the consent of both parents or guardians, or the decision is referred to a judge. 'Therapeutic' abortions, i.e. when there's a likelihood of a child being seriously malformed or the mother's life is at risk, can be performed for up to 20 weeks after conception. Authorisation by a medical specialist is required for all abortions performed 12 weeks after conception. The cost of an abortion is paid for by the heath service, although you can choose to pay for an abortion in a private clinic. Note that the word *aborto* means both miscarriage and abortion.

CHILDREN'S HEALTH

If you're registered with the national health service, you can choose a paediatrician (*pediatra*) from a list at your local ASL. Paediatricians generally treat children up to the age of 14 (although some parents prefer to use their family doctor). Children are given a vaccination record booklet (*libretto delle vaccinazioni*) and are required to have vaccinations against diphtheria and tetanus (*antidifterico-tetanica* or *DT*), polio (*antipolio*) and hepatitis B (*antiepatite B*) at three months, with boosters at 5 and 11 months. A polio booster is required at three years, and diphtheria and tetanus just before entry into primary school. A booster for hepatitis B is necessary at the age of 12. Vaccinations are provided free of charge and are compulsory.

Although not compulsory, vaccinations against whooping-cough, measles, mumps, German measles and HIB (which can cause serious illnesses such as meningitis) are also recommended. A whooping-cough vaccination (*anitpertosse*) can be administered in combination with the diphtheria and tetanus vaccinations (called *DTP*). Some doctors recommend a multiple vaccination (called *MPR*) against measles (*morbillo*), mumps (*parotite*) and German measles (*rosolia*), between the age of 12 and 15 months, although it has been suggested that this vaccination can cause autism.

Italian hospitals have paediatric units where children aged up to 17 are treated. Wards are usually well stocked with games, toys, books and other children, and facilities are provided for one parent (usually the mother) to stay overnight. Mothers with children under one year must usually provide milk, bottled drinking water (if required), nappies and changes of clothes, although food is provided. Children requiring long-term hospitalisation are usually given school lessons in hospital by volunteer teachers.

When you are travelling in Italy, you should take proof of your children's immunisations with you, with official translations obtainable from Italian consulates.

DENTISTS

Italy has few dentists (*dentisti*) per head of population in comparison with doctors, and treatment can be astronomically expensive, which means that many Italians wait until they have serious problems before making an appointment. Few dentists speak English; you can contact your country's embassy or local consulate for a list of English-speaking dentists in your area. Your employer, colleagues or neighbours may also be able to recommend a dentist. Dentists are listed in yellow pages under *Dentisti*. However, only names and addresses are listed and information such as specialities and surgery hours isn't provided.

Dentists' surgery hours vary considerably but are typically from 8.30am until 1pm, and from 4.00 to 7.30pm, Mondays to Fridays. Dentists come under the category of specialists in Italy and, as with doctors, if you wish to pay the national health service *ticket* (i.e. a maximum of €40) you must obtain a referral from your family doctor and choose a dentist who's registered with the SSN. Note, however, that private dentists generally have a better reputation than those working for the state and many Italians pay for private treatment, particularly for cosmetic work (public health dentists don't tend to have the most modern dental equipment).

Always check exactly what treatment has been recommended and how much it will cost before committing yourself – you must be wary of unnecessary treatment, which is a common practice in all countries. Private dentists generally charge between €80 and €130 per visit, which may include a number of treatments, e.g. a scale and polish, and a filling. For more extensive work, such as the removal of teeth or root canal treatment, bills can be astronomical. As with private doctors, it's usual to pay a dentist before a course of treatment begins. If your family requires expensive dental treatment, e.g. crowns, bridges, braces or false teeth, it's worthwhile checking whether treatment is cheaper abroad, e.g. in your home country.

OPTICIANS

As with other medical practitioners, it isn't necessary to register with an optician or optometrist (*ottico*). You simply make an appointment with the practitioner of your choice, although it's wise to ask your friends, colleagues or neighbours if they can recommend someone. Opticians are listed in the yellow pages under *Ottici* and eye specialists under *Oculisti*. Prices for spectacles (*occhiali*) and contact lenses (*lenti a contatto*) aren't controlled, but the eye care business is competitive, so it's wise to shop around and compare costs. A pair of spectacles typically costs between €100 and €160, which may include €80 for the frame. Italy lacks large optical chains where spectacles can be made on the spot or within 24 hours, although if you have a prescription you can sometimes buy ready-made reading spectacles from pharmacies. Always obtain an estimate for lenses and ask about extra charges for fittings, adjustments, lens-care kits and follow-up visits.

To receive free treatment under the national health service, you must have your eyes examined by an eye specialist or oculist (*oculista*). You must first obtain a referral from your family doctor, which you take to an oculist, who usually works in a state hospital or local ASL building. An oculist can make a more thorough test of your eyesight than an optician, and is able to test for certain diseases that can be diagnosed from eye abnormalities, e.g. diabetes and some types of cancer. If glasses are necessary, he will write a prescription to take to an optician.

It's recommended to have your eyes tested before arriving in Italy and to bring a spare pair of spectacles and/or contact lenses with you. You should also bring a copy of your prescription in case you need to obtain replacement spectacles or contact lenses urgently.

SOCIAL SERVICES & COUNSELLING

Social services are an important aspect of health, particularly for anyone thinking of retiring to Italy. In comparison with many other European countries, there's a marked lack of social and home-nursing services for the elderly in Italy. You will almost certainly need to pay privately for a home help, although many towns provide a visiting service for housebound elderly invalids. There are a number of private, purpose-built retirement developments, but few state nursing homes or hospices for the terminally ill (the majority of which are run privately by nuns).

Italy's provision for the disabled has improved in recent years due to a recent law making special access for disabled people compulsory for all public buildings, including banks, offices and schools. In addition, motorway service stations, major tourist sites and hospitals must provide toilets that accommodate wheelchairs. Wheelchair services are provided at most airports, although it's wise to enquire in advance. For further information about assistance for disabled people, contact the Associazione Italiana Assistenza Spastici, Via Cipro, 4/H, Rome (☎ 06-3973 1829).

The national health service provides free counselling and advice on health and relationship problems through its network of local family health centres (*consultorio*). Services usually include marriage and family, psychiatric and sexual counselling, and legal advice (for divorce and separation). Advice on contraception and family planning, and ante-natal care for pregnant women are also provided. Appointments can be made directly without the need for a doctor's referral. Counselling for the disabled and elderly is sometimes also available.

Many provinces have special telephone helplines for women (*telefono rosa*) and children (*telefono azzurro*), where confidential help can be obtained, e.g. in cases of physical and sexual abuse; numbers are listed at the front of telephone directories. The free national helpline number for those experiencing a crisis (*SOS Salute*) is ☎ 167-822 150.

A nation-wide drugs information service is available at local *Servizio per Tossicodipendenti* (*Ser. T*) offices, which also run comprehensive rehabilitation programmes for drug addicts, including medical and psychological support, free HIV testing, methadone treatment, and accommodation and employment in rehabilitation centres. *Ser. T* offices also organise drugs awareness programmes in schools. To find your nearest office, contact your local health authority. A free phone number is usually available between 8am and 2pm and there's also a free national helpline number for drugs-related problems (☎ 167-166 00).

Information and free medical assistance for alcoholics (*servizi di alcologia*) are available through your local health authority. There are also many branches in Italy of the Association of Alcoholics Anonymous (Associazione degli Alcolisti Anonimi), together with its related groups for the children of alcoholics (AchoA and Al-ateen) and relatives (Al-anon).

Advice on a range of health issues, e.g. rape and other forms of sexual abuse, family therapy, women's health (including pregnancy testing, smear tests and menopause treatment) and IVF treatment are available at around 30 Associazione Italiana per l'Educazione Demografica (AIED) centres, which are run by a private foundation that seeks to promote social and cultural awareness of sexual issues. An annual subscription is normally payable, after which treatment is provided at a reduced cost.

SEXUALLY-TRANSMITTED DISEASES

As in most western countries, AIDS (*AIDS* or *SIDA*) is on the increase: by 2002 the total number of AIDS cases in Italy (population 60 million) was 49,333, compared with 18,334 cases in the UK (population 58 million) and 20,898 in Germany (80 million). Condoms (*preservativi*) can be purchased in packets from chemists'; department stores and supermarkets generally don't stock them and you're unlikely to find many vending machines. Family planning centres and family doctors don't generally issue them free either. Free and anonymous testing for HIV (pronounced *akka-ee-vee*), which is conducted at least one month after patients have been at risk, is available at departments of infectious diseases (*malattie infettive*) in public hospitals and other public health centres. A doctor's referral isn't usually required, although if you're a visitor to Italy and aren't in possession of a national health card, you may need to obtain a *straniero temporaneamente presente* (*STP*) card from your local health authority declaring that you're temporarily resident. Confidential advice can also be obtained from the free AIDS helpline (☎ 167-861 061).

For the testing and treatment of other sexually transmitted diseases (*malattie a trasmissione sessuale*), e.g. hepatitis B and C, syphilis and gonorrhoea, you must be referred by your family doctor and pay the *ticket* price. AIED centres offer information and testing for all STDs, as well as advice on a range of other health issues (see **Social Services & Counselling** above).

SMOKING

Italy has some 14 million smokers (nearly 25 per cent of the population) and, not surprisingly, this results in a high incidence of smoking-related diseases (including 100,000 deaths per year). Many Italians start smoking at an early age, cigarettes are inexpensive (as little as €2.50 for 20) and, in keeping with the Italians' sense of individual liberty, the government has, until recently, made little effort to persuade people to stop smoking. Another reason for this may be that the cheapest cigarettes (known as *nazionali*) are manufactured by the state!

However, in a radical move designed to protect the health of passive smokers, the government recently introduced a draconian anti-smoking law, and smoking is now banned in all enclosed spaces, including schools, offices, banks, shops, hospitals, airports, railway stations and work places. Smoking is also banned on public transport, other than in carriages reserved for smokers, and on all Italian domestic flights and Alitalia international flights. Employers must provide separate areas equipped with extractor fans for employees who smoke, and bars and restaurants must provide separate areas for smoking customers (*fumatori*) and non-smoking customers (*non fumatori*). Those who break the law can be fined between €25 and €160 (although first time offenders are likely only to be asked to extinguish their cigarettes) and employers who fail to enforce it can be fined up to €3,100.

SPAS

When you've had a surfeit of *la dolce vita*, a variety of health cures is available at Italy's many spas (*terme*). Italy has over 100 spas, attracting millions of visitors each year. Many offer not only treatment for ailments such as rheumatism, arthritis, respiratory complaints, skin diseases and obesity, but also 'health care tourism' packages, which include beauty treatments, hydromassage, heliotherapy (sun treatment), inhalatory treatments or just relaxation. Many spas stress the scientific aspect of the treatments they offer, listing the mineral composition of their waters and sometimes the scientific research conducted there. All spas have qualified doctors.

Your family doctor can prescribe treatment at a spa centre and, if you're registered with the national health service, you pay only the cost of the *ticket*. However, the SSN doesn't pay for board and lodging. Spas can usually be visited on a daily basis for a fee of between €5 and €10. Maximum immersion time is usually around 20 to 30 minutes, followed by a rest period of a similar duration.

BIRTHS & DEATHS

Births and deaths in Italy must be registered within seven days at the registry office (Ufficio di Stato Civile) of the town (*comune*) where they take place. Registration applies to everyone irrespective of their nationality and whether they're residents or visitors. In the case of hospital births, registration is done by the hospital or clinic where a child is born. If you give birth at home, you must complete the registration yourself. An Italian birth certificate (*certificato di nascita*) is issued automatically.

In the event of a death, all interested parties must be notified. If a death takes place in a hospital, the attending doctor completes a certificate stating the cause of death (*constatazione della morte*); you should make several copies of this, as they're required by banks and other institutions. If a death occurs at home, you should call your family doctor or the local *guardia medica*. If there are suspicious circumstances, you should call the *polizia mortuaria* by ringing 113 and they will arrange for a post mortem examination (autopsy). As with births, deaths must be registered in the town where the death occurred, although the undertakers (see below) usually do this for you.

When a death occurs, it's important to find a reliable undertaker as soon as possible, particularly as they handle most of the documentation. Funerals in Italy are among the most expensive in Europe, frequently costing around €2,600, and it's important to obtain personal recommendations and check that an undertaker abides by the Italian Code of Conduct for Undertakers (*codice italiano di comportamento per le imprese funebri*). You're recommended to ignore recommendations given by hospital staff (who may be getting a commission) or people hanging around hospital mortuaries offering their services.

Bodies can be buried in three ways in Italy – in a family tomb, in an individual tomb (*loculo*) or in a communal burial ground (*campo comune*) – and they can also be cremated. Plots for family tombs are expensive (between €2,600 and €5,200), whereas *loculi*, which are layered blocks of marble tombs, can be bought for between €500 and €1,000 (usually for an initial period of around 30 years, after which the 'lease' is renewable). Interment in a communal burial ground is free but considered demeaning by many Italians, as the remains can be exhumed after just ten years (there's an acute shortage of cemeteries in Italy). Embalming isn't usually available.

Cremation is becoming increasingly popular, not least because it's paid for by the local municipality, although crematoria are few and far between. If the deceased hasn't requested cremation, a family member must make a formal request via a notary to the registry office. Families usually either keep the ashes in the family tomb or *loculo*, lease a special urn from the *comune* or dispose of the ashes in the local *campo comune*, which is free of charge. Note that it's illegal to keep ashes at home or dispose of them in any other way.

The body or ashes of a deceased person may be sent to another country. You need to provide the funeral agent with the documents relating to the death and the identity of the deceased, so that he can obtain the necessary permits. It generally takes from four to seven days to arrange shipment. When a death occurs at home, the body is prepared for shipment or burial in the home, as Italian law forbids undertakers to store them.

13.

INSURANCE

The Italian government and Italian law provide for various obligatory state and employer insurance schemes (see **Social Security** on page 274), and family allowances. Most Italians and EU residents and their families qualify to receive medical treatment under the Italian social security system. If you don't qualify, it's **essential** to take out private health insurance, which may be obligatory for some people. Even if you do qualify for social security benefits, you should bear in mind that these are fewer and less generous than in many other EU countries and in most cases you would be unwise to rely solely on state benefits to meet your needs.

You should ensure that your family has full health insurance during the interval between leaving your last country of residence and obtaining health insurance in Italy. One way is to take out a travel insurance policy (see page 289). However, it's better to extend your present health insurance policy than to take out a new policy (most policies can be extended to provide international cover). This is particularly important if you have an existing health problem that won't be covered by a new policy.

Other compulsory insurance (*assicurazione*) includes third party car insurance (see page 226), third party liability insurance for tenants and homeowners, and mortgage life insurance if you have a mortgage (depending on the amount borrowed). If you lease a car or buy one on credit, a lender will insist that you have comprehensive car insurance. Voluntary insurance includes supplementary pensions, disability, health, household, dental, travel, car breakdown and life insurance. However, insurance is generally more expensive in Italy than in many other European countries, policies also attracting various taxes and 20 per cent VAT, and the average Italian is more prone to taking risks than many other nationalities and carries less insurance than, for example, northern Europeans (although the market has grown considerably in the last decade, particularly in private health insurance and pensions).

It's unnecessary to spend half your income insuring yourself against every eventuality from the common cold to being sued for your last euro, but it's important to insure against any event that could precipitate a major financial disaster, such as a serious accident or your house being demolished by a storm. As with anything connected with finance, it's important to shop around when buying insurance. Just collecting a few brochures from insurance agents or making a few telephone calls **could save you a lot of money**. Regrettably, you cannot insure yourself against being uninsured or sue your insurance agent for giving you bad advice.

In all matters concerning insurance, you're responsible for ensuring that you and your family are legally insured in Italy. If you wish to make a claim, you may be required to report the incident to the police within 24 hours (in some cases this may be a legal requirement). If you're unsure of your rights, it's wise to obtain legal advice for anything other than a minor claim. **Italian law is likely to differ from that in your home country or your previous country of residence, so never assume that it's the same.**

INSURANCE AGENTS & COMPANIES

Italy had a relatively undeveloped insurance market until the 1980s, when many foreign companies stepped in to fill the vacuum and now control a large slice of the market. There are numerous Italian and foreign insurance companies to choose from, either providing a range of insurance services or specialising in certain fields only. Some foreign insurance companies operating in Italy cater particularly for the needs of expatriates, major insurance companies having offices or agents in all main cities (there are also 'direct' telephone insurers). Insurance agents, brokers (*agente*) and companies are listed in the yellow pages under *Assicurazioni* and many advertise in the expatriate press in Italy. Most insurance companies or brokers will provide a free appraisal of your family's insurance needs.

There are many independent brokers in Italy, who can offer you a choice of policies and save you money. However, as in many countries, it's often difficult to obtain completely independent, unbiased insurance advice, as brokers may be influenced by the commission offered for selling a particular policy. As with all financial matters in Italy, be careful who you choose as your broker and the company you insure with, as a number of companies have gone bust in recent years and insurance fraud isn't unknown. **When buying insurance, particularly car insurance (see page 226), shop until you drop!** Obtain recommendations from friends, colleagues and neighbours (but don't believe everything they tell you!). Compare the costs, terms and benefits provided by a number of companies before making a decision. Note that premiums (*premio*) are sometimes negotiable. **However, the most important point is whether an insurance company pays claims fully and promptly, or, as many do, delays paying for as long as possible and fights every euro of a claim.**

The entire insurance industry has been going through a crisis in recent years and (at long last) is becoming more consumer-driven. One major change in recent years has been the advent of telephone and Internet insurers, which allow you to obtain and compare estimates in minutes. Some Internet brokers allow you to compare rates online (🖥 www.diagramma.it) or you can contact individual insurance companies such as Genertel (☎ 800-202 020, 🖥 www.genertel.it), Linear (☎ 800-992 222, 🖥 www.onlinear.it), Lloyd 1885 (☎ 800-999 999, 🖥 www.lloyd1885.it) and Zuritel (☎ 800-247 247, 🖥 www.zuritel.it).

While buying insurance over the phone or on the Internet is a great convenience, you need to exercise some caution, particularly if you're buying a policy from an insurance company that you aren't familiar with. Not all insurance companies are equally reliable or have the same financial stability, and it may be better to insure with a large international company with a good reputation than with a small Italian company, even if this means paying a higher premium. You can check whether a company is registered in Italy with the ISVAP, the Italian insurance industry trade Association (☎ 06-421 331, 🖥 www.isvap.it).

INSURANCE CONTRACTS

Read insurance contracts carefully before signing them. If you don't understand Italian, ask someone to check a policy and don't sign it until you fully understand the terms and the cover provided. Policies often contain traps and legal loopholes in the small print, particularly exclusion clauses, so if you cannot understand a policy it's recommended to obtain professional advice before signing on the dotted line.

Always check the notice period required to cancel (*annullare*) a policy. Policies are usually automatically extended for a further period if they aren't cancelled in writing by registered letter two months before their expiry date. Most Italian insurance policies are valid for ten years, with the exception of motor polices, which run for one year. If possible, you should insure with a company, whose contracts are valid for one year and renewable annually. **If you haven't paid your renewal premium within ten days of the expiry date, your insurance may become invalid (therefore, in the case of motor insurance, you would be driving without insurance!).** You may cancel an insurance policy before the term has expired if the premium is increased, the terms are altered (e.g. the risk is diminished), or an insured object is lost or stolen. This must, however, still be done in writing and by registered post. Cancellation is also permitted at short notice under certain circumstances beyond your control. If you're changing insurance companies, the new company will be happy to cancel your old policy for you and simply give you a standard letter to sign.

If you wish to make a claim, you must usually inform your insurance company in writing by registered letter within two to five days of the incident (e.g. accidents) or 24 hours in the case of theft. Thefts must be reported to the local police within 24 hours, as the police report (*denuncia*) usually constitutes irrefutable evidence of your claim. Like insurance companies everywhere, some Italian companies do almost anything to avoid paying in the event of a claim and use any available loophole. In fact, Italian insurance companies have taken the art of delaying payments or not paying claims at all to unimaginable heights, which is why it's essential to deal with only reputable companies (not that this provides a guarantee). **It isn't unusual for legitimate insurance claims to take years to be resolved – and even then for the outcome to be unsatisfactory.**

If you have a problem with a claim or other problems with an Italian insurance company that you cannot resolve, contact the Italian Insurance Industry Trade Association (ISVAP) in Rome (☎ 06-421 331, ⌨ www.isvap.it).

SOCIAL SECURITY

Italy has an extensive social security (*previdenza sociale*) system covering the vast majority of the population. Social insurance provides benefits for unemployment, sickness and maternity, accidents at work and occupational diseases, as well as old-age, invalidity and survivor's pensions, and family allowances. It **doesn't** include the national heath service (Servizio Sanitario

Nazionale/SSN), which is funded from general taxation (see page 254). The system is run by a number of state agencies, which have been brought together under the umbrella of the National Institute for Social Security (Istituto Nazionale della Previdenza Sociale/INPS). All resident employees and self-employed workers pay social security contributions (*contributi previdenziali*), with a few exceptions (see **Eligibility & Exemptions** on page 276).

If you're an employee (*lavoratore dipendente*), your employer completes all the necessary formalities for registering with social security. Employee's contributions are deducted at source from their gross salary by their employer, who pays around two-thirds of pension contributions, while the remaining third is paid by the employee. For other types of social insurance, the employee's contributions are negligible. The standard total social security contribution made by employees is around 10 per cent of their gross salary, while the employer's contribution is around 35 per cent of an employee's salary (making a total of some 45 per cent). There are different contribution rates for employees in industry, commerce and agriculture, and for workers (*operai*), office staff (*impiegati*) and managers (*dirigenti*), who also receive different benefits. For managers in industry, an income ceiling applies for certain types of social security contributions, such as disability, old age pension and survivor's benefits.

The self-employed (*lavoratori autonomi*) must register and make contributions either to a separate organisation (called a *cassa*), which is a social security fund allied to their profession, or directly with the INPS. Self-employed people who make contributions to their own *cassa* include architects, accountants, lawyers, engineers, surveyors, medical specialists and other freelance professionals, who each have different rates of contributions. The self-employed who make contributions to INPS may be part-time employees (*collaboratori*), such as university students, freelance workers (*indipendenti*), including small businessmen, shopkeepers, traders, tenant farmers, sharecroppers and smallholders, or employees of relatively new industries (e.g. computer consultancies) who don't yet have their own *cassa*.

In certain circumstances where contributions aren't made, they're credited by the state. These are known as accredited contributions (*contributi accreditati*). For example, contributions are automatically credited for periods of unemployment where an employee has paid contributions for unemployment benefit (*indennità di disoccupazione*), for periods of military service, maternity leave, and illness of not less than a week and no longer than 12 months, after making the relevant application to INPS. Applications for notional contributions during periods of illness must be accompanied by a statement from your employer.

If you disagree with a decision taken and notified in writing by a social security body, you may lodge an appeal within certain time-limits, which must be lodged by registered letter (with advice of delivery). If the appeal is dismissed or no decision is taken within 90 days, you may then appeal to the ordinary courts, which in the first instance means the magistrate's court for employment matters (*pretore del lavoro*). The time-limit is three years in the case of pensions and one year in the case of temporary benefits.

Contributions In Other EU Countries: If you've paid regular social security contributions in another EU country for two full years before coming to Italy (e.g. to look for a job), you're entitled to social security cover for a limited period from the date of the last contribution made in your home country. You're also entitled to be covered by the national health service (see page 254). Form E106 must be obtained from the social security authorities in your home (or previous) country and given to your local social security office in Italy. If you're receiving an invalidity pension or other social security benefits on the grounds of ill-health, you should establish exactly how living in Italy affects those benefits. In some countries there are reciprocal agreements regarding invalidity rights, but you must confirm that they apply in your case.

Eligibility & Exemptions

Generally if you work for an employer in Italy, you're insured under Italian social security legislation and won't have any liability for social security contributions in your home country or country of domicile. Italy has reciprocal social security agreements with some 40 countries (including all EU countries, Canada and the US) whereby expatriates may remain under their home country's social security scheme for a limited period. Agreements normally apply for a maximum of two years and may usually be extended for up to five years. For example, under an agreement between the US and Italy, an American employee of a US company who is transferred to Italy for up to five years can continue to pay US social security contributions. Similarly, EU nationals transferred to Italy by an employer in their home country can continue to pay social security abroad for one year, which can be extended for another year in unforeseen circumstances. This also applies to the self-employed. However, after working in Italy for two years, EU nationals **must** contribute to Italian social security.

If you or your spouse work in Italy but remain insured under the social security legislation of another EU country, you're able to claim social security benefits from that country and your foreign contributions are taken into account when calculating your qualification for benefits. This is particularly important with regard to state pensions (see page 279). Contact your country's social security administration for information. In Britain information is provided in two booklets, *Social Security For Migrant Workers* and *Your Social Security, Health Care And Pension Rights In The European Community* (SA29), both of which are available from the Department of Social Security, Contributions Agency, Newcastle-upon-Tyne NE98 1YX, UK (☎ 0191-213 5000).

Benefits

Benefits are detailed below. In many cases there are different regulations and payments for workers (*operai*), salaried staff (*impiegati*) and managers (*dirigenti*).

Sickness Benefit

Sickness benefit (*indennità di malattia*) is payable for an illness or accident that results in an absence from work of at least seven days and is paid for a maximum of 180 days. The amount payable is calculated from your average daily earnings during the month preceding your illness and is equal to around 50 per cent of your earnings for the first 21 days and two-thirds of earnings for the remaining days. However, if you're hospitalised and don't have any dependants, the benefit is equal to 40 per cent of your average earnings. If you have an accident at work, you receive full pay during the recovery period; if an injury prevents you from working permanently, you receive an invalid pension. Sickness benefit is generally paid by the employer, who recovers the payment from the INPS, but in certain cases is paid directly by INPS. Sickness benefit doesn't apply to the self-employed. See also **Sick Leave** on page 61.

Maternity Benefit

Italian maternity benefit (*per maternità*) is among the most generous in the world and is equal to 80 per cent of your salary, which is paid for a total of five months before and immediately following a birth. Mothers are also entitled to receive a reduced benefit of 30 per cent of their salary for six months (called *congedo facoltativo*) during the year following the birth. An application for maternity benefits must be made at your local INPS office; you require a medical certificate (*certificato medico*) confirming your pregnancy and a statement from your employer certifying that you've stopped work due to pregnancy. After the birth you must provide the INPS with a copy of the birth certificate (*certificato di nascita*) and a certificate of family status (*certificato di stato di famiglia*), available from the registry office (Ufficio Anagrafe) in your *comune*. See also **Parental Leave** on page 61.

Disability Benefits

All workers and many other employees are covered against work-related illnesses (e.g. occupational diseases) and accidents. Disability benefits (*indennità di inabilità*) include salary for temporary disability and pensions for permanent disability. Temporary disability benefit is 60 per cent of your average daily wage during the two weeks preceding the accident or onset of illness. Permanent disability benefits vary according to the seriousness of the disability and may take the form of a lump sum payment (for minor disability) or an annuity (for major disability). Those who are totally disabled also qualify for a 'constant attendance supplement' of €369.40 per month. Disability benefits don't apply to the self-employed. For details of permanent disability benefit, see **State Pensions** on page 279.

Family Allowance

If you're an employee and the only wage earner in your family, you can apply for family allowance (*assegno familiare*) if your salary falls below a certain level, which varies according to the number of people in the family. Levels change regularly and up-to-date figures can be found on the website of the Istituto Nazionale della Previdenza Sociale (💻 www.inps.it). Family allowance in 2002 was between €771 and €932 per month, depending on family size and circumstances. An application form is available from your employer or an INPS office and must be accompanied by a certificate of family status (*certificato di stato di famiglia* – see **Parental Leave** on page 61). The form is given to your employer who pays the allowance with your salary.

Unemployment Benefits

There are various kinds of unemployment benefit (*indennità di disoccupazione*), as detailed below.

- **Ordinary Benefit** – To qualify for ordinary benefit (*indennità ordinaria*), you must have worked for at least a year and contributed for at least the previous two years. Benefit is available for a maximum of 180 days (six months) and is paid from the eighth day after termination of work, provided that an application is made within the first seven days. However, applications can be made up to 90 days after ceasing work. Benefit is calculated at 30 per cent of your average earnings during the previous three months, but cannot exceed a certain maximum, which was €932.82 per month in 2002.

- **Reduced Benefit** – If you've worked for at least 78 days in the previous year (including public holidays) but less than a year in total, or have made two years' voluntary contributions, you qualify for reduced benefit (*indennità ridotta*). Benefit is calculated at 30 per cent of your average net earnings during the previous three months, but the entire amount received, which is paid as a lump sum, cannot exceed €932.82.

- **Special Allowance** – A special allowance (*trattamento speciale*) is awarded to employees who have been made redundant in the agriculture and construction industries, and is currently a maximum of around €20 per day. Contributions paid in other EU member states are taken into account when making an application for benefit.

An application for unemployment benefit must be made at your local INPS office or the employment office (Ufficio di Collocamento) with your notice of dismissal and a certificate of family status (*certificato di stato di famiglia* – see **Parental Leave** on page 61). You're issued with an unemployment registration card (*attestato di iscrizione*). If you're unemployed in another EU country, you retain the right to your unemployment benefit (under certain conditions) for up to three months while looking for work in Italy. The country paying your employment benefit issues you with form E303, which you must take to an INPS office in Italy. If you return home before the end of the three months, you continue to receive your unemployment benefit in your home country. The self-employed and those who have never worked in Italy or resign from their job don't qualify for unemployment benefit.

In addition to unemployment benefits, Italy has a state fund for employees in industry whose companies put them on temporary redundancy through no fault of their own (e.g. market crisis, natural disaster, etc.), called *Cassa Integrazione Guadagni* (*CIG*), which is designed to 'integrate' employees' earnings until work is resumed. There are two types of *CIG*:

- **Ordinary CIG** comprises 80 per cent of your salary for hours not worked, e.g. if an employer agrees to provide five hours' work in a 35-hour week, 80 per cent of the salary for the remaining 30 hours is remunerated. This cannot exceed a monthly maximum, which in 2002 was €776.12 per month, or €932.82 per month if monthly income exceeded €1,679.07.

- **Extraordinary CIG**, which is designed to cover special situations, e.g. when a production line is being reorganised or converted and work must temporarily cease, lasts for 36 months in cases of reorganisation or conversion and 12 months in cases of company crisis. Benefit is the same as for ordinary *CIG* above.

In both cases, if the market hasn't changed, companies aren't obliged to take back employees, so *CIG* often becomes the start of unemployment benefit. See also **Dismissal & Redundancy** on page 66.

State Pensions

State pensions comprise old age, invalidity and survivor's pensions (*pensione di vecchiaia, di invalidità ai superstiti*). Total state pension contributions are around 28 per cent of gross salary, of which an employee pays approximately 9 per cent. There are various state or semi-state entities that collect contributions and pay pensions on behalf of particular groups. All employees and certain categories of self-employed people (who pay obligatory contributions to INPS) are entitled to a state pension, which is paid by the INPS.

Other employees and self-employed people receive a pension through a separate, semi-private (*para-statale*) organisation responsible for their profession. These include the INPDAI for industrial managers, the INPADAC for commercial managers, the INPGI for journalists and the ENPALS for those employed in the entertainment industry. The National Fund for the Liberal Professions provides pensions for a wide range of professionals, including doctors, chemists, veterinary surgeons, engineers, architects, surveyors, lawyers, tax advisers, employment consultants, notaries, customs agents and accountants.

There are three kinds of old age pension:

- A **full earnings-related pension** (*pensione di anzianità*) is paid provided you've contributed for a minimum of 35 years and are at least 57 years old when you make your pension claim or have made a minimum of 37 years' contributions (increasing to 38 years in 2004, 39 years in 2006 and 40 years in 2008) irrespective of your age, and have ceased to work. A new type of *pensione di anzianità* affects those who commenced employment on or after 1st January 1996 and those who were 18 or under on 31st December 1995. A third of your gross income goes towards a personal sum, which, together with contributions from your employer (in the case of employees), forms the basis on which your pension is ultimately calculated. For those who worked before 1st January 1996 but who made less than 15 years' contributions before 1993 or less than 18 years' contributions before 1996, a combined system (*sistema misto*) of pension calculation applies.

- A **standard old age pension** (*pensione di vecchiaia*) is paid to employees at the age of 60 (women) or 65 (for men). You must have contributed for at least 20 years to earn a partial pension, which is calculated from your last ten years' income (see below).

- A **social pension** (*pensione sociale*) is for people who have never made any social security contributions and are without any means of income; benefit is currently around €360 per month.

The amount of old age pension payable depends on your number of years' contributions. To qualify for a full pension, you must have made at least 156 weekly contributions or 36 monthly contributions in the previous five years, or 260 weekly contributions or 60 monthly contributions in total. Insurance contributions made in other EU member states can be taken into account when reaching this total. You can choose to make a one-off contribution (*riscatto*) to 'redeem' periods when insurance contributions haven't been made. Such periods may include time spent at university or working abroad in countries without a social security agreement with Italy. If you've paid five years' contributions, you can make voluntary contributions (*contributi volontari*) for periods spent raising a family or looking after a handicapped person. If you aren't employed, you can also make voluntary contributions.

The maximum old age pension is 80 per cent of your highest average annual income received in the previous ten years of employment. In the event of the death of a pensioner, a pension is transferred to a surviving spouse or children. Pensions are indexed to the cost of living and increase annually in line with inflation (currently around 2.4 per cent per year). Pensions are paid on the first day of the month following an application to your local INPS office. State pensions aren't taxable.

An invalidity pension is paid if you're totally and permanently unable to work. You become eligible after five years of contributions, including at least three years in the five years preceding a claim; you must have no other form of income. Payments range from €392.69 to €526.46 per month.

A survivor's pension is paid to the spouse of a deceased pensioner; if he or she has two or more children, the survivor is entitled to 100 per cent of the pension, if one child 80 per cent and if no children 60 per cent. A survivor's pension is also payable to dependent children who lose both (pensioner) parents: 100 per cent for three or more children, 80 per cent for two children and 70 per cent for one child.

As in all EU countries, state pensions are under pressure from governments that can no longer afford to pay them, due to a dwindling number of workers who are supporting a growing number of retirees. Italy has particular problems, as state pensions are too generous (for the government – pensions are **never** too high for pensioners!), despite reforms in recent years, and more people receive their income from the state than from the private sector. Italy (along with Japan) has the highest number of retired people as a percentage of population and in 30 years' time some 30 per cent of Italians will be over 65, which will put public finances at serious risk because the ratio of workers to pensioners will be almost equal (currently it's two to one). From 1st January 2001, the government has offered greater incentives for people to invest in private pensions funds (*fondi privati* or *fondi integrativi pensioni*), which it's hoped will shift some of the burden on to private insurance companies (see **Private Pensions** below).

When you reach state pension age, each EU country where you've paid social security for at least a year pays you an old-age pension. For example, if you've worked in three EU countries, you receive three separate old-age pensions. Each pension is calculated according to your insurance record in that country. If you move to Italy after working in another EU country (or move to another EU country after working in Italy), your state pension contributions can be exported to (or from) Italy. Italian state pensions are payable abroad and most countries pay state pensions directly to their nationals resident in Italy. Non-EU nationals who haven't reached pension age can request reimbursement of their pension contributions (plus their employer's contributions) on leaving Italy permanently.

Further information about pensions can be obtained from the Ministero del Lavoro e della Previdenza Sociale, Direzione della Previdenza, Via Flavia, 6, 00187 Rome (☎ 06-46831) and the Istituto Nazionale della Previdenza Sociale, INPS, Via Ciro il Grande, 21, 00144 Rome (☎ 06-59051).

PRIVATE PENSIONS

There are private pension funds in Italy, although they've been rather slow to take off due to their limited tax advantages when compared with those of many other EU countries.

Since 1st January 2001, anyone who invests in either a pension fund or a qualifying insurance policy (*previdenza*) has been able to deduct premiums of up to 12 per cent of their taxable income up to a tax-free limit of €5,170. Premiums are deducted at your top rate of tax. Employees must also take account of their employers' contributions and must allocate to their pension fund an amount of their termination payment (*trattamento di fine rapporto/TFR* or *liquidazione*) equal to 50 per cent of contributions. Employees hired for the first time after 23rd April 1993 must allocate all their *TFR* to a pension fund.

The increased value of a pension fund is taxed at 11 per cent (called a substitute tax), instead of the usual rate of 12.5 per cent for financial income (see **Capital Gains Tax** on page 318). Benefits (*prestazioni*) paid by pension funds are taxed at 12.5 per cent, net of the substitute tax already paid. Pension funds are authorised to pay a lump-sum capital amount of up to 50 per cent on maturity; the other 50 per cent must be taken as an annuity.

You should obtain professional advice before investing in a pension fund or insurance policy, particularly as the legislation regarding private pensions is recent and liable to change.

HEALTH INSURANCE

If you're planning to take up residence in Italy, your family is entitled to subsidised or free medical treatment under the Servizio Sanitario Nazionale (see page 254). However, many residents have a private health insurance policy (*assicurazione sulla salute*), which pays the portion of medical bills that isn't paid by social security. If you aren't entitled to public health benefits, you should have private health insurance, which is mandatory for non-EU residents when applying for a visa or residence permit.

You should avoid a company that reserves the right to cancel (*recesso* or *facoltà di rescessione*) a policy unilaterally when you have a serious illness or when you reach a certain age (shown as *età massima assicurabile* in policies), as it will prove difficult or impossible to find alternative cover. You should also steer clear of a one-year contract, which a company can refuse to renew. Nowadays, policies often have a period (e.g. five years) during which the insurance company cannot exclude you from cover (*rinuncia alla diritto di recessione*), even if you have a serious illness costing the insurance company a lot of money.

When taking out a policy, you must usually choose a maximum limit (*massimale*) on claims, unless it's already fixed. Ensure that it isn't too low and that it includes all members of your family. Obviously, the higher your cover, the higher are your premiums. Companies usually have a 'nuclear' family policy (*polizza per nucleo familiare*) offering substantial discounts. Most policies include optional cover for loss of earnings (*polizza di indennità giornaliera*) if you're unable to work for a period after an illness or accident, which is worth considering, particularly if you're self-employed.

When comparing policies, carefully check the extent of cover and exactly what's included and excluded from a policy (often indicated only in the **very** small print), in addition to premiums and excess charges. In some countries, premium increases are limited by law, although this may apply only to residents of the country where the company is registered and not to overseas policyholders. Although there may be significant differences in premiums, generally you get what you pay for and can tailor your premiums to your requirements. The most important questions to ask are whether the policy provides the necessary cover and whether it's good value. If you're in good heath and able to pay for your own out-patient treatment, such as visits to your family doctor and prescriptions, the best value policy may be one covering only specialist and hospital treatment. To compare policies, it's best to visit an insurance broker offering policies from a number of companies.

If you already have private health insurance in another country, you may be able to extend it to include Italy. If your stay in Italy is limited, you may be covered by a reciprocal agreement between your home country and Italy. If you already have a private health insurance policy, you may find you can save a substantial amount by switching to another company without losing any benefits (you may even gain some). **If you're planning to change your health insurance company, you should ensure that important benefits aren't lost, e.g. existing medical conditions won't usually be covered by a new insurer.** When changing employers or leaving Italy, you should ensure that you have continuous health insurance. If your family is covered by a company health scheme, your insurance probably ceases after your last official day of employment. When changing health insurance companies, it's wise to inform your old company if you have any outstanding bills for which they're liable.

Italian Companies

Most health polices offered by Italian insurance companies are supplementary policies for Italians who are covered by the national health service, and aren't intended for foreigners who aren't covered and are seeking a comprehensive health policy. Most Italian health insurance policies either don't pay family doctors' fees or pay for medicines other than those provided in a hospital or have an excess (deductible), e.g. around €80 for each 'illness', which may exceed the cost of treatment. Most, however, pay for 100 per cent of specialists' fees and hospital treatment in the best Italian hospitals. Private policies vary considerably in price but generally cost from €1,300 to €2,000 per year for a family of four, although they're higher for the elderly. Many companies, retirement groups and other organisations offer lower group rates.

The largest insurers in Italy include the National Insurance Institute (Instituto Nazionale delle Assicurazioni/INA), formerly state owned but now privatised, Europa Assistance, Filo Diretto, Pronto Assistance and Sanicard. Shop around and compare policies, which vary considerably – from good to terrible! Also bear in mind that (as in many countries) Italian insurance companies are reluctant to pay claims. (One of the reasons they don't insist on a medical examination is so that they can refuse to pay a claim because you omitted to tell them you had a heavy cold three years previously.) When completing the questionnaire (*questionario sanitario*) be sure to list **all** previous illnesses, hospitalisation, current ailments and treatment.

Foreign Companies

There are a number of foreign health insurance companies with agents or offices in Italy, including Baltica (Denmark), BUPA International, Exeter Friendly Society, PPP International, Columbus Healthcare and International Health Insurance (Denmark). These companies offer special policies for expatriates and usually include repatriation to your home country and international cover. If you aren't covered by Italian social security and need comprehensive private health insurance to obtain a resident permice, you must ensure that your health policy will be accepted by the authorities. The main advantages of a foreign health insurance policy are that treatment is unrestricted and you can choose any doctor, specialist, clinic or hospital in Italy, and usually abroad also. Policies may include permanent total disability cover of around €150,000 for those in full-time employment, and usually include repatriation and limited world-wide cover, including North America. A policy may also pay for repatriation of your body for burial in your home country.

Some companies offer policies for different areas, e.g. Europe, world-wide excluding North America, and world-wide including North America. A policy may offer full cover anywhere within Europe and limited cover in North America and certain other countries (e.g. Japan). An international policy allows you to choose to have non-urgent medical treatment in another country. Most companies offer different levels of cover; for example, PPP International offers Basic, Standard, Comprehensive and Prestige cover.

A medical isn't usually required for most health policies, although 'pre-existing' health problems are excluded for a period, e.g. one or two years. Usually there's an excess, e.g. around €80 per claim, although it may be possible to choose an increased voluntary excess of up to €800 and receive a discount (e.g. 10 or 20 per cent). An excess may be per visit (i.e. to a doctor or specialist), or per claim or illness. Obviously a 'per claim' policy is better, as the excess then includes a visit to a family doctor, medicines from a chemist's, a consultation with a specialist and hospitalisation, if they're all associated with the same illness. Cover for dental treatment, spectacles and contact lenses may be available as an option, although there may be a hefty excess, which usually means that you're better off paying bills yourself. A basic policy doesn't usually include maternity benefits and may offer no benefits or restricted benefits for out-patient treatment (which means that you must pay for visits to a family doctor); it may also exclude out-patient medicines, dressings, surgical/dental appliances, spectacles, contact lenses and hearing aids. There may also be an annual limit for ambulance costs.

Children (e.g. up to 16) may be included on a parent's policy and children up to a certain age (e.g. 26) may receive a 50 per cent premium reduction. Premiums are usually related to age, although some companies (such as the Exeter Hospital Aid Society) don't relate premiums to age provided you join before a certain age, e.g. 60 or 65. It's impossible to obtain insurance with some companies if you're above a certain age, e.g. 75.

There's always an annual limit on total annual medical costs (which should be at least €400,000 to €800,000) and some companies also limit costs for specific treatment or costs such as specialist's fees, operations and hospital accommodation. Some foreign health insurance policies may not provide sufficient cover to satisfy Italian regulations, and you should check the minimum cover necessary with an Italian consulate in your country of residence.

Claims are usually settled in major currencies and large claims are usually settled directly (*indennità diretto*) by insurance companies, although your choice of hospital may be limited. **Always check whether a company pays large medical bills directly.** If you're required to pay bills and claim reimbursement, it may take you several months to receive your money (some companies are slow to pay). It isn't usually necessary to have bills translated into English or another language, although you should check a company's policy. Most companies provide 24-hour emergency telephone assistance.

The cost of international heath insurance varies considerably according to your age and the extent of cover. Premiums can sometimes be paid monthly, quarterly or annually (credit card payment may be accepted), although some companies insist on payment annually in advance. Annual premiums vary from around €1,000 to over €4,000 for the most comprehensive cover.

DENTAL INSURANCE

It's unusual to have full dental insurance (*assicurazione per i denti*) in Italy, as the cost is prohibitive. Basic dental insurance is provided under social security (see **Dentists** on page 264) and Italian health insurance companies may offer additional cover as an option. Many international health insurance companies offer optional dental cover or extra dental cover for an additional premium, although there are many restrictions and cosmetic treatment is excluded. The amount payable by a health insurance policy for a particular item of treatment is fixed and depends on your level of dental insurance. A list of specific refunds is available from insurance companies.

Some dentists in Italy, including a number of foreign dentists, offer a dental insurance scheme. For a premium of around €80 per year for an adult, you're usually entitled to bi-annual check-ups, a scale and polish, and consultations at any time (possibly including X-rays). Insurance may also entitle members to a discount on the cost of fillings, crowns, bridges, dentures and children's orthodontics. The cost of dental insurance may be dependent on the condition of your teeth. **If you have healthy teeth and rarely pay for more than an annual check-up and a visit to a hygienist, dental insurance offers poor value.**

HOUSEHOLD INSURANCE

There's no requirement to have cover for your home or belongings and most Italians don't bother to insure their home or its contents, although if you have a mortgage (*ipoteca*), your lender will require you to have building (*edificio*) insurance. Nevertheless, it's highly recommended to take out insurance covering damage to the building due to fire, water, explosion, storm, freezing, snow, theft, vandalism and natural catastrophes. Household insurance (*assicurazione sulla casa*) generally constitutes a multi-risk policy for building and contents, although some companies require separate policies for fire and theft (*assicurazione contro furto e fuoco*) and for liability (*assicurazione contro terzi*) and others offer fire and damage (*incendio ed altri danni ai beni*) with an extra premium for theft and liability. Special conditions apply to holiday homes (see below).

It's possible (and legal) to take out building and contents insurance in another country for a property in Italy, although the policy may still be written under Italian law (so always check). The advantage is that you have a policy you can understand and you're able to handle claims in your own language (you may also be more likely to be paid or be paid earlier). This may seem like a good option for a holiday home in Italy, although it may be more expensive than insuring with an Italian company and can lead to conflicts if the building is insured with an Italian company and the contents with a foreign company.

Building Insurance

It's particularly important to have insurance against storm damage in Italy, which can be severe in some areas. Read the small print and check that you're covered for natural disasters such as floods. However, that if you live in an area that's hit by a succession of natural disasters, your insurance may be cancelled. Note also the following:

- Water damage caused by burst pipes due to old age or freezing may be excluded; under Italian law you're required to turn off the water at the mains if a property is left empty for more than 24 hours (although almost nobody does).

- If you use bottled gas, you must inform your insurance company, as there's an extra premium to pay.

- You must also specifically insure electrical systems and major apparatus against risk such as lightning strikes, or an insurance company won't pay.

- Italian policies usually exclude trees in your garden damaging your house and garden walls falling down.

- You cannot insure against earthquakes on an Italian policy, although a foreign insurance provider may offer cover for an exorbitant premium (e.g. Lloyd's of London). If there's an earthquake, the Italian government assumes responsibility, which is limited to the value stated in the land registry (well below a property's actual value), although the insured value of your home is also taken into consideration.

In the event of total loss, building insurance is based on the cost of rebuilding your home. **Make sure that you insure your property for the true cost of rebuilding.** If you have a property restored or modernised, you must obatin a professional valuation on completion for insurance purposes.

Apartments: If you own an apartment or a property that shares common elements with other properties, building insurance is included in your service charges, although you should check exactly what's covered. You must, however, still be insured for third party risks in the event that you cause damage to neighbouring apartments, e.g. through flood or fire. Having insurance also helps you claim against a neighbour if they cause damage to your apartment.

Rented Property: Your landlord usually insists that you have third party liability insurance, as detailed in the rental contract. A lease requires you to insure against 'tenant's risks', including damage you may make to the rental property and to other properties if you live in an apartment, e.g. due to flood, fire or explosion. You can choose your own insurance company.

Contents Insurance

Contents (*contenuto*) are usually insured for the same risks as a building (see above) and are insured for their replacement value. Contents polices are restrictive with regard to security, including locks, window shutters or grilles (all windows less than 3m/10ft from the ground must be barred), armoured doors, etc.. All security requirements must be adhered to or claims are reduced or won't be paid. Note that Italian policies usually exclude loss of frozen food (after a power cut). There's usually an excess of between €125 and €250 for each claim.

You cannot usually insure valuables (e.g. antiques, jewellery and other precious objects) unless they've been valued by an approved Italian expert and they generally need to be stored in a safe, which must be approved by your insurance company. You should insist on a safe being approved by your insurer and a certificate being issued to verify this (otherwise your insurance company is liable to use the argument that your safe was insecure to avoid paying a claim). Valuables are usually covered only when you're present, rather than abroad or on holiday. Due to the many loopholes, you may be better off keeping your valuables in a bank safety deposit box. When claiming for contents, you should produce the original bills (keep bills for expensive items) and bear in mind that imported items may be much more expensive in Italy.

Holiday Homes

Premiums are generally higher for holiday homes due to their high vulnerability (particularly to burglaries) and are usually based on the number of days per year a property is inhabited and the interval between periods of occupancy. Cover for theft, storm, flood and malicious damage may be suspended when a property is left empty for more than three weeks at a time. It's possible to negotiate cover for periods of absence for a hefty surcharge, although valuable items are usually excluded. If you're absent from your property for long periods, e.g. more than 60 days per year, you may also be required to pay an excess on a claim arising from an occurrence that takes place during your absence (and theft may be excluded). You should read all small print in policies. **Where applicable, it's important to ensure that a policy specifies a holiday home and not a principal home.**

In areas with a high risk of theft (e.g. most major cities and resort areas), you may be required to fit extra locks and other security measures. Some companies may not insure holiday homes in high risk areas. It's unwise to leave valuable or irreplaceable items in a holiday home or a home that's vacant for long periods. **Some insurance companies do their utmost to find a loophole which makes you negligent and relieves them of their liability.** Always check carefully that the details listed in a policy are correct, or your policy could be void.

Premiums

Premiums are usually calculated on the size of the property (either the habitable area in square metres or the number of rooms) rather than its value. Usually the sum insured (house and contents) is unlimited, provided the property doesn't exceed a certain size and is under a certain age. Premiums depend on the area, although you should expect the premium for a policy that includes theft to be around double what you would expect to pay in another western European country. The cost of multi-risk property insurance in a low-risk area is around €90 per year for a property with one or two bedrooms, €160 for three or four bedrooms and around €325 per year for five or six bedrooms. Premiums can be much higher in high-risk areas. If you have an index-linked policy, cover is increased each year in line with inflation.

Claims

If you wish to make a claim, you must usually inform your insurance company in writing (by registered letter) within two to five days of an incident or 24 hours in the case of theft. Thefts should also be reported to the local police within 24 hours, as the police statement (*denuncia*), of which you receive a copy for your insurance company, usually constitutes irrefutable evidence of your claim. **Check whether you're covered for damage or thefts that occur while you're away from the property and are therefore unable to inform your insurance company immediately.**

THIRD PARTY LIABILITY INSURANCE

Many people have third party liability insurance (*assicurazione contro terzi*) in Italy. This covers all members of a family and includes damage done or caused by your children and pets – for example, if your dog or child bites someone.

Where damage is due to severe negligence, benefits may be reduced. Check whether insurance covers you against accidental damage to your home's fixtures and fittings. Third party liability insurance can be combined with household insurance (see above). The cost of third party liability insurance when included in household insurance is around €170 per year and you may need to pay an excess, e.g. the first €75 to €150 of a claim.

HOLIDAY & TRAVEL INSURANCE

Holiday and travel insurance (*assicurazione sul viaggio*) are recommended for all who don't wish to risk having their holiday or travel ruined by financial problems or to arrive home broke. As you probably know, anything can and often does go wrong with a holiday, sometimes before you even get started (particularly when you **don't** have insurance). The following information applies equally to residents and non-residents, whether you're travelling to or from Italy or within Italy. **Nobody should visit Italy without travel (and health) insurance.**

Travel insurance is available from many sources, including travel agents, insurance companies and brokers, banks, motoring organisations and transport companies (airline, rail and bus). Package holiday companies and tour operators also offer insurance policies, some of which are compulsory, overpriced **and don't provide adequate cover.** You can also buy 24-hour accident and flight insurance at major airports, although it's expensive and doesn't offer the best cover. Before taking out travel insurance, you should carefully consider the range and level of cover you require and compare policies. Short-term holiday and travel insurance policies may include cover for holiday cancellation or interruption, missed flights, departure delay at both the start and end of a holiday (a common occurrence), delayed, lost or damaged baggage, lost belongings and money, medical expenses and accidents (including evacuation home), personal liability and legal expenses, and default or bankruptcy, e.g. a tour operator or airline going bust. You may also need cover for transport strikes!

Always check any exclusion clauses in contracts by obtaining a copy of the full policy document, as all relevant information won't be included in an insurance leaflet. High risk sports and pursuits should be specifically covered and **listed** in a policy (there's usually an additional premium). Special winter sports policies are available and more expensive than normal holiday insurance ('dangerous' sports are excluded from most standard policies). Third party liability cover should be €3 million in North America and €1.5 million in the rest of the world. **However, this doesn't usually cover you when you're driving a car or other mechanically propelled vehicle.**

Health Cover

Medical expenses are an important aspect of travel insurance and you shouldn't rely on insurance provided by reciprocal health arrangements, charge and credit card companies, household policies or private medical insurance (unless it's an international policy), none of which usually provide adequate cover, although you should take advantage of what they offer. The minimum medical insurance recommended by experts is €400,000 for Italy and the rest of Europe and €1.5 million for the rest of the world (many policies have limits of between €2.25 million and €7.5 million). If applicable, check whether pregnancy-related claims are covered and whether there are any restrictions for those over a certain age, e.g. 65 or 70 (travel insurance is becoming increasingly expensive for those aged over 65, although they don't usually need to worry about pregnancy – particularly the men!).

Visitors

Travel insurance for visitors to Italy should include personal liability and repatriation expenses. If your travel insurance expires while you're visiting Italy, you can buy further insurance from a local insurance agent, although this won't include repatriation expenses. Flight and comprehensive travel insurance are available from insurance desks at most airports, including travel accident, personal accident, world-wide medical expenses and in-transit baggage.

Cost

The cost of travel insurance varies considerably according to where you buy it, how long you intend to stay in Italy and your age. Generally the longer the period covered, the cheaper the daily cost, although the maximum period covered is usually limited, e.g. to six months. With some policies, an excess must be paid for each claim; with others, the excess applies only to certain items, such as luggage, money and medical expenses. As a rough guide, travel insurance for Italy (and most other European countries) costs from around €35 for one week, €50 for two weeks and €80 for a month for a family of four (two adults and two children under 16). Premiums may be higher for those aged over 65 or 70.

Annual Policies

For people who travel abroad frequently, whether on business or pleasure, an annual travel policy usually provides the best value, but carefully check exactly what it includes. Many insurance companies offer annual travel policies for around €150 to €250 per year for an individual (the equivalent of around two to three months' insurance with a standard travel insurance policy), which are excellent value for frequent travellers. Some insurance companies also offer an 'emergency travel policy' for holiday homeowners who need to travel abroad at short notice to inspect a property, e.g. after a severe storm or burglary. The cost of an annual policy may depend on the area covered, e.g. Europe, world-wide (excluding North America) and world-wide (including North America), although it doesn't usually cover travel within your country of residence. There's also a limit on the number of trips per year and the duration of each trip, e.g. 90 or 120 days. An annual policy is usually a good choice for owners of a holiday home in Italy who travel there frequently for relatively short periods. **However, carefully check exactly what's covered (or omitted), as an annual policy may not provide adequate cover.**

Claims

If you need to make a claim, you should provide as much documentary evidence as possible to support it. Travel insurance companies gladly take your money, but they aren't always so keen to pay claims and you may need to persevere before they pay up. Always be persistent and make a claim **irrespective** of any small print, as this may be unreasonable and therefore invalid in law. Insurance companies usually require you to report a loss (or any incident for which you intend to make a claim) to the local police or carriers within 24 hours and obtain a written report. Failure to do so may mean that a claim won't be considered.

LIFE INSURANCE

Although there are worse things in life than death (like spending an evening with a life insurance salesman), your dependants may rate your death without life insurance high on their list. Many Italian companies provide free life insurance (*assicurazione sulla vita* or *polizza assicurativa/vita*) as an employment benefit, although it may be accident life insurance only. You can take out life insurance or an endowment policy with numerous Italian and foreign insurance companies. Note that Italian policies are usually for life **insurance** and not for **assurance**. (An assurance policy covers an eventuality that's certain to occur, e.g. your death, so a life assurance policy is valid until you die; an insurance policy covers a possible event, e.g. an accident).

In certain cases, life insurance premiums are tax-deductible and a life policy can be useful as security for a bank loan and can be limited to cover the period of the loan. See also **Mortgage & Registration Tax** on page 319.

A life insurance policy intended to take advantage of Italian law is (obviously) best taken out in Italy. However, Italian insurance companies are notoriously slow in paying out on policies that have matured, such as endowment policies (Italy is the only country where the beneficiaries of life policies are likely to die before getting paid!).

It's recommended to leave copies of all insurance policies with your will (see page 319) and with your lawyer. If you don't have a lawyer, keep a copy in a safe deposit box. A life insurance policy must usually be sent to the insurance company upon the death of the insured, with a copy of the death certificate (see **Births & Deaths** on page 268).

14.

FINANCE

Italy is one of the highest taxed countries in the EU. (It's also estimated to have the highest number of tax dodgers, including many of Italy's most famous names – tax evasion is **the** national sport.) There seems to be a tax stamp (*bollo*) for everything in Italy (the Beatles must have had Italy in mind when they wrote their song *The Tax Man*). To make matters worse, Italian tax law is inordinately complicated (it has been simplified in recent years, although you wouldn't believe it) and the taxes, regulations and procedures are constantly changing (just when you think you understand them they change everything and hit you with new taxes). It's important to check all tax information, including the information contained in this book, with an accountant or tax office (but get it in writing) in order to establish that it's correct.

If you plan to live permanently in Italy, you must ensure that your income is and will remain sufficient to live on, bearing in mind currency devaluations and exchange rate fluctuations (if your income isn't paid in euros), rises in the cost of living (see page 321), and unforeseen expenses such as medical bills or anything else that may reduce your income (such as stock market crashes and recessions!). Foreigners, particularly retirees, often under-estimate the cost of living in Italy and some are forced to return to their home countries after a few years. Note also that Italy is one of the highest taxed countries in the European Union (EU) when both direct and indirect taxes (including social security) are taken into consideration. However, the cost of living in Italy is still lower than in many other EU countries, inflation was around 2.4 per cent in 2003 and for many the quality of life/cost of living ratio is unsurpassed.

Competition for your money (*denaro*) is stiff, with financial services offered by commercial and savings banks, foreign banks, the post office, investment brokers and a variety of other financial institutions. Compared to many other western countries, particularly the UK and USA, Italy hasn't traditionally been a credit economy, and Italians have preferred to use cash rather than credit cards or even cheques. The use of plastic money (credit, charge, debit and cash cards) has become increasingly popular in recent years, although it's still some way below most other EU countries.

If you're planning to invest in property or a business in Italy that's financed with money earned or held in a currency other than euros, it's important to consider both present and possible future exchange rates (don't be too optimistic!). If you wish to borrow money to buy property or for a business venture in Italy, you should carefully consider where and in what currency it should be raised. Note that it's difficult for foreigners to obtain business loans in Italy, particularly for new ventures, and you shouldn't rely on it. On the other hand, if you earn your income in euros, this may affect your financial commitments abroad, particularly if the currency is devalued. List all your probable and possible expenses, and do your homework thoroughly **before** moving to Italy – afterwards it may be too late!

When you arrive in Italy to take up residence or employment, ensure that you have sufficient cash, travellers' cheques, credit cards, luncheon vouchers, coffee machine tokens, gold coins, diamonds, etc. to last at least until your first pay day, which may be some time after your arrival. During this period you will also find an international credit card (or two) useful.

FISCAL CODE

All residents of Italy need a fiscal code (*codice fiscale*), which Italians receive at birth. This is required to apply for a job, open a bank account, register a car, buy or rent a home, and even to pay utility bills. You can obtain a fiscal code card from your local tax office (*intendenza di finanza*), where you must present your passport and a copy of the pages containing your particulars. Codes for individuals comprise letters and figures (figures only for companies). The code is made up of the first, third and fourth consonants of your surname (or fewer if there aren't enough), the year and month of your birth (the months being represented by the letters A to L), and your day of birth (1 to 31 for men, 41 to 71 for women). So, for example, if your name is Joe Bloggs and you were born on 1st January 1950, your fiscal code would be BGGS1950A1. Each *comune* has its own number for fiscal code purposes, although the country of birth is shown for foreigners. Husbands and wives have separate codes, as a wife in Italy retains and uses her maiden name after she is married.

You should inform your local tax office when you move home, although you retain the same fiscal code. Your fiscal code must be used on all official correspondence with the tax authorities and on tax declarations. It's useful to keep a note of your code with you at all times, as you never know when you may be required to provide it. If you lose your fiscal code card, the easiest way to obtain a new one is via the Finance Ministry's website (🖳 www.finanze.it).

ITALIAN CURRENCY

On 1st January 1999 the euro (€) was introduced in Italy (plus Austria, Belgium, Finland, France, Germany, Ireland, Luxembourg, the Netherlands, Portugal and Spain) and is now the official currency. Euro notes and coins were introduced on 1st January 2002, although the lira continued to circulate until 1st July 2002, when it was withdrawn (€1 = 1,936.27 lire).

The euro is divided into 100 cents (*centesimi*) and coins are minted in 1, 2, 5, 10, 20 and 50 cents, and 1 and 2 euro denominations. Coins all have a common European face with a map of the European Union and the stars of the European flag, while the obverse is different for each member country. Italian coins have the following designs: the Castel del Monte (1 cent), the Mole Antonelliana tower (2 cents), the Flavian amphitheatre (5 cents), Botticelli's 'Birth of Venus' (10 cents), a Boccioni sculpture (20 cents), Marcus Aurelius (50 cents), a drawing by Leonardo da Vinci (€1) and Dante by Raphael (€2). Coins are minted by individual countries, although they can be used throughout the euro zone irrespective of where they were made.

Euro banknotes are printed in 5, 10, 20, 50, 100, 200 and 500 denominations. The design of the notes was subject to considerable debate and contention, and the winning design depicts 'symbolic' representations of Europe's architectural heritage. None of the 'representations' on any of the notes are supposed to be actual buildings, bridges or arches, although there have been numerous claims in the press and elsewhere that the structures shown are actually landmarks in certain countries.

The euro symbol (€) is generally available on most computer keyboards and calculators unless you're using pre-1997 (or so) equipment or software. Financial software in most of Europe can be easily upgraded to make use of the symbol if it isn't already incorporated into the current release. The Microsoft website (⌨ www.microsoft.com) has keyboard and operating system updates available for downloading, although if you've installed any updates to make your system Y2K compatible, you're probably already euro-ready, at least as far as basic fonts are concerned.

IMPORTING & EXPORTING MONEY

There are no exchange controls in Italy and no restrictions on the import or export of funds. An Italian resident is permitted to open a bank account in any country and to export unlimited funds. You may import or export up to €10,330 in any combination of foreign currency, Italian currency, travellers' cheques and securities without formality. Amounts over €10,330 (e.g. to buy a home) must be declared to the Exchange Controls Office (Ufficio Italiano dei Cambi) in order to prevent money laundering and provide statistical data for the Banca d'Italia.

When transferring or sending money to (or from) Italy you should be aware of the alternatives and shop around for the best deal. One way to do this is via a banker's draft (*assegno circolare*), which should be sent by registered post. Note, however, that in the unlikely event that it's lost or stolen, it's impossible to stop payment and you must wait six months before a new draft can be issued. Bank drafts aren't treated as cash in Italy and must be cleared, as with personal cheques. One of the safest and quickest methods of transferring money is to make a direct transfer or a telex or electronic transfer (e.g. via the SWIFT system in Europe) between banks. A 'normal' transfer should take three to seven days, but in reality can take much longer and an international bank transfer between non-affiliated banks can take weeks! A SWIFT telex transfer **should** be completed in a few hours, funds being available within 24 hours. The cost of transfers varies considerably, not only commission and exchange rates, but also transfer charges (such as the telex charge for a SWIFT transfer).

It's usually quicker and cheaper to transfer funds between branches of the same bank than between non-affiliated banks. Italian banks (along with Portuguese and Spanish banks) are among the slowest in Europe to process bank transfers and you should expect them to take at least twice as long as a bank says it will. It isn't unusual for transfers to and from Italy to get 'stuck' in the pipeline, which allows the Italian bank to use your money for a period interest free. Except for the fastest (and most expensive) methods, transfers between international banks are a joke in the age of electronic banking, when powerful financiers can switch funds almost instantaneously.

Always check charges and exchange rates in advance and agree them with your bank (you may be able to negotiate a lower charge or a better exchange rate). Shop around a number of banks and compare fees. Some foreign banks levy a flat fee for electronic transfers, irrespective of the amount. British banks charge between GB£10 and GB£45 for 'express' electronic transfers taking from one to five days or longer. When you have money transferred to a bank in Italy, make sure that you give the account holder's name, the account number, the branch number and the bank code. If money is 'lost' while being transferred to or from an Italian bank account, it can take weeks to locate it. If you plan to send a large amount of money to Italy or abroad for a business transaction such as buying property, you should ensure that you receive the commercial rate of exchange rather than the tourist rate.

You can also send money by international money order from a post office or with a telegraphic transfer, e.g. via Western Union, the quickest and safest method, but also the most expensive. Western Union transfers can be picked up from a post office in Italy (and 100 other countries) just 15 minutes after being paid into an office abroad. Money can be sent via American Express offices by Amex cardholders. Postcheques (see page 134) can be cashed at any post office in Italy and most credit and charge cards can be used to obtain cash advances. It may be possible to pay some bills by personal cheque, although these take a long time to clear (a number of weeks) and fees are high. **However, most Italian banks don't accept cheques drawn on foreign banks.**

Most banks in major cities have foreign exchange windows and there are banks or exchange bureaux (*ufficio di cambio*) with extended opening hours at airports, major railway stations and in all major cities. Here you can buy or sell foreign currencies, buy and cash travellers' cheques, and obtain a cash advance on credit and charge cards. At airports and in tourist areas in major cities, there are automatic change machines accepting up to 15 currencies, including US$, GB£ and Swiss francs. **However, airports (and change machines) usually offer the worst exchange rates and charge the highest fees (e.g. handling charges).**

There are many private exchange bureaux in major cities and resorts with longer business hours than banks, particularly at weekends. Most offer competitive exchange rates and low or no commission (but always check). They're easier to deal with than banks and, if you're changing a lot of money, you can usually negotiate a better exchange rate. Never use unofficial money changers, who are likely to short change you or leave you with worthless foreign notes rather than euros. Banks tend to offer the best exchange rates and the post office the lowest charges. The post office charges a flat rate of €0.50 per transaction (irrespective of the amount), while banks charge €1.30 or more. The exchange rate (*tasso di cambio*) against the euro for most major international currencies is listed in banks and daily newspapers. Exchange rates are better when obtaining cash with a credit or debit card, as you're given the wholesale rate, although there's a 1.5 per cent charge on cash advances and ATM transactions in foreign currencies.

If you're visiting Italy, it's safer to carry travellers' cheques (*assegni turistici*) than cash. You can buy travellers' cheques from any bank, usually for a fee of 1 per cent of the face value. You can buy euro travellers' cheques, although it may be better to buy cheques in a major currency such as US$ or GB£, which can be used anywhere in Europe. However travellers' cheques aren't as easy to cash in Italy as in some other countries, e.g. the USA, and they're difficult to change in rural areas. They aren't usually accepted as cash by businesses, except perhaps hotels, restaurants and shops in Rome and other major cities, which usually offer a poor exchange rate. Fees and rates vary considerably when cashing travellers' cheques in Italy. Some banks charge €0.50 per cheque with a €1.50 minimum, while the post office charges €1 for amounts up to €50 and €2.60 above €50. Buying large denomination cheques saves on per-cheque exchange charges. Note that American Express and Thomas Cook offices don't charge for cashing their own cheques. Banks usually offer a better exchange rate for travellers' cheques than for banknotes.

Always keep a separate record of cheque numbers and note where and when they were cashed. American Express provides a free, three-hour replacement service for lost or stolen travellers' cheques at any of their offices world-wide, provided you know the serial numbers of the lost cheques. Without the serial numbers, replacement can take three days or longer. Most companies provide toll-free numbers for reporting lost or stolen travellers' cheques in Italy.

One thing to bear in mind when travelling anywhere isn't to rely on one source of funds only.

BANKS

There are three kinds of bank in Italy: ordinary commercial or credit banks, co-operative banks (*banchi popolari cooperative*) and co-operative credit banks (*banche di credito cooperativo*). As in other countries, co-operative banks were established to provide loans (particularly home loans) to their customers. Co-operative credit banks are rural and artisan savings banks funded and owned by farmers and craftsmen. They comprise the largest number of banks (over 500) in Italy, but because their average size is very small they account for just a tiny percentage of total deposits. The Banca d'Italia is owned by the public sector banks and is the only bank permitted to issues notes in Italy.

There are some 900 banks (*banche*), around 200 of which are large (*grandi*), including around 50 branches of foreign banks (mostly in Rome and Milan). The remaining 700 or so are primarily local banks with few branches. The number of banks in Italy is continually decreasing as banks merge or are taken over.

The Banca Nazionale del Lavoro, Cassa di Risparmio, Banca Commerciale Italiana, Banca di Roma, Banco di Napoli and Banco di Sicilia all have nationwide branch networks. The top ten banks hold some 35 per cent of total bank assets. Creditwest, a joint venture between Credito Italiano and the British National Westminster Bank, has around 30 branches in Rome, Milan and Naples. The post office serves as a savings bank for many Italians and foreign residents, although non-residents aren't permitted to open a post office account.

Bank opening hours vary according to the bank and town, and are generally from 8 or 8.30am until 1 or 1.30pm and for one to one and a half hours in the afternoon, e.g. from 2.30 or 3pm until 4 or 4.30pm, Mondays to Fridays. Some branches in major cities also open from 9am to noon on Saturdays. On the day before a public holiday, banks usually open only in the morning. Offices at major airports and railway stations have longer opening hours for changing money and cashing travellers' cheques, and there are also exchange bureaux in major cities and resorts with extended opening hours.

Italian banks have traditionally levied some of the highest charges in the world, although they've been reduced in recent years. The interest rates charged by many Italian banks are still exorbitant, particularly for business and consumer loans. The interest rates levied on credit cards are also excessive. However, lenders are now required to publish the highest rates they charge and the market average, so that borrowers can make comparisons. Shop around and compare rates before signing any contracts or taking out a loan (banks must also publish their conditions).

Italy has traditionally had one of the least efficient and most ponderous banking services in Europe, where even the simplest operation was inordinately complicated and time-consuming. However, banking has become highly automated in recent years, although Italian banks still lag behind those in many other European countries in terms of efficiency, customer service, and the range and quality of services provided.

On the other hand, Italians banks are quite safe and most deposits are covered by a Bank Deposit Insurance Fund (*Fondo Interbancario di Tutela dei Depositi*). Branches of EU banks operating in Italy can join an Italian deposit guarantee plan and increase the amount of financial protection they offer clients above and beyond the protection provided by their home country's guarantee plan. If a bank from a non-EU country is licensed to operate in Italy, the Italian branch must be part of the Italian deposit guarantee plan unless they're members of an equivalent foreign plan. The maximum amount reimbursed to each depositor is limited to the very precise figure of €103,291.38.

Opening An Account

You can open a bank account in Italy whether you're a resident or a non-resident. If you're a non-resident, you're entitled to open a non-resident account (*conto estero*) only. Only foreign currency or imported euros can be paid into a non-resident account, which pays higher interest than resident accounts. There's no withholding tax on interest earned on deposits in non-resident accounts, as there is for resident euro accounts (when withholding tax is deducted at source). If you're a non-resident, it's possible to survive without an Italian account by using cash, travellers' cheques and credit cards, although this isn't wise and is an expensive option. If you have a second home in Italy, you can have all documentation (e.g. cheque books and statements) sent to an address abroad. Some Italian banks also provide written communications in English.

You're considered to be a resident of Italy (*residenti valutari*) if you have your main centre of interest there, i.e. you live or work there more or less permanently. To open a resident's account you must usually have a residence permit (*certificato di residenza*) or evidence that you have a job in Italy.

It's best to open an Italian bank account in person, rather than from abroad. Ask your friends, neighbours or colleagues for their recommendations and just go along to the bank of your choice and introduce yourself. You must be aged at least 18 and provide proof of identity, e.g. a passport, and your address in Italy (a utility bill usually suffices). Before choosing a bank, it's wise to compare the fees charged for international money transfers and other services, which can be high.

If you wish to open an account with an Italian bank while abroad, you must obtain an application form from a branch of an Italian bank (either in Italy or your home country). You need to select a branch from the list provided, which should be close to your home or place of business in Italy. If you open an account by correspondence, you must provide a reference from your bank, including a certificate of signature or a signature witnessed by a solicitor or lawyer. You also need a photocopy of the relevant pages of your passport and a euro draft to open the account.

It isn't recommended to close your bank accounts abroad even when you're living permanently in Italy, unless you're absolutely certain that you won't need them in the future. It's cheaper to keep some money in local currency in an account in a country that you visit regularly, rather than pay commission to convert euros. Many foreigners living in Italy maintain at least two accounts: a foreign account (possibly offshore) for international transactions and a local account with an Italian bank for day-to-day business.

All banks provide credit and debit or ATM cards (called Bancomat cards) to obtain cash throughout Italy and also abroad, usually via the CIRRUS and NYCE networks. However, it's unwise to rely solely on ATMs (called Bancomats) to obtain cash, as they often run out of money or are out of operation. Note also that daily withdrawals with a debit card are generally limited to €300.

Cheque Accounts

The normal bank account for day-to-day transactions in Italy is a cheque (*assegno*) or current account (*conto corrente/interno*). Non-EU residents need Italian residency and a fiscal code (see page 295) to open a current account. Couples can open a joint account (*conto corrente cointestato*) and some banks have special accounts and deals for children, pensioners, students and women. Always shop around and compare fees and benefits before opening an account. When opening a cheque account, you should request a debit (Bancomat) card, which can be used to pay for goods and pay bills throughout Italy. You receive a cheque book (*libretto di assegni*) and your debit card, which you must usually collect in person from your branch, around two to three weeks after opening an account.

Interest is paid on cheque accounts quarterly, although it may be as little as 0.5 per cent. Many banks offer accounts where the balance above a sum of your choice (e.g. €2,500) is automatically invested in mutual funds. There's a fee of around €1 for a cheque book containing ten cheques, although some banks issue them free of charge, and a fee for each cheque you write (which is around €0.80 or more when charges, duty and insurance are included). Current account charges vary according to factors such as the number of cheques you write and the average balance maintained and may be negotiable. Charges are higher for non-resident than resident accounts. Each entry on your bank statement costs you between €0.80 and €1.50, although most banks allow you 100 free operations per year (which includes every withdrawal made with a debit card).

Cheques (*assegni*) may be crossed (*sbarrato*) or open (*non-sbarrato*). Cheques require endorsement on the back before they can be paid into an account. Note that open cheques are freely negotiable and even crossed cheques can be endorsed to a third party (up to €10,350), although you can write not transferable (*non trasferibile*) on the back of a cheque to prevent it from being endorsed. Cheque guarantee cards (*carte di garanzia*) are available in Italy, but few people accept personal cheques even with a guarantee card and you're unlikely to be able to use your cheque book with businesses outside your local area, except utility companies and other businesses you deal with regularly.

To obtain cash at a bank counter, you must complete a form or write a cheque made out to yourself (*me medesimo*, usually written as *m.m.*, or *me stesso*), which can usually be done only at your own branch. All cheques must be written in Italian and not in English and in blue or black in. When writing the amount in words, no capitals are used and all words are connected. When writing figures in Italy (or anywhere in continental Europe), you should cross the down stroke of the number 7 in order to avoid confusion with the number 1, which is often written with a leading upstroke and resembles a seven to many non-Europeans. Like other Europeans, Italians write the date with the day first followed by the month and year; for example, 1.9.04 is 1st September 2004 and not 9th January 2004. **The conventional US form 1/9/00, with the month first and slashes between the digits, is unknown and must never be used!**

Most banks now have tellers who can cash cheques, thus eliminating the previous two-step operation where you presented the cheque/form at one counter and were given a receipt to take to a cash desk (*cassa*) to obtain your money.

It's illegal to bounce cheques (*assegno a vuoto*) in Italy, for which you can be banned from holding a bank account and prosecuted. You should also take care not to become overdrawn, which can be expensive (overdrafts may be possible for a hefty interest rate). Post-dating cheques is also against the law, and all cheques can be presented for payment on the day they're written irrespective of their date. The time taken to clear cheques (after which the funds are credited to your account and start earning interest) varies from two days for a cheque drawn on the same bank to a week or longer for a cheque drawn on a different bank. You can stop payment of a cheque only when it has been lost or stolen (not simply because you've changed your mind), when a report must be made to the local police.

Bank statements (*estratto conto*) are issued monthly or quarterly (you can usually choose) and contain your account details such as your bank, branch and account number at the top. This information is required when payments are to be made directly to or from your account, e.g. by standing order (*ordine di pagamento*) or direct debit (*domiciliazione*). Regular bills (such as utility bills) are best paid by direct debit, for which there's a charge of around €0.80. If you're a non-resident, it's recommended to keep an emergency amount on deposit for unexpected (or unexpectedly high) bills. Bills can also be paid in cash at banks by completing a payment slip (*richiesta di bonifico*).

Offshore Banking

If you have a sum of money to invest or wish to protect your inheritance from the tax man, it may be worthwhile investigating the accounts and services (such as pensions and trusts) provided by offshore banking centres in tax havens such as the Channel Islands (Guernsey and Jersey), Gibraltar and the Isle of Man (around 50 locations world-wide are officially classified as tax havens). Offshore banking has had a good deal of media attention in recent years, during which it has also been under investigation by the EU. The major attractions are that money can be deposited in a wide range of currencies, customers are usually guaranteed complete anonymity, there are no double taxation agreements, no withholding tax is payable and interest is paid tax-free. Many offshore banks also offer telephone (usually 24 hours per day, seven days per week) and Internet banking.

A large number of American, British and other European banks and financial institutions provide offshore banking facilities in one or more locations. Most institutions offer high-interest deposit accounts for long-term savings and investment portfolios, in which funds can be deposited in any major currency. Many people living abroad keep a local account for everyday business and maintain an offshore account for international transactions and investment purposes. However, most financial experts advise investors not to invest their life savings in an offshore tax haven until they know what their long-term plans are.

Offshore accounts have minimum deposits levels, which usually range from around €700 to €14,000, with some as high as €140,000. In addition to large minimum balances, accounts may also have strict terms and conditions, such as restrictions on withdrawals or high early withdrawal penalties. You can deposit funds on call (instant access) or for a fixed period, e.g. from 90 days to a year (usually for larger sums). Interest is usually paid monthly or annually; monthly interest payments are slightly lower than annual payments, but they have the advantage of providing a regular income. There are usually no charges, provided a specified minimum balance is maintained. Many accounts offer a cash or credit card (e.g. MasterCard or Visa) that can be used to obtain cash from cash machines (ATMs) throughout the world.

When selecting a financial institution and offshore banking centre, your first priority should be for the safety of your money. In some offshore banking centres, all bank deposits are guaranteed under a deposit protection scheme, whereby a maximum sum is guaranteed should the financial institution go to the wall (the Isle of Man, Guernsey and Jersey all have such schemes). Unless you're planning to bank with a major international bank, you should check the credit rating of a financial institution before depositing any money, particularly if it doesn't provide deposit insurance. All banks have a credit rating (the highest is 'AAA') and a bank with a high rating will happily tell you what it is (but get it in writing). You can also check the rating of an international bank or financial organisation with Moody's Investor Service. You should be wary of institutions offering higher than average interest rates; if it looks too good to be true it probably will be!

DEBIT, CREDIT & CHARGE CARDS

Debit, credit and charge cards are referred to collectively as credit cards in Italy, which has over 30 million in circulation, almost two-thirds of which are debit cards. Real credit cards (which allow you to pay the balance over a period of time) have been slow to gain acceptance in Italy, where many people still prefer to pay for purchases in cash or with a debit card. However, in the last decade there has been a marked increase in the popularity of credit cards, particularly due to their usefulness in shopping via the telephone or Internet or abroad. Most so-called 'credit' cards issued in Italy function more like charge cards, in that payments for purchases are due when billed and cannot be paid over a period of several months or years. The most common credit cards in Italy are CartaSì, MasterCard and Visa, which are available from most banks. You can also obtain an American Express or Diners Club card direct from these companies.

All Italian banks issue debit/ATM cards known as Bancomat cards, for which there's an annual fee of between €10 and €20; most banks also charge you between €0.80 and €2 for each purchase you make with the card, which explains why most Italians prefer to use cash.

A credit card in Italy costs between €35 and €110 per year, depending on the type of card and the level of service you choose. Some cards include travel or other forms of insurance, either as part of the annual fee or as an add-on feature. When you apply for a credit card, you're required to indicate the bank account you wish to use to pay your monthly balance, and the contract includes a standing order payment to permit the card company to debit payments automatically from your account. You receive a statement of your monthly charges around ten days before the date that the amount due is debited from your account, so you have an opportunity to review the statement and dispute any incorrect payments or charges.

Most credit cards allow you to withdraw cash from ATMs that are part of their network, although there's a charge for each transaction. It's sometimes possible to make deferred payments on travel costs (mostly air fares and hotel bills) charged to your card, but only over a few months (normally two or three months maximum). Before obtaining a credit or charge card, compare the costs and benefits.

If you maintain a bank account abroad, it's wise to retain your foreign credit cards. One of the advantages of using a credit card issued abroad is that your bill is usually rendered or your account debited up to six weeks later, thereby giving you interest-free credit – except when cards are used to obtain cash, when interest starts immediately. You may, however, find it more convenient and cheaper to be billed in euros than in a foreign currency, e.g. US\$ or GB£, when you must wait for the bill from outside Italy and charges vary with exchange rate fluctuations.

If you lose a bank or credit card, you must report it immediately to the issuing office, or within 24 hours at the latest. You also need to report the theft to the police and obtain a copy of the report (*dununcia*). If the theft isn't reported and the card blocked within 24 hours, insurance cover no longer applies and any purchases made by a thief won't be reimbursed. If you lose a Visa, CartaSì or MasterCard (all operated by Servizi Interbancari), you must report it within 24 hours (☎ 800-018 548 within Italy or ☎ +39-02-3488 4001/2333 from abroad). If you lose a card abroad, you must report the loss to the local police and fax the police report within 48 hours to Servizi Interbancari (☎ +39-02-3488 4140 or +39-02-4141 4110) or send it by registered post with proof of receipt. A free replacement card is sent to you by Servizi Interbancari or your bank within a few weeks, or you can request an emergency replacement within 24 hours, for which there's a fee of €10.

Even if you don't like credit cards and shun any form of credit, they do have their uses. For example, no-deposit car rentals, no pre-paying hotel bills (plus guaranteed bookings), obtaining cash 24-hours per day, simple telephone and mail-order payments, greater safety and security than cash, and above all, convenience. They're particularly useful when travelling abroad and you need some form of credit card if you wish to make purchases over the Internet. Note, however, that not all Italian businesses accept credit cards, particularly small businesses, and you should check in advance.

MORTGAGES

Mortgages or home loans (*mutuo ipotecario* or simply *mutuo*) are available from all major Italian banks and many foreign banks. Mortgages from Italian banks can take some time to be approved (although approval is now much quicker than it used to be) and you may be able to obtain better terms and a bigger loan from a foreign lender. Italian mortgages are repaid using the capital and interest method (repayment); endowment and pension-linked mortgages aren't offered.

Italian loans can have a fixed or variable interest rate (*tasso*). When comparing rates, the fixed rate (*tasso fisso*) is higher than the variable rate (*tasso variabile*) to reflect the increased risk to the lender. The advantage of a fixed rate is that you know exactly how much you must pay over the whole term.

Interest rates in Italy have traditionally been high and Italian lenders' margins and fees are among the highest in Europe (mortgages may also contain restrictive clauses). The Eurozone interest rate was 2.5 per cent in spring 2003, with most mortgage rates around 1 to 2 per cent higher. The first banks to offer low rate home loans in Italy were the British banks, Abbey National and Woolwich, followed by the Banco Popolare di Milano (BPM) and Rolo. Loans are also now available from telephone mortgage lenders such as Banca Manager, who offer a fast response and lower fees than most traditional banks. When looking for a mortgage, shop around for the best deal.

Those seeking a first mortgage are usually offered the best deals. Many lenders offer low-start mortgages, which are fixed (*tasso/rata d'ingresso*) for two or three years, after which they may change to a variable rate. Some banks offer lower interest rates to attract buyers in certain areas. You can have a clause in your mortgage whereby you aren't required to accept an increase of over 10 per cent in your payments or more than the standard of living index (i.e. inflation). Any additional amount owed is added to your loan or the loan period is extended. It's possible to assume the mortgage (*accollo del mutuo*) of a vendor.

Up to the mid-1990s, Italian banks rarely lent more than 50 per cent of the value of a property, but the maximum loan has now risen to 85 per cent for buyers of a principal home (*mutuo prima casa*). It may be possible to obtain a larger (e.g. 90 per cent) mortgage for a property requiring restoration (*mutuo per ristrutturazione*). The maximum loan for a second home is generally around 50 or 60 per cent (see **Mortgages For Second Homes** below).

Most banks don't have a maximum limit for mortgages, but some have minimum limits of between €50,000 and €100,000. Mortgage repayments are generally limited to a maximum of around 30 per cent of your net income. Some foreign lenders apply stricter rules than Italian lenders regarding income, employment and the type of property on which they lend, although some are willing to lend more than an Italian lender. It isn't wise to over-stretch your finances when taking out a mortgage. If you default on your mortgage repayments, your property can be repossessed and sold at auction, although most lenders are willing to negotiate and arrange lower repayments if borrowers get into financial difficulties.

Loans are usually repaid over a shorter period (*durata*) in Italy (e.g. 10 or 15 years) than in countries such as the UK and US, but some Italian banks now offer mortgages for up to 30 years.

If you're buying a new property off-plan and therefore making payments in stages, a bank will provide a 'staggered' mortgage, where the loan is advanced in instalments as required by the contract. During the period before completion, interest is payable on a monthly basis on the amount advanced by the bank (plus life insurance). When the final payment has been made and the loan is fully drawn, the mortgage enters its normal amortisation period (*periodo di ammortamento/durata del mutuo*).

It's possible to obtain a mortgage guarantee from most lenders, valid for two to four months, during which period you're guaranteed a mortgage for a specified sum, subject to an acceptable property valuation. The deposit paid when signing the preliminary contract (*compromesso di vendita*) is automatically protected under Italian law should you fail to obtain a mortgage.

To obtain a mortgage from an Italian bank, you must provide proof of your monthly income and all out-goings, such as existing mortgage payments, rent and other loans or commitments. Proof of income usually includes three months' pay slips for employees, confirmation of income from your employer, and tax returns. If you're self-employed, you require an audited copy of your balance sheets and trading accounts for the past three years, plus your last tax return. If you want an Italian mortgage to buy a property for commercial purposes, you must provide a detailed business plan (in Italian).

There are various fees (*spese istruttoria*) associated with mortgages. All lenders charge an arrangement fee for establishing a loan, usually around 1 per cent of the loan amount. There's a registration tax of 2 per cent of the mortgage value, plus interest, and a fixed payment of around €110. A fee is also payable to the notary (*notaio*) for registering the charge against the property. Most lenders also impose an 'administration' fee of around 1 per cent of the loan value.

It isn't usual to have a survey in Italy, where an Italian lender may value a property or simply accept the fiscal value, although foreign lenders usually insist on a valuation before they grant a loan. It's customary in Italy for a property to be held as security for a loan taken out on it, i.e. the lender takes a first charge on the property.

Mortgages For Second Homes

It's more difficult for non-residents to obtain a mortgage for a second home in Italy than for residents, and usually only 50 or 60 per cent of its value can be borrowed. Interest rates for non-residents are also usually higher than for residents. However, if you have spare equity in an existing property (either in Italy or abroad), it may be more advantageous to re-mortgage (or take out a second mortgage on) that property than to take out a new mortgage for a second home. It involves less paperwork and therefore lower legal fees, and a plan can be tailored to your requirements. Depending on the equity in your existing property and the cost of your Italian property, this may enable you to pay cash for a second home.

It's also possible to obtain a foreign currency mortgage (i.e. not in euros). However, you should be wary of taking out a foreign currency mortgage, as interest rate gains can be wiped out overnight by exchange rate swings and devaluations. If you have a foreign currency mortgage, you must usually pay commission charges each time you make a transfer to pay your mortgage or remit money to Italy. However, some lenders transfer mortgage payments to Italy each month free of charge or for a nominal fee.

It's generally recognised that you should take out a loan in the currency in which you're paid or in the currency of the country where a home is situated. In this case, if the foreign currency is devalued, you have the consolation of knowing that the value of your Italian property will have increased by the same percentage, when converted back into the foreign currency. When choosing between a euro loan and a foreign currency loan, be sure to take into account all charges, fees, interest rates and possible currency fluctuations. **However you finance the purchase of a second home in Italy, you should obtain professional advice from your bank manager and accountant.**

If you let a second home, you may be able to offset the interest on your mortgage against rental income, but pro rata only. For example, if you let an Italian property for three months of the year, you may be able to offset a quarter of your annual mortgage interest against your rental income.

VALUE ADDED TAX

Value added tax (VAT or the 'voracious administration tax') is called *imposta sul valore aggiunto (IVA)* in Italy. Most prices of goods and services in Italy are quoted inclusive of VAT, but sometimes they're given exclusive of tax, e.g. for office supplies and business equipment. There are a number of exempt goods and services in Italy, including exported goods, services supplied outside the country, ships and aircraft, interest, insurance, shares and bonds, postal and medical services, and businesses. Non-profit organisations are also exempt from VAT. The following rates of VAT apply to other goods and services:

Rate	Percentage	Applicable To
Reduced	4%	Consumer goods; basic foodstuffs; newspapers, magazines and books; property (excluding luxury homes); meals in company restaurants, schools and canteens; home care assistants for the sick; equipment for the disabled
Intermediate	10%	Non-basic and non-luxury foodstuffs and drinks; hotel bills; cinema tickets; ornamental plants; tickets for urban public transport (except air, rail and boat travel); satellite and cable TV
Standard	20%	Luxury food and drink; clothing, fabric and textiles; raw materials and semi-finished building products; recorded music and films; petrol and other fuels; telephones and telephone bills; electrical appliances; cars, motorcycles and boats; cigarettes; leather and fur; gold jewellery; perfume, cosmetics and soaps

If you're in business or self-employed, you usually need a VAT number (*partita IVA*) and must charge VAT on all your services and goods. You must maintain accounts in officially stamped books (*registri*), which are used to calculate the tax payable. Where applicable, you must apply for a VAT number from your local VAT office (*ufficio IVA*) within 30 days of starting business. The VAT number of companies is also used as their fiscal code (see page 295).

Businesses with a turnover of more than €185,950 (services) or €516,528 (goods) must pay their VAT monthly, while others can choose to pay quarterly. VAT paid on a monthly basis must be paid by the 18th of each month. If you pay quarterly, VAT is payable by the fifth day of the second month after the end of the fiscal quarter, e.g. VAT for the first quarter, ending 31st March, is due on 5th May. You must pay interest at 0.5 per cent on the amount payable in the fourth quarter. An annual VAT declaration must be completed by 5th March of the following year. Even if you have no income, you should file an annual return in order to prevent suspicion of fraud and to keep your VAT number active (if you don't file, it could be cancelled). There are huge fines and even prison sentences for avoiding VAT.

INCOME TAX

Italy has a pay-as-you-earn (PAYE) system of income tax (*imposta sul reddito delle persone fisiche/IRPEF*), whereby employees' tax is withheld at source by employers. The tax year is the same as the calendar year and income is taxed in the year in which the payment or advantage is received. Each person is taxed individually and, although a married couple may file a joint tax return, they're taxed separately.

Italian income tax has traditionally been among the highest in the EU and, although the rates have been reduced in recent years, it's still above the EU average. On the other hand, tax allowances are more generous than in some other countries (see **Allowances** on page 311 and **Credits** on page 313). If you're able to choose the country where you're taxed, you should obtain advice from an international tax expert. Moving to Italy (or another country) often offers opportunities for legal 'favourable tax planning'. To make the most of your situation, it's recommended to obtain professional income tax advice before moving to Italy, as there are usually a number of things you can do in advance to reduce your tax liability, both in Italy and abroad. For example, you may be able to avoid paying tax on a business abroad if you establish both residence and domicile in Italy before you sell. On the other hand, if you sell a foreign home after establishing your principal residence in Italy, it becomes a second home and you may then be liable for capital gains tax abroad. Be sure to consult a tax adviser who's familiar with both the Italian tax system and that of your present country of residence. You should inform the tax authorities in your former country of residence that you're going to live permanently in Italy.

Tax evasion (*l'evasione fiscale*) is rife in Italy, where avoiding taxes is more popular than soccer (Italians may not be world champions at soccer, but they certainly are when it comes to tax evasion). The worst offenders are businesses and the self-employed, and it's common knowledge that tax inspectors accept bribes to 'turn a blind eye' to tax evasion. The tax authorities may estimate your taxable income based on your perceived wealth. All taxpayers must list (on a one-page *riccometro* form) their possessions and liabilities, such as homes, cars, boats and motorbikes, whether they employ household help, whether their spouse works, and whether they have dependent family members. This information is used to determine your financial situation and whether you're entitled to certain social services. Therefore, if you're a millionaire and declare the income of a shop assistant, it would be wise not to live in a *palazzo* and drive a Ferrari! Severe sanctions, including larger fines, were introduced for tax evasion in 2000.

Further information about Italian income tax is available from local tax offices in Italy.

Liability

Your liability for Italian income tax depends on where you're domiciled. Your domicile is normally the country you regard as your permanent home and where you live most of the year. A foreigner working in Italy for an Italian company who has taken up residence in Italy and has no income tax liability abroad is considered to have his tax domicile (*domicilio fiscale*) in Italy. A person can be resident in more than one country at any time, but can be domiciled only in one country. The domicile of a married woman isn't necessarily the same as her husband's but is determined using the same criteria as anyone capable of having an independent domicile. Your country of domicile is particularly important regarding inheritance tax, as there's no longer any inheritance tax in Italy see **Mortgage & Registration Tax** on page 319. Double taxation treaties (see below) contain rules that determine in which country an individual is resident. Generally, you're considered to be an Italian resident and liable to Italian tax if **any** of the following applies:

- Your permanent home (i.e. family or principal residence) is in Italy;
- You spend over 183 days in Italy during any calendar year (Note that many countries, e.g. Britain, limit visits by non-residents to 183 days in any one year or an average of 91 days per tax year over a four-year period);
- You carry out paid professional activities or employment in Italy, except when secondary to business activities conducted in another country;
- Your centre of vital economic interest, e.g. investments or business, is in Italy.

If you're registered as a resident (*residenza anagrafica*) in your *comune*, you're automatically liable to income tax in Italy.

If you intend to live permanently in Italy, you should notify the tax authorities in your present country (you will be asked to complete a form, e.g. a form P85 in Britain). You may be entitled to a tax refund if you depart during the tax year, which usually necessitates the completion of a tax return. The authorities may require proof that you're leaving the country, e.g. evidence of a job in Italy or of having purchased or rented a property there.

If you're in doubt about your tax liability in your home country, contact your nearest embassy or consulate in Italy.

If you move to Italy to take up a job or start a business, you must register with the local tax authorities soon after your arrival. This is done at your local tax office (*intendenza di finanza*).

Double Taxation Treaties: Italian residents are taxed on their world-wide income, subject to certain treaty exceptions. Non-residents are normally taxed only on income arising in Italy. The US is the only country that taxes its non-resident citizens on income earned abroad (American citizens can obtain a copy of a brochure, *Tax Guide for Americans Abroad*, from American consulates). Citizens of most other countries are exempt from paying taxes in their home country when they spend a minimum period abroad, e.g. a year. Double taxation treaties are designed to ensure that income that has already been taxed in one treaty country isn't taxed again in another treaty country. The treaty establishes a tax credit or exemption on certain kinds of income, either in the country of residence or the country where the income was earned. Where applicable, a double taxation treaty prevails over domestic law. Italy has double taxation treaties with over 60 countries, including all members of the EU, Australia, Canada, China, the Czech Republic, Cyprus, Estonia, Hungary, Iceland India, Israel, Japan, Latvia, Lithuania, Malaysia, Malta, Mexico, New Zealand, Norway, Pakistan, the Philippines, Poland, Romania, RSA, Russia, Singapore, the Slovak Republic, Sri Lanka, Switzerland, Turkey, and the US.

Taxable Income

Taxable income in Italy is officially divided into the following six categories, each of which is defined by law: employment, self-employment, business, property (land and buildings – see below), capital (principally dividends and interest), and 'miscellaneous' income. Income from employment includes bonuses (annual, performance, etc.), stock options, interest-free loans, overseas adjustments, cost of living allowances, housing allowance, education allowance, tax reimbursements and car allowance. Taxable income also includes contributions to profit sharing plans, storage and relocation allowances, language lessons provided for a spouse, personal company car, payments in kind (such as free accommodation or meals), home leave or holidays (paid by your employer), children's education, and property and investment income (dividends and interest).

Some income, such as certain social security benefits, isn't subject to income tax. However, income also includes unemployment benefits, redundancy pay, pensions, and benefits for cessation of employment (e.g. severance pay) over and above the minimum required by law. Benefits in kind are valued for tax purposes at their fair market value.

Residents are taxed on their world-wide income and non-residents on income earned in Italy only.

Although the tax rates in Italy are relatively high, your net income tax can be considerably reduced by allowances and credits, as explained below.

Property Income: All property owners in Italy (whether residents or non-residents) must pay income tax based on a property's imputed income. Income from land and buildings is based on their cadastral value (*rendita catastale*), which is a nominal value attributed by the land registry (*catasto*). The value of land is calculated by multiplying the average ordinary income (fixed by the *catasto*) by the surface area, taking into consideration the location of the land. The value of buildings is calculated by multiplying the surface area by an amount (fixed by the *catasto*) that takes into consideration their location, age, condition and official category (see page **Property Taxes** on page 317).

Income tax is also payable on rental income from an Italian property, even if you live abroad and the money is paid there. All rental income must be declared to the Italian tax authorities whether you let a property for a few weeks to a friend or 52 weeks per year on a commercial basis. Rental income is taxed as ordinary income (see **Tax Rates** on page 312). You're eligible for allowances such as repairs and maintenance, security, cleaning costs, mortgage interest (Italian loans only), management and letting expenses (e.g. advertising), local taxes, insurance and depreciation. You should seek professional advice to ensure that you're claiming everything to which you're entitled. Many people find that there's little tax to pay after deducting their expenses.

Property is also liable to a number of property taxes (see page 317).

Allowances

The following allowances can be made against taxable employment income:

- Mandatory social security contributions (see page 274);
- Contributions up to €5,164.57 to Italian qualified pension funds;
- Reimbursement for travel and accommodation for business trips up to a maximum of €46.48 within Italy and €77.47 abroad;
- Reimbursement for laundry, parking and telephone costs for work away from home;
- Reimbursement for food provision by an employer to his or her employees;
- Reimbursement for remuneration in kind (e.g. transport to and from the workplace provided by an employer);

- Share purchase plans granted under certain conditions;
- Maintenance payments to a spouse (from whom the taxpayer is legally separated or divorced);
- Expenses related to property income (see **Property Income** above).

A tax credit of up to 19 per cent of the expenses mentioned below is also granted:

- Interest on a mortgage on a principal residence (*prima casa*) or land in Italy, provided that the loan is taken out in a European Union country, up to a maximum of €3,615.20;
- Medical expenses in excess of €129.11 for general medical expenses and €129.11 for specialist medical treatment, for both the taxpayer and his dependants;
- Funeral expenses up to a maximum of €1,549.37;
- Tuition expenses at universities up to the equivalent cost of attendance at a state establishment;
- Premiums which are for life insurance and health insurance, up to a total of €1,291.14;
- Veterinary expenses exceeding €129.11 up to €387.34;
- Contributions to non-profit entities up to €2,065.83.

Personal 'allowances' are in fact granted in the form of tax credits (see **Credits** below).

Tax Rates

Italian income tax is levied at the following rates on taxable income:

Taxable Income (€)	Tax Rate (%)
Up to 10,329.14	18
10,329.14 – 15,493.71	24
15,493.71 – 30,987.41	32
30,987.41 – 69,721.68	39
Over 69,721.68	45

In addition to the above state tax, regional tax is payable at between 0.9 and 1.4 per cent, depending on the region, and municipal tax at up to 0.5 per cent.

Credits

Personal allowances are granted in the form of tax credits, which are deducted from the amount of tax to be paid. Since 2002 the credits for employees (known officially as dependent workers), the self-employed (referred to as independent workers) and pensioners have been different, as shown in the tables below. In the case of couples, one spouse's tax credit may be used to offset tax payable by the other spouse.

Dependent Workers (Employees)

Taxable Income (€)	Tax Credit (€)
Up to 6,197.48	1,146.53
6,197.48 – 6,352.42	1,084.56
6,352.42 – 6,507.36	1,032.91
6,507.36 – 7,746.85	981.27
7,746.85 – 7,901.79	903.80
7,901.79 – 8,056.73	826.33
8,056.73 – 8,211.66	748.86
8,211.66 – 8,263.31	686.89
8,263.31 – 8,779.77	650.74
8,779.77 – 9,296.22	614.58
9,296.22 – 9,812.68	578.43
9,812.68 – 15,493.71	542.28
15,493.71 – 20,658.28	490.63
20,658.28 – 25,822.84	438.99
25,822.84 – 30,987.41	387.34
30,987.41 – 31,142.35	335.70
31,142.35 – 36,151.98	284.05
36,151.98 – 41,316.55	232.41
41,316.55 – 46,481.12	180.76
46,481.12 – 46,687.70	129.11
46,687.70 – 51,645.69	77.47
Over 51,645.69	51.65

Independent Workers (Self-Employed)

Taxable Income (€)	Tax Credit (€)
Up to 4,699.76	573.27
4,699.76 – 4,803.05	516.46
4,803.05 – 4,957.99	464.81
4,957.99 – 5,112.92	413.17
5,112.92 – 7,746.85	361.52
7,746.85 – 7,901.79	309.87
7,901.79 – 8,263.31	247.90
8,263.31 – 8,779.77	211.75
8,779.77 – 9,296.22	175.60
9,296.22 – 9,812.68	139.44
9,812.68 – 15,493.71	103.29
15,493.71 – 30,987.41	51.65

Pensioners

Taxable Income (€)	Tax Credit (€)	
	Under 75	Over 75
Up to 4,855.37	98.14	222.10
4,855.37 – 9,297.52	61.98	185.95
9,297.52 – 9,555.78	-	92.97
9,555.78 – 9,814.04	-	46.48

Dependent Spouses

A dependent spouse (i.e. someone earning less than €2,840.51) can claim a credit of between €422.23 and €546.18, depending on a couple's taxable income (as shown in the table below).

Taxable Income (€)	Tax Credit (€)
Up to 15,493.71	546.18
15,493.71 – 30,987.41	496.60
30,987.41 – 51,645.69	459.42
Over 51,645.69	422.23

There's also a tax credit of €303.68 for the first dependent child under 18 and €336 for subsequent children, if household income is below €51,645.69.

Tax Returns

The tax year in Italy is the same as the calendar year. If you're a resident, you must file an income tax return (*dichiarazione dei redditi*) unless **any** of the following applies:

- You have no income;
- Your income is exempt from tax, e.g. a war, old age or invalidity pension;
- You've already paid tax at source on income, e.g. dividends, bank interest, mortgage interest;
- You're an employee and are taxed on a PAYE basis and have no other income.

Non-residents with income arising in Italy must also file a tax return. The tax system is based on self-assessment and the tax office won't send you a tax return or chase you to complete one. Tax returns are available free from your local council (*municipio*) or can be purchased from a tobacconist or stationer. They can also be downloaded from the Ministry of Finance's website (🖳 www.finanze.it). Declarations can also be made from abroad by registered post. Many people can obtain free income tax assistance at a Centro Assistenza Fiscale (CAF), including pensioners, part-time workers, certain categories of self-employed people, the disabled and those receiving unemployment benefit. See also **Using A Commercialista** below.

You must file a different tax return according to whether you're employed or self-employed, as explained below:

Employees: The tax return for most taxpayers is the *modello 730*, which covers the following categories of people: employees, pensioners, members of co-operatives, anyone with a fixed-term contract (*tempo determinato*) which extends through the months of March to June, and members of the clergy and elected government officials who have received compensation payments. Those with additional income from land and property, dividends earned from corporations and income derived from on-going work also use the 730. Income subject to taxes other than income tax, such as capital income, income from occasional autonomous work, inherited income received on an on-going basis, life insurance and accident policy premiums if policies are redeemed before five years, non-taxable *TFR* (redundancy payments), and taxes and fees that have been used as deductions (and reimbursed) in the previous year, can also be declared on form 730.

A married couple may file a joint tax return (both must sign) but are taxed separately, although payment is joint. The disadvantage of filing a joint return is that although the assessment may be raised against only one of a couple, there's a common responsibility for payment. A couple can use form 730 if their income is earned solely from land and/or property and the total amount is less than €2,840.51. Otherwise, they must use the *Unico* form (see **Self-Employment** below).

Self-Employed: If you're self-employed (e.g. an artisan, merchant or artist) or a professional with a VAT number, you must file a *Unico* form. This is a multifunctional, colour-coded (light blue, orange, green and dark blue) form that replaced form 740 in 1998. The various coloured sections denote the type of tax. The basic *Unico* form has four pages, but there are 14 other pages comprising a total of 44 sections. No additional documentation such as expense receipts or medical expenses need be attached.

Filing

Modello 730 returns for the previous year must be filed between the 1st May and the 30th June. If you've completed your own form, you may hand it in at a bank or post office and no longer need to file it at the local *comune* or send it to a service centre (*intendenza di finanza*), which are listed in telephone books. However, forms completed by professionals using computer systems must be handed in or sent to a service centre. *Unico* forms should be presented between 1st June and 31st July at a bank, post office or Centro Assistenza Fiscale (CAF) office (a kind of citizens' advice bureau for tax matters, listed in telephone books and on the CAF website, 🖳 www.caaf-cia.it); it shouldn't be taken or sent to a service centre office. Late filing within 30 days of the due date is subject to a penalty of 15 per cent of the tax due; after 30 days penalties range from 120 to 245 per cent of the tax due! You should keep copies of tax returns and receipts for six years.

Payment

Advance tax payments must be made equal to 98 per cent of the tax paid for the previous year or the amount due for the current year (whichever is less). Forty per cent of the advance tax payments (called an *acconto*) must be made by 31st May and the remaining 60 per cent by 30th November. If you've earned less than your advance payment, you can claim a refund, although tax rebates can take years to be paid. Income tax can be paid in two six-monthly instalments, or in seven instalments (provided you don't pay VAT), in which case annual interest of 6 per cent is payable. Payment is due on the last day of each instalment period or (for those who pay VAT) on the 15th of the month. A portion of the total interest due (where applicable) must accompany each instalment. If you choose to pay in instalments, it must be noted on your income tax return.

Payments up to 20 days overdue attract a surcharge of 0.5 per cent; between 20 and 60 days, the surcharge is 3.75 per cent; if you're over 60 days late, you must pay a further surtax of 30 per cent plus 5 per cent annual interest.

Using A Commercialista

Because of the complexity of the Italian tax system, it's wise to use a *commercialista* (a combination of accountant and lawyer) to prepare your tax return, particularly if you're self-employed (obligatory unless you have a doctorate in Italian bureaucracy!). A *commercialista*'s fees are relatively low, although you should obtain a quotation, and he can also advise you on what you can and cannot claim regarding allowances and expenses.

PROPERTY TAXES

Property tax (*imposta comunale sugli immobili/ICI* – pronounced 'itchy') is paid by everyone who owns property or land in Italy, whether resident or non-resident. It's levied at between 0.4 and 0.7 per cent of a property's fiscal value (*valore catastale*), the rate being decided by the local municipality according to a property's size, location, age, condition and official category (*categoria*), as shown in the property deeds (*rogito*). Categories are decided by the land registry (*catasto*) according to the type of property (*abitazione di tipo*) as follows:

Category	Property Type
A/1	*Signorile* (refined)
A/2	*Civile* (civilian)
A/3	*Economico* (economical)
A/4	*Populare* (working class)
A/5	*Ultrapopulare* ('ultra-working class')
A/6	*Rurale* (rural)
A/7	*Villini* (small detached)
A/8	*Ville* (detached)
A/9	*Castelli, palazzi di eminenti pregi artistici o storici* (castle or building of eminent historic or artistic importance)
A/10	*Uffice e studi privati* (private offices and studios)
A/11	*Alloggi tipici dei luoghi* (typical housing of the region)

A property's category has a relatively small influence on the amount of tax payable. If a property is unfit for habitation, the tax is reduced by 50 per cent.

Property tax is usually paid in two instalments: 90 per cent by 30th June and the remaining 10 per cent between 1st and 20th December (for uninhabitable properties, the figures are 45 per cent and 5 per cent respectively). If it isn't paid on time, you can be fined in the form of a surcharge or additional tax (*sopratassa*) of up to 200 per cent of the amount due. The form for paying tax is complicated and many people (particularly foreigners) employ a *commercialista* (see above) or agent to do it for them. You can also pay property tax from abroad using registered post, addressing payment to the tax office of your *comune*. Payments must be up-to-date when a property is sold and you should check this before buying.

Other property-related taxes include communal services (*servizio riscossione tributi ruoli*) for owners of condominiums and other community properties, refuse tax (*tassa communale dei rifiuti*) and water charges (see page 117). Property owners also pay income tax on their property, which is based on its cadastral value (see **Property Income** on page 311).

CAPITAL GAINS TAX

Capital gains tax (*imposta comunale sull'incremento di valore degli immobili/INVIM*) has been abolished for new property owners. Where applicable, CGT is payable to the local community and varies from 3 per cent to 30 per cent according to the capital gain made on a sale, as shown in the table below.

Capital Gain	CGT Payable
Up to 20%	3–5%
20–50%	5–10%
50–100%	10–15%
100–150%	15–20%
150–200%	20–25%
Over 200%	25–30%

CGT is reduced by 50 per cent when a property is sold to a principal residence (*prima casa*) buyer.

The capital gain is the difference between the purchase and sale prices declared in the deeds of sale (*rogito*), less expenses for renovation, improvements, repairs, etc., and is based on the increase in the cadastral value (*rendita catastale*) of a property, not the increase in its market value. It isn't wise to under-declare the value (too much), or the authorities may arbitrarily assess a new sale price (although you can appeal against this). Where applicable, CGT is deducted from the amount payable to the vendor by the notary (*notaio*) handling the sale. Calculating GCT is complicated and it's recommended to employ a *commercialista* (see page 317) to assess the sum payable.

A new capital gains tax was introduced on 1st January 1999 and applies to gains made on stocks and shares. The tax is levied at two rates, 12.5 and 27 per cent, according to the type of gain and is based on the value of your assets at the beginning of the year. Capital gains from managed (as opposed to speculative) savings are subject to CGT at 12.5 per cent, levied on the actual gain (selling price less purchase price re-valued to account for inflation), and capital losses are deductible from capital gains and may be carried forward for five years. Gains derived from qualified sales are subject to CGT at 27 per cent. (A qualified sale is a sale of more than 2 per cent of the issued shares of a company quoted on the primary or secondary markets, or of more than 5 per cent of the shares of a non-listed company.) Capital losses cannot be recovered for qualified sales. The increased value of a pension fund is taxed at 11 per cent (called a substitute tax) instead of the usual rate of 12.5 per cent.

MORTGAGE & REGISTRATION TAX

There's no inheritance of gift tax on inheritances and gifts received after October 25th 2001. However, a mortgage and registration tax of 3 per cent applies to inherited property and gifts.

Inheritances: Any property inherited is subject to mortgage and registration tax on the cadastral value of the property, which is reduced to €129.11 if the property is the first home of the heir or beneficiary.

Gifts: Gifts are also subject to a mortgage and registration tax, although in the case of gifts to distant relatives or unrelated people, registration tax is levied at 7 per cent (for property) or 15 per cent (for land) on amounts above €185,759.91.

WILLS

It's an unfortunate fact of life that you're unable to take your hard-earned assets with you when you take your final bow (or come back and reclaim them in a later life!). All adults should make a will (*testamento*) irrespective of how large or small their assets. The disposal of your estate depends on your country of domicile (see **Liability** on page 309). As a general rule, Italian law permits a foreigner who **isn't** domiciled in Italy to make a will in any language and under the law of any country, provided it's valid under the law of that country. However, if there's any conflict of law, the law of the country where the testator was a citizen at the time of his death applies. A will must be in writing (but not necessarily in the hand of the testator).

Note, however, that 'immovable' property in Italy, i.e. land and buildings, **must** be disposed of in accordance with Italian law. All other belongings in Italy or elsewhere (defined as 'movables') may be disposed of in accordance with the law of your home country or domicile. Therefore, it's important to establish where you're domiciled under Italian law. One solution for a non-resident wishing to avoid Italian inheritance laws may be to buy a home through a company, in which case the shares of the company are 'movable' assets and are therefore governed by the succession laws of the owner's country of domicile.

Italian law gives the immediate family, i.e. spouse, children and parents (called the *legittima*) an absolute right to inherit a share of an estate and it isn't possible to disinherit them. However, a foreigner who wishes to dispose of his estate (other than immovable property) according to the laws of his home country can state this in an Italian will.

There are three types of Italian will, as follows:

- **Holographic Will** – The only requirements of a holographic will (*testamento olografo*) are that it must be written entirely in your own handwriting and signed and dated by you. This is a popular and common type of will in Italy because of its simplicity (no witnesses are required) and that fact that it's free. For anyone with a modest Italian estate, e.g. a small property in Italy, a holographic will is sufficient. However, legally it's the worst type of will you can have, as it can easily 'disappear' or be forged.

- **Public Will** – A public will (*testamento pubblico*) is the safest type of will in Italy. It's prepared and recorded by a notary (*notaio*) and becomes part of his public records. It must be witnessed by two people (of any nationality), who must sign it in the presence of the notary, who also signs. Two copies are made; one for the testator and one for the notary. The notary may also write or oversee the writing of a public will.

- **Secret Will** – A secret will (*testamento segreto*) is written by the testator or a third person and handed to a notary in a sealed envelope. The testator declares the authenticity of the sealed will in the presence of the notary and two witnesses, none of whom actually see the will. Secret wills are rare in Italy.

Where applicable, the rules relating to witnesses are strict and, if they aren't followed precisely, a will may be rendered null and void. In Italy, marriage doesn't automatically revoke a will, as in some other countries, e.g. Britain. Wills aren't made public in Italy and aren't available for inspection.

If you have a large estate in Italy, it's wise to consult a lawyer (*avvocato*) when drawing up a will. It's possible to make two wills, one relating to Italian property and the other to any foreign property. Experts differ on whether you should have separate wills for Italian and foreign property, or a foreign will with a codicil (appendix) dealing with your Italian property (or vice versa). However, most lawyers believe that it's better to have an Italian will for your Italian property (and a will for any country where you own immovable property), which will speed up and reduce the cost of probate in Italy. If you have an Italian and a foreign will (or wills), make sure that they don't contradict one another. Note also that a will written in a foreign language must be translated into Italian (a certified translation is required) and proven in Italy in order to be valid there.

You need someone to act as the executor of your estate, which can be particularly costly for modest estates. Under Italian law, the role of the executor is different from that in many other countries. Your bank, lawyer or other professional will usually act as the executor, although this should be avoided if possible, as the fees can be astronomical. It's recommended to make your beneficiaries the executors, as they can then instruct a lawyer after your death should they require legal assistance. Note that probate (the proving of a will) can take a long time in Italy.

Keep a copy of your will(s) in a safe place and another copy with your lawyer or the executor of your estate. Don't leave them in a safe deposit box, which in the event of your death is sealed for a period under Italian law. You should keep information regarding bank accounts and insurance policies with your will(s), but don't forget to tell someone where they are!

Italian inheritance law is a complicated subject and it's important to obtain professional legal advice when writing or altering your will(s).

COST OF LIVING

No doubt you would like to try to estimate how far your euros will stretch and how much money (if any) you will have left after paying your bills. Inflation in Italy in 2003 was around 2.4 per cent and the country has enjoyed a relatively stable and strong economy in recent years. Salaries are generally reasonable and Italy has a high standard of living, although the combined burden of social security, income tax and indirect taxes make Italian taxes among the highest in the European Union (EU).

Anyone planning to live in Italy, particularly retirees, should take care not to underestimate the cost of living, which has increased considerably in the last decade. Italy is a relatively expensive country by American standards, and it's one of the most expensive countries in the EU, although there's a huge disparity between the cost and standard of living in the prosperous north and central regions of Italy, and the relatively poor south. Luxury and quality products are expensive, as are cars, but wine and spirits are inexpensive. Food costs almost twice as much in Italy as it does in the US, but is similar overall to most other western European countries, although you may need to modify your diet. However, you should be wary of cost of living comparisons with other countries, which are often wildly inaccurate and usually include irrelevant items which distort the results.

It's difficult to calculate an average cost of living in Italy, as it depends on your circumstances and lifestyle. It's possible to live frugally in Italy if you're willing to forego luxuries and live off the land. Shopping for selected 'luxury' items (such as stereo equipment, electrical and electronic goods, computers, and photographic equipment) abroad can also yield significant savings.

A list of the approximate **minimum** monthly major expenses for an average single person, couple and family with two children is shown in the table below. If you work in Italy, you must also take into account social security contributions (see page 274) and income tax (see page 308). The numbers in brackets refer to the notes following the table.

ITEM	MONTHLY COSTS (€)		
	Single	Couple	Family Of Four
Housing (1)	410	650	820
Food (2)	180	325	410
Utilities (3)	55	80	110
Leisure (4)	110	160	180
Transport (5)	110	110	135
Insurance (6)	55	110	120
Clothing	55	110	220
Total	975	1,545	1,995

NOTES

1. Rent or mortgage payments for a modern or modernised apartment or house in an average suburb, excluding major cities and other high-cost areas. The properties envisaged are a studio or one-bedroom apartment for a single person, a two-bedroom property for a couple and a three-bedroom property for a couple with two children.

2. Doesn't include luxuries or liquid food (alcohol).

3. Includes electricity, gas, water, telephone, pay (satellite) TV and heating costs.

4. Includes all entertainment, restaurant meals, sports and holiday expenses, plus newspapers and magazines.

5. Includes running costs for an average family car, plus third party insurance, annual taxes, petrol, servicing and repairs, but excludes depreciation or credit purchase costs.

6. Includes 'voluntary' insurance such as private health insurance, household, third party liability, travel, car breakdown and life insurance.

15.

LEISURE

Italy is one of the most beautiful countries in Europe, possibly the most attractive of all, with more than its fair share of ravishing landscapes and stunning historic towns. It's a country of huge variety, offering something for everyone: magnificent beaches for sun-worshippers, beautiful unspoiled countryside for nature lovers, a wealth of magnificent ancient cities and towns for history enthusiasts (virtually every town is a history book of battles and religious milestones), an abundance of mountains and seas for sportspeople, vibrant night-life for the jet set, fine wines for oenophiles and superb cuisine for gourmets, a profusion of culture, art and serious music for art lovers, fabulous designer goods for shopaholics, and tranquillity for the stressed.

Italy is a fascinating mix of modernity and industry (it's one of the world's top ten economies) and deep-rooted traditions and customs. Few other countries in the world offer such an exhilarating mixture of culture, history, tradition, sophistication and style – all of which can be enjoyed in fine weather for much of the year, particularly in the south. Italians live *la dolce vita* to its full pleasurable limits and, as any newcomer finds, love to celebrate and throw elaborate parties. Wherever you go in Italy, you will be attracted by the Italian lifestyle, the very essence of relaxation, combining an easygoing pace with some of the world's finest food and wine.

Not surprisingly, tourism is huge business in Italy, which is ranked second in the world (after France) in revenue from foreign tourism. The country welcomes some 30 million foreign visitors annually, representing over 100 million overnight stops and receipts in excess of €25 billion. People from all walks of life have been drawn to Italy for centuries, ever since the Romans founded one of the world's greatest civilisations, and the country has been part of the essential 'grand tour' for generations. Rome (the 'Eternal City'), Florence and Venice are among the world's most visited cities. However, although tourism contributes much to the country's economy, it's also responsible (along with pollution and poor management) for the decline of some of Italy's most priceless treasures. Draconian measures to combat excessive tourism and to save Italy's attractions are continually being proposed, particularly since the year 2000, when the capital was close to collapse. One Italian politician even proposed that a 'No Vacancies' sign be posted at Italy's border!

However, there's plenty to explore outside the most famous cities, and out of the high season even the most popular destinations aren't so crowded. You will be enraptured by the constantly varying scenery, charming villages and towns set in magnificent landscapes dotted with olives and vines, hundreds of tiny coves glistening in pristine waters or sheltering picturesque fishing ports, sandy beaches, and ancient hill towns where time appears to have stood still for centuries. There are stunning art throughout the country, displayed in monasteries, churches and palaces (works of art themselves), and countless museums house collections bequeathed by the region's richly varied inhabitants, from the Etruscans and Romans to the great Renaissance artists. Tuscany alone has more classified cultural monuments than most countries and each region retains relics of an artistic tradition widely acknowledged as the world's richest. There are spectacular cathedrals and churches throughout the country, including St Peter's in the Vatican and *Il Duomo* in Milan, a lasting testimony to Italy's rich architectural heritage.

Rome, known for centuries as the 'capital of the world' (*caput mundi*), is one of Europe's most visited cities and its inhabitants maintain a frantic, modern pace of life surrounded by ancient monuments. Tuscany and its gently rolling hills are home to Florence, the birthplace of the Renaissance and a mecca for culture and art-lovers for centuries, where visitors flock to admire its incredible artistic wealth. On the Veneto is Venice, flooded in winter by the lagoon and throughout the year by tourists keen to explore its romantic waterways and sumptuous palaces. Verona, of Romeo and Juliet fame, and Padua with its unique frescos are also found in the north, along with Milan, Italy's industrial and design centre, an intensely modern city that provides an interesting contrast with more traditional cities further south.

Turin, home to the Fiat empire, is another industrial, cosmopolitan city in the north, while nearby Piedmont and Valle D'Aosta are a winter wonderland with a number of fashionable ski resorts. The Italian Riviera is lined with chic coastal resorts, every bit as glamorous and cosmopolitan as their French counterparts, while Capri in the south has a unique charm and beauty, and is one of Italy's most romantic spots. Sicily, the largest island in the Mediterranean, is a land of timeless beauty and world-famous monuments that are testimony to the many races who conquered and inhabited the island through the ages.

The main aim of this chapter, and indeed the purpose of the whole book, is to provide information that isn't found in standard guidebooks. General tourist information is available in numerous Italian and foreign guidebooks. The Michelin *Green Guide to Italy* contains a wealth of information about each region, its history, architecture and art, while the *Michelin Escapade Pocket Guides* concentrate on individual cities, including itineraries, maps and colour photos. The annual *Michelin Red Guide* is the most comprehensive hotel and restaurant guide available, and is priceless for both residents and visitors. It contains all the latest information, including prices, opening times, facilities (including those for children and the handicapped) and town plans.

Good general English-language guides include the *Baedeker Guide to Italy*, *Fodor's Italy*, *Frommer's Italy*, *Lonely Planet's Italy* and *The Rough Guide to Italy* (see **Appendix B** for a comprehensive list). There are also numerous local publications that provide information about local and national events such as *RomaC'è*, *Time Out*, *Wanted in Rome* and *Where Rome* in Rome, and *Firenze Spettacolo* and *Vista* in Florence and Tuscany. In Rome and Milan, the newspaper *La Repubblica* publishes the *TrovaRoma* and *TrovaMilano* weekly entertainment supplements, and all newspapers provide cinema, theatre and concert listings.

TOURIST OFFICES

The Italian National Tourist Board, Ente Nazionale Italiano di Turismo/ENIT, Via Marghera, 2–6, 00185 Rome (☎ 06-49711, 🖳 www.enit.it) is responsible for planning and promoting tourism. ENIT maintains offices in Argentina, Austria, Belgium, Canada, Denmark, Finland, France (2), Germany (3), Greece, Holland, Ireland, Japan, Portugal, South Africa, Spain (2), Sweden, Switzerland (2), the UK and the US (3), as well as offices at Italy's major border posts and airports. The national travel agency, Sestante-Compagnia Italiana di Turismo, known as CIT or Citalia outside Italy, has offices throughout the world and provides extensive information on travelling in Italy, including hotel and train bookings.

Regional Tourist Offices (Ente Provinciale per il Turismo/EPT or Azienda di Promozione Turistica/APT) are located in around 20 provincial capitals and provide information about the local region and towns. In most large towns and cities there are the useful and approachable Informazioni e Assistenza ai Turisti (IAT) or Azienda Autonoma de Soggiorno e Turismo (AAST), which provide information about the local area, including maps, public transport and the opening times of local attractions. In smaller towns look for Ufficio Turistico or Pro Loco offices. In major tourist cities there's also a useful tourist office for students, Centro Turistico Studentesco (CTS), which provides a free accommodation service and information about student discounts. Airports and main railway stations usually have a tourist information office and some main cities have street tourist guides during high season. Most tourist offices answer telephone or written requests for information.

The quality and quantity of tourist information dispensed by tourist offices varies considerably, as do office opening hours. Offices in main towns are usually open from around 8.30am to 7pm, while smaller offices close for lunch from about 12.30 or 1pm to 3pm. Most offices open from Mondays to Fridays and in major cities and resorts offices also open at weekends during summer. Many offices provide an accommodation service, for which there may be a small fee.

National, regional and local tourist authorities publish free brochures and pamphlets in many languages. However, it's recommended to collect information before visiting Italy, as local offices often run out, and local and regional offices don't provide information about places outside their area. Staff at tourist offices in larger towns and main tourist areas speak English. Since 30th December 1999, Italy has operated a National Call Centre (☎ free 800-117 700 or ☎ 06-8741 9007 from abroad) daily from 8am to 11pm except Christmas Day and Easter Sunday, when it operates from 8am to 6pm. The Call Centre has operators who can supply information in Italian, English, French, German and Spanish relating to safety, health care, accommodation, events and shows, museums and exhibitions, transport and traffic, useful phone numbers, information point, and tourist and religious assistance

A wealth of information about Italy is available on the Internet, where the best websites include 🖳 www.italiantourism.com, 🖳 www.travel.it, 🖳 www. dolcevita.com, 🖳 www.goitaly.about.com, 🖳 www.initaly.com, 🖳 www.itwg. com, 🖳 www.italytour.com, 🖳 www.travel.org/italy.html and 🖳 www.travel europe.it. Most cities and regions also have websites dedicated to them such as 🖳 www.comune.roma.it, 🖳 www.romeguide.it, 🖳 www.virtualrome.com, 🖳 www.florence.ala.it and 🖳 www.doge.it (Venice).

HOTELS

There are some 38,000 hotels in Italy, catering for all tastes and budgets, ranging from humble hostels to villas and converted medieval palaces. If you want to rub shoulders with real Italians, start at the bottom end of the accommodation chain rather than the top. The 20 regional boards in the country classify hotels and other accommodation in Italy using stars (one to five) or classes, as described below:

Category	Description
1*/4th class (*pensione*)	Basic facilities; no en suite bathroom or toilet
2*/3rd class (*pensione*)	Slightly better facilities; usually en suite bathroom or toilet
3*/2nd class (*pensione*)	As above but with more facilities, such as a telephone and TV
4*/1st class (*albergo*)	Excellent facilities, e.g. room service, laundry, etc.
5*/deluxe (*albergo*)	The best in hotel facilities

Note that hotels are classed according to their facilities rather than their quality, so accommodation within the same category can vary considerably; there are also differences in criteria from one region to another. Sometimes a hotel may have a lower rating than it deserves simply because the local tourist office hasn't upgraded it yet or it has chosen to remain in a lower category to avoid paying higher taxes (a popular Italian pastime). Hotels can legally increase their charges twice per year, although many don't, and room rates must be displayed on the inside of the door in each room. Before you accept a room, it's wise to view it so that you know exactly what you get for your money. A rough guide to room rates is given below:

Star Rating	Price Range (€)
1*	25–40
2*	40–50
3*	50–65
4*	65–80
5*	80+

The prices quoted above are for a double room for one night (prices in Italy are usually quoted per room and not per person), inclusive of tax and service charges. As in most countries, single rooms are rare and only marginally cheaper than doubles. Value added tax at 9 per cent is added to all hotel bills except those in five-star hotels, where VAT is charged at 12 per cent. Some room rates include breakfast (*colazione*), so if you don't want to have breakfast in the hotel you should make this clear when booking. (Breakfast is usually far better value at a local bar or café.) Some hotels provide a small safe for your valuables, although there may be a modest charge for this service.

Rates are fixed in agreement with the provincial tourist board and vary according to the class, season, services available and the locality, with hotels in large towns, cities and coastal resorts the most expensive. Prices in Florence and Venice are particularly high, and you receive worse value there than in most other cities. However, these two cities apart, relatively cheap accommodation can usually be found, mostly in the old quarters, close to the main square or churches, although older hotels may not have heating and frequently have problems with electricity and plumbing. Few hotels in Italy, apart from the most expensive, provide air-conditioning, even in the hottest summer months.

Room sizes vary considerably. In city centres, even top class hotels may have relatively small rooms. A double room (*camera doppia*) usually contains two single beds rather than a double bed; if you want a double bed, ask for a *camera matrimoniale*. Many hotels have 'family' rooms for three or four guests at greatly reduced rates, or provide extra beds for children in a double room with no extra charge. An extra bed for an adult normally costs a minimum of 15 per cent of the double room rate.

Hotels don't usually have private garages, although some do provide parking – check whether this is covered or not and that a hotel has insurance for parking facilities.

April to October is high tourist season in the most popular Italian cities and resorts (December to March in ski resorts), and hotel bookings should be made well in advance, particularly in Florence, Milan, Rome and Venice. You should confirm your booking by fax or telephone before arrival. Some hotels require a deposit (*caparra*) – a booking is considered valid as soon as a deposit is paid – which should be refunded if a booking is cancelled at least 14 days in advance or 30 days in advance during the high season. In major cities, you may be obliged to book for a minimum of three nights, particularly in July and August.

It's illegal to have unregistered guests in hotels and you're required to produce identification when you register, usually in the form of a passport. Under Italian law, it's compulsory for a hotel to provide you with a receipt (*ricevuta fiscale*) for final payment when you leave and you should keep this receipt until you return home or leave the country. While not all hotel proprietors speak English, most are used to dealing with English-speaking clients.

There are various Italian chain hotels, with prices usually at the upper end of the scale, as well as the usual large international hotels such as Intercontinental and Hilton. Chains include Ciga, among the oldest in Italy with a turn-of-the-century opulence, Relais et Châteaux, which operates historic hotels usually situated in castles, villas or monasteries with excellent but expensive facilities, Agip, a Forte group partner that operates a chain of mid-range hotels and motels throughout the country, Jolly and Best Western.

There are a number of hotel booking services in Italy, including Centro Prenotazioni Hotel Italia, which provides a nation-wide, free booking service (☎ 167-015 772, 💻 www.hotelme.it), while Hotel Reservations (☎ 06-99100 from 7am to 10pm) provides the same service in Rome via its offices at the city's airport and railway stations. There also useful 'day hotels' (*albergo diurno*) at railway stations in major cities, open daily between 6am and midnight, where showers, hairdressing, cleaning and laundry facilities are provided. Tourist services, guides and ticket sales are also available.

Most guidebooks include a selection of hotels and there are a number of Italian hotel guides. The most comprehensive hotel (and restaurant) guide is the *Michelin Red Guide Italy*, which also lists weekly closing days and seasonal opening. The *Guida Touring Alberghi e Ristoranti d'Italia* published by the Touring Club Italiano is also a much respected guide, as is the new Gambero guide, *Tuttiitalia* (Arcigola Editore), which includes restaurants. Hotel guides in English include *Alistair Sawday's Special Places to Stay* by Susan Pennington, *High Quality Bed and Breakfast in Italy* (Le Lettere), *Karen Brown's Italy: Charming Inns & Itineraries* by Clare Brown and others (Fodor) and *Hello Italy! A Hotel Guide to Italy, Rome, Venice, Florence & 23 Other Italian Cities* by Margo Classe (Wilson). Local administrations publish lists of hotels and other accommodation, and most provincial and regional tourist organisations publish hotel guides.

BUDGET ACCOMMODATION

There's a wide variety of budget accommodation in Italy, including hostels (*locande* or *alberghi*), guesthouses (*alloggi* or *affittacamere*), and rooms and lodgings. *Locande* and *affittacamere* aren't included in the hotel star classification system and usually provide quite basic facilities, although in some areas, such as Isole Eolie and the Alps, the standard of this type of accommodation can be excellent. You can expect to pay between €15 and €30 for shared facilities and dormitory beds in hostels. Food is sometimes provided, although you should be aware that in major resorts, such as Rimini on the Adriatic coast and anywhere on the Italian Riviera, you may be obliged to pay for half or full-board.

Bed and breakfast (B&B) accommodation in private houses, inns and apartments is also available in Italy, although it isn't as common as in many northern European countries. The guide, *Dolce Casa*, provides a comprehensive list of B&B accommodation with a description of each establishment; room rates range from €15 to €60 per person per night.

For a more historic experience, you can stay in many Italian monasteries and convents, where, in return for inexpensive accommodation, you're expected to make your own bed and clean up after meals. There's usually a curfew, rooms are single sex and cost between €15 and €30 per night, or slightly less than a one-star hotel. To facilitate entry, a letter of introduction from your priest, vicar or rabbi is recommended, although many institutions accept Catholic guests only. For further information, contact the local tourist office or the provincial archdiocese (*arcivescovado*) or obtain a copy of *Bed & Blessings Italy: A Guide to Convents and Monasteries Available for Overnight Lodging* by Anne and June Walsh (Paulist Press). The religious organisation, Associazione Cattolica Internazionale al Servizio della Giovane-Protezione della Giovane, Via Urbana, 158, 00184 Rome (☎ 06-4890 4523) helps women travellers find cheap accommodation in its own hostels and convents, where there's a 10.30pm curfew.

'Farm holidays' (*agriturismo*) are also popular, particularly in Adige, Apulia, Trentino-Alto Veneto and Tuscany, where there are over 1,600 farms to choose from. Under the scheme, farmers let converted barns and cottages for a minimum of a week for around €275. Alternatively, and often on a nightly basis, you can rent a room in the farmhouse with full board (usually four-course meals of wholesome farm food) from around €15 to €35 per night. Note, however, that one-night stays may be unavailable in high season, when you may need to book for a minimum of a week. Some farms also offer facilities such as swimming pools, tennis courts and horse riding. For more information and a list of properties contact Agriturist, Corso Vittorio Emanuele, 101, 00186 Rome (☎ 06-6852 342), which publishes an annual guide, *Guida dell'Ospitalità Rurale, Agriturismo e Vancanze Verdi*, listing farm holiday accommodation facilities by region. Another useful guide is *Guida alle Vacanza in Campagna* published by the Touring Club Italiano. Regional and provincial tourist offices can also provide information about local facilities.

If you're a student, you may be able to find a room in university accommodation in the main cities in July and August, although you must book well in advance. City tourist offices can provide information, or contact the local Centro Turistico Studentesco e Giovanile (CTS).

The Club Alpino Italiano, Via E. Petrella, 19, 20124 Milan (☎ 02-2057 231) operates around 500 mountain huts (*rifugi*). For €8 to €14 per night you can stay in stunning natural surroundings but in spartan accommodation. You may get a bed if you turn up on spec, but it's recommended to book (better than sleeping rough!). Note that prices are subject to a 20 per cent surcharge from 1st December to 30th April.

There are some 50 youth hostels in Italy providing cheap and cheerful accommodation, usually in dormitories. You must usually provide a sleeping bag or sheet, which can also be hired at hostels, and there may be kitchen and laundry facilities. Security in hostels is often lax, so you should keep your valuables with you at all times. Most hostels have curfews, daytime lockouts, and separate quarters for men and women. The minimum age for children, who must be accompanied by an adult, is eight. To stay at a hostel belonging to Hostelling International (HI) you must be a member. Annual membership is available from HI affiliates abroad or from the Associazione Italiana Alberghi per la Gioventù/AIG, Via Cavour, 44, 00184 Rome (☎ 06-487 1152), which provides a free fax booking service at its major hostels and food and transport discounts. If you book accommodation at a youth hostel, you should expect to pay a deposit of around 30 per cent of the total price.

Most tourist guides include budget accommodation and there are a number of books written especially for those on a tight budget, including *Cheap Sleeps in Italy* by Sandra Gustafson (Chronicle).

SELF-CATERING

If you want to explore an area thoroughly or wish to relax in comfortable surroundings away from the hustle and bustle of cities, self-catering accommodation is a popular and usually affordable option. Most areas in Italy, particularly Sicily, Tuscany, Umbria and Veneto, have a wide range of self-catering properties, including apartments, farmhouses and villas. If you fancy somewhere with a touch of historic *ambience*, you can even choose a renaissance villa, a Venetian palace or a medieval castle apartment – just a few of the many historic buildings available for rent. Standards vary considerably, from dilapidated, ill-equipped apartments to luxury villas with every modern convenience. You don't always get what you pay for and some properties bear little resemblance to their descriptions.

Lets are usually on a weekly basis from Saturday to Saturday, prices varying according to the time of year – in high season it can be an expensive option. However, a villa can sometimes sleep up to 15 people, which reduces costs for a large party or a number of families. Rates usually include linen, gas and electricity, although heating in winter, e.g. gas or electric heaters, is usually charged extra. **Beware of gas heaters with faulty ventilation ducts, as they're responsible for a number of deaths in self-catering accommodation.** Extra beds, cots and high chairs may be provided on request, and TVs can sometimes be rented for a small cost per week.

Properties in resort areas usually have a swimming pool, although apartments and townhouses may have a shared pool. Most are also located close to a beach and are in use from around May to September. Some properties have an indoor heated swimming pool and other facilities such as tennis courts. Most holiday apartments are fairly basic, often with tiny kitchens and bathrooms (perhaps with a shower only), and have a combined lounge/dining room, a patio or balcony and are basically equipped. If you need special items such as a cot or high chair, you should mention it when booking. Properties are, however, generally well-stocked with cooking utensils, crockery and cutlery, although you should check, as you may need to buy a good kitchen knife, a teapot, egg cups, a pepper mill or a filter coffee machine. Most people take a few essential foods and supplies with them and buy fresh food on arrival.

Unless a company or property has been highly recommended, it's best to book through a reputable organisation such as a tourist agency. Local and national newspapers advertise properties for rent in their small ads section (*piccola pubblicità – affittasi appartamento*) and tourist offices may be able to provide a list. The National Estate Agents Association, FIAIP, Via Monte Zebio, 30, 00195 Rome (☎ 06-3219 798) can provide information, as can the specialist company Cuendet & Cie Spa, Strada di Strove, 17, 53035 Monteriggioni (☎ 05-7757 6330, 💻 www.cuendet.com). Most companies send catalogues on request. It's essential to book if you want accommodation during the high season (July and August) or over a holiday weekend, e.g. at Easter. There's usually a 25 per cent deposit, the balance payable on arrival. Normally you must arrive by 5pm on your first day and vacate the property by noon on your day of departure. Outside the high season, self-catering accommodation can usually be found on the spot by asking in bars and restaurants or by obtaining a list from the local tourist office.

There's also an accommodation option in Italy called a *residence*, half-way between a hotel and a self-catering flat, where kitchen facilities are provided but there's also a restaurant. Information about these can be found in the ENIT annual accommodation lists for each region, available from ENIT offices abroad or from their head office in Rome (see page 327).

Among the numerous self-catering rental agencies in Italy are The Best in Italy (💻 www.thebestinitaly.com), Best of Sabina (💻 www.bestofsabina.it), Elegant Etruria (💻 www.dbws.com/etruria/hime.htm), Homes International (✉ homesint@tin.it), Milligan & Milligan Rentals (💻 www.italy-rentals. com), Toscana Ville Castelli and Golf (💻 www.toscanaitaly.it) and Tuscany Net (💻 www.tuscany.net).

CAMPING & CARAVANNING

Camping is popular in Italy, where there are over 2,000 campsites throughout the country, although most are open only from April to September. Campsites are graded from one to four stars according to their facilities and comfort, and range from small sites with basic facilities to huge complexes with supermarkets, swimming pools and tennis courts. Sites are usually in scenic locations near mountains or lakes and tend to be quite a distance from major cities. They can be expensive, as rates are calculated per person, site and vehicle. Average prices range from €5 to €7.5 per adult, €3 to €5 per child under 12 (children under three are admitted free) and around €6 for the site. Many campsites accommodate caravans and motor caravans as well as tents.

Some campsites require campers to have an international camping carnet, which can usually be purchased on site or obtained from the Italian Camping and Caravanning Federation, Federazione del Campeggio e del Caravanning/Federcampeggio, PO Box 23, 50041 Calenzano (FI) (☎ 055-882 391). In summer, when campsites are at their busiest, you should arrive at the site before 11am to ensure a place.

Camping outside campsites is usually prohibited unless you have permission from the landowner. When camping 'wild', you shouldn't light fires or leave litter.

Federcampeggio publishes the *Guida Camping d'Italia* and a free map of campsites offering discounts to holders of an international camping carnet, plus the annual *Guida Touring Campeggi e Villagi Turistici* in association with the Touring Club Italiano, (TCI), Corso Italia, 10, 20122 Milan (☎ 02-85261).

FESTIVALS

Like all southern Europeans, Italians use any excuse for a holiday and all cities, towns and villages stage an annual festival (*festa*), often lasting several days. It's well worth planning your visit to a region of Italy to coincide with the local celebrations. The vivid and colourful celebrations are usually of religious or historical origin.

Italy's colourful history provides a variety of backdrops for celebrations, of which medieval and renaissance events are among the most popular subjects. You can expect to see pageants, tournaments, crossbow and jousting events, battles and family feuds all re-enacted by local townsfolk richly dressed in period costume. There are numerous events dating back to medieval and renaissance times, including the Palio bareback horse races in Sienna (held on 2nd July and 16th August), the 'firing of the cart in Florence', the Feast of the Redeemer and the historical regatta in Venice, the Sardinian Cavalcade in Sassari, the feast of the almond blossom in Agrigento (Sicily), the Race of the Candles and Palio of the Crossbow in Gubbio (Umbria), and the Regata of the Four Ancient Maritime Republics (which rotates between Pisa, Venice, Amalfi and Genoa). Other unmissable events include carnival (*carnevale*) in Venice and Verona, Corpus Christi in Spello (Umbria) with its *Le Infiorate* flower festival in June, the football match and magnificent 16th century costume parade (*Calcio Storico Fiorentino*) in Florence on 24th June, and the Epiphany toy and sweet fair in Rome at Piazza Navona (from Christmas to the 5th January).

Religious festivals are often more serious affairs (they usually have strong pagan roots), especially at Easter, when solemn processions of white-robed, hooded figures and flagellants parade through the streets behind a statue of the local patron saint. One of the most spectacular religious festivals is held at Cocullo (Abruzzo) in May, when a statue of the local patron saint, San Domenico, is carried around the streets draped in live snakes. There are also many flamboyant Easter celebrations, including those at Chieti, Florence and Taranto and in many towns in Sicily. Festivals honouring patron saints are particularly colourful events and include the Feast of San Nicola in Bari, the Feast of San Gennaro in Naples and the Feast of St Antonio in Padua. Passion plays are also popular.

At Christmas, most churches are decorated with cribs or nativity scenes (*presepi*) and Epiphany (*Epifania*), celebrated on the 6th January, is an important event, particularly for children, who are visited at night by an old woman (*La Befana*) on a broomstick who leaves presents or coal according to whether a child has been good or bad. Pilgrimages are popular, the Vatican being, of course, the most popular Catholic pilgrimage destination, particularly during Catholic

Jubilee years, while another place of homage, the shrine of the Madonna di Polsi in Aspromonte (Calabria), attracts around a million pilgrims annually.

Many towns and cities stage festivals of the performing arts, the most famous being the Spoleto two-week summer festival – a combination of film, theatre, classical music and ballet performed within the walled streets of the town.

Italy also stages literally hundreds of food festivals (*sagre*), where local food and wine flow freely, wine and truffle festivals being among the most popular. Local newspapers and tourist offices are good sources of information for these. For a full list of celebrations, contact ENIT (see page 327), which publishes a comprehensive list of events in its booklet, *An Italian Year*. Local and regional tourist offices also provide information.

MUSEUMS, GALLERIES & CHURCHES

Bellini, Botticelli, Canaletto, da Vinci, Donatello, Giacometti, Giotto, Michelangelo, Palladio, Raphael, Tintoretto, Titian . . . of all the European nations, Italy has made the greatest contribution to painting and sculpture, and the country's fragmented political history has led to a rich regional diversity in the arts. The Italian renaissance, left a magnificent legacy of painting and sculpture that decorates Italian museums, buildings and churches throughout the country (it's said that Italy is home to half the world's great art).

There are some 70 state-owned museums and art galleries in Italy, in addition to countless private collections. Among the many highlights are the Accademia and Collezione Peggy Guggenheim in Venice, the Galleria degli Uffizi and Galleria dell'Accademia (home to Michelangelo's *David*) in Florence, and the Musei Vaticani (the world's largest museum complex, housing one of Italy's most important art collections and incorporating the Sistine Chapel with its unique frescoes by Michelangelo), the Borghese Gallery and the Museo Nazionale di Villa Giulia in Rome. The Borghese Gallery, which reopened in 1997 after more than a decade of restoration, can be visited by just 400 or so people at a time and you must make an appointment (☎ 06-32810).

State-run museums are usually open from Tuesdays to Saturdays from 9am to 1 or 2pm and Sundays from 9am to 1pm. They usually close on Mondays. Privately owned museums operate much the same hours, but may open briefly in the afternoons. Entrance fees usually range from €1.5 to €5, although costs are considerably higher (e.g. €7) for major exhibitions. Those under 18 and over 60 are allowed free entry, although proof of age (e.g. a passport) must be provided. Information regarding opening times, entrance fees, special events and the location of museums is provided by tourist offices, and can also be obtained via the Internet (💻 www.museionline.com). You can also book tickets to a number of state-run museums and archaeological sites via the Internet (💻 www.beni culturali.it).

Because so many of Italy's Renaissance artists relied heavily on the Catholic Church for patronage, most Italian churches are 'art galleries' in their own right and you may be amazed to discover the treasures inside even the smallest and most insignificant-looking of churches. Churches are usually open to visitors from around 7 or 8am to noon and reopen from 4 to 7 or 8pm, although in remote rural areas, they open only for services and possibly just on Sundays. However, visits are possible at other times by asking at the local tourist or information office. You won't usually need to pay an entrance fee but may be expected to pay your guide if you have one or leave a donation.

When visiting places of worship, you should dress conservatively, i.e. no shorts or uncovered shoulders, and you shouldn't walk around during services. As most of Italy's churches predate their magnificent paintings and frescoes, many are closed for restoration (*chiuso per restauro*) from time to time. If you're making a special trip to a church or historical site, check in advance whether it will be open.

Italian archaeological sites have formed an essential part of the country's tourist attractions since the 18th century, when it became fashionable for young British and German aristocrats to visit ruins around Europe as part of their cultural education. The sites also provide a unique insight into the country's colourful history, particularly the ruins of the ancient world left by the Etruscans, ancient Greeks and, of course, the Romans. Rome is home to several famous sites, including the Forum and the city's most famous landmark, the Coliseum, a massive amphitheatre where the Romans staged gladiator fights and fed Christians to lions.

The towns of Ercolano and Pompeii have unique archaeological sites. Both were buried under volcanic mud and ash from the eruption of nearby Mount Vesuvius in AD79 and their perfectly preserved remains have been an object of fascination for tourists since they were first excavated in 1750. Sites within cities tend to open from 9am to 3pm in winter (7pm in summer), from Mondays to Saturdays, and until 1pm on Sundays throughout the year. Larger sites, such as Pompeii, open earlier and close later e.g. 8am to 7.30pm, Mondays to Saturdays. The entrance fee to most sites is around €7 and there are usually official guides, who charge a small fee. Local tourist offices can provide further information on archaeological sites and they usually offer useful guidebooks for the most important ones.

OPERA

Opera is the quintessential Italian art form – not for nothing was it invented in Italy – and Italy has the world's most demanding fans, who have even been known to boo Pavarotti when he has an off-day! The country provides a rich selection of operatic seasons throughout the year and some of the world's best and most famous theatres. These include the Teatro alla Scala (known as La Scala) in Milan, the Teatro San Carlo in Naples and the Teatro dell'Opera in Rome, which are renowned for the technical perfection of their performances and the magnificent detail of their scenery and costumes. Other major opera houses include the Teatro Petruzzelli (Bari), Teatro Comunale (Bologna), Teatro Massimo Bellini (Catania), Teatro Comunale (Florence), Teatro Comunale (Genoa), Teatro Massimo (Palermo), Teatro Regio (Parma), Teatro Manzoni (Rome), Teatro Comunale Giuseppe Verdi (Trieste), Teatro Regio (Turin) and the Gran Teatro la Fenice in Venice (destroyed by fire in 1996 but being restored).

The opera season runs from December to June, and summer performances are held in magnificent open-air locations, which include the Verona Arena (July/August), the Terme di Caracalla in Rome (July/August), the Arena Sferisterio in Macerata (July), and the Greek theatres of Taormina and Syracuse.

Tickets at La Scala are difficult to obtain, unless you book months in advance, although there are usually seats available in the gallery (up in the clouds) for a modest price. For less celestial seats you should expect to pay from €10 to €200; tickets are available from the box office or by phone (☎ 02-809126, 🖳 www.teatroallascala.org). Tickets at Rome's Teatro dell'Opera cost between €12 and €150.

MUSIC & BALLET

Italians are great lovers of classical and popular music (as well as opera – see above). The country has produced many great classical composers, including Donizetti, Monteverdi (the father of modern opera), Puccini, Rossini, Scarlatti, Verdi and Vivaldi. There are orchestras and chamber music groups in all the major cities, the most famous being Rome's Academy of Saint Cecilia, I Musici, the Scala Philharmonic Orchestra, the Venice Orchestra and Solisti Veneti. These orchestras perform regular concerts in their home cities and on tour. Most concerts are held on Saturdays, Sundays and Mondays, tickets costing in the region of €30 to €50. The Associazione Musicale Romana provides a year-long schedule of festivals and concerts, among the most important of which are the *Maggio Musicale Fiorentino* (May to June) and the Festival of Two Worlds (*Festival dei Due Mondi*) in Spoleto (mid-June to mid-July). For details of these and other musical events, consult the local tourist office or see the Italian music website (🖳 www.musica.it).

Few modern Italian pop singers or groups have made much of an impact outside Italy and the country's biggest claim to pop music fame is probably Mina, who made her mark in the 1960s. The music scene is lively and whether your taste be jazz or acid funk, rock or folk, there's sure to be a bar or club playing your sort of music in most cities, often live. Ask at local tourist offices and see local newspapers for details of concerts and venues. The Festival of Italian Song (*Festival della Canzone Italiana*) held in San Remo in January/February is as popular and prestigious in Italy as the Grammy Awards in the US or the Brit Awards for pop music in the UK.

Ballet is also popular in Italy and most major opera houses have ballet seasons, including Italy's main company, the Rome Opera Ballet, which performs at the Teatro dell'Opera. Italy stages a world-renowned International

Ballet Festival at Nervi (near Genoa) in July. Prestigious companies and troupes from throughout the world regularly perform in Rome, where there are also open-air performances in summer.

THEATRE

Italy boasts a vast number of theatres throughout the country, among the most famous of which are the Ponchielli in Cremona, the Carlo Felice in Genoa, La Scala in Milan, Politeama in Palermo, the Opera Theatre in Rome, the Regio Lingotto in Turin and the Fenice in Venice. In summer, the amphitheatre in Verona and the Terme di Caracalla and Coliseum in Rome offer a series of spectacular plays. There's a strong tradition of theatre in Italy dating back thousands of years, and theatres offer a wide variety of plays and musicals, which are performed in Italian unless there's a visiting company from abroad. Local tourist offices and newspapers provide information on theatrical events, as do billboards and town hall notice boards.

CINEMA

Italy has one of the healthiest film industries in Europe and has produced many great film directors, including Bernado Bertolucci, Federico Fellini, Vittorio Gassman, Sergio Leone and Luchino Visconti, as well as actors and actresses such as Sophia Loren, Gina Lollobrigida and Marcello Mastroianni. For many years, Rome's Cinecittà film studios were the leading film production centre in Europe, producing Italian classics such as Fellini's *La Dolce Vita* as well as many international productions. Today, the film studios and Italian cinema in general are facing difficult times, in common with those in most other European countries. However, Italy retains a small film industry that's widely respected throughout the world, with many young and promising directors, such as Benigni, Pieraccioni and Troisi.

Italians are keen filmgoers and almost every large town and city has several cinemas, many with multi-screens. However, most foreign-language films are dubbed into Italian and it's difficult to find screenings of foreign films in their original language. Nevertheless, in the major cities there's usually at least one cinema showing foreign-language films without subtitles, although the film may be shown on one day per week only (exceptions include the Pasquino cinema in Rome and the Astro in Florence, which show English-language films daily). There are regular film shows at foreign cultural centres, where films are shown in their original language.

Cinema tickets usually cost around €6.50, although prices are reduced on Wednesdays and increased at weekends and on public holidays. Check local newspapers for details of programmes and performance times.

There's no formal film classification system, but the words *vietato ai minori di 14 anni* ('children under 14 not admitted') indicate that a film has violent or sexually explicit content.

The Venice Film Festival in August/September is the world's oldest film festival (established 1932) and its prestigious prizes are highly rated in the international film world, particularly the Venetian Golden Lion award for best film, which is one of the industry's highest accolades. Tickets, however, are difficult or impossible to come by.

SOCIAL CLUBS

There are several expatriate clubs and organisations in most major cities, catering for all nationalities. In addition to a multitude of social, sports and special interest clubs, there are also branches of international clubs in most towns, including American Women's and Men's Clubs, Anglo-Italian Clubs, Business Clubs, chambers of commerce, International Men and Women's Clubs, Political Organisations, Lion Clubs and Rotary Clubs. Club listings and announcements are made in English-language and other expatriate publications, and most embassies and consulates in Italy maintain lists. Most clubs organise a variety of activities and pastimes such as bridge and whist, sports activities, appreciation of the arts, outings, dinner dances and other informal social events. Membership fees vary tremendously and some clubs offer short-term membership. Many clubs provide important information for new arrivals, organise free or inexpensive Italian-language classes and provide foreign newspapers to keep in touch with home.

Joining a club is one of the best ways to meet people and make friends in Italy. Ask at the local tourist office, town hall or library for information.

GAMBLING

Like most people Italians aren't averse to placing the odd wager, and for those who aren't football stars, famous fashion designers or business tycoons, there are plenty of opportunities (but, alas, little chance) to win millions of euros on the weekly state lottery, which also offers many smaller prizes. You can check your numbers in the *Giornale Ufficiale*. Other lotteries and prize draws include *Gratta e Vinci* (scratch and win – or more often, lose!), *Totocalcio* and *Totogol* (similar to the British football pools), *Superenalotto*, *Totip* and *Lotto*. Prize money varies from game to game, as do your chances of winning, which are about the same as your chance of being struck by lightning. Don't forget to check your tickets, as every year millions of euros are unclaimed by prize winners. Should you be one of the lucky few, you will be even happier to know that all winnings are tax-free!

There are also numerous TV shows offering large cash prizes; needless to say, the Italian equivalent of 'Who Wants To Be A Millionaire' is among the most popular. There's even a national association of game players (Associazione

Nazionale Concorsisti Italiani) with some 200 members, which publishes a newsletter with the latest information on how to win radio and TV games.

If the lottery and game shows aren't glamorous enough for you, you may wish to visit a casino (*casinò*, which also means 'brothel'!). There are a number in Italy, situated in Campione d'Italia on Lake Lugano, San Remo in Imperia (Liguria), St Vincent in Aosta (Val d'Aosta) and Venice, where the glamorous Palazzo Vendramin Calergi is open all year round, while the Lido Casino provides opportunities to lose your money from June to September only. Both establishments are convenient stops on the Vaporetto ferry, the 'Casino Express'. The San Remo Casino is reminiscent of many turn of the century establishments, with decor to match, while the Casinò de la Vallée in St Vincent is one of the largest in Europe. Black ties and evening wear are usually obligatory for entry to casinos, as are passports, as Italian nationals are barred unless they're employed there (others must visit France or Switzerland for a flutter). Opening hours tend to be from around 2pm to 2am or 3pm to 4.30am and the entrance fee is around €10.

Although for the majority of people gambling is harmless fun, the country also has a huge problem with gambling addiction, particularly slot machines, and there are a number organisations that work tirelessly to repair the damage caused by unbridled speculation.

NIGHTLIFE

Italians are gregarious by nature and their lifestyle revolves almost exclusively around socialising. All towns and cities are constructed around squares (*piazze*), where people meet and congregate, particularly in the evenings. Bars and cafés remain open long into the evening, often into the small hours (see below). Many bars in major cities have live music in the evenings and in recent years many 'pub type' establishments have opened. These are more sophisticated than a typical British or Irish pub and are more like a night-club without the music, with drinks usually more expensive than elsewhere. British and Irish bars, and 'atmospheric' pubs have also recently appeared on the scene, particularly in Rome and northern cities.

Discos (*discoteche*) in Italy tend to be enormous establishments with several floors and different kinds of music being played in various areas. Unfortunately, the prices generally match the size and discos are often prohibitively expensive. In towns and small cities you can expect to pay around €20 for entry, although in large cities or on the Italian Riviera you can pay up to €60! As a small recompense, your first drink is usually included in the entrance fee, although subsequent drinks may cost between €5 and €10. Most discos open around 10.30pm until the small hours, although there are also discos on Saturday and Sunday afternoons for the under 16s. Night-clubs (*locali notturni*) are generally smaller and less expensive than discos, with entrance occasionally free or up to around €10. The choice of music is more limited in night-clubs and the clientele tends to be older. In the major cities there's also a wide variety of gay and lesbian bars and clubs.

Local newspapers and entertainment magazines are the best source of information on nightlife, particularly in the major cities where the best and most 'in' places change constantly. Student and youth departments also publish information about local entertainment. Also, don't neglect to ask your friends and colleagues to recommend their favourite bars, discos and clubs.

BARS & CAFES

The foreign custom of 'going out for a drink' isn't particularly popular in Italy, where most people consume alcohol only with meals, although many Italians have a *grappa* or brandy with their morning coffee. Nevertheless, bars and cafés are plentiful in Italy and are an essential part of daily life. In fact, there's an ever-increasing range of bars and pubs springing up throughout the country; in Rome alone, there are over 300 watering holes. Most bars are similar in appearance – a pristine chrome bar, bright lights and a photograph (or two) of the local football team on the wall – and serve snacks and ice cream as well as drinks all day (they also admit children).

When you enter a bar, your first decision is whether to stand or sit; once you've chosen, there's no going back! Table (*tavola*) or terrace (*terrazzo*) service is usually twice as expensive as standing – a tariff list (*listino prezzi*) must, by law, be posted behind the bar. If you choose to stand, you must usually order from the cashier (*cassa*), who gives you a receipt (*scontrino*) that you present to the bartender, although in smaller bars you may be able to order first and pay when you leave. If you decide to sit, you must wait to be served. It isn't done to order from the cashier and then sit down; if you do the waiter will have his suspicions about your nationality confirmed instantly!

Coffee (*caffè*) is an institution in Italy and is served in many ways. Among the most common are:

- *espresso* – a small, **very** strong black coffee;
- *caffè lungo* – also small and black, but weaker;
- *corretto* – black mixed with a liqueur, usually grappa;
- *macchiato* – black with a spoonful of milk 'foam' on top;
- *caffè latte* – a large coffee with lots of milk;
- *cappuccino* or *cappuccio* – coffee with with cream and chocolate on top, often served lukewarm and drunk only for breakfast or between meals in Italy (only foreigners insist on it being served after dinner!)

A *decaffeinato* or *Hag* usually consists of a sachet of decaffeinated coffee and a cup of warm milk (decaf isn't popular in Italy). Some names for coffee vary from region to region, although all have little in common with the pale imitations dished up in many other countries. An *espresso* costs around €0.75 and a *cappuccino* around €1.25.

Italians aren't great tea drinkers and, if you ask for tea, you should be prepared to receive a glass of lukewarm water with a teabag beside it. If you want proper tea, ask for boiling water, *molto caldo* or *bollente* and bring your own teabag! Other hot drinks include chocolate (*cioccolata*), thick enough to eat with a spoon.

Beer is a popular drink with Italians, particularly among the younger generation, and British and (in particular) Irish-style pubs have mushroomed in recent years. Italian beers include Moretti, Frost and Peroni, which are served in bottles containing one-third or two-thirds of a litre and on draught (*alla spina*). Prices average around €1 for a small (*piccola*, 20cl) beer, €1.30 for a medium (*media*, 40cl) beer and around €1.80 for a large (*grande*, 66cl) beer – although prices depend very much on the establishment and whether you sit or stand. Beers from a wide range of other countries are also widely available.

Wine (*vino*) is served by the glass, costing from around €0.75 to €1.10, although you can pay up to €8 for a glass of vintage wine in a wine bar. For information about Italian wine, see page 386.

Non-alcoholic drinks include *granita*, an ideal summer drink made with fresh lemon or other fruit juice and crushed ice. Carbonised drinks are also popular throughout Italy. Bars and cafes in Italy are obliged (by law) to provide a free glass of tap water for anyone who wants it, irrespective of whether you buy anything else.

Bars usually serve a wide range of snacks, from sandwiches to basic hot meals. Snack bars (*paninoteche*) specialise in made-to-order sandwiches with a vast choice of fillings, which are usually displayed behind the counter. The different sandwiches available include:

- *tramezzino* – thin white sandwich bread cut into triangles;
- *panini* – a crusty, French bread stick;
- *schiaccitta* – a large, round salted cracker which, when filled, is cut into portions;
- *toste* – a toasted sandwich, which in bars is usually limited to cheese and/or ham but usually comes in a variety of flavours in a *paninoteche*.

RESTAURANTS

There are countless restaurants (*ristoranti*) and eating places in Italy, including the following:

- *tavola calda* (literally 'hot table') – a cheap, self-service establishment;

- *osteria* – essentially a wine bar offering a small selection of dishes;
- *rosticceria* – serving mainly cooked meats and a selection of take-away foods;
- *trattoria* – traditionally a family-run establishment, simpler in cuisine and less expensive than a *ristorante* proper, although the two have become interchangeable terms and you find little difference between them, except perhaps in price (a *trattoria* usually being cheaper).

Small grocery shops (*alimentari*) also sell sandwiches to take away. Another popular snack is portions of pizza (*taglio di pizza*). Ice-cream (*gelato*) is sold in a *gelateria*, although good home-made (*produzione propria*) ice cream isn't as easy to find as it used to be – a tell-tale sign is a *gelateria* with a queue of Italians outside.

Restaurants rarely open for lunch before 12.30pm and for dinner before 7.30pm (up to an hour later in the south), and they usually close on one day per week, generally a Sunday or Monday.

Many restaurants offer a choice of cheaper set meals. The tourist menu (*menù turistico*) or meal of the day (*menù del giorno*), sometimes called simply the 'fixed price menu' (*menù a presso fisso*), often includes two courses (e.g. pasta and a meat dish), but not drinks, for around €10 to €15. The à la carte menu is divided into starters (*antipasto*), usually salads or cold meats, a first course (*primo platto*) of pasta or rice, the main course (*secondo*), a fish or meat dish accompanied by vegetables (*contorno*), cheese (*formaggio*), and finally the dessert course (*dolci* or *frutta* – as one of the options is usually fruit). You aren't obliged to partake of all the courses on offer but you should order at least two, as few restaurants look kindly on diners who limit themselves to a plate of pasta or salad.

If you want water with your meal, tap water (*acqua semplice*) is safe to drink just about everywhere and you can order this free with your meal. However, you must be sure to specify this, or the waiter may bring you mineral water (*acqua minerale*), which Italians usually drink alongside their wine. Mineral water is available fizzy (*gassata*) or still (*non gassata*).

Italians usually drink wine with a meal. Most drink house wine (*vino della casa*) or the local wine (*vino locale*) when dining out, although even good quality wines are relatively inexpensive in all but the most upmarket restaurants. You should expect to pay around €7 for an average bottle in a restaurant or around double the supermarket price. Note, however, that many restaurants (e.g. *trattorie*) often stock only a limited selection of wines and mostly cheaper varieties. You can also order wine by the carafe (*caraffa/vinosfuso*) and in quarter (*quartino*) and half litre (*mezzo litro*) measures.

Before a meal, many Italians like to have a Campari with soda and ice or prepared fruit cocktails, usually non-alcoholic (*analcolico*). After a meal, as a *digestivo*, liqueurs are popular and include *limoncello*, which is pure alcohol infused with lemons, the herb-based *amaro*, *strega* and *galliano*, the widely popular *grappa*, a strong, clear liqueur made from grape skins (whose bitter taste is certainly an acquired one!), *amaretto* (almond based), *sambuca* (a sweet liqueur made from aniseed) and *maraschino*, made from the cherries after which it's named.

The bill (*conto*) usually includes a cover charge (*coperto*) of between €0.75 and €3 per person, which may include bread (*pane e coperto*). There may be an added service (*servizio*) charge of around 10 to 15 percent. Tipping is often a casual affair, with bills rounded up to the nearest banknote rather than a specific percentage added. **It's unusual for Italians to share restaurant bills, so beware if you suggest going out for a meal with a large group of friends!**

Restaurant guides are plentiful in Italy and most book shops have a section on gastronomy, including excellent guides such the Touring Club Italiano's *Guida Touring Alberghi e Ristoranti d'Italia*, *La Guida d'Italia* (l'Espresso) and Gambero Rosso's *Ristoranti d'Italia*. For English-speakers, the *Michelin Red Guide* to Italy is invaluable, while those on a tight budget may be interested in *Cheap Eats in Italy* by Sandra Gustafson (see also **Appendix B**).

Italian Cuisine & Eating Habits

Cooking (and eating) is an art form in Italy – one that stretches back thousands of years. Painted tombs show Etruscans enjoying huge banquets and the Romans were notorious for their hours of dining on delicacies such as flamingo tongues, peacock and crane. The modern Italian is no less interested in food and eating is one of the nation's greatest pleasures – Italian cuisine (*cucina*) is one of the finest in the world: light and healthy, yet full of flavour. The fact that Italy's status unified nation is somewhat recent explains the huge regional differences in cuisine. In the north, many dishes are reminiscent of France – rich and creamy and, surprisingly, often butter-based – while as you move south the dishes become hotter and spicier, and are cooked in olive oil rather than butter. However, most Italian cuisine is based on a few essential ingredients, notably pasta (see page 384).

When most people think of Italian food, they think of pasta dishes such as spaghetti Bolognese, lasagne and tortellini, which originated in Emilia-Romagna. Each region and many towns in Italy have their own pasta specialities, using a multitude of different shapes, sizes and colours. Short, tubular pasta, such as penne or macaroni (*maccheroni* in Italian), is best with rich, thick, meaty sauces, whereas long pasta, such as spaghetti and tagliatelle, is ideal with creamy or light sauces.

In the north of the country, pasta is often replaced by other staples such as *polenta*, a mixture of maize flour and water, which is slowly boiled and then sometimes fried, or rice, which is widely used in dishes such as risotto. Another Italian dish popular throughout the world is pizza, which originated in Naples – the most famous, Pizza Margherita, contains tomatoes, mozzarella and basil and is named after a former queen of Italy.

As well as these world-famous dishes, Italy boasts a vast range of regional and local culinary delights, such as cured ham (*prosciutto*) from Palma, Liguria's pesto served with sun-dried tomatoes and *foccacia* bread, Venetian risotto, a rice dish served with seafood or meat, Sienna's famous *panforte*, a rich fruity Christmas cake, Sardinia's spit-roasted piglet, Sicily's delicious desserts such as *cannoli*, zabaglione, *granita*, marzipan and cassata – a rich sponge-based dessert with ricotta cheese, liqueur and fruit – and, of course, Italian ice-cream (*gelato*), which is reputed to be the best in the world.

Italians are particularly fond of salad, especially green salads, which may include chicory, celery, cress, artichokes, radicchio, rocket and tomatoes. Italy produces an amazing variety of cheeses, including mozzarella (used in pizzas), parmesan, gorgonzola, pecorino, ricotta and provolone. Salami or pork products are another speciality, including the famous hams of Parma, *mortadella* from Bologna, San Daniele from Friuli and *speck* from Trentino-Alto Adige.

Italian eating habits are similar to those of other southern European countries. Breakfast (*prima colazione*) is continental style: a coffee (maybe a cappuccino) and a pastry, often taken standing in a bar or café. Lunch (*pranzo*), served between 1 and 3pm, is traditionally the main meal of the day and a social occasion, when the world's affairs are discussed and put to rights (Italy's affairs usually take a little longer to fix); as many as four courses may be served. However, as modern living (and the outside world) encroaches ever deeper into the Italian culture, the long lunch tradition is gradually being eroded as more and more businesses work continuous days. Dinner (*cena*) is served from 7 or 8pm onwards and is traditionally a simpler meal than lunch, although it's hardly a snack and usually consists of a cooked meal.

LIBRARIES

The library structure in Italy is generally poor and nowhere near as good as those in the UK and US. Libraries are likely to be small, rather inefficiently run places, where locating a book can take weeks rather than minutes. However, there's a large state-owned library in every city, which may have a small foreign-language section. To become a member you must provide identity and a number of photographs. State-owned libraries are usually open from around 10am to 5pm or sometimes a little later on a couple of days per week.

Rome and Florence house the most English-language libraries, and American universities and English-language churches usually operate their own libraries. The British Council also has a library at its branches; the Harold Acton Library in Florence is one of the largest English-language libraries in continental Europe. Expatriate associations and clubs often run book-lending clubs or libraries (e.g. the Santa Susanna Lending Library in Rome), and foreign embassies house reference libraries, although you need an appointment to use these. Most private libraries require annual membership, for which there's usually a small fee. Ask at local consulates and expatriate clubs for information.

16.

SPORTS

The Italians' passionate love of sport usually involves watching rather than participating, although Italy has a proud record in international competition in many sports, notably football, basketball, cycling, motor racing, skiing and boxing. Sports such as football (especially), motor racing and cycling attract vast numbers of ardent supporters, and if you have the opportunity to attend one of these major sporting occasions it will certainly be an experience to remember. On arrival in Italy it won't take you long to realise the importance of sport in a country where *La Gazzetta dello Sport* (💻 www.gazzetta.it) is by far the biggest selling daily newspaper. However, when it comes to working up a sweat, you won't see as much evidence of this as you do in many other countries. For example, you see few joggers on the streets and the general fitness craze that has swept many countries in the last decade or so has, to a large extent, passed Italy by. Schools don't need to offer sport as part of their curriculum and although some do provide sporting activities, many have poor facilities and are unable to do so. However, appearances can be deceptive and there are plenty of opportunities to take part in amateur sport around the country, although you may just need to look a bit harder to find them.

Italians tend to be serious about their sport, as they're about anything that involves dressing up and looking their best. If you want to blend in with the crowd, it isn't the done thing to turn up in a pair of old shorts and an ill-fitting T-shirt advertising your favourite beer (or a university you never attended). Whatever their chosen sport, Italians invariably look the part and have the latest and best equipment, plus the most fashionable attire, even if they're beginners or incompetent. Sports equipment is generally reasonably priced in Italy, although fashionable designer sports wear can be expensive. However, if you time your purchases for the low season and during sales, or by buying last season's gear, a considerable amount can be saved.

Tourist and information offices can put you in touch with local sports clubs and facilities, but they cannot usually provide comprehensive information. Sports shops (*articoli sportivi*) are usually a good source of information about local sports facilities, and clubs (*associazioni e federazioni sportive*) may be listed in the yellow pages (*pagine gialle*) or the English yellow pages (see page 446). Alternatively you can contact the national federation for your chosen sport (some federations are listed in this chapter) or the Italian Olympic Committee, Comitato Olimpico Nazionale Italiano/CONI, Foro Italico, 00195 Rome (☎ 06-36851). If you have access to the Internet, you will find a wealth of information about Italian sports (try 💻 www.datasport.it).

AERIAL SPORTS

There are flying clubs and schools throughout the country offering flying and gliding opportunities and training, although flying is an expensive sport in Italy. Those arriving from North America in particular notice that prices are much higher, due in part to the much higher cost of aviation fuel and higher landing fees. You must be licensed before you can fly solo and all craft must be registered with the Aeroclub Italiano, Via Roberto Ferruzzi, 38, 00143 Rome (☎ 06-5195 7042, 💻 www.aeci.it).

Other aerial sports such as hang-gliding (*deltaplano*), paragliding (*parapendio*), parachuting and hot-air ballooning are all popular in Italy, particularly in the Alps and Dolomites, where the main season runs from June to October. For obvious reasons, all such activities require beginners to undergo an extensive training programme leading to internationally recognised qualifications. However, it's usually possible to try these sports by taking a tandem flight with a qualified instructor for a reasonable fee to see whether the freedom of the skies appeals as much in reality as it does in theory! For further information about free flying, especially hang-gliding and paragliding, contact the Federazione Italiana Volo Libero, Via Salbertrand, 50, 10146 Turin (☎ 011-744 991, 💻 www.fivl.it).

CYCLING

Cycling (*ciclismo*) is a hugely popular sport, despite the fact that some two-thirds of the country is mountainous and temperatures in summer are often too high for anyone but the most dedicated riders. Cycle racing has a huge following in Italy, which is organised at all levels – Italy has a long record of producing world-class riders. The 'Tour of Italy (*Giro d'Italia*), Italy's answer to the *Tour de France* and one of the world's most prestigious cycling races, has been held annually since 1909, interrupted only by the two world wars. The race is held in May and attracts large crowds along the route – it's well worth making the effort to take in a stage. Cycling clubs can frequently be seen on tours throughout the country, especially at the weekends, with the brightly-clad riders seemingly oblivious to the gradients. However, it's noticeable that groups are almost exclusively male, despite the fact that cycling is popular among women and there's also a women's *Giro d'Italia*, which follows a route in the north of over 1,200km (745mi) in June to July each year.

For those with lesser ambitions, the largest area of flat land in Italy is the Po delta in the north, which provides an ideal area for cycling and is noted for its stunning scenery. Most towns have specialist cycling shops that sell or hire bicycles and provide spares, assistance, and advice about routes and local cycling clubs. A popular choice in mountainous regions is to use a cable car to take your bike to the top of a mountain, from where you take a 'leisurely' ride back down.

Dedicated cycle tracks (*pista ciclabile*) are something of a rarity, although there are some in national parks and a few in towns around the country. There have been some recent initiatives to create cycle tracks and cycling pressure groups are pressing for further progress. Cycling as a means of transport has also received welcome publicity in recent years during a series of car-free Sundays, which have been operating in hundreds of towns and cities once per month to draw attention to (and help combat) traffic pollution. With cars banned from town centres on these days, the strangely quiet streets are full of cycles and a few horses. A new initiative in Florence is bicycle taxis, which operate in the city centre and carry two passengers.

The price of a basic bicycle starts at around €120 and for a mountain bike at some €250, although prices are much higher for racing models that can run to €1,500 or more (top Italian makes include Bianchi and Campagnolo). Shop around and compare prices and features. If you're after a standard bicycle you could also try large supermarkets and hypermarkets, where prices are generally lower. Bikes should be fitted with an anti-theft device such as a steel cable or chain with a lock, as bicycle theft is rife in Italy. Bicycle rental is available in many towns and resorts, although it isn't always obvious where to go (ask at the local tourist or information office). Rental costs vary according to the model, with a basic cycle starting at around €12 per day and a good mountain bike costing €30 or more per day.

The regulations concerning the transportation of cycles on trains have recently changed and it's now possible to take your bicycle with you on all classes of train for a fee of from €3.5 to €7, depending on the distance. At the time of writing, cycles were transported free of charge on car-free Sundays (see above), although this may change (check at the local railway station for the current situation).

A glance at any major city in Italy will confirm, cities aren't ideal places for cycling due to the volume of traffic and the level of pollution. Most Italians don't use bicycles in town centres, but rely instead on scooters or motorbikes, whose large numbers add greatly to the apparently random (and real) confusion of the traffic flow! If you do cycle in traffic it's wise to wear a face-mask, although, according to medical experts, they offer little or no protection against carbon monoxide. It's important not to underestimate the dangers of cycling (particularly for children) in Italy's cities and towns, where many cyclists are killed and injured each year. Helmets are essential attire, particularly for children, as are reflective clothing and bright (preferably flashing) lights at night. Head injuries are the main cause of death in cycle accidents and you should buy a quality helmet that has been tested and approved.

For further information about cycling contact the Italian Cycling Federation, Federazione Ciclistica Italiana, Via Marsala, 8, 00185 Rome (☎ 06-3685 8171) or check the Internet (e.g. 🖳 www.cycling.it).

FISHING

Italy offers abundant fishing opportunities, both fresh and salt water, and over two million people take part in the sport annually. The many lakes, rivers and mountain streams provide the opportunity to fish for trout, carp, perch, pike and other species. For freshwater fishing, you require a special annual licence and must be a member of the Federazione Italiana della Pesca Sportiva, Viale Tiziano, 70, 00196 Rome (☎ 06-3685 8238), which administers over 90 per cent of Italy's inland waters. You also require a special licence to fish in most waters (e.g. €8 per day) or only when you actually catch something – in some areas there are park rangers who charge you a small fee based on the size and weight of your catch.

No licence is required for sea fishing and you can join a deep-sea fishing excursion or hire your own boat at many ports. Spear fishing is legal and popular in many places, but regulations forbid the use of scuba tanks and nets for underwater fishing. Underwater fishing is permitted only during daylight, when (by law) no more than 5kg (11lb) of fish and shellfish may be caught per day.

FOOTBALL

Football or soccer (*calcio*) is Italy's national sport and by far the most important in Italy, occupying almost the entire first half of each issue of *La Gazzetta dello Sport*. Italian football fans (*tifosi*) are among the most dedicated and fervent in Europe, and are matched in their fanaticism only by the Spanish. No football fan should pass up the opportunity to experience the passions aroused by a first class match (*partita*). Italian regional pride is much in evidence on the terraces, which is only briefly forgotten when watching the national team (*azzurri*). Italy has a proud tradition in international football and has won the World Cup on three occasions, in 1934, 1938 and 1982 (second only to Brazil and equal with Germany), although results have been disappointing in recent years.

Matches are often packed with incident, both on and off the field, in a drama that provides first class entertainment. Despite the chanting and passion though, there's little threat of the physical violence that's associated with the game in some other countries. The concept of having several beers (or a dozen) before a match is foreign to Italian supporters, who are more likely to have a coffee, and drunkenness at matches is practically unknown, despite the sale of alcohol inside many grounds.

Italy claims to have the best league in the world (although Spain's *Seria A* has a strong case), with some of the world's most famous clubs (the likes of Inter-Milan and Juventus are household names) and biggest stars. First class matches attract huge attendances and Italy's top clubs have been among the most successful in Europe (although until 1996 they were officially non-profit organisations). After a hiatus in the late 90s and early 21st century when Spanish and English clubs dominated in European competition, the Italians returned to the fore in 2003, with the Champions League final contested between two Italian sides, AC Milan and Juventus (the former won, on penalties).

The Italian league consists of four main divisions: *Serie A, B, C1* and *C2. Serie A* is the top division with 18 teams, with ticket prices costing from around €15 to €80. The season runs from around the end of August to June, with a mid-winter break in December-January. At the end of the season the top team in Serie A wins the championship (*campionato*) and '*Lo Scudetto*', while the bottom four teams are relegated to *Serie B*. Matches are played on Sundays, usually in the afternoon, although they sometimes take place in the evening. It's a common sight on a Sunday to observe Italian families out for an afternoon stroll, only to notice that the men in the group have radios pressed to their ears so as not to miss any of the action! The season culminates with the Italian Cup (*Coppa Italia*) final in June.

For those more interested in playing than watching, even small towns usually have several clubs and there are leagues and competitions at every level. Five-a-side football is also popular, as is eight-player *calcio* (*calciotto*) and pitches can be rented at most sports centres. Many companies have five-a-side teams and arrange matches on an informal basis or enter competitions held at a local sports centre. The local tourist or information office may be able to put you in touch with a local club, some of which advertise in the yellow pages. Alternatively you can contact the Federazione Italiana Giuoco Calcio, Via Gregorio Allegri, 14, 00198 Rome (☎ 06-8491 2132, 🖳 www.fige.it).

There are a number of websites where you can obtain latest football results and information such as 🖳 www.dossier.net and most clubs have their own websites, e.g. 🖳 www.inter.it (Inter Milan) and 🖳 www.juventus.it (Juventus).

GOLF

Although you may not automatically think of golf when you think of Italy, there are many 9 and 18-hole courses around the country, particularly in the north where there's more flat land available. As in most European countries, golf is generally a sport for the wealthy and it hasn't caught on with the masses despite the best efforts of Constantino Rocco and a number of other Italian professional players to popularise the sport. It's usually necessary to join a club, many of which have long waiting lists, although there are a number of public courses where anyone can play a round for a fee. Some private clubs also allow visitors with a handicap card to play for green fees. Further information can also be obtained from the Italian Golf Federation, Federazione Italiana Golf, Via Flaminia, 388, 00196 Rome (☎ 06-394 641).

HIKING

Hiking (*escursionismo*), which includes anything from a gentle ramble through the countryside to serious hill walking, is popular in Italy, where there are numerous opportunities for walkers of all standards. The most popular areas include the Alps, the Apennines (particularly in the Parco Nazionale d'Abruzzo and the Sila Massif in Calabria) and Tuscany (e.g. the Alpi Apuane), along with the coastlines of Liguria and Amalfi, and the Italian lakes in the north. Those seeking challenges can find plenty on some of the alpine routes, although there are also alpine paths suitable for beginners and families with young children. Those who enjoy more remote hiking, may wish to try the interior of Sardinia (e.g. Gennargentu) or Sicily, where you need to be well prepared as you're likely to be on your own should any problems arise. Alternatively, you could follow the volcanoes' route, which includes walks to the summits of two of Europe's most active volcanoes, Etna and Stromboli. Many resorts in the Alps advertise green weeks (*settimane verde*), which include accommodation and activities for summer visitors, similar to the white weeks offered to skiers in the winter.

The main organisation for hiking (as well as sports such as mountaineering and climbing) is the Italian Alpine Club (Club Alpino Italiano/CAI – see address below). It has a membership of around 400,000, making it by far the largest alpine club in the world, and includes a network of some 450 local hiking clubs throughout Italy. The CAI is responsible for trail marking, which is generally of a high standard, particularly in northern and central Italy. It also operates around 600 mountain refuges (*rifugi*), providing accommodation and meals to walkers, a highly regarded mountain rescue service, and produces maps and a range of other publications. Trekking Italia is another organisation that organises weekend and week-long treks in many regions of Italy and abroad. For information contact the Associazione Amici del Trekking e della Natura, Via Molino delle Armi, 31, 20123 Milan (☎ 02-8372 838, 🖳 www.trekkingitalia.com).

The main hiking season is from May to October, although there are opportunities to walk all year round in many areas. In the northern mountains, walking is often hampered by snow from November to April or later, and the official 'season' may last only from June to September. In contrast, winter and spring are the ideal time for walking in much of the central and southern parts of the country, although even in the south there can be snow on higher land in winter and early spring. Alpine routes are at their busiest in August and anywhere south of Tuscany is likely to be too hot for comfortable walking in summer. If you're hiking for more than a day you need to arrange overnight accommodation. In Italy it's unusual for hikers to carry tents and camp in the wild, which is, in any case, forbidden in most areas. However, in the more remote areas of Sicily and Sardinia camping equipment is useful (see **Camping & Caravanning** on page 334).

If you're hiking in a mountain area between mid-June and September you can stay at one of the network of *rifugi*, which are numerous in the northern mountains, but much less common in central and southern areas. *Rifugi* may be run by the CAI (see above) or privately operated, with prices at CAI *rifugi* from around €12 to €30 for bed and breakfast. Accommodation may be in dormitories, although a limited number of private rooms are usually available. **Rifugi can be fully booked at peak times which means that they may either send you on to the next refuge (which could be several hours walk away) or you may end up sleeping on the floor.** If possible, it's therefore wise to book in advance. Details of the location and phone numbers of *rifugi* are available from local tourist offices or the *Guida Escursionistica per Valli e Rifugi* series of guides published by the CAI.

Bookshops in major towns and cities stock hiking maps and books, and shops in hiking areas stock a wide range of local maps and books. The largest scale maps are usually 1:25,000, which show paths and *rifugi* as well as topographical features and buildings. These include the *Tabacco* series for the north-east and the Dolomites, the *Instituto Geografico Centrale* series covering north-west Italy and the Alps, the *Edizioni Multigraphic Firenze* series for central and southern Italy, and the *Kompass* range, which covers most of the country. Tourist offices are also a good source of information about routes, including places of interest and the local flora and fauna.

The Touring Club Italiano (TCI) and Club Alpino Italiano publish a series of comprehensive walking guides, Guide dei Monti d'Italia, containing maps. A number of English-language hiking guides are available, including *The Independent Walker's Guide to Italy* by Frank W. Booth (Interlink), *Walking and Eating in Tuscany & Umbria* by James Ladsun & others (Penguin) and *Walking in Italy* by Helen Gillman and others (Lonely Planet), which contains suggested walks throughout the country ranging from two hours to six days in duration, plus a wealth of general information about walking in Italy. Cicerone Press publish a number of walking guides, including *Walking in the Dolomites* and *Walking in the Central Italian Alps*, both by Gillian Price.

If you wish to join a local walking club or require further information about walking in Italy, contact the Club Alpino Italiano, Via E Petrella, 19, 20124 Milan (☎ 02-2057 231, 🖳 www.cai.it).

Safety

The following notes are designed to help you survive a walk on the wild side:

- If you're going to take up hiking seriously, a good pair of walking shoes or boots is mandatory and widely available in sports shops. Always wear proper walking shoes or boots where the terrain is rough. Break in a new pair of boots (and rusty muscles) on some gentle strolls before setting out on a marathon hike across the Alps.

- Don't over-exert yourself, particularly at high altitudes where the air is thinner. Mountain sickness usually occurs only above 4,000m (13,000ft), but can also happen at lower altitudes. If you aren't particularly fit, take it easy and set a slow pace. It's easy to over-exert yourself and underestimate the duration or degree of difficulty of a hike. Start slowly and build up to those weekend marathons. If you're unfit, use chair lifts and cable cars to get to high altitudes.

- **Don't attempt a major hike alone as it's too dangerous.** Notify someone of your route, destination and estimated time of return. Check the conditions along your route and the times of any public transport connections (set out early to avoid missing the last cable car or bus). Take into account the time required for both ascents and descents. If you're unable to return by the time expected, let somebody know if you can (a mobile phone may come in handy). If you realise that you're unable to reach your destination, for example, due to tiredness or bad weather, turn back in good time or take a shorter route. If you get caught in a heavy storm, descend as quickly as possible or seek protection, e.g. in a refuge hut.

- Check the weather forecast. Storms can strike surprisingly quickly, even in summer, and particularly in the mountains. Be aware of the dangers of electrical storms and don't shelter under isolated trees and other objects that could easily be struck by lightening.

- Hiking, even in lowland areas, can be dangerous, so don't take any unnecessary risks. There are enough natural hazards, including bad weather, rock-falls, avalanches, rough terrain, snow and ice, and wet grass, without adding to them. **There is only one dangerous snake in Italy, the viper, which is common throughout the country with the exception of Sardinia.** Anti-venom injections are widely available in pharmacies, but you can minimise your chances of being bitten by wearing boots, socks and long trousers when walking through undergrowth, and not sticking your hands into holes and crevices. Don't walk on closed tracks at any time, particularly in the spring when there may be a danger of avalanches or rock falls. During the hunting season, warning signs may be posted in certain areas, which are best avoided (many hunters shoot at anything that moves!).

- Wear loose-fitting clothes in several layers so that you can cover up or peel layers off as required. A first-aid kit (for cuts and grazes), compass, identification, maps, small torch and Swiss army knife may also come in handy, as will a water bottle and some rations to keep you going. Children should be equipped with a loud whistle in case they get lost.

- Take sun protection, for example a hat and sunglasses, and sun and barrier cream. This is especially important if you're hiking in the mountains, as you burn more easily at high altitude due to the thinner air. Use a total sun-block on your lips, nose and eyelids, and take a scarf or handkerchief to protect your neck from the sun. You may also need to protect yourself against ticks and mosquitoes in some areas. You should also be aware of the *calabrone*, a large wasp found in Italy whose sting can provoke a severe allergic reaction in some people.

HUNTING

The hunting (*la caccia*) season in Italy extends from September until February for most animals and until March for migratory birds. Game is public property and you can hunt in most places provided you're at least 100m (328ft) from a house and don't damage crops. There are an estimated 800,000 regular hunters (mostly using shotguns), mainly in Tuscany and Sardinia. Popular prey includes wild boar, rabbit, hare and many species of birds, including songbirds, many of which are protected in other countries. Hunters are a powerful lobby group in Italy, although hunting is controversial and many protests take place on the opening day of the season; however, to date the pro-hunting lobby has managed to overcome all efforts to have it banned.

If you take part in hunting, you must ensure that you're aware of the regulations governing which species can be shot. Enthusiasm for hunting has resulted in many animals becoming rare, endangered or extinct, and new laws have been introduced to provide greater protection for many birds and animals. In recent years, further measures have been taken to protect animals in regions hit by fires and drought. Campaigns against hunting are led by the World Wildlife Fund (WWF) and the Animal Rights League, who are active in trying to ensure that hunting regulations are adhered to. During the 1999/2000 hunting season, WWF volunteers apprehended some 1,000 illegal hunters, many of whom were seeking to shoot or trap protected birds of prey, especially falcons.

For further information about hunting in Italy, contact the Federazione Italiana Caccia, Viale Tiziano, 70, 00196 Rome (☎ 06-3685 8354).

MOTOR SPORTS

Italy is synonymous with cars, being the home of such famous names as Alfa Romeo, Ferrari, Fiat, Lamborghini, Lancia and Maserati, and a love of cars is almost mandatory among Italian males. Italians (both male and female) are passionate supporters (*tifosi*) of Formula One motor racing, especially the Ferrari team, although this is one sport where there are definitely more opportunities for watching than taking part – unless, of course, you take into account the endless possibilities presented on Italy's roads, which many Italians use as a racetrack!

Italy has a proud history in motor racing and has produced many world champions. Two Formula One Grand Prix races are staged annually in Italy, at Monza and Imola (where Ayton Senna was killed in 1994). In April the San Marino race, although not technically an Italian event, is held on Italian soil at Imola, south-east of Bologna (not far from the home of Ferrari at Modena). There are many links between Ferrari and the Imola track, where the stadium, Autodromo Enzo e Dino Ferrari, is named after the founder of Ferrari and his son. The Italian Grand Prix is held in September at Monza (🖳 www.monzanet.it), where there has been motor racing since 1922. The Formula One *Autodromo* lies within a vast, attractive park on the edge of Monza, although it's little more than a northern suburb of Milan these days. Tickets for Grand Prix meetings can be obtained from the venue, although they don't come particularly cheap, varying from around €40 to well over €250. Michael Schumacher won the Formula One Drivers' World Championship in 2000 driving a Ferrari – their first championship in 21 years – and is still dominating the sport.

Rallying

There are many opportunities to get involved with rallying in Italy, where you can take part in one of the many events organised by local motor clubs or just watch the experts in the major national races such as the famous San Remo Rally held in October each year. Contact local automobile clubs for information about what's available in your area.

Motorcycle Racing

This is another enormously popular sport, which has had a long love affair with Italian superbikes such as Ducati, Moto Guzzi and MV Agusta. Mopeds and motor bikes are such a common means of everyday transport for millions of Italians that it would be strange if this didn't spill over into a love of motorcycle racing. If you wish to take part in something a little more organised than the daily race to work, contact the Federazione Motociclistica Italiana, Viale Tiziano, 70, 00196 Rome (☎ 06-3685 8371).

ROCK-CLIMBING & CAVING

If you love the mountains but find hiking doesn't provide you with sufficient challenges, mountaineering (*alpinismo*), rock climbing (*roccia*) or caving (*speleologia*) may be for you. Italy provides many opportunities for these sports, particularly in the Alps, where there are challenges available to suit all levels of experience. If you're new to these sports it's recommended to join a club to 'learn the ropes' before heading for the mountains. Although not for beginners, one relatively easy introduction to rock-climbing is via the *Vie Ferrate* (literally 'iron ways'), which consist of permanently fixed iron ladders, pegs and cables onto which climbers can attach their karabiners. These were established as far back as the late 19th century and provide access to routes that would otherwise be too difficult.

There are climbing clubs in most towns, many of which are affiliated to the mountaineering section of the Club Alpino Italiano (CAI), Via E Petrella, 19, 20124 Milan (☎ 02-2057 231, 🖳 www.cai.it), which has some 800 official mountaineering and climbing instructors. The Federazione Arrampicata Sportiva Italiana, Via San Secondo, 92, 10128 Turin (☎ 011-5683 154) can also put you in touch with mountain-climbing schools that provide training and organise climbing expeditions for all ages. Even if you have experience you probably need to hire a guide in an unfamiliar area, who can be found through mountaineering schools or independently at many alpine resorts. Don't take unnecessary risks and ensure that you have the appropriate equipment and experience for a planned climb or expedition. Many climbers lose their lives in the mountains each year, often due to inexperience or recklessness. The mountain rescue service, staffed by 7,000 members of the CAI, rescues many climbers each year, many of whom are inadequately equipped or inexperienced for the route they're attempting.

Caving

Italy has been an important centre of European caving or 'spelunking' (*speleologia*) for over a century and the sport has enjoyed increasing popularity in recent decades. There are over 10,000 documented caves in Italy, in areas as diverse as Lombardy, Marche, Sardinia and Tuscany, although the greatest number are to be found in Umbria. Umbria was the original focus of caving and includes Monte Cucco, one of the deepest cave systems in the world, and the 'Avenue of the Great Wells' – a series of large underground wells regarded by caving enthusiasts as Italy's most spectacular geological feature. Further north, a popular alpine system is *Pioggia Bella*, which has seven entrances and offers a through trip of over six kilometres.

Those taking part in caving expeditions range from trained members of the various caving organisations in Italy to those wishing to experience a guided weekend adventure in the geological underworld of fossils, rivers and unusual creatures, including bats and cave fish. It's important to have the appropriate training, equipment and conditioning, and to be accompanied by an experienced guide to explore this dark and silent world (best avoided by those who suffer from claustrophobia). Even an 'easy' cave system requires you to scramble over rocks, bend over double (possibly for hours) to traverse low passages or wriggle and squeeze your body through narrow channels. In more difficult caves you may need to use rock-climbing skills and rope systems to cross underground lakes or may even be required to swim under water. Newcomers can attend an introductory guided weekend, which are arranged in the easier caves, with all equipment provided by the organisers.

For further information contact the Centro Nazionale di Speleologia, Via Galeazzi, 5, 06021 Costacciaro (☎ 075-9170 400) or the Gruppo Speleologico CAI Perugia, Via Santini, 8, 06128 Perugia (☎ 05-5847 070).

RACQUET SPORTS

Tennis is by far the most popular racquet sport, where there's a wealth of both public and private courts available. Italian tennis clubs usually operate on a membership basis, so you need to join or be invited as a guest by a member, and membership can be expensive. There are also public facilities in most towns and cities owned by the commune (*comune*) where you can rent a court by the hour or obtain a season pass (*abonnamento*). Tennis is a popular after-school activity for children and tennis lessons are widely available for all ages and standards, including residential courses. Most courts are clay (*terra rossa*) or hard (asphalt). Professional tennis enjoys a large following and the country stages a number of top tournaments, including the Italian Open, which is held in Rome in May (on clay) and is the precursor to the French Open. The country has had reasonable success in international events and has a number of top male and female players. If you want to find a club in a particular area, contact the Italian Tennis Federation, Federazione Italiana Tennis, Viale Tiziano, 70, 00196 Rome (☎ 06-3685 8210).

Squash has a relatively small following in Italy where there are a small number of squash clubs in major cities (see the yellow pages), and sometimes facilities are also provided at tennis clubs and sports centres. Specialist clubs may require you to be a member, but often you can rent a court without joining. Squash courses or individual sessions of instruction are usually provided, typically costing around €15 for a 45-minute lesson.

Badminton has only been introduced in the last decade or so, although there are now clubs in most major cities, many of which participate in national tournaments and international competitions. Many clubs offer free use of equipment and coaching for members. Most clubs meet in the evenings at local sports centres, where basic membership costs start at around €30 per year plus a fee of around €3 per visit to pay for court hire and equipment.

Table tennis is popular throughout Italy, where tables and bats can be hired for a nominal cost at sports centres and other sports clubs, e.g. tennis and squash clubs, where tournaments are organised at all levels and for all ages. Table tennis tables are also provided in social and other clubs, and even on beaches in summer.

RUGBY

In a country so fanatical about football, rugby was always going to have a hard time getting established. Rugby union (played between teams of 15 players) was introduced in northern Italy by workers returning from France in the late 1920s, and it's still strongest in the northern regions. Over the last 15 years or so it has become increasingly popular, aided by government moves to promote the sport. In particular, major tax breaks were provided for companies wishing to invest in rugby clubs and teams. Sponsorship money poured in and the growth of the game was assured, which was accompanied by an influx of foreign stars to Italian clubs.

At the national level, the Five Nations tournament (England, France, Ireland, Scotland and Wales) was expanded in 2000 to become the Six Nations when Italy was admitted.

Most Italian towns of any size boast a rugby club, a total of around 430 competing in one of the country's many leagues and knockout competitions that take place between September and April. For information about local clubs, contact the Italian Rugby Federation, Federazione Italiana Rugby, Via Leopoldo Franchetti, 1, 00194 Rome (☎ 06-3610 821, 🖳 http://edit.fedrugby.it).

SWIMMING

Not surprisingly given the climate, swimming (*nuoto*) is a popular sport and pastime in Italy, although the country has fewer indoor swimming pools (*piscina*) than you may expect. Sea swimming is popular in summer, when the water temperature can reach around 27°C (81°F) and a dip provides a welcome break from the blazing summer sun. However, although many Italians get into the water to cool off, this often has more to do with posing than swimming, evidenced by the number of people who take their mobile phones into the sea with them – held carefully above the water level, needless to say! Most beaches are public, with the best (white sand) beaches on the Adriatic coast, where the Lido off Venice is Italy's most fashionable bathing resort. Expect to pay around €1.50 for a beach chair, up to €6 per day to hire a basic lounger and up to €15 per day for an elaborate sun bed with an umbrella.

Sometimes you must join a club to use a swimming pool, although there are also many public pools where you pay an entrance fee. In summer there are many open-air public pools, some of which are heated and covered in winter and used all year round. Hotel pools are also sometimes open to non-residents, but these tend to be expensive. If you join a swimming club, you will find that there are numerous local and national competitions in which you can take part. Swimming lessons are also widely available through clubs and at public pools. The local tourist or information office can inform you about local swimming facilities. **In most pools you're required to wear a swimming cap, which is often compulsory, irrespective of how much (or little) hair you have!** Private clubs with pools are listed under *Impianti Sportivi e Ricreativi* in the yellow pages. There are a number of water parks (*parchi aquatici*) throughout the country, offering pools, slides, wave machines and games, although these are usually outdoor facilities and therefore open only in summer. They tend to get very busy and aren't ideal for serious swimming, but are good for a family day out.

For more information about swimming, contact the Italian Swimming Federation, Federazione Italiana Nuoto, Piazza Lauro de Bosis, 2, 00196 Rome (☎ 06-3219 001).

WATERSPORTS

In Italy you're never far from the sea, which has had a key influence on much of Italian life. Many regions take pride in their long and illustrious maritime history as explorers (Christopher Columbus came from Genoa), traders and warriors. Given the climate, the length of the coastline and the large lakes in the north, it will come as no surprise to discover that watersports are popular in Italy. Messing about in boats is a favourite pastime and sailing boats, motorboats, canoes and kayaks can be hired at many coastal and lake resorts. Water-skiing (*sci acquatico*) and windsurfing are also popular, both along the coast and on inland lakes, particularly Lake Garda, where the north end around the Riva del Garda is noted for its strong winds. Equipment and wetsuits – highly recommended at most times of the year – can be rented at resorts. For details about water-skiing clubs contact the Federazione Italiana Sci Nautico, Via Piranesi, 44/b, 20137 Milan (☎ 02-7529 181).

Boating

Sailing (*vela*) in yachts and dinghies is popular throughout Italy, where even small coastal towns often have a marina. Dinghy sailing is also popular on the major lakes, particularly Lake Garda, which is the biggest and often provides better wind conditions than the smaller lakes. Sailing has received a further boost in recent years by the prominent Italian attempts to win the America's Cup. So far success has proved elusive, but the challenge has raised the profile of the sport in Italy considerably.

Motor boats are also popular as they cater for the Italians' love of speed. Many resorts have prominent sailing and yacht clubs, through which boats can usually be rented and courses taken. Generally these require you to be a member and costs vary widely; enquire at a tourist office about the facilities available locally or contact the relevant sports federation (see below).

Boating holidays are popular in Italy, mainly on yachts and motor boats, and you can also charter a boat directly provided you have a licence (*patente nautica*) or are willing to hire a captain, or even an entire crew if your budget stretches to it. **Before anchoring at a marina in Italy, you must obtain permission from the harbour master (*capitaneria di porto*).** Weekly and weekend sailing courses and holidays are featured in the magazine *Avventure nel Mondo* and advertised in sailing magazines. If you're chartering a boat without a captain, you need a guide to harbours such as the 'Pilot' series (published in England by Imray, Laurie, Norie & Wilson Ltd., 🖳 www.imray.com), which includes most Italian ports. A list of sailing clubs and information about courses is available from the Italian Sailing Federation, Federazione Italiana Vela, Viale Brigata Bisagno, 2, 16129 Genoa (☎ 010-589 431, 🖳 www.federvela.it) or via the Internet (🖳 www.velanet.it). For information about motorboat clubs and racing, contact the Federazione Italiana Motonautica, Via Piranesi, 44/b, 20137 Milan (☎ 02-701 631).

For those who like to drool over incredibly expensive boats that they will probably never be able to afford (unless you have very deep pockets), a huge boat show (*Salone Nautico*) is staged in Genoa in October each year. It offers an entertaining day out, if only to marvel at the way a fortunate few live, and is a good place to make contact with sailing organisations and discover the range of boating holidays available in Italy and beyond. Entry is free for foreigners on production of your passport.

Canoeing, kayaking and rowing (*canottaggio*) are also popular (which is one of the world's leading rowing nations), both on lakes, rivers and along the coast. For information, contact the Italian Rowing Federation, Federazione Italiana di Canottaggio, Viale Tiziano, 70, 00196 Rome (☎ 06-366 596, 🖳 www.canottaggio.org) or the Federazione Italiana Canoa e Kayak, Viale Tiziano, 70, 00196 Rome, ☎ 06-36851), who can provide a list of clubs that rent equipment and provide training.

Diving

Scuba-diving is well established in Italy, where it developed under the auspices of the Italian Federation of Divers. Some of the best scuba-diving (*immersioni* or *subacquee*, often shortened to *sub*) in the Mediterranean is in Italian waters and diving is popular almost everywhere along the coast. However, the best diving areas are in the Ligurian Sea, south of Genoa in the area stretching from the Portofino peninsula to the Cinque Terre and beyond, and around the Italian islands of Capri, Sardinia and Sicily. The area around the Portofino peninsula has recently been designated a marine nature reserve, with fishing and other activities restricted. The area has a rocky coast and boasts a wide range of interesting marine life (it's particularly noted for its large number of red fan corals), and provides an excellent environment for fish and invertebrate life. However, there are few large fish, due in part to the fact that spear fishing continues to be popular in Italy (outside the marine park), although there's evidence of greater numbers of larger fish in the area since the park was established.

A particular attraction at San Fruttuoso is the submerged bronze statue of the Christ of the Deep (*Cristo degli abissi*). This famous statue of Christ with outstretched arms was placed in the bay at a depth of 18 metres in 1954, as a memorial to those who have died at sea. On a calm day the statue can be seen from a boat on the surface, but the view from close up under the water is much more impressive. In August an annual festival takes place at the statue to honour seafarers.

The islands of Sardinia and Capri also offer good diving, with plenty of marine life and several interesting wrecks. Wreck diving is popular in Italy, where even sunken aircraft survive well due to the Mediterranean being an enclosed sea without strong tides. Wrecks suitable for scuba-divers include a number of war and merchant ships dating back a few centuries, as well a number of German and British warplanes. If you want to see larger fish and mammals, you should head for Sicily, which has the advantage of being further out in the Mediterranean.

Beginners need to enrol on a diving course of which there's a wide variety available, including those offered by the major training organisations such as PADI, SSI and CMAS. If you're already a trained diver, a local dive centre will ask to see your certification card, after which you're able to join them on trips to local dive sites and further afield. If you don't have your own diving equipment, it can be hired at local dive centres. The water temperature varies around the coast, but can fall to around 14°C (57°F) in winter, rising to as high of 25 to 27°C (77 to 81°F) in summer. Local divers generally wear semi-dry suits in cooler temperatures, while in summer a wet suit is sufficient (suits can be hired in most areas).

In recent years, independent dive centres have developed all along the coast and on the islands of Elba, Sardinia and the Maddalena archipelago, noted for its crystal-clear waters. These tend to advertise in the local press and on roadside posters, and many also advertise in Italian, English and American diving magazines. Information about scuba-diving and dive centres can also be obtained from the Federazione Italiana Pesca Sportiva e Attività Subacquee, Via Tiziano, 70, 00196 Rome (☎ 06-3685 8290).

Free diving (*apnea*) is a specialist sport involving a number of different disciplines. They have in common the concept of breath-hold diving, i.e. diving on a single breath of air without scuba equipment. It is popular in Italy, due in part to the publicity surrounding the success of Italians such as Umberto Pelizzari in extending the depth limits reached in this sport. Most diving magazines in Italy include articles about *apnea* and have advertisements for courses. Needless to say, it's a sport that requires extensive training and you need to be fully aware of the dangers. Blackouts and convulsions are common, even among the top competitors in the sport, and can result in death unless the right backup is available. If you're interested, speak to the experts at a local diving centre or the Federazione Italiana di Attività Subacque (see above).

WINTER SPORTS

Winter sports really mean skiing or snowboarding in Italy, although most winter sports are catered for in Italian resorts. The country has over 2.5 million keen skiers, who are joined each year by millions of foreign visitors from around the world. Both alpine or downhill (*sci alpino* or *lo sci*) and cross-country skiing (*sci di fondo*) are well catered for in Italy (most resorts provide facilities for both), although downhill skiing is far more popular with the macho Italians. Italy has some of the best ski resorts in Europe and each year hosts the middle stages of the World Ski Cup.

The best-equipped and most famous ski resorts are in the Alps, conveniently situated close to the northern cities of Milan, Turin and Genoa. However, skiing is also possible locally if you live in Rome, Florence or Naples at smaller (and cheaper) resorts in the Apennines (*Appennini*), the Abruzzi (at resorts such as Campo Felice and Roccardo) and even in Sicily, where you can ski on Mount Etna, famous for its active volcano. For snowboard fanatics, the best resort in the area of Rome is Campo Imperatore (L'Aquila). The Italian alpine resorts are arranged in a number of distinct geographical areas, each of which have extensive networks of interlinked resorts. The main areas include the Dolomites (Dolomiti) in the Trentino-Alto Adige and Veneto-Friuli regions, the Milky Way (Via Lattea) in the western Alps, and the Aosta Valley (Valle d'Aosta) and Lombardy in the north.

In the east, the Dolomite Superski area is the largest in the world and takes in many popular resorts, including Campitello Matese, Canazei, Cortina d'Ampezzo and Selva. It offers spectacular scenery and includes over 40 ski resorts, some 450 ski lifts and an incredible 1,200km (circa 750mi) of runs (pistes). All lifts can be accessed with a single pass and the computerised lift system eases the ascent up the mountains, with runs to suit all abilities and a large number of ski schools. An unusual ski tour in the Dolomites is the 77km (48mi) Great War Route (*Giro della Grande Guerra*), which wends its way among the most spectacular peaks of Trentino, Alto Adige and Veneto, and explores some of the major sites where the Italian, German and Austrian forces fought between 1915 and 1918. A map of the route is available at tourist offices in Alleghe, Arraba, Cortina D'Ampezzo, Pescul and San Cassiano, enabling skiers to guide themselves along the route, which never exceeds red (intermediate) grade.

In Lombardy, in the north of Italy, the main resorts include Aprica, Bormio, Lavigno, Madesimo, Ponte di Legno (one of Italy's highest resorts) and San Simeone (good for beginners). Further west are the Milky Way and the Aosta Valley. The Milky Way, close to the French border, is based on the resorts of Clavire, Sauze D'Oulx and Sestriere, and has over 200km (124mi) of slopes and links with French resorts. The Aosta valley is situated in the north-west of Italy, running from the Mont Blanc tunnel towards Turin, where the main resorts include Cervinia, Courmayeur and La Thuile, among the most fashionable and expensive in Italy. Cervinia is linked to the famous Swiss resort of Zermatt, from Courmayeur you can ski the famous 'Vallée Blanche' (which runs down to Chamonix in France), while La Thuile borders the French ski area of La Rosire, which is included in the ski pass.

The ski season generally lasts from December to late March, although at higher altitudes and in good years it can be longer. There's also year-round skiing on glaciers, which include Marmolada in the Dolomites, Monte Bianco (Mont Blanc) and Monte Cervino (the Matterhorn) in the Aosta Valley. The Italian ski slopes are generally on the sunny south side of the Alps and therefore subject to less reliable snowfalls than the northern slopes in other alpine countries, thus reducing the length of the season. This is overcome in many resorts by using snow machines, which help keep runs open when the weather doesn't oblige. Before booking, it's wise to consult a good ski guide or a travel agent regarding the snow record at the time of year you plan to ski (or, better still, delay booking until you can be sure of good snow conditions).

The most southerly skiing in Italy is on Sicily's Mount Etna, which rises to a height of over 2,600m (8,539ft), where the short season generally runs from January to late March. This area has become more popular in recent years, thanks to its breathtaking views and general lack of queues, and it now has nine lifts serving the southern and north-eastern faces of the mountain. The cost of a daily lift pass is a modest €16, which may include the added 'bonus' of volcanic dust from Mount Etna, which regularly blackens the snow but doesn't call a halt to the skiing. If the rumbling gets too much for your liking, Sicily's beaches are just 45 minutes away by car, so it's possible to enjoy skiing and sea swimming on the same day.

Ski packages, known as white weeks (*settimane bianche*), can be purchased from travel agents or you can contact resort or regional tourist offices directly in your areas of interest. Packages include accommodation and may also include equipment hire, lift passes and tuition, if required. This is usually the most economical way to book a skiing trip lasting for more than a few days. However, if tuition or equipment hire aren't included in a particular package, they can easily be arranged on arrival at a resort.

It's important to check the snow conditions, as it's hardly worth skiing when there's little snow or snow conditions are bad, e.g. salt or slush. When snow cover is poor many runs are closed, particularly those down to the valley or bottom station, and you must endure a lot of queuing and walking between lifts. Many resorts have installed snow-making equipment (snow cannons) and are therefore able to guarantee that a limited number are (nearly) always open. However, when snow conditions are bad and most runs are closed, the overcrowding can be horrendous. Information about snow conditions is published in many Italian newspapers and the English-language *International Herald Tribune* (IHT), which includes a weekend ski report on Thursdays. There are also numerous Internet sites containing ski information (e.g. 💻 www. complete-skier.com) and most resorts have their own websites, as do regional tourist associations.

Alpine Skiing

The alpine skiing (*sci alpino*) season in Italy generally runs from December to late April. Alpine skiing is much more expensive than cross-country, as the equipment (skis, boots and clothing) costs more and you also need to budget for the cost of a lift pass. However, it's possible to hire much of the equipment until you decide whether this is the sport for you. It's difficult to estimate the cost of equipment as it depends very much on what you buy, although €250 is a rough minimum per person for skis, bindings, boots, poles and clothes. It's possible to spend much more than this, but you should bear in mind that many a would-be skier has invested a lot of money in new equipment only to find that he doesn't like skiing.

If you're a beginner, it's recommended to hire equipment such as skis and poles (from €30 for six days) and boots (from €13). This still leaves you needing to buy a ski suit, gloves and goggles/sunglasses (at a cost of around €110 or more), as these cannot be hired. If you plan far enough in advance, you can save money by shopping during end of season or pre-season sales, or by buying second-hand equipment (often little used and available via ski clubs). Take precautions against having your ski equipment stolen – when you must leave it unattended, a good tip is to mix your skis and poles with those of your friends.

Ski-lift passes can cost over €30 per day for an adult in a top Italian resort and skiing in some resorts, particularly at weekends (Sundays are the worst), entails a lot of queuing. In many resorts you can buy a limited area ski-lift pass or a half-day pass, e.g. from noon, which is cheaper than buying a day pass for a whole area (you need to be an Olympian or Superman to ski a large area in one day). You can buy a ski-lift pass in most resorts from 1 to 21 days or for the whole season – the longer the period, the cheaper the daily cost. **Be aware, however, that in bad weather conditions, which occur quite often, many runs are closed and there's usually no compensating reduction or refund in the price of ski-lift passes.**

It's wise to leave the top resorts to the experts and frequent some of the smaller, cheaper areas, at least until you're sufficiently skilled and fit enough to take full advantage of the more difficult runs. That isn't to say that the bigger, more expensive resorts don't provide good value. A top resort may offer up to ten times the number of lifts and prepared runs of a small resort, while charging 'only' an extra 25 to 50 per cent for a ski-lift pass.

If you're a newcomer to alpine skiing, it's definitely worth enrolling at a ski school (*scuola sci*) or taking lessons from an expert (*maestro di sci*) for a week or two to learn the basics – and it's much safer than simply launching yourself off the nearest mountain, both for yourself and other skiers. Good skiing is all about style and technique, and the value of coaching cannot be over-emphasised. Private and group lessons are available at all resorts, and English is widely spoken by instructors in Italy. The cost of beginners' ski lessons in a small group starts from around €10 for a two-hour session, with individual lessons starting from around €25 per hour.

You can book a skiing holiday at a travel agency or contact resort tourist offices directly (many are on the Internet) if you're planning to make your own way to a resort and just require accommodation. Accommodation in ski resorts is much more expensive during holiday periods (Christmas, New Year and Easter), when the runs are also very crowded. During public and school holiday periods, the crowds of school children may drive you crazy, both on and off-piste, particularly when queuing for ski-lifts. It goes without saying that these periods are best avoided, if possible. Mondays are usually the best days (congestion-wise) to ski in resorts close to the major cities. All large and many smaller resorts provide baby-sitting services or a ski nursery school, although most schools won't accept children below the age of five.

Preparation

It's certainly wise to do some preparation and take a few precautions before attacking the ski slopes:

- **Ski Exercises** – It's recommended to perform special ski exercises for a few weeks before taking to the runs. This helps to increase your general flexibility and strength, and prepares your body for the unique demands of skiing. It also ensures that you don't ache quite so much after a day on the runs. Most ski books contain recommended exercises. Remember, grossly unfit skiers are a danger to everyone – not least themselves.

- **Insurance** – Check that your group is fully insured for ski accidents, including helicopter rescue. Many annual insurance schemes exclude skiing, unless you pay an additional premium to have it specifically included. Even then, the type of skiing covered may be limited and off-piste skiing may be excluded.

- **Piste Plan** – Always obtain a piste plan on arrival in a resort and check the connecting runs, so as not to get lost or take the wrong runs. In Italy runs are graded as follows: green = beginners, blue = easy, red = intermediate and black = difficult. Incidentally, if you ski over a border, the system is the same in Austria and France, but there are no green graded runs in Switzerland. Unfortunately piste plans aren't always easy to read. There's sometimes a lot of walking between lifts and what appears on the plan to be the top of a lift may turn out to be the bottom. Without a piste plan it's possible to end up by mistake on one of those dreaded 'north face of the Eiger' blackest-of-black runs. A piste plan also lets you know what kind of lift is available for each run. Italian resorts have a mix of button (single tow) lifts, T-bars, chair-lifts and cable cars.

- **Clothing** – Besides proper ski clothes (jacket, trousers and gloves), long johns, thermal underwear, inner gloves, special socks, scarves and woollen hats may be necessary. However, it's wise to adopt a policy of multiple layers rather than heavy underclothes, as on a sunny day you may want to be able to peel off layers. Once you're past the falling-over stage, a small rucksack or a bum-bag can be useful for carrying small items (such as cameras or sun-cream) or additional clothing. A one-piece ski suit is best for beginners, as it keeps out the snow when you fall over. Lightweight clothes and gloves can be worn on warmer days (gloves should always be worn to protect hands from injury). *Après ski* boots with non-slip rubber soles, e.g. moon boots, are essential and inexpensive.

- **Skin & Eye Protection** – Your skin and eyes need protection from the sun and glare when skiing (snow blindness is rare, but not unknown). It's easy to get sunburnt at high altitudes, even in winter. Use a total block-out cream for your lips, nose and eyelids, even when the sun doesn't appear particularly bright. When skiing in bright sunlight, special ski sunglasses with side protection or mirror lenses are best. Buy the best you can afford. A loop connected to the sunglasses and hung around your neck helps prevent their loss in a fall and is also handy to hang them from when you aren't wearing them. However, don't wear dark sunglasses or goggles that inhibit your vision in poor visibility, e.g. when it's snowing, as it makes it difficult to see the bumps and dips. **You can have a dangerous fall if you hit an unseen bump (or a fellow skier) at high speed.**

Safety

Safety is of paramount importance in any sport, but it's particularly important when skiing, where the possibility of an accident is ever present (one in every ten skiers suffers some sort of injury). In recent years, skiing-related deaths and serious injuries have increased considerably as slopes have become more crowded and skiers have looked further afield for more daring and dangerous thrills. Around 200 skiers die annually in Europe and a further 100,000 are injured. **Accident insurance is essential when skiing anywhere.**

Equipment

While it's unnecessary to wear the latest ski fashions, it's important to have suitable, secure and safe equipment, particularly bindings and boots. Although the latest high-tech bindings are a great help in avoiding injuries, the correct settings are vital. They should be set so that in the event of a fall, you part company with your skis before your leg (or part thereof) parts company with your body. Beginners' bindings must be set so that they release fairly easily, but not so easily that they open each time a turn is attempted. If you own your own equipment, you should have your skis and bindings serviced each season by a qualified ski mechanic (any ski shop can do this). If you're using rented or second-hand skis, double check that the bindings are set correctly and release freely in all directions. If you aren't entirely happy with rented equipment, never hesitate to request adjustments or an exchange. Remember to have details of your height in metres and your weight in kilogrammes when you hire your skis, as you're asked for this information so that the bindings can be set correctly. Young children should wear safety helmets at all times as soon as they're able to use normal runs and lifts.

Ability & Injuries

Try to ski with people of the same standard or with an experienced skier who's willing to ski at your pace, and don't be in too much of a hurry to tackle those black runs. It isn't obligatory to ski from sunrise to sunset, although some fanatics may try to convince you otherwise. Stop skiing and rest when you feel yourself flagging. A sure sign is when you keep falling over for no apparent reason (unless you've had a large liquid lunch!). Most ski accidents happen when skiers are tired. If you injure yourself, particularly a knee, it's important to stop skiing and seek medical advice as soon as possible. If you attempt to ski with an injury or before an injury has had time to heal, you risk aggravating it and doing permanent damage. It's better to ride down in the cable-car than on a stretcher!

Weather

Unless you're an expert skier, it's best to avoid skiing in bad weather and in poor snow conditions. When snow cover is poor or runs are icy, the danger of injury increases dramatically – particularly for beginners and intermediates, who often find it difficult or impossible to control their skis.

Avalanche Warnings

NEVER ignore avalanche warnings (*avviso di valanghe*) or attempt to ski on a closed (*chiusa*) run or anywhere there's a danger of avalanches (information is available at ski lift stations). Avalanches on open runs are extremely rare as the overloaded slopes overlooking runs are blasted with explosives to remove excess snow. Don't ski off-piste (*fuoripista*) unless you're an experienced skier and always hire an experienced local guide in an unfamiliar area. Each year over 150 skiers are killed in avalanches in the Alps, usually when skiing off-piste. You can buy a small radio transmitter that helps rescuers locate you if you're buried in an avalanche (some also have a flashing light system). They're expensive but many off-piste skiers consider their lives are worth the cost and most guides insist upon them. You can also wear an ABS air balloon rucksack, which inflates like a car air-bag to protect you in the event of an avalanche (although experts are undecided on their effectiveness). **Never ski off-piste on your own.**

Restricted Areas

Only ski where it's permitted. In some areas, off-piste skiing is forbidden (*vietata*) to protect plants and wildlife. Many animals hibernate in winter and others need to preserve their precious reserves of fat. You won't help their chances of survival by disturbing and frightening them. Trees are planted in many areas to help prevent avalanches and are easily destroyed by careless skiers. Some areas are designated as nature conservation areas and you can be fined for skiing there.

Cross-Country Skiing

Although cross-country skiing (*sci di fondo*) doesn't have the glamorous jet-set image of alpine skiing, it's popular with Italians. It appeals to both young and old, particularly those whose idea of fun is a million miles away from hurtling down a hill at 100kph (62mph) with a thousand metre drop on one side and a glacier on the other. Cross-country skiing can be enjoyed at any pace and over any distance, and therefore has great attraction both for those who aren't very fit or keen athletes. It can be exhilarating, particularly if you make the effort to learn the correct technique and persevere beyond the beginners' stage. It's also rates highly as a total body workout and is claimed by many to be one of the best forms of exercise.

Compared with alpine skiing, cross-country skiing has the advantages of cheaper equipment, lower costs, fewer broken bones and no queues. No expensive ski-lift passes are necessary and essential equipment costs as little as €120 for skis, bindings, poles, boots and gloves. No special clothing is necessary apart from gloves and boots, provided you have a warm pullover and tracksuit. You can, of course, buy more expensive equipment and special clothing.

Prepared cross-country trails, usually consisting of two sets of tracks (*piste per sci di fondo*), are laid on specially prepared and signposted routes, where you ski in the direction of the arrows. There are cross-country ski trails in many ski resorts in Italy, some of which are floodlit for night skiing. You can enjoy cross-country skiing anywhere there's sufficient snow, although using prepared trails is easier than making your own (as is common in Scandinavia).

Heli-Skiing

Many Italian ski resorts offer heli-skiing, which is a version of off-piste skiing that involves being taken to your starting point by helicopter. Most skiing is off-piste and therefore you need to be an expert skier and many heli-ski operators won't take groups without a guide. Italy is the only alpine country that lacks nation-wide legislation governing heli-skiing, although regulations vary from region to region. For example, in the Trentino-Alto Aldige region, heli-skiing is possible only within strict guidelines, while in the Valle d'Aosta the rules are more flexible. The absence of legislation may change in future in response to calls from environmentalists for restrictions on heli-skiing above a height of 1,500m (4,921ft) in the Alps and above 1,000m (3,280ft) in the Apennines. Contact a tourist office in the region where you plan to ski for the latest information. Costs vary according to the length of the flight to your drop off, the number in your party and whether or not you take a guide. However, you should expect to pay at least €110 per person for small groups of four or five people. For groups of ten or more, costs can fall to as little as €50 per person.

Off-Piste Skiing

Off-piste (*fuoripista*) skiing is possible in many areas and is the stuff of dreams for many skiers. Virgin powder snow and the lack of crowds are the main attractions, as well as the sheer challenge of skiing away from marked trails. To participate you must be an advanced skier able to handle black runs with confidence and must take careful note of any warnings, particularly those concerning avalanches. Many avalanches are caused by off-piste skiers each year and off-piste skiing is banned in some areas for environmental or safety reasons. It's wise to take a guide with you when skiing in an unfamiliar area (see also **Avalanche Warnings** on page 371).

Snow Surfing Or Snowboarding

Increasingly popular throughout Italy, snow-boarding has a cool image and is a popular alternative for many, predominantly younger, thrill-seekers. With your feet attached across a single board you surf down the mountain in soft boots and without poles. Snowboarders often share runs with skiers, although in some resorts there are separate runs. Despite being accepted as an Olympic sport, snowboarding still merits little attention from the world's press, although these days it's finding it easier to attract sponsors keen to associate themselves with the sport's image of freedom and individuality. Equipment hire is available at most resorts for a daily cost of around €10 for a board and €4 for boots, while lessons cost around €13 for two hours. Information about facilities can be obtained from resort and regional tourist offices or a guide book such as the *Good Skiing and Snowboarding Guide* (published in the UK by Which?).

Ice Skating

Ice skating (*pattinaggio sul ghiaccio*) is possible in many ski resorts during the winter season and also year round in major cities. In resorts, rinks are often outdoors and therefore subject to the vagaries of the weather. Instruction for beginners is usually available, which can significantly reduce the amount of time spent hanging on to the edge of the rink or a companion, before you gain the confidence to glide off across the ice. Elsewhere, opportunities for ice-skating are surprisingly limited, although most major cities have at least one indoor ice rink.

For further information about winter sports, contact the Italian Winter Sports Federation, Federazione Italiana Sport Invernali, Via Paranesi, 44/b, 20137 Milan (☎ 02-75731). Information about snow and road conditions is available on the Internet at the Snowlinker on the Fileita website (🖳 www.fileita.it). Snow conditions are also available by telephone (☎ 144-661 902). The XX Olympic Winter Games will be held in Turin in 2006 (🖳 www.torino2006.org).

OTHER SPORTS

The following is a selection of other popular sports in Italy:

Athletics: Most towns and villages have athletics (*atletico*) clubs and organise local competitions and sports days.

Basketball: Basketball (*pallacanestro* or simply *basket*) is a surprisingly popular sport. It was introduced by the Americans after the second world war and Italy is now ranked second in the world to the US in the sport. The professional basketball season runs from September to May, and there are amateur clubs in many towns that provide courses for beginners. For information, contact the Federazione Italiana Pallacanestro, Via Vitorchiano, 113, 00189 Rome (☎ 06-3685 6514, 🖳 www.fip.it).

Bowls: Bowls (*bocce*) is widely played throughout the country and is the Italian equivalent of lawn bowls. There are *bocce* pitches (*bocciodromo*) in most towns and villages where frequent competitions are held; indeed for some, predominantly older men, it seems to comprise almost a full-time occupation.

Boxing: Boxing is popular throughout the country, particularly as a spectator 'sport'. Boxing clubs and gymnasiums for budding professionals are common in the main cities.

Gymnasiums Or Health Clubs: Most towns have at least one gymnasium (*palestra*) offering a wide variety of classes, including aerobics, step, yoga, stretching, dance, martial arts and power sculpting. Costs vary tremendously according to the facilities provided and the amount of competition in the area. Many first class hotels also have fitness rooms.

Gymnastics: Another popular sport, where classes are held for all ages at gymnasiums and sports centres.

Horse Riding: Horse riding (*equitazione*) is popular but expensive. There are many riding schools and clubs in rural areas, and you can also hire horses from some farms. Many riding holidays are available, either from specialist holiday operators or as part of the 'agri-tourism' (*agriturismo*) scheme, where accommodation and riding facilities are provided on working farms. Information can be obtained from the Federazione Italiana di Sport Equestri, Viale Tiziano, 74, 00196 Rome (☎ 06-3685 8350).

Jogging & Running: Both of these are quite popular, although you wouldn't think so from the relatively few joggers seen on the streets. There's an extensive annual programme of competitive races throughout the country, ranging from a few kilometres up to full marathons.

Martial Arts: For those brought up on a diet of Bruce Lee, unarmed combat such as Aikido, Judo, Karate, Kung Fu, Kushido, Taekwon-Do and T'ai Chi Ch'uan, are taught and practised in many sports centres and private clubs around the country.

Roller Skating & Skate-Boarding: Rinks are provided in large towns and winter ice-skating rinks may also be used for roller skating (*pattinaggio a rotelle*) in the summer. Much practising is done on the pavements, which can add a touch of excitement (and danger) to a daily stroll (*passeggiata*).

Ten-Pin Bowling: This sport is growing in popularity and there are ten-pin bowling centres in most major towns and cities, however, it's a relatively expensive sport in Italy.

Volleyball: A popular, fun sport for all the family, played both indoors and outdoors (e.g. beach volleyball).

Water Polo: Water polo (*pallanuoto*) is popular both as an amateur and professional sport (the season runs from March to July). Amateur club games take place at local swimming pools.

Miscellaneous Sports: Many foreign sports and pastimes have a group of expatriate fanatics in Italy, including American football, baseball, *boules*, cricket, Gaelic sports (hurling, Gaelic football), hockey (ice and grass), handball, lacrosse, *pelota* and softball. For information enquire at libraries, tourist and information offices, expatriate social clubs, and embassies and consulates.

17.

SHOPPING

Italy is one of the world's great shopping countries and Italian shops are designed to seduce you with their artful displays of beautiful and exotic merchandise. Shopping is both an art form and a pleasure in Italy, particularly food shopping, most Italians preferring to shop in traditional small family stores (*botteghe*) rather than faceless supermarkets. The major cities, where even the smallest shop windows are a delight, are a shopper's paradise. It's difficult to say which is Italy's finest shopping city; some say Milan or Rome, with their streets packed with designer boutiques, while others plump for Florence or Venice with their more traditional shops – all have their unique attractions.

Italian design has long been internationally acclaimed for its practicality, simplicity and elegance, and Italian products are also synonymous with craftsmanship, quality and style (not to mention expense!). Nowadays luxury designer (*firmato*) products are part and parcel of Italian everyday life, whether they take the form of a gleaming red Ferrari or Lamborghini, a classic Armani suit, a Louis Vuitton suitcase, Gucci shoes or Rayban sunglasses. Legions of foreign shoppers flock to Italy each year to buy top quality Italian labels, particularly those at the forefront of *haute couture* such as Armani, Ferretti, Gucci, Ungaro, Valentino and Versace. Consumerism rates more highly among Italians than in most other European countries and Italians are dedicated shoppers, all aspiring to own luxury goods, particularly designer clothes.

As well as the factory produced designs, Italy is also famous for its handicrafts and hand-made goods, and each region has its specialities. Among the best buys are clothing, shoes, luggage, contemporary art, prints, engravings, leather goods, jewellery (particularly gold), perfumes, ceramics, pottery, mosaics, marble, basketwork, straw goods, brass, fabrics, linens, glassware, porcelain, china, furniture, soft furnishings, inlaid wood, carvings, antiques, lace, embroidery and paper goods. Italy is also famous for its food (ham, cheese, pasta, olive oil, etc.) and drink (wine, spirits and liqueurs).

Shop staff in Italy vary from cordial and helpful to rude and dismissive, and queuing isn't a practice that's very well understood. Getting served is usually a free for all and you must speak up when it's your turn, or you'll be trampled by 'sweet' little old ladies!

You should try to avoid offering a shopkeeper a €50 or €100 note when you're buying something costing a couple of euros and should also avoid using a credit card to pay for items costing less than around €15 (you may not be permitted to do so anyway). In Rome and other major cities and resorts, where there are many tourists, you must be wary of pickpockets and bag-snatchers. **Never** tempt fate with an exposed wallet or purse or by flashing money around.

There are a number of books for dedicated shoppers in Italy, including Frommer's *Born to Shop Italy* by Suzy Gersham and George McDonald (Macmillan), *Made in Italy* by Annie Brody and Patricia Schultz (Workman), *Bargain Hunting in Italy*, *Designer Bargains in Italy* and *Lo Scoprioccasioni* (the bargain hunter's bible in Italian, but easy enough to understand) – the last three written by Theodora van Meurs. Catalogue shopping is available via Skymail (☎ 02-5530 3366), which also offers magazine subscriptions.

Sales

Sales (*saldi*) are an important event in the Italian shopping calendar and, although there aren't massive queues of shoppers outside department stores from the early hours of the morning, sales are nonetheless popular with bargain hunters. There are three kinds of sale in Italy, all of which are strictly regulated by local and national laws. The main sales are held twice a year: between 7th January and 7th March and between 10th July and 10th September. Shops don't need to hold their sales for the whole of these periods, but sales must start and end within these periods. Only seasonal products (including fashion) can be sold at a discount, and sale prices must be displayed in shop windows.

Promotional sales (*vendite promozionali*) can be held at any time of the year, although clothes, shoes and accessory outlets cannot hold promotional sales during the 40 days immediately preceding the main winter and summer sales. The discount and original prices must be displayed on all goods. When a business is closing down or moving to a new address, a closing down sale is permitted (*liquidazioni*) for a maximum of six weeks, although this may be extended in certain cases.

As with all purchases, you should choose your goods carefully before buying in a sale and be aware of your rights. Bear in mind that you may find it difficult to pay with a credit card during sales periods, as many shops refuse to accept them, although this is an illegal practice.

SHOPPING HOURS

Italians don't generally 'convenience shop' at all times of the day and night, and retail hours reflect this, although the only law limiting opening hours is one passed in 1998 that forbids retailers from opening for more than 13 hours daily between 7am and 10pm and on more than eight Sundays annually (even this restriction is relaxed in resort and tourist areas). Shopping hours vary according to the region, city or town and the type of shop. However, in general, shops open Mondays to Saturdays from around 8.30 or 9am to 12.30 or 1pm and from 3.30 or 4pm to 7.30 or 8pm, although in some cities (particularly in the south) and during summer months, shops may not open until 5pm and may remain open until 9pm and afternoon shopping is virtually non-existent in small towns.

This long lunchtime break (*pausa* or *siesta*) may come as a surprise to many foreigners. The *pausa* makes good sense in the summer, when it's often too hot to do anything at midday and it allows time for lunch, traditionally the most important meal of the day for Italians. However, in winter you find yourself shopping in the dark, a practice that may seem odd to some foreigners. In the major cities there's a growing tendency for shops to stay open all day and larger shops and department stores open from 9am to 7pm continuously (*orario continuato/non-stop*).

Most shops close on Wednesday or Thursday afternoons depending on the region, and department stores and supermarkets usually also close on Monday mornings, although this is becoming less common in the larger cities. Most shops close on Sundays throughout the country, although this tendency is changing and many supermarkets in tourist and coastal areas now open on Sunday mornings. However, even in popular tourist areas, many small shops close for holidays for a few weeks in summer; August is the most popular month, especially around 15th (*Ferragosto*).

FOOD

Most Italian cuisine is based on fresh local produce, and shopping for food is a daily ritual carried out with great diligence (not to mention pleasure) by Italian women (mainly). The range and quality of fresh food is far greater than in many other countries, as is the number of specialist outlets from which you can buy food. Italian women are demanding and choosy when buying produce, which tends to be seasonal and not available all year round. Traditionally, food shopping has been done in small specialist food shops and at food markets, rather than at large supermarkets. However, as the number of Italian women working outside the home increases, more are shopping in supermarkets.

A general store or grocer's (*alimentari*) sells basic foods, fresh bread, dairy products, ham and other cured meats, wine, and usually fresh fruit and vegetables. A *drogheria* sells dry goods, foodstuffs and household cleaners. An *erboristeria* sells health foods, organically grown produce and wholemeal food, which may also be sold in *drogherie* and chemists'. For a list of health food shops, look in the yellow pages under *Alimentari Dietetici* or *Macrobiotici e Biologici*. A *gelateria* sells the world-famous Italian ice cream – for the best home-made ice cream look for the sign *produzione propria*. A *latteria* sells milk (fresh, long-life and sterilised) and milk products such as cheese, yoghurt and butter. It may also sell other basic food products. A *rosticceria* is a good place to buy ready cooked food such as roast chickens and meat, and ready prepared dishes such as lasagne and pizzas. Other specialist food shops are described below.

The cost of living in Italy is one of the highest in Europe and the prices of some foods may come as a shock to foreigners, particularly items such as Parma ham and certain Italian cheeses, which are more expensive in Italy than abroad! Generally, meat and fish are expensive, but fruit, vegetables, dairy foods, olive oil and wine are cheaper than in many other countries. If you wish to save money on your weekly food bill, where you shop is as important as what you buy. Generally, it's better to shop at markets and small shops patronised by Italians, although this is more time consuming than shopping at supermarkets. Obviously it helps if you speak some Italian, but it's easy enough to point to what you want and say *un chilo* (a kilo) or *mezzo chilo* (half kilo). Village shops can be expensive and it may be cheaper to travel to the nearest town to buy food.

Italians don't care much for foreign food and are conservative in their taste, preferring simple, fresh (i.e. Italian) ingredients. You won't, therefore, find a huge selection of foreign food in most shops, although larger supermarkets may have a small section and in the major cities there are specialist foreign food shops. If you insist on buying imported produce, your food bill will rocket.

Shopping in Italy often involves an Italian idiosyncrasy: you must order what you want from the assistant behind the counter, pay the bill for your purchases at a separate cash register (*cassa*), and then return to the counter with your receipt (*scontrino*) and collect your shopping (the system was invented by bureaucrats!). This takes some getting used to and involves a lot of queuing, although the time can be profitably spent conversing with your fellow-shoppers and improving your Italian!

Each time you make a purchase, ensure that you receive a fiscal receipt (*scontrino fiscale*) – it's illegal for most shopkeepers (newsagents, tobacconists and petrol stations are excluded) not to give you one and for you not to have one. The tax police (*Guardia di Finanza*) can fine you for leaving a shop without a receipt, even for small items such as a can of drink. This draconian law was due to be abolished in 2002, but was still in force in spring 2003.

An interesting book (in Italian) for budding gourmets is *Itinerari del Prodotto Tipico Italiano,* published by Agriturist, C Vittorio Emanuele, 101, 00186 Rome (☎ 06-6852 342, 💻 www.agriturist.it), which explains the various categories of wine, cheese, olive oil, meat, and fruit and vegetables grown and produced in Italy. It also contains itineraries throughout the country where you can sample local produce, which must be one of the most pleasurable ways to discover Italian cuisine. Other interesting books include *Italy for the Gourmet Traveler* by Fred Ponklin (Little Brown) and *Celebrating Italy* by Carol Field (Harper Perennial). There are many websites devoted to Italian cuisine, including 💻 http://italianfood.about.com, 💻 www.cucina-italiana.com 💻 www.gambero rosso.it and 💻 www.mangiarebene.com.

Meat

There are several kinds of meat shop in Italy: a *macelleria* sells most kinds of meat, including beef (*manzo*), veal (*vitello*), pork (*carne di maiale*) and chicken (*pollo*) as well as eggs (*uove*); a *salumeria* sells cured, smoked and roast meats and sometimes fresh pork; a *polleria* sells chicken (*pollo*), rabbit (*coniglio*) and game (*selvaggina*); and a *macelleria equina* sells horse meat (*carne di cavallo*).

Veal is generally regarded as the best meat in Italy and specialities are prepared in numerous different ways throughout the country, the most famous of which is *ossobuco* – stewed slices of veal shin bone with the marrow left in the bone. Pork, which is generally considered a winter food and isn't widely available in summer, and pork products from the north are the best, while roast suckling pig (*porchetta* or *porcheddu*) is a speciality in many regions, including Sardinia and Umbria. Thin slices of rare beef (*carpaccio*) served as a starter with oil or shavings of parmesan cheese is a popular dish, while lamb (*agnello* or *abbacchio*) is popular in the south (less so in the north), although you may find the cuts smaller than you're used to. Easter is the main season for lamb and a particular speciality is Sardinian milk-fed lamb. Italians, like most Latins, eat a variety of small song birds, including skylarks (*allodole*) and thrushes (*tordi*).

Cooked Meat: Cured ham (*prosciutto*) is the main type of ham consumed in Italy and famous throughout the world for its subtle, delicate taste. Ham is cured in many parts of Italy, although the best comes from Parma. Italians eat it on its own or as a starter with melon. Cooked and smoked ham are also popular. Other cooked meats include an infinite variety of sausages (*salsiccia*) and salami, which vary from region to region. Cold meats are sold in a variety of stores, including *salumerie, rosticcerie* and *alimentari* (general grocery stores).

Fish

Fish (*pesce*) and other seafood (*frutti di mare*) are popular in Italy, particularly in Sicily and the south and anywhere near the coast, and most towns have at least one fish shop (*pescheria*). Common seafood includes anchovies (*acciughe*), served fresh and usually fried (not salted and from a tin except when on pizzas), clams (*vongole*), a favourite in Naples, where they form part of the famous spaghetti sauce, cod (*merluzzo*), crab (*granchio*), lobster (*aragosta*), usually prohibitively expensive, mackerel (*sgombro*), mussels (*cozze*), octopus (*polpo*), oysters (*ostriche*), prawns (*gamberi*), usually served grilled, particularly in Rome, sardines (*sarde*), served with pasta and a popular dish in Palermo, sole (*sogliola*), squid (*calamari*), and swordfish (*pesce spada*) and tuna (*tonno*), both usually served as thick steaks and grilled. Tinned fish is also popular and a huge variety is available.

Bread & Cakes

Bread (*pane*) is sold in a *panifici* or *panetterie* and is usually baked on the premises each morning. General stores and most supermarkets also have a bread counter. Bread is usually white and similar to a French stick, although wholemeal (*integrale*) bread is also available and there are many regional variations. Bread rolls (*panini*) and croissants (*cornetti*) can be bought from a *panetteria*, as can other baked goods, both sweet and savoury. For cakes, pastries and home-made sweets, you must go to a *pasticceria*.

Fruit & Vegetables

Much of the Italian diet is based on fresh fruit (*frutta*) and vegetables (*verdura*), of which there's a huge variety, although most produce is seasonal and isn't usually available all year round. Apart from produce that isn't grown in Italy, imported fruit and vegetables are found only in a few delicatessens and specialist food shops. Fruit and vegetables can be purchased from greengrocers (*verduraio, fruttivendolo* or *ortolano*), where you can choose what you want, or from a supermarket, where you may have to buy pre-packed, family-sized portions of second grade (*seconda scelta*) produce and the selection may be more limited, although prices generally lower. Markets usually offer better quality **and** value (see page 384).

Olive Oil

As in all Mediterranean countries, olive oil (*olio d'oliva*) forms an important part of the Italian diet and is the base for most savoury dishes, although in Lombardy butter is used in preference for cooking. Although Italy isn't the world's largest producer of olive oil, it's the world's biggest exporter, the US being its main customer. There are several grades of olive oil, including the finest quality extra virgin (*extra vergine*), which is a golden-green colour, virgin and plain olive oil. The cheapest olive oils are blends of lower grade oils (called *olio lampante*) that are best avoided. The best oils are cold-pressed (*spremitura a freddo*), low in acidity and expensive.

Fine olive oil is produced throughout the country: Tuscany's oil is widely recognised as among the world's best and is used by many top chefs. Some areas have been awarded a *denominazione d'origine controllata* (*DOC*) quality classification, and a few have the higher *denominazione d'origine controllata e garantita* (*DOCG*), e.g. Montalcino. Olive oil can be purchased direct from the producers, where you can often taste it before you buy. It has varying acidity: low acidity, e.g. 0.4° or 0.5°, is good for salads and odourless in cooking, while acidity of 1° usually means a fuller flavour.

Cheese

A cheese shop (*negozio del formaggio*) sells countless varieties of cheese (*formaggio*) from throughout Italy, Lombardy being one of the largest cheese-making areas. Perhaps the most famous and certainly the most distinctive Italian cheese is parmesan (*parmigiano*), which is used eaten grated with most kinds of pasta. Parmesan is made throughout the provinces of Modena, Parma and Reggio Emilia and in parts of Bologna and Montova (all in Emilio Romagna). The best quality (and most expensive) parmesan comes from Parma and Reggio Emilia and has *Parmigiano Reggiano* stamped on the rind; less expensive parmesans are called *grana padano*. The older parmesan cheese is, the more expensive it becomes, the most expensive being called *stravecchione* (very old).

Other cheeses include *gorgonzola*, a piquant, blue-veined cheese that originates from the town of Gorgonzola near Milan and is generally an after-dinner cheese, *mascarpone*, a rich soft cheese used in sweet dishes, *mozzarella*, a rubbery and delicately flavoured (tasteless?) cheese which is usually used as a topping for pizzas or as a stuffing for vegetables, and *ricotta*, a soft white cheese used in salads and many other dishes and to fill pasta such as *tortellini* (salted ricotta/*ricotta salata* is popular in the south). Regional specialities include *burrata*, a buttery cheese from the south, the mild *caciotta*, *fontina* from Piedmont, used in fondues (*fonduta*), and *pecorino*, a hard, strong cheese made with sheep's milk.

Pasta

Pasta is a staple of the national diet and forms part of most Italian meals, although in the north cornmeal (*polenta*) or rice (*riso*) is often substituted for pasta; a *risotto* is a dish made with rice. Pasta tends to be served before the main course rather than as part of the main course itself, in one of four ways: on its own or 'dry' (*pasta asciutta*) with a sauce, in soups (*pasta in brodo*), baked (*pasta al forno*), and 'filled' (*pasta ripiena*). There's an almost infinite variety of shapes and sizes of pasta, each with its own name, which may vary from one region to another. Common types of pasta include the universally known *lasagne*, *spaghetti*, *tagliatelle* and *fettucine* as well as tube pastas such as *fusilli* (corkscrew shaped), *farfalle* (bow shaped) and *maccheroni*. Pastas for soup are usually small, e.g. *conchigliette* (shell shaped) or *vermicelli* (literally 'little worms'). Filled pastas include *cannelloni* (cylindrical in shape), *tortellini* (small and circular) and *ravioli*.

Packet or dried pasta is made of good quality durum wheat and water, whereas fresh egg pasta (*pasta all'uovo*) is made with eggs and flour. Egg pasta is usually served with richer, creamier sauces than those accompanying dry pasta. For Italians, cooking pasta is an art: it must be cooked for exactly the right amount of time so that it's firm with a slightly chewy consistency (*al dente*). Different regions have their own specialities and throughout the country the same types of pasta may be served with different sauces. Generally speaking, in the north the sauces are richer, often creamy and are served with red meat such as the world famous *ragù bolognese* from Bologna, while in the south more vegetables and seafood are included.

MARKETS

Markets (*mercati*) are a common sight throughout Italy and are an essential part of daily life. They're colourful, entertaining and worth a visit even if you don't plan to buy anything. Some towns have markets on one or two days per week only (usually on the same days each week), while larger towns and cities may have a daily produce market from Mondays to Saturdays. There are also Sunday markets, particularly antique and flea markets in some places. In major cities, such as Milan and Rome, there are markets specialising in 'exotic' produce and goods, such as African, Chinese and Jewish produce.

There are three kinds of market in Italy: indoor markets, permanent street markets (*mercati comunali coperti*) and travelling open-air street markets that move from town to town on different days of the week. The most popular wares in open-air and street markets are clothing, leather goods, bric-a-brac and household products. Prices are generally lower than in shops, although much depends on your bargaining skills. You should beware of bargain-priced branded goods, such as watches, perfume, clothes and leather goods, as they're usually fakes. There's often a large central market (*mercato centrale*) in cities and most towns have indoor or covered markets. Markets usually operate from early in the morning to around 1pm on weekdays and all day on Saturdays.

A variety of goods is sold in markets, including food, plants, clothes (markets are a good source of inexpensive clothes), footwear, crockery, hardware, cookware, fabrics, ceramics, cassettes and CDs, carpets, jewellery, watches and leather goods. Specialist markets in Rome and other main cities sell antiques (*mercati dell'antiquariato*), books, clothes, stamps, flowers and animals (for pets). Famous markets include the flower market at San Remo, which caters for wholesalers throughout Europe.

Food markets are extremely popular in Italy and are usually divided into sections for fresh fruit and vegetables, meat, fish, cheese and cooked meats, olives and olive oil. Produce is always fresh and generally cheaper than in supermarkets, particularly if you buy what's in season and locally produced. You should arrive early in the morning for the best produce, although the best prices may be had at the end of the morning, when stall-holders are packing up and remaining food is sold cheaply.

Produce is usually marked with its price per kilogram and you should order by the kilo (*chilo*), half kilo (*mezzo chilo*) or in multiples of 100g (*ettogrammo*), although some produce is sold by the piece (*parte*). Some haggling over food prices may take place, although usually the marked price prevails. The law in Italy requires market vendors to give you a printed receipt for your purchases and you should ask for one if it isn't forthcoming.

You may be allowed to handle food products, although some vendors may object to this, particularly if the produce is delicate, but you can ask to try a piece before you buy. When buying fruit and vegetables in markets, check that the quality of the produce you're given is the same as that displayed, which isn't always the case. A queue at a particular stall is usually a sign of good quality and value. Local people also sell home-grown produce on the fringes of markets and also by the roadside in rural areas.

Antique markets (*mercati dell'antiquariato*) and flea markets (*mercato delle pulci*) are common throughout Italy, although you shouldn't expect to find many (or indeed, any) bargains in the major cities, where the best items are usually snapped up by dealers. However, in small towns you can turn up some real bargains. You should never assume that because something is sold in a market it's automatically a bargain, particularly when buying antiques (*antiquariato*), which may not be authentic. You should also beware of buying stolen antiques, the theft of which is widespread. The most famous antiques markets include those held in the Piazza Grande in Arezzo on the first weekend of the month, the Piazza Bellini in Naples and the Ponte di Mezzo in Pisa, the last two being held on the second weekend of the month. Others include Bergamo (third Sunday of the month), Lucca (third weekend of the month), Milan (last Sunday of the month), Modena (last weekend of the month), Ravenna (third weekend of the month) and Turin (second Sunday of the month). Rome has a permanent antiques market with around 20 stalls at the Piazza Fontanella Borghese. Italy's best flea markets are found on Rome's Porta Portese (in the Trastevere quarter) on Sundays (with 4,000 stall-holders, it's the largest in Europe) and in Florence at the Mercato delle Pulci on the last Sunday of the month. To find out more about antiques markets in your local area, pick up a copy of *Gazzetta dell'Antiquario* (which lists all markets), or enquire at local tourist offices and town halls.

ALCOHOL

Drinking forms an essential part of *la dolce vita* and no meal is complete without accompanying wine (*vino*) and a concluding liqueur (*digestivi*). Italy produces a wide variety of alcoholic beverages, including many excellent wines, some good beers, and a huge variety of spirits and liqueurs. Imported spirits and beers are generally available, although considerably more expensive than native drinks.

Italy is among the few European countries to have seen an overall reduction in the nation's alcohol consumption during the 1990s. While beer has become an increasing favourite, particularly among young people, Italy remains a predominantly wine-drinking nation, with spirits reserved for special occasions.

Health Warning: Considering the ready availability of alcohol and the frequency with which it's drunk, it may come as a surprise to foreigners that Italians don't have a huge problem with alcoholism or drunkenness, which is more than can be said for many tourists and foreign residents. In fact, Italians drink far less alcohol than many other Europeans and drunkenness, especially in women, is much frowned upon in Italian society. Children are introduced to alcohol at an early age and it's common to see them tasting a small amount at social gatherings. However, when Italians go out socially, they rarely overindulge and often order soft drinks rather than alcohol. In contrast, expatriates who like the odd drink (or two) should carefully control their alcohol intake, as alcoholism is prevalent among foreign residents.

Wine

Italy is the world's largest wine-producing country and consumption per head is second only to France. Italians are justifiably proud of their wine and find it difficult to believe any other is better (not that many Italians have ever tasted foreign wine or even wines from outside their local region – like most major wine-producing countries, Italy is extremely parochial). Over 1.6 million hectares (around 4 million acres) of farmland are dedicated to vineyards – more than for food production. Italian wines vary from dry (*secco*) to sweet (*dolce*) and include whites (*bianco*) and reds (*rosso*). The country produces relatively few rosés (*rosato*) or sparkling wines, although two of the latter are among its most famous wines.

Classification: In 1965, laws introduced to regulate Italian wine production prescribed three official classifications, which must be displayed on labels. *Vino da tavola* means simply 'table wine', which although not known for its quality can be surprisingly good, particularly the Sicilian Corvo reds and whites. *DOC* (*denominazione di origine controllata*) means that a wine has been produced according to certain rules and specifications, although it's no guarantee of quality. *DOCG* (*denominazione di origine controllata e garantita*) means a wine has met the same specifications as for a *DOC* but has also been tested by government inspectors. There are only some 50 *DOCG* wines in Italy.

Production Areas: Virtually no part of Italy (including the islands) is without its wine producers, which range from among the largest and most sophisticated in the world to small farm plots producing no more than a few hundred bottles per year. The following is a summary of the types of wine produced in each main wine-producing region (see **Appendix E**):

- Puglia (Apulia) in the south-west produces more wine than any other Italian region, *Castel del Monte* (made in white, rosé and red versions) being the best known.

- Campania has been producing its wines from the volcanic soil of Mount Vesuvius for over 2,000 years, although the wines from this region aren't of particular note nowadays; the most famous include *Lacrima Christi* (literally 'Christ's tear'), a red wine favoured (particularly in Naples) to accompany seafood, *Falerno* and *Gragano*, a dark red.

- Emilia-Romagna produces the world-famous *Lambrusco*, a sparkling usually red wine which can be of poor quality unless it comes from one of the four *DOC* zones. Other wines of note from the region include red *Sangiovese* and *Albana*, a sweet white.

- Lazio is one of the major wine-producing areas in Italy and produces seven types of wine, including *Cecubo*, *Colli Albani* and *Frascati*, which are mostly white and dry, and best drunk young. *Frascati*, the region's most famous wine, is also made in a dessert variety.

- The Marche region on the east coast produces *Verdicchio dei Castelli di Jesi*, characterised by its unique amphora-shaped bottle, a delicate white regarded by some as one of the best wines to accompany fish.

- The Montefalco area in Umbria produces some excellent *DOC* reds.

- Piedmont is said to produce the best wines in Italy, including the classy, traditional red *Barolo* and *Barbaresco*, both of which need ageing and rank among the most expensive in Italy. World-famous sparkling *Asti* is also produced here, as is vermouth.

- Sardinia produces white *Vernaccia*, which is similar to sherry and comes in two versions: dry, served as an aperitif, and sweet, which is a dessert wine.

- Sicily, known as the 'paradise of the grape', produces many different red and white wines from the volcanic soil of Etna. Marsala, a fortified dessert wine, is the most famous of Sicilian wines and is often used in cooking. Other Sicilian wines of note include the red and white *Corvo*, which, although not *DOC* wines, can be quite expensive.

- The Trentino-Alto Adige region produces more *DOC* wines than anywhere in Italy and its 20 varieties, which are influenced by nearby Austria's wine making techniques, styles and preferred grape varieties, include some excellent whites such as *Riesling, Terlano* and *Pinot Bianco*. The area also produces some high-quality reds (*Kalterersee, St Magdalene* and *Lagrein Dunkel*) and some outstanding sparkling wines such as *Spumante Trentino Classico*. The rare *vin santo*, a rich dessert wine, is also worthy of note in this area.

● The red wines of Tuscany are justly famous and rate among the world's best. *Chianti* is the best known; the finest is classified as *Chianti Classico* (with a black cockerel on the bottle), although the cheapest can be dreadful. Two other good Tuscan reds (and among Italy's most expensive wines) are *Vino Nobile di Montepulciano*, aged for four years before bottling, and *Brunello di Montalcino*. *Vin santo* is a dessert wine made from sun-dried grapes (and often served to visitors at all times of day).

● Umbria is known for its dry white wines, of which the most famous is *Orvieto*, although *Grechetto*, a reasonably-priced white, is making its mark on the domestic market.

● Veneto produces a number of world-famous wines, some of them developed using French and German grape varieties, including *Bardolino, Soave* and *Valpolicella*, as well as several kinds of cabernets.

Buying Wine: You can buy wine from supermarkets and hypermarkets, where prices are usually reasonable, although there may not be a particularly good range of quality wines and storage can be a problem. In the major cities and wine-producing areas there are wine shops such as the *bottiglieria* and the more specialist *enoteca*, where there's usually an excellent choice and you can often sample wines before you buy. Most wine is reasonably priced in Italy, a good wine costing in the region of €8 per bottle, although prices rise to over €16 or more for an outstanding vintage. If you want to save money, you can buy wine directly from producers, whose signs '*Vendita Diretta*' (direct sales) line the roads in wine-producing areas. At some producers, you can have your own bottles filled with wine, which helps reduce the price, although the wine isn't usually of the best quality. Note that you shouldn't leave wine in a car for long periods during hot weather, which ruins it.

Wine Tasting: Wine tasting is a wonderful pastime for aspiring oenophiles and is a great way to see Italy – but beware of drinking to excess if you're driving! Wine festivals are held throughout Italy, where tasting is usually free and wine flows freely. The most notable festivals include Bolzano in late March, Città della Pieve and Panicale in Umbria in April, Orvieto in June, and Tivoli in October. Consult local tourist offices for information. The Movimento del Turismo del Vino (Italian Wine Tourist Movement) can provide information about over 300 wine producers catering specifically to visitors. Wine tasting courses are held in major cities throughout Italy by the Associazione Italiana Sommeliers (known affectionately as Vino Vino), Viale Monza, 9, 20125 Milan (☎ 02-2846 237, 🖳 www.sommelier.it) or you can sign up for wine tasting tours organised by wine producers or the Touring Club Italiano, Corso Italia, 10, 20122 Milan (☎ 02-85261, 🖳 www.touringclub.it).

Further Information: There are many books dedicated to Italian wine, including the *Italian Wine Guide* (Abbeville Press), *Wines of Italy* by Burton Anderson (Mitchell Beazley) and the annual *Vini d'Italia* (Arcigola Editore), also published in English as *Italian Wines* (or *The Slow Food Guide to Italian Wines*), the most comprehensive guide to Italian wine, ranking over 11,000 wines! Winetel Italy (🖳 www.winetel-italy.com) has information and statistics on Italian wines and producers. Other interesting websites include 🖳 www.agriline.it, 🖳 www. enotime.com, 🖳 www.il-vino.com, 🖳 www.vinoclub.it and 🖳 www.ware.it.

Spirits & Liqueurs

Although Italians are fond of a pre-dinner aperitif, much less in the way of spirits is consumed in Italy than in many other European countries, and rather than have a whisky or brandy after a meal, most Italians prefer home-grown liqueurs (see below). All the best known brands of spirits are readily available in Italy, plus a number of cheaper Italian brands, although these aren't of such good quality. A bottle of Italian brandy (the main brands are *Stock* and *Vecchia Romagna*) costs around €8, while well known brands of imported spirits (gin, scotch whisky, rum and vodka) usually cost around €15 for a 70cl bottle.

Before a main meal, fortified wines such as *Campari*, *Cinzano* and *Martini* are popular, often served with soda and ice. These aperitifs cost in the region of €8 for a 70cl bottle. There's also an artichoke-based drink, *Cynar*, often drunk as an aperitif, although it's something of an acquired taste. After-dinner drinks usually consist of an Italian liqueur, of which there's a great variety, including *Amaro*, *Galliano* and *Strega*, all bitter and herb-based, *Amaretto*, almond-based and very sweet, *Mistrà* and *sambuca*, aniseed liqueurs usually drunk with coffee, *maraschino*, made from the cherries from which it takes its name, and *grappa*, the Italian 'firewater', which comes in many varieties and is made from juniper berries, grapes or plums. There are numerous *grappa* outlets in Italy and it's probably Italy's cheapest liqueur, but be warned before you rush out to buy a bottle – it's another acquired taste! As well as an being after-dinner drink, *grappa* is a popular way to start the day, often drunk by Italians with their morning coffee (if this doesn't get you going, nothing will!).

Beer

Beer (*birra*) in Italy is usually of the lager type and is sold in 33cl, 75cl and 1 litre bottles. The main Italian brands include *Dreher*, *Moretti* and *Peroni*, all of which are of good quality. There are also darker beers, called *birra nera* or *birra rossa*, which look rather like British stout or bitter, although their taste isn't as malty. Many imported beers are sold in supermarkets, although they cost up to three times as much as Italian beers.

SUPERMARKETS & HYPERMARKETS

Although supermarkets (*supermercati*) are on the increase in Italy, they aren't as prevalent as in other countries such as America, Britain and even France, and hypermarkets (*ipermercati*) account for just 6 per cent of the Italian food market (compared with almost 50 per cent in France). There are several supermarket chains, including the Co-op, Esselunga, Euromercato, GS, Pam, SMA, Standa and Unes. Supermarkets usually provide parking for customers and are open all day without a break for lunch. **Plastic bags (*sacchetti*) aren't always provided free and may cost 5 or 10 cents**, so it's recommended to follow the Italian custom and take your own bags with you. Shopping trolleys usually require a 50 cent coin, which is returned when you take the trolley back to a storage area.

Discount supermarkets (*i discount*) have recently sprung up on the outskirts of cities throughout Italy and include chains such as Lidl and In's Discount. Foods sold here are mainly basic, unbranded, non-perishable items that are usually good value.

DEPARTMENT STORES

There are several department stores (*grandi magazzini*) in Italy with branches throughout the country, including Coin, Esselunga, La Rinascente, Metro, Standa and Upim. La Rinascente (🖳 www.rinascente.it), established in the early 1900s, is Italy's largest and best department store and has two outlets in Rome and its flagship store in Milan. La Rinascente stocks a variety of goods, including the best and most famous Italian and international products, such as clothing, accessories, furniture and household goods. It provides an excellent service for foreign shoppers, including multilingual information counters and international shipping and tax refunds, and all major credit cards are accepted. La Rinascente stores have continuous opening hours from 9am to 7.30pm, Mondays to Saturdays.

Coin, Esselunga, Metro, Standa and Upim have more outlets than La Rinascente and are generally cheaper, although they aren't as stylish or upmarket. They're usually open from 9am to 7pm, Mondays to Saturdays, although some smaller branches may close for lunch.

In Italian department stores you can browse to your heart's content without feeling obliged to buy anything or being accosted by over-zealous shop assistants – an important advantage over small shops.

CLOTHES

Fashion

Italy is renowned for its high fashion, synonymous with elegance and style, and since World War II has vied with France for the number one spot (much 'French' fashion is designed and manufactured in Italy, despite what the label may say). Italian fashion designers rank among the best in the world and include such household names as Armani, Dolce & Gabbana, Fendi, Ferragamo, Ferretti, Gianfranco Ferre, Gucci, Moschino, Ungaro, Valentino and Versace, whose collections attract legions of shoppers annually.

Most Italians have at least a few designer garments and many are even prepared to go without basics in order to have the best in design. Such design excellence doesn't come cheaply and prices are generally very high, but then so is the quality, and an item made in Italy usually lasts for many years (classic design rarely goes out of fashion). *Haute couture* (*alta moda*) commands very high prices and Italian fashion is no exception, much of the merchandise costing far more than you would expect to pay for clothes in other countries. However, the high prices are matched by high quality and garments usually last for many seasons. Prices tend to be fixed (*prezzi fissi*) and bargaining is usually a waste of time and effort unless you're buying a large number of garments or a particularly expensive item. If you're after bargains, the sales in January and July are a must, as it's possible to make huge savings (see **Sales** on page 379).

You may see some shops with signs saying *Ingresso Libero* (Browsers Welcome), but in most smart Italian boutiques browsing isn't permitted; therefore, unless you know exactly what you're after, it's probably better to go to a department store where you can sift through clothes to your heart's content with no risk of disapproving glares from shop assistants.

There are many websites for those interested in Italian fashion, including ⌨ www.modaitalia.net, ⌨ www.modaonline.it, ⌨ www.made-in-italy.com/fashion/indexhtm and ⌨ www.dolcevita.com.

Milan: Milan (considered on a par with Paris) dominates the Italian fashion scene and has the largest choice of boutiques, followed by Rome and Florence. Most Italian and international designers have studios and boutiques in Milan, and twice a year (in spring and autumn) major fashion shows are staged in the city: the *Milanocollezioni* and the *Milanovendemoda* (contact the Milan tourist office for information, ☎ 02-7252 4300).

Milan is the dynamo behind the Italian fashion industry and it's from here that many of Italy's international designers made their way to fame and fortune. The heart of the city's fashion scene is found within the shopping area called the Golden Triangle, on the Via Montenapoleone, one of the country's most exclusive shopping streets, where the finest Italian clothes, shoes and accessories are on display in almost every shop window. Window shopping is a delight here (and, due to the prohibitively high prices, the only kind of shopping most people are likely to do!). Should you be inclined to try something on and you want the shop assistants to take you seriously, you need to look as if you've got millions to spend. Fashion shop assistants in Milan treat you according to how much money they think you're likely to spend!

Poorer mortals (or outside the sales season) go to Corso Buenos Aires, where some 400 shops sell affordable but still fashionable clothes, although you must beware of fake merchandise in some shops. Discount stores (*blocchisti*) sell last year's fashions at reduced prices and you can pick up bargains at stores such as L'Emporio Isola, Gastone Stockhouse and Vestistock Due. Another place to look for bargains in Milan is at wholesale clothing warehouses, mostly based around the Stazione Centrale, some of which offer good prices to retail shoppers.

Rome: Clothes shopping is no less elegant in Rome, where the Via Borgognona and Via Condotti are meccas for wealthy, well-dressed women from around the world. After you've done your window shopping here, you can find more affordable garments in side streets; discount stores such as Discount System and Labels-for-Less offer both women's and men's clothes for around half their original price.

Florence: Florence was once Italy's fashion capital, a mantle now assumed by Milan; however, the city still boasts a large number of boutiques and certainly has prices to match those in Milan and Rome. The main fashion boutiques and shoe shops are situated around the Via dei Tornabuoni, where everyone who's anyone in the Italian fashion industry is represented.

Clothes Shops

La Rinascente department stores (see page 390) stock many top Italian and international fashion labels as well as their own line of quality clothing, *Ellerre*, for men, women and children. Other national chains of clothes shops, still of high quality but without the bank-busting prices, include Benetton, Conbipel, Metro (inexpensive clothes for men, women and children), Oviesse (inexpensive men's clothing), Sisley (also sells children's clothes) and Stefanel (for women). Etam and Elena Miro sell clothes for larger women. Many cities and towns have used and new clothes markets, e.g. the Via Sannio in Rome. There are also 'antique' (i.e. secondhand) clothing shops and charity shops in many cities, where you can often pick up bargains.

Clothes sizes in Italy aren't usually uniform and may vary from designer to designer. In general, you may find the sizes smaller than you're used to and women's shoes in particular are manufactured with a small foot in mind. If you aren't the same size as the average Italian and live in northern Italy, it may be worthwhile crossing the border into Switzerland, where sizes tend to be larger. See **Appendix D** for a comparison between European, British and North American sizes.

NEWSPAPERS, MAGAZINES & BOOKS

Newspapers and magazines in Italy are distributed via state-licensed outlets or kiosks (*edicole*), of which there are many, particularly in the major cities. In common with other Latins, Italians aren't generally such avid newspaper and magazine readers as, say, Americans and Britons, although the readership of books, newspapers and magazines is much higher in northern and central Italy than in the south. The average daily newspaper circulation of all newspapers is around 6 million, although many Italians read free copies in libraries, cafés and bars. There's no tradition of newspaper delivery other than by post and you won't see any Italian newsboys or girls.

The press reflects the strong regional allegiances in Italy; there are few national newspapers. The centre-left *La Repubblica* (Rome) and the more right-wing *Corriere della Sera* (Milan), which includes an English-language section, *Italy Daily*, are Italy's best-selling and most widely read newspapers. *L'Unità*, the Democratic Left's paper, while not particularly widely read, is considered to be one of the most readable newspapers. Regional newspapers include *La Nazione* (Florence), *La Stampa* (Turin), *Il Messaggero* and *Il Tempo* (Rome), *Il Mattino* (Naples), *Il Secolo XIX* (Genoa), and *La Sicilia* and *Giornale di Sicilia* (Sicily), all of which have healthy readerships within their own regions.

Italy doesn't have popular 'tabloid' newspapers, the nearest thing to which are the specialist sports newspapers, *Corriere dello Sport* and *La Gazzetta dello Sport*. Note that, in Italy, 'sport' is usually a euphemism for Italy's most important news topic, soccer.

The traditional hefty Sunday newspaper complete with colour supplements is virtually non-existent in Italy; many news kiosks are closed on Sundays. English-language newspapers can be purchased in most large cities and towns, although at much inflated prices (sometimes as much as three times their home cover price) and usually a day or so after publication. However, certain newspapers published in Europe such as *The Times, Financial Times, The Guardian* and the *International Herald Tribune* are usually available on the day of publication.

Italian magazines and periodicals satisfy all tastes and interests – there are some 10,000 to choose from – and often come with gifts, e.g. CDs or videos. International publications such as *Newsweek* and *The Economist* are available at kiosks, and the Italian equivalents, *L'Espresso* and *Panorama*, provide extensive coverage of national and international current affairs. Other quality publications include *Vogue Italia* (fashion), *Domus, Arca, Bazaar* and *Abitare* (design), *AD* and *FMR* (lifestyle), and *Airone* (nature). Like their European counterparts, Italians avidly devour anything concerning the private (or not so private) lives of the famous (not for nothing are freelance photographers who pursue celebrities named after the Italian *paparazzi*), and 'gossip' magazines such as *Oggi* and *Gente* are extremely popular. Most major newspapers and magazines have websites.

English-language newspapers and magazines are published in many areas and contain a wealth of information about Italian culture, current affairs, national and local events, restaurants, bars, entertainment, services and shops, as well as providing expatriates with vital information. These include *A Guest in Milan* (monthly), *Yes Please* (Milan, quarterly), *Metropolitan* (Rome), *Time Out* (Rome, monthly), *Wanted in Rome* (bi-monthly), *Where Rome* (monthly) and *Vista* (Tuscany).

There's an English-language book shops in most cities in Italy and a number in major cities. Most, however, are fairly small with limited stock, although they can order any book in print. Book shops are also a useful source of information for foreign residents: they often have notice boards where advertisements can be placed and distribute leaflets and free publications to the expatriate community. Among the main English-language book shops in Italy are the American Bookstore (☎ 02-878 920) in Milan and, in Rome, the Economy Book and Video Center (💻 www.booksitaly.com), the Anglo-American Book Co. (💻 www.aab.it) and the English Bookshop (☎ 06-3203 301). There are also secondhand book shops in most large towns that buy, sell and exchange second-hand books.

The largest Italian book shop chain, Feltrinelli, has international branches in Bologna, Florence and Rome, which stock a good selection of books in English and other languages. Other Feltrinelli branches usually stock some English-language books and all stores keep English textbooks for language teachers. Book fairs and second-hand book markets for collectors are regularly staged in the major cities. Books aren't particularly expensive in Italy, where a new paperback costs around €9 and there's a proliferation of inexpensive paperbacks (*libri economici*) costing around €5.

FURNITURE & FURNISHINGS

Furniture (*mobili*) is generally more expensive in Italy than in many other European countries, although a wide range of modern and traditional furniture is available. Modern furniture is popular and is sold in furniture shops in industrial zones and in hypermarkets throughout Italy, although there are few nation-wide chains of discount shops. Department stores also sell a wide range of (mostly up-market) furniture. UnoPiu and DuePiu have huge factory outlets north of Rome selling wooden furniture, garden and conservatory furniture (such as rattan and bamboo items), DIY furniture and household goods. They produce beautiful catalogues and you can order by telephone (☎ 0761-7581 for a catalogue). Tucano and Oltrefrontiera have a wide selection of furniture and home furnishings, many imported from around the world. Inexpensive chain stores include Coin, Habitat, Home Shop, Rinascente, Standa and Upim. At the other end of the scale, a number of international designer companies have elegant boutiques in Italy, including Biggie Best, English Home and Designers Guild.

Most stores make deliveries or loan or rent self-drive vans at reasonable rates. Pine furniture is inexpensive and popular. Beware of buying complicated home-assembled furniture with indecipherable instructions and too few screws. If you want reasonably priced, good quality, modern furniture, you need look no further than Ikea, a Swedish company manufacturing furniture for home assembly with a number of stores in Italy. There are also many good carpet stores in Italy, although, like most home furnishings, they can be expensive.

Exclusive modern and traditional furniture is available everywhere, although not everyone can afford the exclusive prices. Many regions of Italy have a reputation for quality hand-made furniture.

Italian furniture and furnishing shops often offer design services (which may be free to customers), and stock a wide range of beautiful fabrics and materials in patterns and colours ideally suited to Italian homes and the climate and conditions.

If you're spending a lot of money, don't be reluctant to ask for a reduction, as most stores will give you a discount. The best time to buy furniture and furnishings is during sales (particularly in winter), when the prices of many items are slashed. Most furniture shops offer special deals on furniture packages for a complete room or home. It's possible for residents to pay for furniture (and large household appliances) interest-free over a year or with interest over a longer period, e.g. five years. It may be worthwhile comparing the cost of furniture in a neighbouring country with that in Italy, although it usually doesn't pay to buy new furniture abroad to furnish an Italian home (particularly as you must usually add transport costs).

If you're looking for old furniture at affordable prices, you may find a few bargains at antique fairs (*fiera d'antiquariato*) and flea markets (*mercato delle pulci*), although genuine antiques are expensive and difficult to find. If you do come across anything worthwhile, you must usually drive a hard bargain, as the asking prices are often ridiculous, particularly in popular tourist areas during the summer. Markets are, however, good for fabric (e.g. for curtains), bed linen and wallpaper. There's a reasonable market for second-hand furniture in Italy and many sellers and dealers advertise in the expatriate and local press (e.g. *Wanted in Rome*). Charity shops are an Aladdin's cave of household goods and furniture (and they hold periodic sales). You can also try the classified ads in newspapers such as *Porta Portese* (Rome – named after the city's famous flea market), *La Pulce* (Florence) and *Secondamano* (Milan) – there are equivalents in most cities.

The kind of furniture you buy depends on a number of factors, including how long you're planning to stay, whether you plan to take it with you when you leave, the style and size of your home, your budget, the local climate, and not least, your taste. If you intend to furnish a second home with antiques or expensive modern furniture, bear in mind that you need adequate security and insurance. If you own a home abroad, it may be worthwhile shipping surplus items of furniture you have abroad (unless you live in Australia!).

DIY: There are do-it-yourself (DIY) hypermarkets in some areas, selling everything for the home, including DIY supplies, furniture, bathrooms, kitchens, decorating and lighting, plus services such as tool rental and wood-cutting. Look for the enormous Brico Io and Brico Centre stores, usually located in shopping centres on the outskirts of large cities. There are salvage and second-hand companies selling old doors, window frames, fireplaces, tiles and other materials that are invaluable when restoring an old home or to add a special touch to a modern home. Note, however, that many modern DIY supplies and materials aren't as easy to find in Italy as in some other European countries and are more expensive, so you may be better off importing them.

HOUSEHOLD GOODS

Household goods in Italy are generally of good quality and there's a large choice. Prices compare favourably with other European countries and bargains can be found at supermarkets and hypermarkets. Not surprisingly in a nation where people spend much of their time in the kitchen (the rest is spent eating!), Italian kitchenware, crockery, cutlery and glasses can all be purchased cheaply, and the quality and design are usually excellent. It's recommended to buy white goods (such as refrigerators and washing machines) in Italy, as imported appliances may not function properly due to differences in the electrical supply (it may also be difficult to have them repaired).

Italian appliances, such as those made by Candy or Zanussi, usually have a good reputation for quality and wear, although German brands are generally better (and more expensive). Most Italian kitchens don't come with cupboards or major appliances when you buy or rent a home (unless you agree to purchase the existing kitchen from the previous tenant/owner), so you don't usually need to worry about whether you can fit an imported dishwasher or washing machine into the kitchen. However, you should check the size **and** the latest Italian safety regulations before shipping these items to Italy or buying them abroad, as they may need expensive modifications (see **Power Supply** on page 111).

If you already own small household appliances, it's worthwhile bringing them to Italy, as usually all that's required is a change of plug. If you bring appliances with you, don't forget to bring a supply of spares and refills such as bulbs for a refrigerator or sewing machine and spare bags for a vacuum cleaner (unless you have a bagless model!). If you're coming from a country with a 110/115V electricity supply, such as the US, you will need a lot of expensive transformers and it's usually better to buy new appliances in Italy. Small appliances such as vacuum cleaners, grills, toasters and electric irons are inexpensive in Italy and are of good quality. **Don't bring a television without checking its compatibility first, as TVs from many countries won't work in Italy (see page 158).**

If you need kitchen-measuring equipment and cannot cope with metric measures, you must bring your own measuring scales, jugs, cups and thermometers (or refer constantly to **Appendix D**). Note also that foreign pillow sizes (e.g. American and British) aren't the same as in Italy and duvets are much more expensive in Italy than in some other countries and therefore worth bringing with you.

HANDICRAFTS

For centuries, Italian craftsmen have produced exquisite hand-crafted articles, many of which are highly sought after. Although recent years have seen an influx of cheaper, mass-produced imitation Italian handicrafts made in such countries as China and the Czech Republic, there remain craftsmen throughout the country making authentic items, which are generally sold at reputable stores and outlets. Each region has a long tradition of particular handicrafts and one of the attractions of exploring Italy is discovering the vast range of products for sale.

Faenza near Bologna is world-famous for its ceramics, which have been produced there since the 12th century, including hand-painted, ornamental earthenware (*faïence*), characterised by its brilliant colours and floral decorations. The Amalfi coast is also famous for its colourful and highly-decorated pottery.

Venetian glass, traditionally made on the island of Murano, is world-renowned, even though much of the glass used in its manufacture is now imported from the Czech Republic. Glass objects, which are sold in over 1,000 outlets in Venice, vary considerably in price and quality, ranging from the exquisite and tasteful to the tacky. Prices may be an indication of quality but are generally higher than what the seller expects to receive. To ensure your purchase is genuine and good value, you should buy from a reputable and reliable dealer such as Pauly & Co., Salviati or The Domus on the island of Murano itself. Carlo Moretti is one of the world's top glass artisans, and his designs, particularly paperweights, can be found at many outlets. However, you should expect to pay high prices for the genuine article, particularly if it's a unique piece.

Venice is also world-famous for its hand-made lace. It fetches high prices in Venice, where you should beware of machine-made lace, usually imported from China but sometimes just as expensive. The only way to be sure of obtaining top-quality, hand-made lace is to buy *Jesurum* lace (named after Michelangelo Jesurum, who rounded a lace-making school in the 19th century). Other Venetian handicrafts include carnival (*carnevale*) masks, which make beautiful souvenirs, and marbled paper (*carta marmorizzata*); both are best bought direct from workshops and manufacturers.

Italy boasts the finest leather craftsmen in the world and Italian leather footwear, luggage, clothing, bags, wallets and purses are universally acclaimed and are among the best value handicrafts you can buy. The finest work in the country is generally found in Florence, where much of the leather is still hand-crafted and comes in a combination of colours. For the best buys, it's recommended to go to a reputable shop such as Beltrami, John F. or, of course, Gucci. If you're looking for good value, small leather items such as purses, wallets and belts, markets are a good place to shop – for example the *Mercato Centrale* and the *Piazza del Mercato Nuovo* in Florence, open daily except Sundays. Milan, where the legendary Salvatore Ferragamo chain has its headquarters, also has a large leather industry and is **the** place to shop for leather footwear.

Prints and engravings are highly prized in Italy, where the tradition dates back to the Renaissance. As with other handicrafts, it's sometimes difficult to distinguish between the mass-produced factory print or engraving and the genuine hand-crafted article. On the other hand, genuine prints usually fetch high prices that aren't always justifiable, so it may not be a bad idea to content yourself with a good reproduction, some of which are works of art in themselves. Rome and Florence are the main cities for art and prints, although markets and antique shops throughout Italy operate a flourishing business. As well as printing, Italians also have a strong tradition of bookbinding and stationery products. Florentine stationery articles, including the traditional marbled paper used to line books and albums, are particularly sought after.

TOBACCONISTS'

Tobacconists' (*tabaccheria*) are easily identified in Italy by a large black 'T' sign outside. After Italian unification in 1861, tobacconists were awarded a monopoly on the sale of tobacco, salt and quinine. Nearly a century and a half later, with salt readily available at food shops and quinine no longer made, tobacco sales is virtually the only remaining monopoly in Italy – and a thriving business for the state (licensed bars called *bar tabacchi* also sell tobacco products). In addition to the major foreign brands of cigarettes, there's an Italian brand called MS (*Monopolio dello Stato*), which is cheaper than imported brands, although less sophisticated.

A pack of 20 cigarettes in Italy costs between €2.50 and €3.30. Tobacconists are also the official outlet for tax stamps (*marche da bollo*), shown by a *Valori Bollati* sign outside, which must be affixed to official documents and application forms. The standard stamp for administrative documents (*atti civili*) costs €10.33. Requests for official documents may need to be made on official lined paper (*carta da bollo* or *carta bollata*) with a tax stamp affixed or *carta semplice* (standard white paper to which you may affix tax stamps), both sold by tobacconists. Tobacconists also sell postage stamps, postcards, public transport and lottery tickets, telephone cards, confectionery and ice cream, a few stationery items, photographic film and souvenirs.

SHOPPING ABROAD

Shopping abroad (e.g. in neighbouring Austria, France, Slovenia or Switzerland) makes a welcome change from all those Italian shops full of tempting and expensive luxuries. It can also save you money and makes an interesting day out for the family. Don't forget your passports or identity cards, car papers, children, dog's vaccination papers and foreign currency. If you're travelling to Switzerland via motorway by car, you need to buy an annual motorway tax sticker at the border costing Sfr40 (around €25). Shopping in Switzerland is popular with Milan and Turin residents, particularly for dairy products and chocolate. Most shops in Swiss and Slovenian border towns accept euros, but usually give you a lower exchange rate than a bank. Whatever you're looking for, compare prices and quality before buying. Bear in mind that if you buy goods that are faulty or need repair, you may need to return them to the place of purchase.

Since 1993 there have been no cross-border shopping restrictions within the European Union (EU) for goods purchased duty and tax paid, provided all goods are for personal consumption or use and not for resale. Although there are no restrictions, there are 'indicative levels' for certain items, above which quantities may be classified as commercial. For example, those entering Italy aged 17 or over may import the following amounts of alcohol and tobacco without question:

- 10 litres of spirits (over 22° proof);
- 20 litres of sherry or fortified wine (under 22° proof);
- 90 litres of wine (or 120 x 0.75 litre bottles/ten cases), of which a maximum of 60 litres may be sparkling wine;
- 110 litres of beer;
- 800 cigarettes, 400 cigarillos, 200 cigars and 1kg of smoking tobacco.

There's no limit on perfume or toilet water. If you exceed the above amounts, you will need to convince the customs authorities that you aren't planning to sell them. There are fines for anyone who sells duty-paid alcohol and tobacco, which is classed as smuggling.

Never attempt to import illegal goods into Italy and don't agree to bring a parcel into Italy or deliver a parcel in another country without knowing exactly what it contains. A popular confidence trick is to ask someone to post a parcel in Italy (usually to a *poste restante* address) or to leave a parcel at a railway station or restaurant. **THE PARCEL USUALLY CONTAINS DRUGS!**

Duty-Free Allowances

Duty-free (*esente da dazio*) shopping was abolished within the EU on 1st July 1999 and duty-free allowances now apply only if you're travelling to Italy from a country outside the EU (which includes neighbouring Slovenia and Switzerland, although Slovenia is due to join the EU on 1st May 2004). For each such journey, travellers aged 17 or over are entitled to import the following goods purchased duty-free:

- One litre of spirits (over 22° proof) **or** two litres of fortified wine (under 22° proof) **or** two litres of wine;
- Two litres of still table wine;
- 200 cigarettes **or** 100 cigarillos **or** 50 cigars* **or** 250g of tobacco;
- 60ml of perfume;
- 250ml of toilet water;
- Other goods, including gifts and souvenirs to the value of €34.62.

  *Non-EU residents are entitled to import 150 cigars.

Duty-free allowances apply to both outward and return journeys, even if both are made on the same day, and the combined total (i.e. double the above limits) can be imported into your 'home' country.

VAT Refunds: If you live outside the EU, you can obtain a VAT refund (20 per cent on most goods) on purchases provided the value of goods purchased in any one shop (excluding books, food, services and some other items) amounts to at least €154.94, including VAT (shops providing this service usually display a 'Tax-Free' sticker in their windows). Large department stores may have a special counter where non-EU shoppers can arrange for the shipment of duty-free goods. An export sales invoice (or 'tax-free shopping cheque') is provided by retailers, listing all purchases. When you leave Italy, your purchases must be validated by customs (*dogana*) staff at the airport, port or railway station, so don't pack them in your checked baggage. Refunds may be made on the spot at 'tax-free' counters or by post, in which case they're usually made within 90 days of the date of purchase. On-the-spot refunds can take some time, which you should allow for before your plane, train or ship leaves. You can choose to have a refund paid to a credit card or bank account or to receive a cheque.

INTERNET SHOPPING

With Internet shopping the world is literally your oyster and savings can be made on a wide range of goods, including books, clothes, sports equipment, electronic gadgets, jewellery, computers and computer software, and services such as insurance, pensions and mortgages. Huge savings can also be made on holidays and travel. Small high-price, high-tech items (e.g. cameras, watches and portable and hand-held computers) can usually be purchased cheaper somewhere in Europe or (particularly) in the USA, with delivery by courier within as little as a few days.

When buying goods overseas, however, you should ensure that you're dealing with a bona fide company and that the goods will work in Italy (if applicable). If possible, always pay by credit card when buying by mail-order or over the Internet, which may provide added protection, e.g. British credit card issuers are jointly liable with the supplier. Many card companies claim that the law doesn't cover overseas purchases, although many issuers consider claims up to the value of the goods purchased (and they could also be liable in law for consequential loss). When you buy expensive goods abroad, have them insured for their full value.

When buying goods overseas, also take into account shipping costs, duty and VAT. There's no duty or tax on goods purchased within the European Union or on goods from most other countries worth €34.62 or less. Don't buy alcohol or cigarettes abroad, as the duty is usually too high to make it worthwhile. When VAT or duty is payable on a parcel, the payment is usually collected by the post office or courier company on delivery.

Shopping on the Internet is generally very secure (secure servers, with addresses beginning https:// rather than http://, are almost impossible to crack) and in most cases safer than shopping by phone or mail-order. There are literally thousands of shopping sites on the Internet, including Taxi (🖳 www.mytaxi.co.uk), which contains the Internet addresses of 2,500 world-

wide retail and information sites, 🖥 www. shopguide.co.uk and 🖥 http://
content.virgin.net (which has a good directory of British shopping sites).

RECEIPTS

Receipts (*scontrino*) in Italy are important legal documents and not only is it
illegal for the shop not to give you one, it's also illegal for customers not to
possess one for the purchases they've made. This practice is supposed to help
stamp out tax fraud, a favourite Italian pastime, and the Italian tax police
(*Guardia di Finanza*) can fine any customers leaving a shop without a receipt. A
receipt is also necessary should you need to return any purchases for exchange
or a refund. Once you've made a purchase, you have eight days in which to
return it to the shop, although goods bought in sales are exchanged only if
they're faulty or defective, so you should examine any planned purchase
carefully. If there's a fault, you must return the goods with the receipt and a
written complaint stating the nature of the defect. If you're dissatisfied with the
shop's response to your complaint, you should take the complaint to the local
police, who have a commercial department (*polizia annonaria commerciale*), or to
the local council (*assessorato al comercio*).

CONSUMER PROTECTION

The law protects consumers' rights to health, quality and security of products
and services, and to adequate information and accurate publicity. In order to
ensure such protection, legal actions may be brought by individuals and by
recognised consumer associations. The foremost Italian consumer protection
organisation is called Altro Consumo-Informazione Indipendente per i
Consumatori, Altroconsumo, Via Valassina, 22, 20159 Milan (☎ 02-668 901,
🖥 www.altroconsumo.it). You must take out a subscription in order to receive
their monthly magazine (it isn't sold at news kiosks), which also entitles you to
use their Internet consultant service (✉ associati@altroconsumo.it).

18.

ODDS & ENDS

This chapter contains miscellaneous information, including everything you ever wanted to know about tipping and toilets (but were afraid to ask). Most of the topics covered are of general interest to anyone living or working in Italy, although admittedly not all are of vital everyday importance. However, buried among the trivia are some fascinating snippets of information.

CITIZENSHIP

Any child born of an Italian father or mother is automatically Italian, as is a child born in Italy of unknown or stateless parents, or if the child doesn't obtain the citizenship (*cittadinanza*) of its parents under the law of their country. A foreigner married to an Italian citizen can apply for Italian citizenship six months after marriage if living in Italy, or three years after marriage if living abroad. A foreign resident who isn't married to an Italian can apply for citizenship after ten years residence or after only four years if he is a European Union national, and stateless people resident in Italy and foreigners serving the Italian state can apply after five years. A foreigner with a parent or grandparent who was an Italian citizen at birth qualifies for citizenship after living in Italy for two years after their 18th birthday or, if born in Italy, before they reach the age of 18. A child born to foreign parents in Italy doesn't automatically acquire Italian citizenship, but has the right to it provided it's requested before the child reaches the age of 18. It's no longer necessary to have to choose between your parents' nationality and Italian, as Italy now recognises dual nationality (*doppi cittadinanza*).

In order to obtain Italian citizenship, you must apply to the Minister of the Interior (*Ministro degli Interni*) through the mayor of the commune (*comune*) where you live or through an Italian consulate abroad. A concession tax must be paid and the procedure ends with the applicant swearing loyalty to the republic and observance of the constitution and laws of the state. As with most things involving bureaucrats in Italy, the process of applying for and obtaining Italian citizenship is a long drawn out affair often taking years, which will stretch your patience beyond endurance. The documents required vary according to your situation and nationality (it's allegedly easier for those married to Italians) – up to 12 documents may be required, many of which must be on official paper (*bollo*), translated by an official translator, authenticated or legalised. A list of the necessary documents is available from your local government office (*prefettura*). After making an application, the authorities have 18 months to make a decision.

As mentioned above, Italy recognises dual citizenship, although anyone with dual citizenship arriving in or leaving Italy must do so with an Italian passport or identity card.

CLIMATE

Italy generally has a temperate climate influenced by the Mediterranean and Adriatic Seas, and the protective Alps encircling the north. The islands of Sicily and Sardinia, and southern Italy enjoy a mild Mediterranean climate, as does the Italian Riviera. Italy has warm dry summers and relatively mild winters in most regions, although there's a marked contrast between the far north and the south. Rome is generally recognised as the dividing point between the colder north and the hotter southern regions. The best seasons throughout the country are spring and autumn, when it's neither too hot nor too cold in most regions.

Summers are generally very hot everywhere, when thunderstorms are common in inland areas, with average temperatures in July and August around 24°C (75°F). Summers are short and not too hot in alpine and the northern lake areas, while the Po Valley has warm and sunny summers, but can be humid. Summers are dry and hot to sweltering the further south you go (too hot for most people), although sea breezes alleviate the heat in coastal areas. In Rome and further south, the *scirocco* wind from Africa can produce stifling hot weather in August, with temperatures well above 30°C (86°F).

Winters are relatively mild in most areas with some rainy spells. However, they're very cold (but usually sunny) in the alpine regions, where snowfalls are frequent. The first snowfall in the Alps is usually in November, although light snow sometimes falls in mid-September and heavy snow can fall in October. The Alps shield northern Lombardy and the lakes area (including Milan) from the extremes of the northern European winter. Fog is common throughout the north from the autumn through to February and winters can be severe in the Po Valley, the plains of Lombardy and Emilia-Romagna. Venice can be quite cold in winter (it frequently snows there) and it's often flooded (*acqua alta*) when the sea level rises and inundates the city. Florence is cold in winter, while winters are moderate in Rome where it rarely snows. The Italian Riviera and Liguria experience mild winters and enjoy a Mediterranean climate as they're protected by both the Alps and the Appennines (*Appennini*). Sicily and southern Italy have the mildest winters, with daytime temperatures between 10 to 20°C (50 to 68°F).

Rainfall is moderate to low in most regions and is rare anywhere in summer. The north and the Adriatic coast are wetter than the rest of Italy. There's a lot of rain in the central regions of Tuscany and Umbria in winter, although they suffer neither extreme heat nor cold most of the year. There's a shortage of water in many areas during summer, when the supply is often turned off during the day and households are limited to a number of cubic metres per year.

Average daily maximum/minimum temperatures (in Centigrade) for selected towns are show below:

Location	Spring (April)	Summer (July)	Autumn (October)	Winter (January)
Brindisi	18/11	29/21	22/15	12/6
Cagliari	19/11	30/21	23/15	14/7
Milan	18/10	29/20	17/11	5/0
Naples	18/9	29/18	22/12	12/4

Palermo	20/11	30/21	25/16	16/8
Rome	19/10	30/20	22/13	11/5
Venice	17/10	27/19	19/11	6/1

A quick way to make a **rough** conversion from Centigrade to Fahrenheit is to multiply by two and add 30. Weather forecasts (*previsioni del tempo*) are broadcast on TV and radio stations and published in daily newspapers. Weather reports are also available by telephone (📠 144-661 911) and on the TV Videotel 'teletext' service.

Earthquakes & Volcanic Eruptions

Italy is prone to earthquakes and volcanic eruptions (see **Geography** on page 408). There has been a government campaign in recent years to inform people and allay their fears about earthquakes, although it has probably had the opposite effect! Officially, some 3,000 towns out of a total of 8,000 are in constant threat from earthquakes. These communities contain some ten million homes, at least two-thirds of which aren't earthquake proof (even those that are supposedly 'earthquake proof' often aren't). The regions most at risk are Calabria, Friuli-Venezia-Giuila, Marche and Sicily. The area extending from Tuscany to Basilicata (with the exception of Puglia) has a medium to high risk, while all other regions are low or low to medium risk.

CRIME

The crime rate in Italy varies considerably from region to region and is around average for Europe. Violent crime is rare in most areas, although muggings do occur in resort areas and cities. Despite the fearsome reputation of the Mafia, there's actually **less** violent street crime such as muggings and robbery with violence in most parts of Italy than in many other European countries, and it's generally a very safe place for children. Sexual harassment and assault can be a problem for women in some areas, although most men draw the line at cat-calls and whistles. Foreigners should take care when travelling in the south of Italy, where highway robbery and kidnappings of foreigners occasionally take place.

Housebreaking and burglary are rife, where vacant 'holiday' or second homes are a popular target. Many residents keep dogs as a protection or warning against burglars and have triple-locked and steel-reinforced doors. However, crime in rural areas remains relatively low and it's still common for people in villages and small towns not to lock their cars and homes (in some small villages you still see the keys left nonchalantly in the front door).

Car theft and theft from cars is widespread in cities, where foreign-registered cars are a popular target, particularly expensive models, which are often stolen to order and spirited abroad. Theft of small items such as radios, luggage, mobile phones, cameras, briefcases, sunglasses and even cigarettes from parked cars is a major problem. Thieves in the south take items from cars at gas stations, often by smashing car windows. It's also possible to have your belongings stolen from an occupied vehicle while waiting in traffic or stopped at traffic lights. It's therefore wise to keep the windows closed (weather permitting) in cities and major towns, the doors locked at all times, and to keep all valuables out of sight at all times. When parking a bicycle, moped or scooter, you should also use as many high-security locks as you can carry.

Beware of bag snatchers (*scippatori*) in towns and cities, who operate on foot, scooters, motorcycles or even from cars. Always carry bags defensively slung across your body with the clasp facing the body; make sure it has a strong strap that cannot easily be cut, otherwise you should carry it firmly in your hand. Bags that are worn around the waist ('bum-bags') are vulnerable and should be avoided, as should small back-packs which can easily be cut. One of the most effective methods of protecting your passport, money, travellers' cheques and credit cards is with an old-fashioned money belt (worn under your clothing) or a pouch on a string or strong cord around your neck. It's also recommended to keep some emergency money and a credit card in separate places in case of theft and a copy of important documents such as your passport. Never tempt fate with an exposed wallet or purse or by flashing your money around, and hang on tight to your shoulder bag. Don't carry a lot of cash or expose expensive jewellery, watches or sunglasses when out walking.

Confidence tricksters and hustlers are also rife in Italy, where it's wise to avoid all strangers trying to attract your attention. Many stage accidents, such as spilling something on your clothes (or pointing out something which has been done by an accomplice), in order to rob you. Be alert to any incident that could be designed to attract your attention and keep strangers at arms' length. Don't accept an offer from someone to take your photograph with your camera (they're likely to run off with it); if you must ask someone to take a photo, ask a tourist.

Pickpockets and bag-snatchers are a plague in the major cities, where the street urchins (often Albanians or Gypsies) are highly organised and trained pickpockets (if you get jostled check for your wallet). They try to surround you and often use newspapers or large pieces of cardboard to distract you and hide their roaming hands. Keep them at arm's length, if necessary by force, and keep a firm grip on your valuables. If you're targeted shout 'go away' (*va via!*) in a loud voice – a loud whistle can also be useful to scare off prospective attackers or pickpockets. Always remain vigilant in tourist haunts, queues, on public transport (particularly on night trains) and anywhere that there are crowds. Thieves on crowded public transport slit the bottoms of purses or bags with a razor blade or sharp knife and remove the contents through the bottom.

Italy is infamous for its organised crime and gang warfare, which is rife in some areas, although it has no discernible impact on the lives of most foreigners there (particularly in the north of the country). The term 'Mafia' is used to describe five distinct organised crime groups: the original Sicilian Mafia, the *Camorra* in Naples and Campania, the *Ndrangheta* in Calabria, and the *Sacra*

Corona Unità and *La Rosa* in Apulia. These groups operate both separately and together, and their activities range from drugs and contraband to protection rackets, gambling and prostitution. They also monopolise lucrative contracts in most fields throughout the country and it's estimated that their combined turnover is billions of euros, possibly over 10 per cent of Italy's GNP.

The Mafia holds a death grip on the south of Italy, where business people are often forced to pay protection money (*pizzo*) to the mobsters to ensure their businesses are safe – it's estimated that half the businesses in Naples pay protection money! Loan sharking (*usurai*), lending money at extortionate rates of interest, is common in the south, where an association has been established to help those who cannot borrow money from banks. Despite many high profile arrests in recent years, rumours of the Mafia's demise or loss of influence are premature and they reportedly have their fingers in every facet of government right up to the Prime Minister's office in Rome! In recent years, Albanians, Russians and other foreign gangsters have challenged the Mafia in the north, where they're heavily involved in illegal drugs.

Don't let the foregoing catalogue of crime and mayhem put you off Italy. You can usually safely walk almost anywhere at any time of day or night and there's no need for anxiety or paranoia about crime. However, you should be 'street-wise' and take certain elementary precautions. These include avoiding high-risk areas at night (such as parks and car parks) and those frequented by drug addicts, prostitutes and pickpockets. You can safely travel on the underground (*metrò*) at any time, although some stations are best avoided late at night. When you're in an unfamiliar city, ask a policeman, taxi driver or other local person whether there are any unsafe neighbourhoods – and avoid them!

If you're the victim of a crime, you should report it to the nearest police station (*commissariato di pubblica sicurezza*) or to the local *Carabinieri* immediately – (see **Police** on page 421). You can report it by telephone but must go to the station to complete a report (*denuncia*), of which you receive a copy for insurance purposes. Don't, however, expect the police to find your belongings or even take any interest in your loss. Report a theft to your insurance company as soon as possible.

See also **Car Crime** on page 243, **Household Insurance** on page 285, **Home Security** on page 106 and **Legal System** on page 415.

GEOGRAPHY

Italy covers an area of 301,245km² (116,319mi²) and comprises a long peninsula shaped like a boot, which is instantly recognisable and tends to give the impression that the country is much larger than it actually is (it covers around the same area as the US state of Arizona or the British Isles). The country is 1,200km (750mi) in length and between 150 and 250km (93 to 155mi) in width. Italy has borders with France (488km/303mi), Switzerland (740km/460mi), Austria (430km/267mi) and Slovenia (199km/124mi), and encompasses two independent states within its borders: the Vatican City (116acres/47ha) in

Rome, established in 1929, and the Republic of San Marino (61km²/24mi²) within the Marche region.

It's a land of stark contrasts, including towering mountains and vast plains, huge lakes and wide valleys. It has a wide variety of landscape and vegetation, characterised by its two mountain ranges, the Alps and the Apennines (almost 80 per cent of the country is covered by hills and mountains). The Alps (*Alpi*) form the border in the north, stretching from the Gulf of Genoa (*Golfo di Genova*) in the west to the Adriatic Sea (north of Trieste) in the east. The highest mountain peak is Monte Bianco (Mont Blanc, 4,807m/15,770ft), on the border with France, while the highest peak in the Italian Alps is Monte Rosa (4,634m/15,203ft) on the Swiss border. The Alps are divided into three main groups, western, central and eastern, and are at their most beautiful and spectacular in the Dolomites (*Dolomiti*) in the east.

The Apennines form the backbone of Italy, extending for 1,220km/758mi from Liguria near Genoa to the tip of Calabria and into Sicily. The highest peak in the Apennines is the Corno Grande (2,914m/9,560ft) in the Gran Sasso d'Italia range in Abruzzo. The Apuan Alps (*Alpi Apuane*) in the north-west of Tuscany form part of the sub-Apennines and are composed almost entirely of marble and have been mined since the Roman times. In the south, the Gargano and Sila massifs cross the spur and foot of the boot respectively.

The alpine foothills are characterised by the vast Po Valley and the lakes of Como, Garda and Maggiore. In the north there are large areas of forest and farmland, while the south is mostly scrubland. Lowlands or plains comprise less than a quarter of Italy's total land mass. The largest plain is the Po Valley (bounded by the Alps, the Apennines and the Adriatic Sea), a heavily populated and industrialised area. The Po is Italy's longest river, flowing from west to east across the plain of Lombardy in the north into the Adriatic. Its tributaries include the Adige, Piave, Reno and Tagliamento rivers. Other major rivers include the Tiber (Rome) and the Arno (Tuscany). A coastal plain runs along the Tyrrhenian Sea from southern Tuscany through Lazio into Puglia (Tavoliere delle Puglia), while another smaller plain is Pianura Campana near Mount Vesuvuis. Italy has a number of great national parks, including Abruzzo in the Apennines and the Alpine Gran Paradiso between Valle d'Aosta and Piedmont.

The country is surrounded by sea on all sides except in the extreme north. The Ligurian and Tyrrenian seas bound the west of the peninsula, the Ionian Sea lies off the coasts of Puglia, Basilicata and Calabria in the south, and the Adriatic Sea in the east separates Italy from the former Yugoslavia (now a group of independent states). Italy has a vast and varied coastline of some 7,500km (4,660mi), including its islands, highlights of which include the Amalfi Coast (south of Naples), the crescent of Liguria (the Italian Riviera) and the Gargano Massif (the spur jutting into the Adriatic). Coastal areas vary considerably from the generally flat Adriatic coast to the dramatic cliffs of Liguria and Calabria.

The country encompasses a number of islands, including Sicily (situated across the Strait of Messina), the largest and most densely populated island in the Mediterranean. The islands of Pantelleria, Linosa, Lampedusa lie between

Sicily and Tunisia, and many small islands surround Sicily, offering excellent facilities for scuba-diving and underwater fishing, and spectacular scenery. These include the Lipari group of islands (encompassing Lipari itself plus Vulcano, Panarea and Stromboli), Ustica, Favignana, Levanzo, Marittimo, Pantelleria and Lampedusa. Italy's (and the Mediterranean's) second-largest island is Sardinia (*Sardegna*), situated in the Tyrrhenian Sea to the west of the mainland and south of the island of Corsica (France). It's the country's most sparsely populated region, with a coastline of some 1,300km (800mi), and is one of Italy's most unspoilt regions.

Among Italy's most famous and attractive islands are Capri, Ischia and Procida in the Gulf of Naples. The seven islands of the Tuscan archipelego (off the Maremma coast) are among the most appealing of all the Mediterranean islands and include Elba, Capraia, Pianosa, Montecristo, Gorgona, Giglio and Giannutri. The beautiful island of Elba (where Napoleon was exiled from May 1814 to February 1815) covers an area of 224km^2 (86mi^2), two-thirds of which is woodland, and has some excellent sandy beaches. Other islands include the virtually unknown (five) Pontine islands some 32km (20mi) off the coast of Lazio.

Italy has a number of active volcanoes, including Mount Etna on Sicily (3,274m/10,741ft), Stromboli (on the Isle of Eolie off the west coast of southern Italy) and Vesuvius (near Naples). Etna (last erupted in 2003) and Stromboli are among the world's most active volcanoes, while Vesuvius hasn't erupted since 1944. Italy is also prone to earthquakes and a European fault line runs through the centre north to south down to Sicily. The highest risk areas are in the south, where some 70 per cent of the terrain is susceptible to earthquakes. The country's last major earthquake hit Messina and Reggio di Calabria in 1908, killing some 85,000 people. More recently there have been earthquakes in Friuli (1976), Irpinia, south-east of Naples (1980) and Umbria (1997).

Italy is divided into 20 regions (and 96 provinces), shown on the map in Appendix E.

GOVERNMENT

Italy was a monarchy from its unification in the second half of the 19th century until 1946, when it became a parliamentary republic following a national referendum. It adopted its constitutional charter on the 1st January 1948 that defines the political and civil liberties of the citizens and the parliamentary principles of government. Italy is headed by a president who appoints the prime minister, the elected head of government. The seat of government is Rome, where the president resides in the Palazzo del Quirinale, the chamber of deputies sits in the Palazzo Montecitorio and the senate in the Palazzo Madama.

President

The head of state is the president of the republic, who represents the nation's unity and ensures compliance with the constitution (under the direction of the constitutional court). He is elected every seven years by a college comprising both chambers of Parliament and three representatives from each region, and must gain a two-thirds majority which guarantees that he is acceptable to a sufficient proportion of the populace and the political partners. The minimum age for presidential candidates is 50. The current President, Carlo Azeglio Ciampi, took office in 1999.

His duties include appointing the prime minister, promulgating laws and decrees, calling special sessions of Parliament, delaying legislation, authorising the presentation of government bills in Parliament and, with parliamentary authorisation, ratifying treaties and declaring war. Some of these acts are duties that **must** be performed by him, whereas others have no validity unless countersigned by the government. The president commands the armed forces and presides over the Supreme Council of Defence and the Superior Council of the Magistrature. He may dissolve Parliament (except during the last six months of his term of office) either on his own initiative in consultation with the presidents of both chambers or at the request of the government. Whenever a government is defeated or resigns, it's his duty (after consulting eminent politicians and party leaders) to appoint the person most likely to win the confidence of Parliament, although the candidate is usually designated by the majority parties and the president has limited choice.

Parliament

The Italian Parliament (*parlamento*) is bicameral, consisting of two assemblies: the Senate of the Republic (*Senato della Repubblica*) with 315 members and the Chamber of Deputies (*Camera dei Deputati*) with 630 members. The assemblies enjoy equal powers and are both elected by universal suffrage. In theory, the senate should represent the regions and in this way differ from the lower chamber, but in practice the only real difference between them lies in the minimum age required for the electorate and the candidates: 18 and 25 respectively for deputies and 25 and 40 for senators. Parliament is elected every five years, although in the past, few governments have run their course, with the average length less than one year (see also **Elections** below). The senators and deputies must declare to which parliamentary group they intend to belong to and any political group consisting of at least 10 senators and 20 deputies has the right to be represented in Parliament.

The government is appointed by the president of the republic and is led by the president of the council of ministers (*il Presidente del Consiglio*), more commonly referred to as the Prime Minister. Although the government carries out the executive functions of the state, in emergencies it also has powers to approve laws by decree. Parliament can be dissolved by the president of the republic, e.g. when the prime minister loses a vote of no confidence. Ministerial appointments are negotiated by the parties constituting the government majority and each new government must receive a vote of confidence in both houses of Parliament within 10 days of its appointment. If at any time the government fails to maintain the confidence of either house, it must resign. Splits in the coalition of two or more parties that have united to form a government have caused most resignations in the past.

The most important function of Parliament is ordinary legislation. Bills may be presented in Parliament by the government, by individual members, or by bodies such as the National Council for Economy and Labour, various regional councils, or communes, as well as by petition of 50,000 citizens of the electorate or through a referendum. Bills must be approved by both houses before they become law; thus, whenever one house introduces an amendment to a draft approved by the other house, the latter must approve the amended draft. The law comes into force when published in the *Gazzetta Ufficiale*.

Political Parties

From the end of World War II to the early 1990s, Italy had a multi-party system dominated by two large parties, the Christian Democratic Party (Partito della Democrazia Cristiana/DC) and the Italian Communist Party (Partito Comunista Italiano/PCI), and a number of small but influential parties. The DC was the dominant governing party in various alliances with the smaller parties of the centre and left. The smaller parties ranged from the neo-fascist Italian Social Movement (Movimento Sociale Italiano/MSI) on the right to the Italian Socialist Party (Partito Socialista Italiano/PSI) on the left, while a number of small secular parties occupied the centre. The DC, in various alliances with smaller parties of the centre and left, was the dominant governing party, and the principal opposition parties were the PCI and the MSI.

The Italian party system underwent a radical transformation in the early 1990s as a result of both international and national events. In 1991 the Communist Party became the Democratic Party of the Left (Partito Democratico della Sinistra/PDS) and the DC disappeared altogether. The main result of these changes was the collapse of the political centre and a right-left polarisation of the party spectrum. The post-war party system was radically altered by the fall of communism, by a wave of judicial prosecutions of corrupt officials that involved most Italian political parties, and finally by the electoral reforms of the 1990s. The DC, battered by scandal, was replaced by a much smaller organisation, the Italian Popular Party (Partito Popolare Italiano/PPI), which itself virtually disappeared after elections in 1994.

By that time three new parties had arisen to dominate the political right: Forza Italia (FI), a vaguely neo-liberal alliance created in 1994 by the media tycoon Silvio Berlusconi, the Northern League (Lega Nord/LN), formed in 1991, a federalist and fiscal-reform movement with large support in the northern regions, and the National Alliance (Alleanza Nazionale/AN), which succeeded the MSI in 1994, but whose political platform renounced its fascist past. Meanwhile, the PCI remained an important electoral force under a new name, the Democratic Party of the Left (Partito Democratico della Sinistra/PDS). Thus, the

Italian political spectrum, which had previously been dominated by parties of the centre, became polarised between parties of the right and left.

Regional Government

For administrative purposes, the country is divided into 20 regions (*regioni*, see **Appendix E**), which roughly correspond to the historical regions of the country. The regions are further divided into 96 provinces (*provinci*), which are further subdivided into town councils or communes (*comuni*). The five special status regions (*regioni a statuo speciale*) of Friuli-Venezia-Giuila, Sardinia, Sicily, Trentino-Alto Adige and Val D'Aosta are autonomous or semi-autonomous due to particular ethnic or geographical considerations. They have special powers granted under the constitution and regional assemblies (similar to Parliaments) with a wide range of administrative and economic powers. Apart from these exceptions, Italy's other 15 regions have little autonomy compared with, for example, those in Germany or Spain.

Participation in national government is a principal function of the regions and regional councils may initiate parliamentary legislation, propose referenda, and appoint three delegates to assist in presidential elections. With regard to regional legislation, the five 'special' regions have exclusive authority in certain fields such as agriculture, forestry and town planning, while the other regions have authority within the limits of principles established by state laws. The legislative powers of the regions are subject to certain constitutional limitations, the most important of which is that regional acts may not conflict with national interests. The regions can also enact legislation necessary for the enforcement of state laws when the latter contain the necessary provisions and have administrative competence in all fields in which they have legislative competence. The regions have the right to acquire property and to collect certain revenues and taxes. Regional and local elections are held every five years.

Communes

The organs of the commune (*comune*), the smallest local government unit, are the popularly elected communal council, the communal committee or executive body and the mayor (*sindaco*). The communes have the power to levy and collect limited local taxes and have their own police (*vigili urbani*), although their powers are much less than those exercised by the national police. The communes issue ordinances and run certain public health services, and are responsible for such services as public transportation, refuse collection and street lighting. Regions have some control over the activity of the communes and communal councils may be dissolved for reasons of public order or for continued neglect of their duties. The mayor of a commune, in his capacity as an agent of the central government, registers births, deaths, marriages, and migrations, maintains public order (although in practice this is dealt with by the national police), and can, in an emergency, issue ordinances concerning public health, town planning and the local police. An EU national is entitled to vote in communal elections and stand as a candidate.

Elections

All citizens aged 18 years and over may vote in elections for the Chamber of Deputies, although the age limit is 25 for the Senate. The turnout for elections in Italy is the highest in the EU in all elections, reaching well over 80 per cent of the electorate for parliamentary elections. For almost half a century after World War II, Italy's electoral system was based on proportional representation, a system in which seats in an elected body are awarded to political parties according to the proportion of the total vote they receive. Between 1993 and 1995, however, several changes were made by national legislation and popular referenda. On the national level, the Chamber of Deputies and the Senate are now elected by a combination of proportionality and plurality. Seventy-five per cent of the seats in these two chambers are now filled from single-member districts by individual candidates who win the largest number of votes in each district. The other 25 per cent of the seats are awarded to candidates from party lists on a proportional basis. The number of votes obtained by the winner in single-member districts is fully (for senators) or partially (for deputies) subtracted before allocating proportional seats, thus introducing a further element of proportionality.

In regional elections, voters cast two ballots. The first is cast in a contest for 80 per cent of the seats in the regional council, which are awarded on a proportional basis. The second ballot is employed in a plurality vote; the regional coalition that wins a plurality is awarded all the remaining seats as well as the presidency of the regional government. Split voting is allowed. In provincial elections, only one vote is cast. If a single provincial list wins more than 50 per cent of the votes, seats are divided among all the lists according to their proportion of the vote, and the presidency goes to the head of the winning list. Otherwise, a run-off election must take place between the two most successful lists, with the winner taking 60 per cent of the seats. A similar system is employed in municipal elections in cities with more than 15,000 inhabitants. In this case, however, two ballots are cast, one for mayor and one for the council. Split voting is permitted. In smaller cities, only one ballot is cast and the winning list is awarded two-thirds of the seats as well as the mayoralty.

Referenda

An important feature of the Italian constitution is the right to hold referenda in order to repeal laws or executive orders (except with regard to anything concerning the state budget or the ratification of international treaties) at the request of 500,000 signatories or five regional councils. Referenda have been used extensively since the 1970s to make possible a wide range of institutional and civic reforms. Referenda are provided for with regard to all regional legislation and some regions have a provision for holding ordinary referenda. The constitution also provides that 50,000 members of the electorate may jointly present to Parliament a draft bill. Important referenda held in the past include those on abortion, divorce, nuclear power and electoral reform.

European Parliamentary Elections

EU nationals aged over 18 who are resident in Italy are permitted to vote and, if aged over 25, can stand as a candidate in European elections for Members of the European Parliament (MEPs). If you wish to exercise your right to vote, you must request an application (for registration on the supplementary list drawn up by the municipality) from the mayor of the municipality in which you're resident not later than 90 days before polling day. You may be required to show your identity documents and give your last address in your home EU country in order to verify that you're an EU citizen. As far as elections to the European Parliament are concerned, you lose the right to vote in your EU country of origin if you choose to vote in Italy.

LEGAL SYSTEM

Italian law is codified and based on Roman law, particularly regarding civil law. The codes of the Kingdom of Sardinia in civil and penal affairs, derived from the French Napoleonic model, were extended to the whole of Italy when Italy was unified in the mid-19th century. The revised 1990 penal code replaced the old 'inquisitory' system with an accusatory system similar to that of common-law countries. Besides the codes, there are innumerable statute laws that integrate the codes and regulate areas of law, such as public law, for which no codes exist. Under the Italian constitution, the judiciary is independent of the legislature and the executive, and therefore jurisdictional functions can be performed only by ordinary magistrates and judges cannot be dismissed. The Italian judicial system consists of a series of courts and a body of judges who are civil servants. The judicial system is unified, with every court being part of the national network. The highest court in the central hierarchy is the Supreme Court of Appeal, which has appellate jurisdiction and gives judgements only on points of law. The 1948 constitution prohibits special courts with the exception of administrative courts and military court-martials, although a vast network of tax courts has survived from an earlier period.

The Italian legal system is inordinately complicated and most lawyers (*avvocato*) and judges (*giudici*) are baffled by the conflicts between different laws, many dating back centuries, added to which European Union directives simply serve to complicate matters further. There are literally thousands of laws, most of which are ignored, and newcomers must learn where to draw the line between laws that are enforced and those that aren't or are only weakly enforced. It sometimes appears that there's one law for foreigners and another for Italians, and fines (*multe*) are commonplace. The legal system grinds **very** slowly and it takes years for a case to come to court; the average time between indictment and a court judgement is ten years, and eight out of ten convictions involving prison terms never take effect.

This means that you should do everything possible to avoid going to court, by taking every conceivable precaution when doing business in Italy, i.e. obtaining expert legal advice in advance. If things go wrong, it can take years to achieve satisfaction and in the case of fraud the chances are that those responsible will have either gone broke, disappeared or even died! **Even when you have a foolproof case there's no guarantee of winning and it may be better to write off a loss as experience.** Local courts, judges and lawyers frequently abuse the system to their own ends and almost anyone with enough money or expertise can use the law to their own advantage.

Civil Courts

Civil justice is applied in disputes between private bodies and in some cases also between private and public administrations. Civil justice is dispensed by justices of the peace (*giudici conciliatori/guidice di pace*), judges (*pretori*), tribunals (*tribunali*), appeal courts (*corti d'appello*) and the supreme court (*corte di cassazione*). The *conciliatori* and *pretori* are single-person organs, while the *tribunali* and *corti* are collective organs comprised of variable numbers of members. A justice of the peace generally has jurisdiction in all civil law cases concerning property up to a maximum value of €2,600 (similar to a small claims' court in other countries). The supreme court (*corte di cassazione*) deals with the control of the proper application of the law by appellate judges.

Criminal Courts

The criminal legal process involves judges, tribunals and assize courts (*corte d'assise*), which include juries (*giudici popolari*), unlike other courts which are composed entirely of lawyers. Once a trial has been concluded and judgement passed, a party found guilty can appeal the decision to an appeal court. If the appeal fails, it may be possible to appeal to the supreme court, but only on the grounds of the wrong interpretation or application of the law by the judge.

Administrative Courts

Administrative courts have two functions: the protection of legitimate interests (*interessi legittimi*), that is the protection of individual interests directly connected with public interests, and the supervision and control of public funds. Administrative courts are also provided by the judicial sections of the council of state, the oldest juridical-administrative advisory organ of government. The court of accounts has both an administrative and a judicial function, the latter primarily involving fiscal affairs. The losing party has the option of requesting a review of the entire case by the council of state (*consiglio di stato*) in Rome, whose judgement is final.

Arrest

If you're arrested in Italy, you have no right to see a lawyer (*avvocato*) before a hearing before a judge, but may give the name of your lawyer in writing. You have the right to silence and need only state your name, date and place of birth, and whether you have been arrested before in Italy. You have the right to notify your local consulate who can provide the names of English-speaking lawyers or lawyers speaking other languages. You can be held for a maximum of three days before a hearing must take place before a judge, when you must be represented by a lawyer (if you don't provide the name of a lawyer one will be appointed by the court), after which you're usually permitted to go free provided you're deemed unlikely to flee, be a danger to society or destroy evidence. **In serious cases it can be difficult to obtain bail and you can be held for up to three years without trial!**

Lost Property Or Documents

If you lose or have something stolen in Italy, you should make a report (*denuncia*) to the local *Carabinieri* (see **Police** on page 421), rather than the office in the town where you live. This is important if you want to make a claim on an insurance policy, as the police report provides evidence of your loss.

MARRIAGE & DIVORCE

To be married in Italy, a couple must appear with two witnesses and make a declaration of their intention to marry before the civil registrar (*ufficiale di stato civile*) of the town where the marriage is to take place. The couple must present all necessary documents at the time of their declaration, which must be translated into Italian and certified by an Italian Consular Officer. These include your passport, birth certificate, a final divorce (*sentenza di divorzio*) or annulment decree or death certificate (if previously married) and, if either party is aged under 18, a sworn statement of consent to the marriage by the parents or legal guardians. You also need the inevitable fiscal stamp! You may also need to obtain a 'certificate of no impediment' (*nulla osta*) from a consulate stating that according to the laws to which the citizen is subject in their home country, there's no obstacle to his or her marriage. Presentation of this declaration allows the authorities to reduce the time before a marriage licence is granted from three weeks to around four days. **A divorced woman must wait nine months or obtain a special dispensation from a local court before she can remarry in Italy, because she could be pregnant by her former husband at the time of the divorce.**

After the declaration is made, it's usually necessary for banns (*pubblicazioni matrimoniali*) or the announcement of the forthcoming marriage, to be posted at the local town hall (*comune* sometimes referred to as *municipio*) and church (for a church wedding) for two consecutive Sundays before the marriage occurs if either party is Italian or resident in Italy. However, banns are waived by the civil registrar if neither party to the marriage is Italian or is residing in Italy. The couple may be married in a civil or religious ceremony on the fourth day following the second Sunday on which the banns are posted (or any time after banns have been waived). Over 75 per cent of weddings in Italy are still performed in church.

A civil ceremony is usually performed by the mayor or civil registrar at the local town hall in front of two witnesses. There's nothing to pay apart from the fiscal stamp (€10.33). If a religious ceremony is performed by a Roman Catholic priest, a separate civil ceremony is unnecessary, but the priest must register the marriage with the civil registrar in order for it to be legal. Catholic churches require that both parties are baptised and confirmed Catholics, and attend a church 'pre-matrimonial course'. The authorities require the presence of a translator if neither party speaks Italian. Due to the special requirements that apply to marriages performed by non-Roman Catholic clergymen, the latter usually insist on a prior civil ceremony before performing a religious ceremony in order to ensure the legality of the marriage.

Family law has seen many reforms in recent decades, including the abolition of the husband's status as head of the household and the legalisation of divorce and abortion. Couples married in Italy must choose between shared ownership (*comunità dei beni*) and separate ownership (*separazione dei beni*) of their worldly goods in the event of divorce or death (which can have important consequences). Foreigners from countries without matrimonial regimes are usually shown as having married without regime or the equivalent of *separazione dei beni*. A wife isn't required to take her husband's name upon marriage and most generally retain their maiden names until death, although most women are known by their husband's surname. However, some wives append their husband's surname to their own and some even put it in front.

Divorce has been possible in Italy only since 1970. You can be divorced in Italy if your marriage took place there or if one of a couple is Italian or a resident in the country. With the exception of divorce by consent, divorce is a complicated matter in Italy and is best avoided if it can be accomplished abroad, which is possible when one of a couple isn't Italian or you were married abroad. **For two non-Italians or when only one partner is Italian, foreign law may take precedence over Italian law.** A couple divorcing by consent must wait three years to be divorced and couples not divorcing by consent must wait five years after fault has been proved. The other difference is the cost; divorce by consent costs little or nothing, while a contested divorce costs many thousands of euros. When a couple decide to divorce, they go before a judge who offers them the choice of a reconciliation or a formal separation (*separazione formale*) for one year. Financial matters should also be dealt with at this time. The mother is usually given custody of the children, with access for the father, and once they reach the age of ten they can (within certain guidelines) decide which parent they want to live with. Catholics who no longer wish to be married but equally don't want to get divorced, can obtain a formal judicial separation.

MILITARY SERVICE

The Italian armed forces number around 270,000 comprising the army (circa 165,000), air force (65,000), navy (40,000) and central staff (30,000). The strength of the armed forces is being reduced and is expected to number 215,000 by 2005. Italy also has reserve forces numbering around 300,000 (circa 240,000 army, 35,000 navy and 25,000 air force). The 115,000 *Carabinieri* police force (see page 421) is also part of the army, although future control is expected to pass from the Ministry of Defence to the Ministry of the Interior when it's deployed for public order. Defence spending fell in the 1990s and is currently around €15,500 million per year, which includes the paramilitary *Carabinieri* police force. Italy, which has no nuclear weapons, is a member of the North Atlantic Treaty Organisation (NATO) and is home to a number of NATO military bases (from where the Kosovo military campaign was largely conducted in 1999).

Italy has compulsory military service (conscription) for men for a period of ten months, which is to be phased out by 2005 when the country plans to have fully professional armed forces (children born after 1987 are released from the call up – *la chiamata*). Conscripts currently comprise around 135,000 (50 per cent) of the total armed forces, which will drop from the current 270,000 to around 215,000. Young men called up for military service can choose to do alternative social services, which often involves working for charitable organisations run by the Roman Catholic Church (not surprisingly, the church is opposed to the ending of conscription). Women have recently been accepted in the armed forces and can also train as front-line airforce pilots, but are still excluded from serving on submarines and in the *Carabinieri*.

PETS

If you plan to take a pet (*animale domestico*) to Italy, it's important to check the latest regulations. Make sure that you have the correct papers, not only for Italy, but for all the countries you will pass through. Particular consideration must be given before exporting a pet from a country with strict quarantine regulations, such as Britain. If you need to return prematurely, even after a few hours or days, your pet must go into quarantine, e.g. for six months in Britain. However, on 28th March 2000, Britain introduced a pilot 'Pet Travel Scheme (PETS)', which has replaced quarantine for qualifying cats and dogs. Under the scheme, pets must be micro-chipped (they have a micro-chip inserted in their neck), vaccinated against rabies, undergo a blood test and be issued with a 'health certificate' ('passport'). **Note that the PETS certificate isn't issued until six**

months *after* the above have been carried out! Pets must also be checked for ticks and tapeworm 24 to 48 hours before embarkation on a plane or ship.

The scheme is restricted to animals imported from rabies-free countries and countries where rabies is under control – 22 European countries plus Bahrain, Canada and the USA. However, the current quarantine law will remain in place for pets coming from Eastern Europe, Africa (including the Spanish enclaves of Ceuta and Melilla), Asia and South America. The new regulations cost pet owners around £200 (for a micro-chip, rabies vaccination and blood test), plus £60 per year for annual booster vaccinations and around £20 for a border check. Shop around and compare fees from a number of veterinary surgeons. To qualify, pets must travel by sea via Dover, Plymouth or Portsmouth, by train via the Channel Tunnel or via Gatwick or Heathrow airports (only certain carriers are licensed to carry animals). Additional information is available from the Department of the Environment, Food and Rural Affairs (DEFRA, formerly the MAFF) by phone (☎ UK 0845-241 1710) or via email (✉ pets.helpline@ defra.gsi.gov.uk).

There's no quarantine for pets in Italy, but they need a health certificate issued by an approved veterinary surgeon. Dogs and cats need a rabies vaccination not less than 20 days or more than 11 months prior to the date of issue of the health certificate. Those aged under 12 weeks are exempt, but must have a health certificate and a certificate stating that no cases of rabies have occurred for at least six months in the local area. British owners must complete an *Application for a Ministry Export Certificate for Dogs, Cats and Rabies Susceptible Animals* (form EXA1), available from the Department of the Environment, Food and Rural Affairs (DEFRA), Animal Health (International Trade) Area 201, 1A Page Street, London SW1P 4PQ, UK (☎ 0870-241 1710). A health inspection must be performed by a licensed veterinary officer before you're issued with an export health certificate (bilingual, Italian-English) that's valid for 30 days. Animals may be examined at the Italian port of entry by a veterinary officer. If you're transporting a pet by ship or ferry, you should notify the shipping company. Some companies insist that pets are left in vehicles (if applicable), while others allow pets to be kept in cabins. If your pet is of nervous disposition or unused to travelling, it's best to tranquillise it on a long sea crossing. Pets can also be transported by air.

At the age of three months, a dog must be registered at the local 'dog bureau' (*anagrafe canina*) and some municipalities issue dog tags. Italian regulations require dogs to be tattooed on their body (not just their ear) as a means of registration, although a new micro-chip identification system is being introduced and will eventually replace tattooing. Tattooing must be done by a veterinary surgeon (*veterinari*) or the local health authority (*unita santaria locale*), who do it for free. Dogs and cats don't need to wear identification discs in Italy and there's no system of licensing (a dog tax was abolished because most people claimed their dogs were working animals and refused to pay it). However, it's recommended to fit your dog with a collar and a tag containing your name, address and telephone number. Lost dogs are taken to the local pound and unidentified dogs may be put down if the owner cannot be found. All dogs must be kept on a leash and muzzled (if dangerous) when in a public area in towns or on public transport, but not in the country. You must usually pay full fare on public transport for a dog that isn't carried and in some towns large dogs may be prohibited altogether from travelling on public transport.

If you intend to live permanently in Italy, dogs should also be vaccinated against certain other diseases such as hepatitis, distemper and kennel cough, and cats immunised against feline gastro-enteritis and typhus. Pets should also be checked frequently for ticks and tapeworm. **There are a number of diseases and dangers for pets in Italy that aren't found in most other European countries, including the fatal *leishmaniasis* (also called Mediterranean or sandfly disease), which can be prevented by using a spray such as DefendDog.** Obtain advice about this and other diseases from a veterinary surgeon (*veterinario*) on arrival in Italy. Take extra care when walking your dog, as some have died after eating poisoned food, which is sometimes laid by hunters to control natural predators. Don't let your dog far out of your sight or let it roam free, as dogs are often stolen or mistakenly shot by hunters.

Health insurance for pets is available from a number of insurance companies (vets fees are high in Italy) and it's wise to have third party insurance in case your pet bites someone or causes an accident. In areas where there are poisonous snakes, some owners keep anti-venom in their refrigerator (which must be changed annually). Although not exactly a nation of animal lovers, pets are rarely restricted or banned from long-term rental or holiday accommodation (but check when renting an apartment).

The unpleasant aspect of Italy's dog population is abundantly evident on the streets of Italian towns and cities, where dogs routinely leave their 'calling cards'. **You must always watch where you walk.** Most dog owners don't take their pets on long country walks, but just to a local park or car park or simply let them loose in the streets to do their business. Poop-scoops must be used in some cities and towns, where you can be fined around €30 for not cleaning up after your dog, although most people ignore this law. Although it's of little consolation, it's supposedly good luck to tread in something unpleasant!

The Ente Nazionale per la Protezione degli Animali (national association for the protection of animals) is the main organisation for animal welfare in Italy and it operates shelters for stray and abused animals, and inexpensive pet hospitals in many cities.

POLICE

There are various police (*polizia*) forces in Italy, most of which are armed (some even brandish machine guns). All police come under the Ministry of the Interior, apart from the *Carabinieri*, which come under the Ministry of Defence in certain matters. A 1981 reform was supposed to merge the two branches, although nothing came of it and there's still considerable duplication of their roles. Both forces are responsible for public order and security, and you can contact either to report a crime; dial 112 (non-emergencies) or 113 (emergencies) for police assistance.

The *Carabinieri* are a special branch of the army (numbering around 115,000), with similar functions to the police, particularly concerning criminal investigation. They deal with national and serious crime, including the Mafia and organised crime, and are Italy's most efficient and professional police force. *Carabinieri* officers are distinguished by their dark blue uniforms with a red stripe down the side of the trousers and white shoulder belts; they also have splendid ceremonial uniforms with long cloaks and Napoleonic hats. They're housed in barracks (*caserma*) in all major towns and cities, drive navy blue cars and also employ helicopters, aircraft and speed boats, and are the best-funded of Italy's police forces. You should report a theft to the *Carabinieri* or the *Polizia di Stato*.

The *Polizia di Stato* or *Polizia Statale* is a national or state police force, with special branches responsible for the security of main roads (*Polizia Stradale*), the rail system (*Polizia Ferroviaria*) and airports (*Polizia Aereoportuale*). Officers wear light blue trousers with a thin purple stripe and a dark blue jacket. They have stations (*questura* or a *commissariati* in smaller towns) in all main towns and cities, and drive light-blue cars with a white stripe and *Polizia* written on the side. If you want to report a theft or obtain a resident permit, you should go to the *Polizia* (*Ufficio Stranieri* for the latter).

The *Vigili Urbani* are municipal (*comune*) or local police, who deal mainly with local traffic control and municipal administration, and consequently aren't very popular (not that any police are popular). Officers wear white helmets and dress in black in winter and blue in summer, drive black and white cars and also use motorcycles and bicycles. Some municipal police speak foreign languages, shown by a badge on their uniforms. Attempts have been made to amalgamate the *Vigili* with the public security police, but the municipalities have resisted such proposals.

The *Guardia di Finanza* (numbering around 65,000) is responsible for enforcing the regulations regarding national and international financial dealings, including counterfeiting, fraud, tax evasion, smuggling and illegal entry. They're particularly active at border crossings, airports and ports, where they operate fast powerboats to apprehend smugglers. Officers wear grey/green uniforms with an insignia of yellow flames on the shoulders (hence their nickname of *fiamme gialle*). Although it's highly unlikely, you could be stopped by an officer of the *Guardi di Finanza* if you leave a shop without a receipt for a purchase.

The *Guardia di Pubblica Sicurezza* (public security guards) is a force of around 80,000 charged with the maintenance of internal public security and order, with the protection of life and property, and with preventing and checking crime and gathering evidence in criminal matters. Although the force is of a semi-military character, it performs all normal police functions and is responsible to the minister of the interior.

POPULATION

The population of Italy is around 58 million, or about the same as Britain and France, with a population density of almost 200 inhabitants per km² (around 500 people per mi²), which makes Italy the fifth most densely populated country in Europe, after the Benelux countries and the UK. This figure, however, doesn't necessarily reveal the distribution of population and of the 96 provinces, only some 40 have a density higher than the national average, with around 70 per cent of the population inhabiting a surface area equal to just one-third of the country. Around two-thirds of the population live in cities.

From antiquity, Mediterranean peoples had highly developed urban centres. For historical as well as geographic reasons, Italy has never been dominated by one city, each region tending to have its own urban centre. Today, there are four cities with a population of over one million (Rome, Milan, Naples and Turin), but many cities have a population of over 100,000. Of these, almost half are on or near the sea; a similar proportion are in the north and the rest are in the centre, south, Sicily and Sardinia. A number of cities have, with increased population and industrialisation, merged with neighbouring cities into enormous metropolitan complexes, sometimes characterised as mega-cities, such as that surrounding Milan. There are now several metropolitan areas, including Milan, Naples, Rome, Turin, Genoa, Florence, Palermo and Bologna.

The most heavily-populated cities and areas include Rome, Milan and Naples (Portici, a suburb of Naples, is one of the most densely populated areas of the world), Liguria, Piedmont and parts of Lombardy, the Veneto and Friuli-Venezia-Giuila. In contrast, many areas, not necessarily mountainous or difficult to reach, are under-populated. The rural population, which at the beginning of World War II accounted for practically half the country's population, has been gradually declining with the massive increase in urbanisation and drift from the countryside. The largest cities include Rome 2.7 million, Milan 1.3 million, Naples 1.1 million, Turin 1 million, Palermo 700,000, Genoa 700,000, Bologna 400,000, Florence 400,000, Bari 350,000, Catania 350,000, Venice 300,000, Messina 250,000 and Verona 250,000. Due to Italy's low birth-rate, at around 9 births per 1,000 population (roughly the same as the death rate) and relatively low immigration, population growth is practically zero (due in part to Italy's prosperous condom industry, despite the Catholic church's ban on non-natural birth control.)

In general, the birth rate and average family size are higher in the south of Italy than in the north, although populations in Molise, Basilicata and Calabria are declining through continued emigration. The mortality rate is slightly lower in the south than in the north, as a result of improved medical care and a younger population; in certain northern regions, especially Liguria, populations are beginning to decrease because the birth rate is falling faster than the mortality rate. As regards the country as a whole, life expectancy has risen during the second half of the 20th century, reflecting higher nutritional, sanitary and medical standards. The majority of the population are between 20 and 70 years old, with decreasing numbers below age ten and increasing numbers aged over 75, especially women.

Traditionally, Italy has been a land of emigration, as witnessed by the massive flows of Italians to North and South America (mainly to the US, Argentina, Uruguay and Brazil) during the 19th and 20th centuries. Between 1875 and 1925, a total of some ten million Italians left the country (around half eventually returned). There were further mass emigrations to Australia, Belgium, France, Germany, Great Britain and Switzerland after the second world war. In this second wave, a total of some 8 million people emigrated, of whom roughly half have returned. At the same time, especially in the 1950s and 1960s, there was a wholesale population movement from the southern and north-eastern regions to the north-west, where industry was actively expanding.

In recent years, Italy's rapid economic growth has attracted many immigrants to the country, mainly from North and sub-Saharan Africa, but also from the Philippines, China, South America and most recently from Albania and the former Yugoslavia. There are over 1.5 million registered immigrants (*extracomunitari*) in Italy, plus many more living illegally. Illegal immigration has led to tougher immigration rules and a more forceful programme of expulsion.

RELIGION

Italy is a Christian country with some 98 per cent of the population belonging to the Roman Catholic church and less than 1 per cent Protestant. The majority of the world's religious and philosophical movements have churches or meeting places in the major cities and resort areas, including English (e.g. Anglican) and American churches. Other religious groups in Italy include around 1.3 million Muslims, 500,000 evangelical Protestants, 150,000 Jehovah's Witnesses, 40,000 Jews, and the Waldensian Evangelical Church and other small groups such as Swiss-Protestant Baptists in Piedmont, plus a number of Eastern Orthodox Albanian communities in the *Mezzogiorno*. The right to freedom of worship is guaranteed under the Italian constitution, although some extreme sects are prohibited and the rising number of Muslims is causing concern to some in the Catholic church. **When visiting a house of worship in Italy, you should avoid wearing shorts and women shouldn't wear short skirts or skimpy tops, although you're rarely refused entry or asked to leave (except at St. Peter's in Rome, where women must cover their shoulders).**

Italy has a unique religious heritage and 2,000 years of Christianity has permeated every facet of Italian life. The Vatican City (116 acres/47 hectares, population around 900) was established in 1929 and is a self-contained sovereign state (the world's smallest) within the city of Rome. The Vatican is the home of the government of the Roman Catholic Church and of the Pope (*il Papa* or *Supreme Pontiff*), the spiritual leader of the world's Roman Catholics. As well as its own peacekeeping force, the Swiss Guard, the Vatican has its own post office, newspaper and radio and TV stations. It also mints its own coins (with the Pope's face) and issues its own stamps.

The Catholic faith enjoys particular privileges, partly by virtue of a historical tradition that has seen the Church of Rome as a constant in government and the organisation of public life. There have traditionally been close relations between the state and the Catholic Church, which remains at the centre of Italian society and political power. However, a concordat signed in 1984 ended the church's position as the state religion, abolished compulsory religious teaching in public schools and reduced state financial contributions to the church. Every town or village has at least one Catholic church and over 95 per cent of Italians are baptised in the Catholic church, although only around a quarter regularly attend mass. However, saints' days, first communions and religious festivals remain popular and the majority of Italians prefer to be married in church. Children usually take their first communion when they're eight or nine years old, usually in April or May, which is an important date in their lives, when they become full members of the Catholic church.

SOCIAL CUSTOMS

All countries have their own particular social customs and Italy is no exception. As a foreigner you will probably be excused if you accidentally insult your host, but you may not be invited again. Note that Italians are much more formal than most foreigners imagine and newcomers should tread carefully to avoid offending anyone.

- When you're introduced to an Italian, you should say good day (*buongiorno*) and shake hands (a single pump is enough). Hello (*ciao!*) is used among close friends and young people, but it isn't considered polite when addressing strangers unless they use it first. Women may find that some men kiss their hand (*baciamano*), although this is rarer nowadays. When being formally introduced to someone the common response is pleased to meet you (*molto lieto*). When saying goodbye, it's a formal custom to shake hands again. It's also customary to say good day or good evening on entering a small shop, waiting room or lift, and good day or goodbye (*arriverderci* or *arrivederla* when formally addressing only one person) on leaving (friends say *ciao!* or cheerio/bye!). *Buongiorno* becomes *buonasera* any time after the lunch break (around 1pm), although if you choose *buonasera* (or *buongiorno*), don't be surprised if the response isn't the same. Good night (*buonanotte*) is used when going to bed or leaving a house in the evening.

- Titles should generally be used when addressing or writing to people, particularly when the holder is elderly. *Dottore* is usually used when addressing anyone with a university degree (*dottoressa* if it's a woman) and employees may refer to their boss as director (*direttore*) or *presidente*. Professionals should be addressed by their titles such as professor (*professore*), doctor (*dottore*), engineer (*ingegnere*), lawyer (*avvocato*), architect (*architetto*) and for the parking attendant (*capo*). If you don't know someone's title, you can use *signore* (men) or *signora* (women) – a young woman may be addressed as *signorina*, although nowadays all women tend to be addressed as *signora*.

- Italian families and close friends usually kiss (*bacio*) when they meet, irrespective of their sex. If a lady expects you to kiss her, she offers her cheek. Between members of the opposite sex the 'kiss' is deposited high up on the cheek, never on the mouth (except between lovers!) and isn't usually really a kiss, more a delicate brushing of the cheeks. There are usually two kisses commencing with the right cheek. It's also common in Italy for male relatives and close male friends to embrace each other.

- When talking to a stranger, particularly older Italians, you should use the formal form of address (*lei*). Don't use the familiar form (*tu*) or call someone by their Christian name until you're invited to do so. Generally the older or more important person invites the other to use the familiar *tu* form of address and first names. The familiar form is used with children, animals and God, but almost never with your elders or work superiors. However, Italians are becoming less formal and younger people often use *tu* and first names with colleagues, unless they're of the opposite sex, when *tu* may imply a special intimacy! It's customary to use *lei* in conversations with shopkeepers, servants, business associates and figures of authority (the local mayor) or those with whom you have a business relationship, e.g. your bank manager, tax officials and policemen.

- If you're invited to dinner by a Italian family (a rare and honoured occasion), you should take along a small present of flowers, pastries or chocolates. Gifts of foreign food or drink aren't generally well received unless they're highly prized in Italy such as malt whisky. Some people say you must never take wine, although this obviously depends on your hosts and how well you know them. If you do bring wine, it's unlikely to be served at a meal, as the wine will have already been chosen. Flowers can be tricky, as some people associate them with certain things (e.g. chrysanthemums for cemeteries). It's common for Italians to send a small note or gift the following day to thank people for their hospitality or kindness.

- Italians say good appetite (*buon appetito!*) before starting a meal. If you're offered a glass of wine, wait until your host has made a toast (*salute!*) before taking a drink. If you aren't offered a (another) drink, it's time to go home. You should, however, go easy on the wine and other alcohol, as if you drink to excess you're unlikely to be invited back! It's common in Italy to invite people to come after dinner (*dopo cena*), e.g. from 9.30pm, for dessert and wine.

Italians dress well and, like the French, seem to have an inborn sense of elegance and style. Presentation and impression are all important to Italians and are referred to as *bella presenza* or *bella figura* (literally 'cutting a beautiful figure'). They generally dress well and appropriately all the time, and tend to be more formal in their dress habits than most northern Europeans and North Americans. However, although they rarely loaf around in shorts or jog pants, they also tend not to go to the other extreme of tuxedos and evening gowns. Italians judge people by their dress, the style and quality being as important as the correctness for the occasion. Italians consider bathing costumes, skimpy tops and flip-flops or sandals with no socks strictly for the beach or swimming pool, and not, for example, the streets, restaurants or shops (although foreigners and their 'eccentric' behaviour are tolerated). They also choose the occasions when they wear jeans carefully, which aren't thought appropriate for a classy restaurant or church (if they aren't the latest designer fashion).

Bella figura refers not only to the way you look, but also to the way you act and what you say. It's similar in some ways to the oriental 'face' and Italians must look good and be seen in the correct light, always appearing to be in control and not show ignorance or be lacking in anything. It's important for foreigners not to show disrespect or ridicule an Italian, even if it means biting your tongue on occasions. (Italians believe that many foreigners are shameless in the way they dress and act in public and have no self respect.)

- You should introduce yourself before asking to speak to someone on the telephone. Although the traditional siesta is facing a battle for survival, it isn't recommended to telephone between the siesta hours (e.g. 2 to 4pm) when many people have a nap (*pisolino*). If you call between these times, it's polite to apologise for disturbing the household if you know people in the household are likely to have a siesta.

- If you have a business appointment with an Italian, he will expect you to be on time, although he will invariably be five or ten minutes late. However, if **you're** going to be more than five minutes late, it's wise to telephone and apologise. Italians usually exchange business cards (*biglietti de visita*) on business and social occasions.

TIME DIFFERENCE

Like most of the continent of Europe, Italy is on Central European Time (CET). This is Greenwich Mean Time (GMT) plus one hour from the last Sunday in October until the last Sunday in March, and GMT plus two hours during daylight saving from the last Sunday in March to the last Sunday in October. Time changes are announced in local newspapers and on radio and TV. The time is given on the telephone 'speaking clock' service number (see your local phone book) and shown on a TV (by pressing the 'time' button). When making international telephone calls or travelling long-distance by air, check the local time difference, which is shown in phone books.

Times, for example, in timetables, are usually written using the 24-hour clock, when 10am is written as 1000 and 10pm as 2200. Midday (*mezzogiorno*) is 1200 and midnight (*mezzanotte*) is 2400. When writing times, Italians put a comma between hours and minutes, e.g. 9,00 is 9am and 21,00 is 9pm. The international time difference in winter (October to March) between Rome at noon (1200) and some major international cities is shown below:

ROME	LONDON	JO'BURG	SYDNEY	AUCKLAND	NEW YORK
1200	1100	1300	2100	2300	0600

TIPPING

Italians aren't large tippers, although it's common practice to round up the bill to an even sum or say 'keep the change' (*tenga il resto*). Hotel, restaurant and café bills usually include a 15 per cent cover (*coperta*) and service (*servizio*) charge plus *IVA* (10 per cent or 20 per cent in top class restaurants), usually shown on the bill as 'all inclusive' (*tutto compreso*) if they're included in the price shown. When it isn't indicated on the menu, most people assume that service is included, although *IVA* isn't always included on menus. Even when service isn't included, Italians rarely leave large tips (*mancia*), although it's customary to leave a few small coins when having a drink standing at a bar. When paying by credit card, a tip is usually left in cash rather than added to the credit card payment. Tips aren't usually left in establishments where you pay at a cash register rather than at the table, or in family-run restaurants where you're a regular customer. The main exception to the tipping rule is in expensive or fashionable establishments, where 'tips' may be given to secure a table (or guarantee a table in future). Many foreigners follow international practice and tip as they would in other countries, e.g. 10 to 15 per cent.

It isn't usual to tip all and sundry, and many people don't tip taxi drivers, porters, hotel staff, car park attendants, cloakroom staff, shoeshine boys and cinema ushers, although you can give a small tip if you wish or, in the case of taxis, round up the fare to the next euro. If someone expects (or hopes for) a tip, often a little basket is provided. Attendants at public toilets usually have set fees (see below). It's isn't customary to tip a petrol station attendant for cleaning your windscreen or checking your oil. Hairdressers or the girl who washes your hair usually receives a tip of around €5. It isn't necessary to tip a porter who charges a fixed price per piece of luggage. An apartment block concierge or porter (*portiere*) usually receives a substantial tip at Christmas, e.g. €25 to €50, depending on how helpful he has been and how much you have used his services. He may also receive tips at other times for special jobs. Postmen aren't tipped in Italy.

If you're unsure whether you should tip someone, ask your Italian neighbours, friends or colleagues for advice – who will probably all tell you something different! Large tips are considered ostentatious and in bad taste (except by the recipient, who will be your friend for life).

TOILETS

Public toilets vary considerably in their age and facilities, and in addition to some of the world's best, Italy also has some of the worst (Italian toilets aren't know for their cleanliness). Toilets may be labelled with a symbol of a man or woman or with the letters WC. Sometimes the wording may be in Italian, e.g. *signori* (men) or *signore* (women) – watch that final letter! – or *uomini* (men) or *donne* (women). If you need to ask where a toilet is, you say *Dov'e' la toilette?*

Public toilets are few and far between, although there are toilets in bars, cafés, restaurants, hotels, department stores, large supermarkets, shopping centres, railway and bus stations, museums and places of interest, on beaches and near markets. The most accessible bathrooms are those found in bars and restaurants, although you shouldn't expect to find toilet paper at most of them (it's recommended to carry some tissues with you). **Some bars (particularly in Rome) charge customers around a euro to use their toilets!** Public toilets are almost unknown outside of bus and railway stations, although major tourist sites have the most modern facilities, where there's usually an attendant who may dispense paper (*carta*) and expects a tip of around €0.50. You may also need to pay extra to use a WC. There are modern coin-operated public toilets with soap, hot water, towels and air-conditioning in some cities and resort areas.

If a building has a septic tank (*fossa settica*), certain items must never be flushed down the toilet, including sanitary towels, paper (other than toilet paper), disposable nappies, condoms or anything made of plastic. You should also never use standard bleaches, disinfectants and chemical cleaners in systems with septic tanks (special brands are available for septic tanks), as they can have a disastrous affect on its operation and create nasty smells.

In private residences, Americans should ask for the toilet (*toilette*) and not the bathroom (*stanza da bagno*), as the toilet is often separate from the bathroom. Most Italian bathrooms have a bidet (*bidé*) in addition to a toilet bowl, which are for 'intimate ablutions' and are also used for washing feet.

19.

THE ITALIANS

Who are the Italians? What are they like? Let's take a candid and prejudiced look at them, tongue firmly in cheek, and hope they forgive my flippancy or that they don't read this bit (which is why it's hidden at the back of the book).

The typical Italian is courteous, proud, undisciplined, tardy, temperamental, independent, gregarious, noble, individualistic, boisterous, jealous, possessive, colourful, passionate, spontaneous, sympathetic, fun-loving, creative, sociable, demonstrative, irritating, charming, aggressive, self-important, generous, cheerful, cultured, polite, unreliable, honourable, outgoing, impetuous, flamboyant, idiosyncratic, quick-tempered, artistic, a gourmet, ungovernable, elegant, irresponsible, hedonistic, lazy and industrious, contradictory, an anarchist, informal, self-opinionated, corrupt, indolent, flexible, patriarchal, frustrating, inventive, sensual, practical, irresistible, impatient, scheming, voluble, friendly, sexist, musical, sensitive, humorous, garrulous, petulant, macho, noisy, happy, fiery, warm-hearted, a suicidal driver, decadent, religious, chauvinistic, an excellent cook, stylish, bureaucratic, dignified, kind, loyal, a fashion victim, extroverted, tolerant, self-possessed, a tax dodger, unabashed, quarrelsome, partisan, a procrastinator, scandal-loving, articulate, a *bon viveur*, conservative, nocturnal, hospitable, spirited, urbanised, confident, sophisticated, political, handsome and a football fanatic.

You may have noticed that the above list contains 'a few' contradictions (as does life in Italy), which is hardly surprising as there's no such thing as a typical Italian. Apart from the differences in character between the inhabitants of different regions such as Campania (Naples), Lazio (Rome), Lombardy (Milan), Sardinia and Sicily, the population also includes a potpourri of foreigners from all corners of the globe. Even in appearance, fewer and fewer Italians match the popular image of short, dark and slim, and the indigenous population includes blondes, brunettes and redheads.

Italy became a unified state only in 1861 and most people have more loyalty to their town, province or region than to Italy as a whole, considering themselves Florentines, Milanese, Neapolitans, Romans or Sicilians first and Italians a distant second, summed up by the word *campanilismo* – literally 'loyalty to your bell-tower'. There's long been a north-south divide (gulf), the more conservative northerners dismissing the less inhibited southerners as lazy, lawless, cunning, corrupt and primitive peasants, while southerners consider northerners to be serious, industrious and money-grabbing foreigners who got rich from exploitation. One of the few things that unites Italians (usually in despair) is the national football team.

Compared with most other European countries of a comparable size, Italy attracted relatively few immigrants in the 20th century (the massive industrial expansion in the north was achieved by the migration of workers from the south) and the country is still trying to come to terms with the huge influx of refugees and immigrants in recent years. Nevertheless, Italians generally live in harmony with their foreign population (*stranieri*) and are among the most tolerant Europeans (particularly when it comes to free-spending tourists).

When Italians and foreigners come into contact, it often results in a profusion of misunderstandings (few foreigners can fathom the Italian psyche), which does little to cement good relations. Italy has the most stifling (and over-staffed) bureaucracy in western Europe (even worse than France and Spain) and any encounter with officialdom is a test of endurance and patience. Government offices (if you can find the right one) often open for only a few hours on certain days of the week, the person dealing with your case is always absent, you never have the right papers (or your file has been lost), the rules and regulations have changed (again), and queues are interminable (take along a copy of Dante's *Inferno* to help pass the time). It's all part of a conspiracy to ensure that foreigners cannot find out what's going on and therefore pay more taxes, fees and fines (or preferably go home).

Official inefficiency has been honed to a fine art in Italy, where even paying a bill or using the postal service (a truly world-class example of ineptitude) is an ordeal. Italians are generally totally disorganised (summed up by the word *casino*, which roughly translates as a shambles but also means a brothel!) and the only predictable thing about them is their unpredictability. They seldom plan anything (if they do, the plans will be changed or abandoned at the last moment), as one of the unwritten 'rules' of Italian life is spontaneity. Don't expect workmen to arrive on time (or at all) – when they do finally turn up they probably won't have the right tools or spares anyway – or jobs to be finished on schedule. Italians are dismissive of time constraints and have no sense of urgency, treating appointments, dates, opening hours, timetables and deadlines with scorn (about the only events which start on time are football matches). Don't plan on doing anything at all in August, when the whole country goes on holiday and all business (apart from tourism) comes to a grinding halt.

Italy is infamous for its corruption (not to mention the *Mafia*), which pervades all levels of society, from the government to the humblest peasant. Tax evasion is **the** national sport and you certainly don't need to be engaged in the hidden economy to be part of it – the 'black' list includes many of Italy's richest and most famous people. In 1985 a bill was introduced to curtail tax evasion among the self-employed, which led to a national strike! Fines are always negotiable, particularly if you argue loud and long enough, as is your tax bill if you know someone who works in the tax office. Bribery (*la bustarella*) is part and parcel of everyday life and everything and every Italian has a price: if you have enough money or contacts you can get anything done; without either, it can take aeons to accomplish even the simplest task. **There's one law for Italians and another for foreigners – particularly foreigners who don't speak Italian.**

Most Italians are anarchists; they generally do what they want when they want, particularly regarding motoring (especially parking), smoking in public places (a 'no-smoking' sign is usually seen as a good reason to light up) and building. Italians (and, it seems, Italian officials) make up their own laws and choose those they wish to obey 'a la carte' (all EU directives are totally ignored). If it wasn't for the large fines for often minor offences, Italians would happily ignore most laws. Most Italians rely on instinct rather than morals or laws!

Italians are unbridled hedonists and are mainly interested in food, football, sex, alcohol and gambling (especially the men). The main preoccupation of Italians is having a good time and they have a zest for life matched in few other countries. They take childish pleasure in making the most of everything, grasping every opportunity to party, and are at their most energetic when making merry. They're inveterate 'celebrators' and when not attending a feast (*festa*), family celebration or impromptu party, they're to be found in bars and restaurants indulging in one of their favourite pastimes – eating and drinking.

Italians have a passion for food, which consists largely of pasta, pasta and pasta, with lashings of tomatoes, garlic and olive oil. They're committed carnivores and eat anything that walks, runs, crawls, swims or flies – particularly Italy's fast-disappearing wildlife. Like other southern Europeans, they eat most of the objectionable bits that other people throw away, including feet, ears, tails, brains, entrails and reproductive organs (Italians could never be called squeamish). Family celebrations routinely last from dawn to dusk, with a constant stream of food and wine – if eating was an Olympic event, the rest of the world needn't bother to turn up! Italians also know a thing or two about drinking, washing down their food with prodigious amounts of wine, and they're the world's largest consumers of whisky.

When not eating and drinking (or singing or watching football), Italians are allegedly making love. Italian men have a reputation as great lovers, although their virility isn't supported by the birth rate, which is one the lowest in Europe. Italian women are beautiful (at least until they marry), although what they see in greasy, crooning, smooth-talking, mummy's boys who only come up to their knees is anyone's guess. The macho image of Italian men has taken a pounding in recent years, as women have stormed most male bastions and today are just as likely to be found in the university, office, factory, professions and the government, as in the home or the church.

Italian men are car fanatics and worship all things automotive (particularly if they're red and made in Modena); they have a passionate and enduring love affair with their cars, which are more important to them than their homes, wives and children. Many Italians are loath to forsake their cars under any circumstances and would rather endure endless traffic jams than resort to public transport. In fact, Italians rarely drive anywhere these days; when they aren't in a traffic jam talking on their mobile phones, they're looking for a parking space. Cars aren't for driving in Italy, but for posing – nothing is guaranteed to draw a crowd in Italy quicker than a blood-red Ferrari or even an exotic foreign machine, provided it looks as if it can do a million kilometres per hour. Italians are among the most ill-disciplined drivers in the world and their frenetic, aggressive driving style is enough to intimidate all but the most battle-hardened motorists. The only way a foreign driver can survive is to drive like an Italian, which means ignoring all signs and road markings, parking restrictions, speed limits and traffic lights, and driving everywhere with their foot to the floor and one hand on the horn.

Enough of this frivolity, let's get down to serious business. Italy is one of the most politically unstable countries in the EU, although this amazingly seems to have little outward effect on the country's economy. There have been numerous changes of government since the second world war (Italy changes its government as often as some people change their socks), largely due to the country's system of proportional representation, which almost guarantees shaky coalition governments (an attempt at electoral reform in recent years doesn't appear to have had much effect). Italians have no time for politicians (who they blame for all their ills), whose public standing has sunk to record lows in the last decade following a succession of scandals, including fraud and involvement in organised crime. Not surprisingly, Italians are the most passionate Europeans and firmly believe in a united Europe and a single currency (so would you if you'd had the lire!).

Among the biggest concerns facing Italians are unemployment, drug addiction, asylum seekers, refugees and illegal aliens, the environment and pollution, pensions, health care, property crime, housing costs and the widening gulf in prosperity between the north and south. However, by far the biggest challenge facing Italy's leaders is how to reform the economy (e.g. debt-ridden public companies and a huge social security deficit) without provoking a revolution.

Despite the country's problems, Italians enjoy one of the best lifestyles and quality of life of any European country, or indeed, any country in the world. The foundation of its society is the family (particularly the mother) and community; Italians are noted for their close family ties, their love of children and care for the elderly, who aren't dumped in nursing homes. In Italy, work fits around social and family life, not vice versa. The real glory of Italy lies in the outsize heart and soul of its people, who are among the most convivial, generous and hospitable in the world. Italy is celebrated for its simple, relaxed way of life, warm personal relationships and time for others, lack of violent crime (excluding gang warfare), good manners and spontaneity – Italians are never slow to break into song or dance when the mood strikes them. For sheer vitality and passion for life, Italians have few equals and, whatever Italy can be accused of, it's **never** plain or boring. Few other countries offer such a wealth of intoxicating experiences for the mind, body and spirit (and not all out of a bottle!). Italy is highly addictive and, while foreigners may complain about the bureaucrats or government, the vast majority wouldn't dream of leaving and infinitely prefer life in Italy to their home countries. **Put simply, Italy is a great place to live (provided you don't need to do business there) and raise a family.**

If you're willing to learn Italian (or at least make an effort) and embrace Italy's traditions and way of life, you're invariably warmly received by the natives, who go out of their way to welcome and help you. Above all, you need to accept Italy as it is, warts and all (life is so much better when you stop banging your head against the wall), and just lie back and enjoy *la dolce vita*.

Viva Italia! **Long live Italy!**

20.

MOVING HOUSE OR
LEAVING ITALY

When moving house or leaving Italy, there are numerous things to be considered and a 'million' people to inform. The checklists contained in this chapter make the task easier and may even help prevent an ulcer or nervous breakdown – provided of course you don't leave everything to the last minute.

MOVING HOUSE

When moving house **within** Italy the following items should be considered:

- If you're renting accommodation, you must give your landlord notice as per your rental contract (see page 105) and have your deposit refunded. Your notice letter should be sent by registered post (*certificado*).

- Inform the following, as applicable:
  - Your employer;
  - Your present town hall and the town hall in your new municipality;
  - Your social security and income tax offices;
  - If you have an Italian registered car or driving licence and are remaining in the same province, you should return your licence and registration document, and have the address changed (see **Chapter 11**). If you're moving to a new province you should inform both your current and new provinces;
  - Your electricity, gas, telephone and water companies;
  - Your insurance companies (e.g. health, car, household, third party liability, etc.), hire purchase companies, lawyer, accountant, and local businesses where you have accounts. Take out new insurance, if applicable;
  - Your banks and other financial institutions such as stockbrokers and credit card companies. Make arrangements for a transfer of funds and the cancellation or alteration of standing orders or direct debits;
  - Your family doctor, dentist and other health practitioners. Health records should be transferred to your new practitioners;
  - Your family's schools. If applicable, arrange for schooling in your new community (see **Chapter 9**). Try to give a term's notice and obtain copies of any relevant school reports and records from current schools;
  - All regular correspondents, subscriptions, social and sports clubs, professional and trade journals, and friends and relatives. Arrange to have your post redirected;
  - Your local consulate or embassy if you're registered with them (see page 92).

- Return any library books or anything borrowed.

- Arrange removal of your furniture and belongings, or rent transportation if you're doing your own removal.

- Ask yourself (again): 'Is it really worth all this trouble?'.

LEAVING ITALY

Before leaving Italy for an indefinite period, the following items should be considered **in addition** to those listed above under **Moving House:**

- Check that your family's passports are valid!
- Give notice to your employer, if applicable.
- Check whether any special entry requirements are necessary for your country of destination, e.g. visas, permits or inoculations, by contacting the embassy or consulate in Italy. **An exit permit or visa isn't required to leave Italy.**
- You may qualify for a rebate on your income tax and social security payments.
- Arrange to sell anything you aren't taking with you (house, car, furniture, etc.) and to ship your belongings. Find out the procedure for shipping your belongings to your country of destination (see page 108). Check with the local embassy or consulate of the country to which you're moving. Special forms may need to be completed before arrival. If you've been living in Italy for less than two years, you're required to re-export all personal effects imported duty-free from outside the EU, including furniture and vehicles (if you sell them you may be required to pay duty).
- If you have an Italian registered car that you intend to take with you, you will need to have it re-registered in your new country of residence and inform the Italian authorities.
- Pets may require special inoculations or may need to go into quarantine for a period (see page 419), depending on your destination.
- Arrange health, travel and other insurance (see **Chapter 13**).
- Depending on your destination, you may wish to arrange health and dental check-ups before leaving Italy. Obtain a copy of your health and dental records.
- Terminate any loans, lease or hire purchase contracts, and pay all outstanding bills (allow plenty of time as some companies are slow to respond).
- You may be entitled to a rebate on your road tax, car and other insurance. Obtain a letter from your insurance company stating your no-claims bonus.
- Make arrangements to sell or let your house or apartment and other property in Italy.
- Check whether you need an international driving licence or a translation of your Italian or foreign driving licence for your country of destination.
- Give friends and business associates in Italy an address and telephone number where you can be contacted abroad.

Buon viaggio!

APPENDICES

APPENDIX A: USEFUL ADDRESSES

Embassies & Consulates

Foreign embassies in Italy are located in Rome; many countries also have consulates in other major cities. Note that business hours vary considerably and all embassies close on their national holidays and on Italy's public holidays. Always telephone to check the business hours before visiting. Selected embassies are listed below:

Albania: Via Asmara, 5, Rome (☎ 06-8621 4475).
Argentina: Piazza dell'Esquilino, 2, 00185 Rome (☎ 06-4742 551).
Australia: Via Alessandria, 215, 00198 Rome (☎ 06-8527 21).
Austria: Via G.B. Pergolesi, 3, 00198 Rome (☎ 06-8440 141).
Belgium: Via dei Monti Parioli, 49, 00197 Rome (☎ 06-3609 511).
Brazil: Piazza Navona, 14, 00186 Rome (☎ 06-6839 81).
Canada: Via GB de Rossi, 27, 00161 Rome (☎ 06-445 981).
Czech Republic: Via Colli Farnesina, 144, 00194 Rome (☎ 06-3296 711).
Denmark: Via dei Monti Parioli, 50, 00197 Rome (☎ 06-3200 441).
Finland: Via Lisbona, 3, 00198 Rome (☎ 06-852 231).
France: Piazza Farnese, 67, 00186 Rome (☎ 06-686 011).
Germany: Via San Martino della Bataglia, 4, 00185 Rome (☎ 06-492 131).
Greece: Via Mercadante, 36, 00198 Rome (☎ 06-8537 551).
Hungary: Via dei Villini, 12/16, 00161 Rome (☎ 06-4423 0567).
India: Via XX Settembre, 5, 00187 Rome (☎ 06-4884 642).
Ireland: Largo Nazareno, 3, 00187 Rome (☎ 06-6782 541).
Israel: Via Quintino Michele Mercati, 14, 00197 Rome (☎ 06-3619 8500).
Japan: Via Sella, 60, 00187 Rome (☎ 06-4879 91).
Netherlands: Via Michele Mercati, 8, 00197 Rome (☎ 06-3221 141).
Poland: Via PP Rubens, 20, 00197 Rome (☎ 06-3224 455).
Portugal: Via Pezzana, 9, 00197 Rome (☎ 06-8073 8 01).
Russia: Via Gaeta, 5, 00185 Rome (☎ 06-4941 649).
South Africa: Via Tanaro, 14/16, 00198 Rome (☎ 06-8525 41).
Spain: Via Garibaldi, 35, 00186 Rome (☎ 06-5800 144).

Switzerland: Via Barnaba Oriani, 61, 00197 Rome (☎ 06-8095 71).

United Kingdom: Via XX Settembre, 80/a, 00187 Rome (☎ 06-4220 0001).

United States of America: Via Vittorio Veneto, 119/A, 00187 Rome (☎ 06-4674 1).

British Provincial Consulates

Bari: Via Dalmazia, 127 (☎ 080-5543 668).

Cagliari: Viale Columbo, 160 (☎ 070-8286 28).

Catania: Via Verdi, 53 (☎ 095-7151 864).

Florence: Piazzo Castelbarco, Lungarno Corsini, 2 (☎ 055-2841 33).

Genoa: Via di Francia, 28 (☎ 010-4168 28).

Messina: Via Cadorna, 14 (☎ 090-6729 24).

Milan: Via San Paolo, 7 (☎ 02-7230 01).

Naples: Via dei Mille, 40 (☎ 081-4238 911).

Palermo: Via Cavour, 121 (☎ 091-3264 12).

Rome: Via XX Settembre, 80a (☎ 06-4220 0001).

Trieste: Via Dante Alighieri, 7 (☎ 040-3478 303).

Turin: Via Saluzzo, 60 (☎ 011-6509 202).

Venice: Accademia Dorsoduro, 1051 (☎ 041-5227 207).

Selected Italian Government Departments

Department of Institutional Reform (Dipartimento delle Riforme Istituzionali, Piazza Monte Citorio, 115, 00187 Rome, ☎ 06-6779 5938).

Department of Public Function (Dipartimento della Funzione Pubblica, Via del Sudano, 49, 00186 Rome, ☎ 06-6899 7366, 🖳 www.funpub.it).

Ministry of Politics, Agriculture and Foresty (Ministero delle Politiche, Agricole e Forestali, Via XX Settembre, 20, 00187 Rome, ☎ 06-4819 868, 🖳 www.politicheagricole.it).

Ministry of Communications (Ministero delle Comunicazioni, Viale America, 201, 00144 Rome, ☎ 06-5444 1, 🖳 www.comunicazioni.it).

Ministry of Cultural Heritage (Ministero per i Beni e le Attivita Culturali, Via del Collegio Romano, 27, 00186 Rome, ☎ 06-6723 1, 🖳 www.beniculturali.it).

Ministry of Education (Ministero dell'Istruzione, dell'Universita e della Ricerca, Viale Trastevere, 76/a, 00153 Rome, ☎ 06-5849 1, 🖳 www.istruzione.it).

Ministry of the Environment (Ministero dell'Ambiente e della Tutela del Territorio, Viale Cristoforo Colombo, 44, 00147 Rome, ☎ 06-5722 8509, 🖳 www.minambiente.it).

Ministry of Foreign Trade (Ministero del Attivita Produttive, Viale Boston, 25, 00144 Rome, ☎ 06-5993 1, 🖳 www.mincomes.it).

Ministry of Foreign Affairs (Ministero degli Affari Esteri, P della Farnesina, 1, 00194 Rome, ☎ 06-3691 1, 🖳 www.esteri.it).

Ministry of Health (Ministero della Salute), Lungotevere Ripa, 1, 00153 Rome, ☎ 06-5994 1, 🖳 www.ministerosalute.it).

Ministry of the Interior (Ministero dell'Interno, Palazzo Viminale, Via Agostino Depretis, 00184 Rome, ☎ 06-4651, 🖳 www.mininterno.it).

Ministry of Justice (Ministero della Grazia e Giustizia, Via Arenula, 70, 00186 Rome, ☎ 06-6885 1, 🖳 www.giustizia.it).

Ministry of Social Affairs (Ministero per la Solidarieta' Sociale, Via V Veneto, 56, 00187 Rome, ☎ 06-4816 11, 🖳 www.affarisociali.it).

Ministry of the Treasury (Ministero dell' Economia e della Finanza, Via XX Settembre, 97, 00187 Rome, ☎ 06-4761 1, 🖳 www.tesoro.it).

Ministry of Teaching, University and Research (Ministero dell' Istruzione, dell'Universita e della Ricerca, Via Trastevere, 76/A, 00153 Rome, ☎ 06-5849 1, 🖳 www.murst.it).

Prime Minister (Presidenza del Consiglio dei Ministri), Palazzo Chigi, Piazza Colonna, 370, 00187 Rome, ☎ 06-67791, 🖳 www.palaz zochigi.it).

Miscellaneous

American Chamber of Commerce in Italy, Via Contù 1, 20123 Milan (☎ 02-8690 661).

British Chamber of Commerce for Italy, Via Dante, 12, 20121 Milan (☎ 02-8777 98/8056 094, 🖳 www.britchamitaly.com).

Dante Alighieri Society, 4 Upper Tachbrook Street, London SW1X 8NX, UK (☎ 020-7828 9660).

European Commission, Information Centre, 8 Storey's Gate, London SW1P 3AT (☎ 020-7973 1992).

Federazione Italiana Lavoratori Emigranti e Famiglie, 96/98 Central Street, London EC1V 8AJ, UK (☎ 020-7608 0125).

Italian Chamber of Commerce and Industry, 1 Princes Street, London W1B 2AY, UK (☎ 020-7495 8191, 💻 www.italchamind.org.uk).

Italian Consulate General, 38 Eaton Place, London SW1X 8AN, UK (☎ 020-7235 9371).

Italian Cultural Institute, 39 Belgrave Square, London SW1X 8NT, UK (☎ 020-7235 1461, 💻 www.italcultur.org.uk).

Italian Cultural Institute, 686 Park Avenue, New York, NY 10021, US (☎ 212-879 4242, 💻 www.italcultny.org).

Italian Embassy, 3000 Whitehaven St, NW, Washington, DC 20008, US (☎ 202-612 4400, 💻 www.italyemb.org).

Italian Embassy, 14 Three Kings Yard, Davies Street, London W1Y 2EH, UK (☎ 020-7312 2200, 💻 www.embitaly.org.uk).

Italian Federation of Professional Estate Agents (FIAIP), Via Monte Zebio, 30, 00195 Rome (☎ 06-3219 798).

Italian Government Travel Office, 630 Fifth Avenue, Suite 1565, New York, NY 10111, US (☎ 212-245 4822).

Italian Institute for Foreign Trade, 37 Sackville Street, London W1X 2DQ, UK (☎ 020-7734 2412).

Italian State Tourist Board, 1 Princes Street, London W1R 8AY, UK (☎ 020-7408 1254).

Italian Trade Commission, 37 Sackville Street, London W1S 3DQ, UK (☎ 020-7734 2412, 💻 www.ice.it/estoro2/londra).

APPENDIX B: FURTHER READING

English-Language Newspapers & Magazines

Dimore-Homes and Villas of Italy, Via Cristoforo Colombo 440-00145 Rome (☎ 06-5422 5128, 🖥 www.dimore.com). Magazine dedicated to luxury homes and properties for sale, with English and Italian text.

English Yellow Pages, Via Belisario 4/B, 00187 Rome (☎ 06-4740 861, 🖥 www.englishyellowpages.it).

Grapevine, Casella Postale 56, 55061 Carraia (LU) (☎ 0583-909 012, 🖥 www.luccagrapevine.com). Monthly English-language magazine for Lucca and the surrounding area.

Hello Milano, (☎ 02-2952 0570, 🖥 www.hellomilano.it). Free online and printed monthly entertainment magazine.

The Informer, Via dei Tigli 2, 20020 Arese (MI) (☎ 02-9358 1477, 🖥 www.informer.it). A monthly online magazine for expatriates, with a subscription required to access much of the site.

International Herald Tribune (🖥 www.iht.com).

International Property Magazine, 2a Station Road, Gidea Park, Romford, Essex RM2 6DA, UK (☎ 01708-450784). Bi-monthly magazine.

Ville e Casali, Edizioni Living International, Via Anton Giulio Bragaglia 33, 00123 Rome (☎ 06-3028 21, ✉ direzione@eli.it). Glossy monthly home magazine containing a catalogue of luxury properties with English summaries of articles and house descriptions.

Wanted in Rome, Via dei Delfini 17, 00186 Rome. (☎ 06-6790 190, 🖥 www.wantedinrome.com). Classied advertisements, jobs, accommodation (rentals, properties for sale, holiday properties), what's on and lifestyle articles.

Where Rome, Via Ostiense 172, 00154 Rome (☎ 06-5781 615, ✉ where rma@alfanet.it). Monthly entertainment magazine.

World of Property, Outbound Publishing, 1 Commercial Road, Eastbourne, East Sussex BN21 3XQ, UK (☎ 01323-726040, 🖥 www.outboundpublishing.com). Quarterly magazine.

Books

The books listed below are just a small selection of the many relating to living or working in Italy. In addition to the general guides listed, there are many excellent regional guides. Some titles may be out of print but may still be obtainable from book shops and libraries; the same book may have different publishers in Britain and the US. Books prefixed with an asterisk are recommended by the author.

Travel

*AA Baedeker's Italy (AA Publishing)

*Alistair Sawday's Special Places to Stay, Susan Pennington (Alistair Sawday)

Bed & Blessings Italy: A Guide to Convents and Monasteries Available for Overnight Lodging, Anne & June Walsh (Paulist Press)

Blue Guide Northern Italy from the Alps to Bologna, Alta MacAdam (Blue Guides)

Blue Guide Tuscany, Alta MacAdam & John Flower (Blue Guides)

*Cheap Sleeps in Italy, Sandra Gustafson (Chronicle)

City Secrets: Rome, Robert Kahn (Little Bookroom)

*Dorling Kindersley Travel Guides: Italy (Dorling Kindersley)

Fodor's Italy (Fodors)

*Frommer's Italy, Darwin Porter & Danforth Prince (Macmillan)

*Frommer's Italy's Best-Loved Driving Tours, Arthur Frommer (MacMillan)

The Guide to Lodging in Italian Monasteries, Eileen Barish (Anacapa Press)

The Independent Walker's Guide to Italy, Frank W. Booth (Interlink)

*Insight Guide: Italy (APA Publications)

*Italian Days, Barbara Grizzuti Harrison (Atlantic Monthly)

*Karen Brown's Italy: Charming Inns & Itineraries, Care Brown & Others (Fodors)

*Let's Go Italy (Griffin)

*Lombardy: The Italian Lakes, John Flower (Philip)

*Lonely Planet Italy, Helen Gillman & others (Lonely Planet)

*Michelin Green Guide Italy (Michelin)

*Rick Steves' Italy, Rick Steves (Avalon)

*The Rough Guide Italy, Ros Belford, Martin Dunford & Celia Woolfrey (The Rough Guides)

*Tuscany, Umbria and the Marche, Michael Pauls & Dana Facaros (Cadogan)

*Venice, Frail Barrier, Richard de Combray (Doubleday)

Venice and the Veneto, James Bentley (Aurum)

Property & Living

*After Hannibal, Barry Unsworth (Penguin)

*Bella Tuscany, Frances Mayes (Bantam)

**Buying a Home in Italy, David Hampshire (Survival Books)

*Desiring Italy, Susan Neunzig Cahill (Fawcett Books)

*Edith Wharton's Italian Gardens, Vivian Russell (Ecco Press)

*Gardens of the Italian Lakes, Judith Chatfield (Rizzoli)

Gardens of Tuscany, Ethne Clark (Weidenfeld & Nicolson)

*Great Houses of Tuscany: The Tuscan Villas (Viking)

The Hills of Tuscany: A New Life In An Old Land, Ferenc Matè (Harper & Collins)

The Hill Towns of Tuscany, Richard Kauffman & Carol Field (Chronicle)

A House in Sicily, Daphne Phelps (Carroll & Graf)

Italian Country Style, Robert Fitzgerald & Peter Porter (Fairfax)

*An Italian Education: The Further Adventures of an Expatriate in Verona, Tim Parks (Avon Books)

*Italian Neighbours, Tim Parks (Fawcett Books)

Italian Villas and Gardens, Paul van der Ree

*Italian Villas and Their Gardens, Edith Wharton (Da Capo)

Italy: A Complete Guide to 1,000 towns and Cities and Their Landmarks (Touring Club Italiano)

Italy: The Hill Towns, James Bentley (Aurum)

*The Most Beautiful Villages of Tuscany, James Bentley & Hugh Palmer (Thames & Hudson)

North of Naples, South of Rome, Paolo Tullio (Lilliput Press)

*A Place in Italy, Simon Mawer (Sinclair Stevenson)

*Private Tuscany, Elizabeth Helman-Minchilli & Others (Rizzoli)

*A Small Place in Italy, Eric Newby (Picador)

*Survival Guide to Milan, Jessica Halpern (Informer)

*Traditional Houses of Rural Italy, Paul Duncan (Collins & Brown)

A Tuscan Childhood, Kinta Beevor (Penguin)

Urban Land and Property Markets in Italy, Gastone Ave (UCL Press)

*Under the Tuscan Sun, Frances Mayes (Broadway Books)

*A Valley in Italy: The Many Seasons of a Villa in Umbria, Lisa St. Aubin de Terán (Harperperennial)

Venice: the Most Triumphant City, George Bull

*Views from a Tuscan Vineyard, Carey More (Pavillion)

*Within Tuscany, Matthew Spender (Penguin)

Food & Drink

The Best of Italy: A Cookbook, Evie Righter (Collins)

*Celebrating Italy, Carol Field (Harper Perennial)

*Cheap Eats in Italy, Sandra Gustafson (Chronicle)

*The Classic Italian Cookbook, Marcella Hazan (Macmillan)

Cooking the Italian Way, Alphonse Bisignano (Lerner)

The Dictionary of Italian Food and Drink, John F. Mariani (Broadway Books)

*Eating and Drinking in Italy, Andy Herbach & Michael Dillon (Capra Press)

Eating in Italy: A Travelers Guide to the Gastronomic Pleasures of Northern Italy, Faith Heller Willinger & Faith Echtermeyer (William Morrow)

Eating Out in Italy, Dianne Seed & Robert Budwig (Rosendale)

*The Edible Italian Garden, Rosalind Creasy (Periplus)

*Essentials of Classic Italian Cooking, Marcella Hazan (Knopf)

*Floyd on Italy, Keith Floyd (Penguin)

Food in Italy, Claudia Gaspari (Rourke)

*The Food of Italy, Waverly Root (Vintage)

*A Food Lover's Companion to Tuscany, Carla Capalbo (Chronicle)

Frommer's Food Lover's Companion to Italy, Marc & Kim Millon (Macmillan)

Guide to Italian Wine, Burton Anderson (Mitchell Beazley)

*Italian Food, Elizabeth David (Penguin)

The Italian Wine Guide (TCI/Abbeville Press)

*Italian Wines, Victor Hazan (Kyle Cathie)

*Italian Wines 2002, Gamberro Rosso (Gambero Rosso)

*Italy for the Gourmet Traveler, Fred Plotkin (Kyle Cathie)

Little Italy Cookbook, David Reggurio & Melanie Acevedo (Artisan)

*Michelin Red Guide Italy (Michelin)

Recipes From Paradise, Fred Plotkin (Little, Brown)

*Slow Food Guide to Italian Wine (GRUB)

A Traveller's Wine Guide to Italy (Aurum Press)

Touring in Wine Country: Northwest Italy, Maureen Ashley (Mitchell Beazley)

A Traveller's Wine Guide to Italy, Stephen Hobley (Traveller's Wine Guides)

Vino, Burton Anderson (Little, Brown)

Walking and Eating in Tuscany & Umbria, James Ladsun & others (Penguin)

Wines of Italy, Burton Anderson (Mitchell Beazley)

*World Food Italy, Matthew Evans & Gabriella Cossi (Lonely Planet)

Miscellaneous

*Agnelli and the Network of Italian Power, Alan Friedman (Mandarin)

The Architecture of the Italian Renaissance, Peter Murray (Schocken)

Business Italy, A Practical Guide to Understanding Italian Business Culture, Peggy Kenna & Sondra Lacy (Passport)

Contemporary Italy, Donald Sassoon (Longman)

The Crisis of the Italian State, Patrick McCarthy (Macmillan)

*D. H. Lawrence and Italy, D.H. Lawrence (Penguin)

Early Renaissance, Michael Levy (Penguin)

*The History of the Decline and Fall of the Roman Empire, Edward Gibbon (Penguin)

History of the Italian People, Guiliano Procacci (Penguin)

A History of Rome, Michael Grant (Simon & Schuster)

*The Honoured Society, Norman Lewis (Eland)

*The Italians, Luigi Barzini (Penguin)

The Last Italian: Portrait of a People, William Murray (Prentice Hall)

Lives of the Artists, Giorgio Vasari (Penguin)

*Lonely Planet: Walking in Italy, Helen Gillman and others (Lonely Planet)

Love and War in the Apennines, Eric Newby (Picador)

The Mafia, Claire Sterling (Grafton)

*Men of Honour: The Truth about the Mafia, Giovanni Falcone (Warner)

The New Italians, Charles Richards (Penguin)

*A Traveller in Italy, H.V. Morton (Methuen)

*A Traveller's History of Italy, Valerio Lintner (Windrush)

Venice, James Morris (Faber)

Walking in the Dolomites, Gillian Price (Cicerone)

Wild Italy, Tim Jepson (Sheldrake)

APPENDIX C: USEFUL WEBSITES

There are dozens of expatriate websites and as the Internet increases in popularity the number grows by the day. Most information is useful, and websites generally offer free access, although some require a subscription or payment for services. Relocation and other companies specialising in expatriate services often have websites, although these may provide only information that the company is prepared to offer free of charge, which may be rather biased. However, there are plenty of volunteer sites run by expatriates providing practical information and tips. A particularly useful section found on most expatriate websites is the 'message board' or 'forum', where expatriates answer questions based on their experience and knowledge and offer an insight into what living and working in Italy (or in a particular region or town) is **really** like. The list of websites below is by no means definitive.

Italian Websites

Alitalia (💻 www.alitalia.it). The site of the country's state airline, including an English-language section.

Datasport (💻 www.datasport.it). A comprehensive site dedicated to Italian sport (in Italian).

Dolce Vita (💻 www.dolcevita.com). Dubs itself 'the insider's guide to Italy' and covers fashion, design, cuisine, travel and events (in English).

In Italy Online (💻 www.initaly.com). Over 4,000 pages of information about Italy, its regions, places to visit and things to do, as well as practical advice about day-to-day living.

Italian Automobile Club (💻 www.aci.it). Italy's leading motoring organisation; the site has plenty of useful information about driving in the country (in Italian).

Italian Government (💻 www.governo.it). The Italian government's website, with information about all aspects of life in the country (in Italian).

Italian Government Tourist Board USA (💻 www.italiantourism.com). The government's site for US visitors is packed with information about Italy (in English).

Italian Institute for Foreign Trade (🖳 www.italtrade.com). An organisation that promotes trade, business opportunities and industrial cooperation between Italian and foreign companies.

Italian Telephone Directory (🖳 http://paginebianche.virgilio.it).

Italian Yellow Pages (🖳 http://paginegialle.virgilio.it). The site has an English-language search facility.

Museums Online (🖳 www.museionline.com). A guide to Italy's museums and their exhibits, including an English version.

Romebuddy.com (🖳 www.romebuddy.com). A general guide to all aspects of living in Rome and Italy.

Travel Italy (🖳 www.travel.it). Contains information about everything from archaeology to thermal spas to religious tourism.

General Websites

Australia Shop (🖳 www.australia.shop.com): Expatriate shopping for homesick Australians.

British Expatriates (🖳 www.britishexpat.com and www.ukworld wide. com): Two sites designed to keep British expatriates in touch with events in and information about the UK.

Direct Moving (🖳 www.directmoving.com): General expatriate information, tips and advice, and numerous links.

Escape Artist (🖳 www.escapeartist.com): One of the most comprehensive expatriate sites, including resources, links and directories covering most expatriate destinations. You can also subscribe to the free monthly online expatriate magazine, Escape from America.

ExpatAccess (🖳 www.expataccess.com): Aimed at those planning to move abroad, with free moving guides.

ExpatBoards (🖳 www.expatboards.com): A comprehensive site for expatriates, with popular discussion boards and special areas for Britons and Americans.

Expat Exchange (🖳 www.expatexchange.com): Reportedly the largest online 'community' for English-speaking expatriates, including articles on relocation and a question and answer facility.

Expat Forum (🖳 www.expatforum.com): Provides cost of living comparisons as well as over 20 country-specific forums.

Expat Mums (🖳 www.expat-moms.com): Information for expatriate mothers.

Expat Network (🖳 www.expatnetwork.com): The UK's leading expatriate website, which is essentially an employment network for expatriates, although it also includes numerous support services and a monthly online magazine, Nexus.

Expat Shopping (🖳 www.expatshopping.com): Order your favourite foods from home.

Expat World (🖳 www.expatworld.net): Information for American and British expatriates, including a subscription newsletter.

Expatriate Experts (🖳 www.expatexpert.com): Run by expatriate expert Robin Pascoe, providing advice and support.

Global People (🖳 www.peoplegoingglobal.com): Includes country-specific information with a particular emphasis on social and political issues.

Living Abroad (🖳 www.livingabroad.com): Includes an extensive list of country profiles, which are available only on payment.

Outpost Information Centre (🖳 www.outpostexpat.nl): Contains extensive country-specific information and links operated by the Shell Petroleum Company for its expatriate workers, but available to everyone.

Real Post Reports (🖳 www.realpostreports.com): Includes relocation services, recommended reading lists and 'real-life' stories written by expatriates in cities throughout the world.

Save Wealth Travel (🖳 www.savewealth.com/travel/warnings): Travel information and warnings.

Trade Partners (🖳 www.tradepartners.gov.uk): A UK government-sponsored site providing trade and investment (and general) information about most countries, including the USA.

The Travel Doctor (🖳 www.tmvc.com.au/info10.html): Includes a country by country vaccination guide.

Travelfinder (🖳 www.travelfinder.com/twarn/travel_warnings.html): Travel information with warnings about danger areas.

World Health Organization (🖳 www.who.int): Health information.

The World Press (🖳 www.theworldpress.com): Links to media sites in practically every country in the world's media.

World Travel Guide (💻 www.wtgonline.com): A general website for world travellers and expatriates.

Yankee Doodle (💻 www.yankeedoodleiow.com): Import American products.

Websites For British Expatriates

British Expatriates (💻 www.britishexpat.com and www.ukworld wide. com): These websites keep British expatriates in touch with events and information in the United Kingdom.

Trade Partners (💻 www.tradepartners.gov.uk): A government-sponsored website whose main aim is to provide trade and investment information for most countries. Even if you aren't intending to do business, the information is comprehensive and up to date.

Websites For Women

Career Women (💻 www.womenconnect.com): Contains career opportunities for women abroad plus a wealth of other useful information.

Expatriate Mothers (💻 http://expatmoms.tripod.com): Help and advice on how to survive as a mother on relocation.

Spouse Abroad (💻 www.expatspouse.com): Information about careers and working abroad. You need to register and subscribe.

Third Culture Kids (💻 www.tckworld.com): Designed for expatriate children.

Women Abroad (💻 www.womanabroad.com): Advice on careers, expatriate skills and the family abroad. Opportunity to subscribe to a monthly magazine of the same name.

Worldwise Directory (💻 www.suzylamplugh.org/worldwise): Run by the Suzy Lamplugh charity for personal safety, the site provides practical information about a number of countries with special emphasis on safety, particularly for women.

APPENDIX D: WEIGHTS & MEASURES

Italy uses the metric system of measurement. Those who are more familiar with the imperial system of measurement will find the tables on the following pages useful. Some comparisons shown are only approximate, but are close enough for most everyday uses. In addition to the variety of measurement systems used, clothes sizes often vary considerably with the manufacturer (as we all know only too well). Try all clothes on before buying and don't be afraid to return something if, when you try it on at home, you decide it doesn't fit (most shops will exchange goods or give a refund).

Women's Clothes

Continental	34	36	38	40	42	44	46	48	50	52
UK	8	10	12	14	16	18	20	22	24	26
USA	6	8	10	12	14	16	18	20	22	24

Pullovers

Pullovers	Women's						Men's					
Continental	40	42	44	46	48	50	44	46	48	50	52	54
UK	34	36	38	40	42	44	34	36	38	40	42	44
USA	34	36	38	40	42	44	sm	med	lar	xl		

Men's Shirts

Continental	36	37	38	39	40	41	42	43	44	46
UK/USA	14	14	15	15	16	16	17	17	18	-

Men's Underwear

Continental	5	6	7	8	9	10
UK	34	36	38	40	42	44
USA	sm	med		lar	xl	

Note: sm = small, med = medium, lar = large, xl = extra large

Children's Clothes

Continental	92	104	116	128	140	152
UK	16/18	20/22	24/26	28/30	32/34	36/38
USA	2	4	6	8	10	12

Children's Shoes

Continental	18 19 20 21 22 23 24 25 26 27 28 29 30 31 32
UK/USA	2 3 4 4 5 6 7 7 8 9 10 11 11 12 13
Continental	33 34 35 36 37 38
UK/USA	1 2 2 3 4 5

Shoes (Women's and Men's)

Continental	35 36 37 37 38 39 40 41 42 42 43 44
UK	2 3 3 4 4 5 6 7 7 8 9 9
USA	4 5 5 6 6 7 8 9 9 10 10 11

Weight

Avoirdupois	Metric	Metric	Avoirdupois
1oz	28.35g	1g	0.035oz
1lb*	454g	100g	3.5oz
1cwt	50.8kg	250g	9oz
1 ton	1,016kg	500g	18oz
2,205lb	1 tonne	1kg	2.2lb

Length

British/US	Metric	Metric	British/US
1in	2.54cm	1cm	0.39in
1ft	30.48cm	1m	3ft 3.25in
1yd	91.44cm	1km	0.62mi
1mi	1.6km	8km	5mi

Capacity

Imperial	Metric	Metric	Imperial
1 UK pint	0.57 litre	1 litre	1.75 UK pints
1 US pint	0.47 litre	1 litre	2.13 US pints
1 UK gallon	4.54 litres	1 litre	0.22 UK gallon
1 US gallon	3.78 litres	1 litre	0.26 US gallon

Note: An American 'cup' = around 250ml or 0.25 litre.

Area

British/US	Metric	Metric	British/US
1 sq. in	0.45 sq. cm	1 sq. cm	0.15 sq. in
1 sq. ft	0.09 sq. m	1 sq. m	10.76 sq. ft
1 sq. yd	0.84 sq. m	1 sq. m	1.2 sq. yds
1 acre	0.4 hectares	1 hectare	2.47 acres
1 sq. mile	2.56 sq. km	1 sq. km	0.39 sq. mile

Temperature

°Celsius	°Fahrenheit	
0	32	(freezing point of water)
5	41	
10	50	
15	59	
20	68	
25	77	
30	86	
35	95	
40	104	
50	122	

Notes: The boiling point of water is 100°C / 212°F.

Normal body temperature (if you're alive and well) is 37°C / 98.4°F.

Temperature Conversion

Celsius to Fahrenheit: multiply by 9, divide by 5 and add 32. (For a quick and approximate conversion, double the Celsius temperature and add 30.)

Fahrenheit to Celsius: subtract 32, multiply by 5 and divide by 9. (For a quick and approximate conversion, subtract 30 from the Fahrenheit temperature and divide by 2.)

Oven Temperatures

Gas	Electric	
	°F	°C
-	225–250	110–120
1	275	140
2	300	150
3	325	160
4	350	180
5	375	190
6	400	200
7	425	220
8	450	230
9	475	240

Air Pressure

PSI	Bar
10	0.5
20	1.4
30	2
40	2.8

APPENDIX E: MAP

The map opposite shows the 20 administrative regions of Italy, which are listed below with the 95 provinces (and their official abbreviations).

Region	Provinces
Abruzzo (*Abruzzi*)	Chieti (CH), L'Aquila (AQ), Pescara (PE), Teramo (TE)
Basilicata (*Lucania*)	Matera (MT), Potenza (PZ)
Calabria	Cantazaro (CZ), Cosenza CS), Reggio di Calabria (RC)
Campania	Avellino (AV), Benevento (BN), Caserta (CE), Naples/Napoli (NA), Salerno (SA)
Emilia Romagna	Bologna (BO), Ferrara (FE), Forli (FO), Modena (MO), Piacenza (PC), Parma (PR), Ravenna (RA), Regio Emilia (RE)
Friuli-Venezia Giuila	Gorizia (GO), Pordenone (PN), Trieste (TS), Udine (UD)
Lazio (*Latium*)	Frosinone (FR), Latina (LT), Rieti (RI), Rome/Roma (ROMA),Viterbo (VT)
Liguria	Genova (GE), Imperia (IM), La Spezia (SP), Savona (SV) Lombardy (Lombardia) Bergamo (BG), Brescia (BS), Como (CO), Cremona (CR), Mantua/Mantova (MN), Milan/Milano (MI), Pavia (PV), Sondrio (SO), Varese (VA)
Marche	Ancona (AN), Ascoli Piceno (AP), Macerata (MC), Pesaro (PS)
Molise (*Molize*)	Campobasso (CB), Isernia (IS)
Piedmont (*Piemonte*)	Alessandria (AL), Asti (AT), Cuneo (CN), Novara (NO), Turin/Torino (TO), Vercelli (VC)
Puglia (*Apulia/ Le Puglie*)	Bari (BA), Brindisi (BR), Foggia (FG), Lecce (LE), Taranto (TA)
Sardinia (*Sardegna*)	Cagliari (CA), Nuoro (NU), Oristano (OR), Sassari (SS)
Sicily (*Sicilia*)	Agrigento (AG), Caltanissetta (CL), Catania (CT), Enna (EN), Messina (ME), Palermo (PA), Ragusa (RG), Syracuse/Siracusa (SR), Trapini (TP)
Tuscany (*Toscana*)	Arezzo (AR), Florence/Firenze (FI), Grosseto (GR), Leghorn/Livorno (LI), Lucca (LU), Massa Carrara (MS), Pisa (PI), Pistoia (PT), Siena (SI)
Trentino-Alto Adige	Bolzano (BZ), Trento (TN)
Umbria	Perugia (PG), Terni (TR)
Val d'Aosta	Aosta (AO)
Veneto	Belluno (BL), Padua/Padova (PD), Rovigo (RO), Treviso (TV), Venice/Venezia (VE), Verona (VR), Vicenza (VI)

INDEX

F

G

H

Q

R

S

T

LIVING AND WORKING SERIES

Living and Working books are essential reading for anyone planning to spend time abroad, including holiday-home owners, retirees, visitors, business people, migrants, students and even extra-terrestrials! They're packed with important and useful information designed to help you **avoid costly mistakes and save both time and money**. Topics covered include how to:

- Find a job with a good salary & conditions
- Obtain a residence permit
- Avoid and overcome problems
- Find your dream home
- Get the best education for your family
- Make the best use of public transport
- Endure local motoring habits
- Obtain the best health treatment
- Stretch your money further
- Make the most of your leisure time
- Enjoy the local sporting life
- Find the best shopping bargains
- Insure yourself against most eventualities
- Use post office and telephone services
- Do numerous other things not listed above

Living and Working books are the most comprehensive and up-to-date source of practical information available about everyday life abroad. They aren't, however, boring text books, but interesting and entertaining guides written in a highly readable style.

Discover what it's *really* like to live and work abroad!

Order your copies today by phone, fax, mail or e-mail from: Survival Books, PO Box 146, Wetherby, West Yorks. LS23 6XZ, United Kingdom (☎/🖨 +44 (0)1937-843523, ✉ orders@ survivalbooks.net, 💻 www.survivalbooks.net).

BUYING A HOME SERIES

Buying a Home books are essential reading for anyone planning to purchase property abroad and are designed to guide you through the jungle and make it a pleasant and enjoyable experience. Most importantly, they're packed with vital information to help you **avoid the sort of disasters that can turn your dream home into a nightmare!** Topics covered include:

- Avoiding problems
- Choosing the region
- Finding the right home and location
- Estate agents
- Finance, mortgages and taxes
- Home security
- Utilities, heating and air-conditioning
- Moving house and settling in
- Renting and letting
- Permits and visas
- Travelling and communications
- Health and insurance
- Renting a car and driving
- Retirement and starting a business
- And much, much more!

Buying a Home books are the most comprehensive and up-to-date source of information available about buying property abroad. Whether you want a detached house, townhouse or apartment, a holiday or a permanent home, these books will help make your dreams come true.

Save yourself time, trouble and money!

Order your copies today by phone, fax, mail or e-mail from: Survival Books, PO Box 146, Wetherby, West Yorks. LS23 6XZ, United Kingdom (☎/📠 +44 (0)1937-843523, ✉ orders@ survivalbooks.net, 🖳 www.survivalbooks.net).

ORDER FORM

ALIEN'S GUIDES / BEST PLACES / BUYING A HOME / DISASTERS / WINES

Qty.	Title	Price (incl. p&p)*			Total
		UK	**Europe**	**World**	
	The Alien's Guide to Britain	£5.95	£6.95	£8.45	
	The Alien's Guide to France	£5.95	£6.95	£8.45	
	The Best Places to Buy a Home in France	£13.95	£15.95	£19.45	
	The Best Places to Buy a Home in Spain	£13.45	£14.95	£16.95	
	Buying a Home Abroad	£13.45	£14.95	£16.95	
	Buying a Home in Britain	£11.45	£12.95	£14.95	
	Buying a Home in Florida	£13.45	£14.95	£16.95	
	Buying a Home in France	£13.45	£14.95	£16.95	
	Buying a Home in Greece & Cyprus	£13.45	£14.95	£16.95	
	Buying a Home in Ireland	£11.45	£12.95	£14.95	
	Buying a Home in Italy	£13.45	£14.95	£16.95	
	Buying a Home in Portugal	£13.45	£14.95	£16.95	
	Buying a Home in Spain	£13.45	£14.95	£16.95	
	How to Avoid Holiday & Travel Disasters	£13.45	£14.95	£16.95	
	Renovating & Maintaining Your French Home	Autumn 2003			
	Rioja and its Wines	£11.45	£12.95	£14.95	
	The Wines of Spain	£15.95	£18.45	£21.95	
				Total	

Order your copies today by phone, fax, mail or e-mail from: Survival Books, PO Box 146, Wetherby, West Yorks. LS23 6XZ, UK (☎/▤ +44 (0)1937-843523, ✉ orders@ survivalbooks.net, ▣ www.survivalbooks.net). If you aren't entirely satisfied, simply return them to us within 14 days for a full and unconditional refund.

Cheque enclosed/please charge my Amex/Delta/MasterCard/Switch/Visa* card

Card No. __ __ __ __   __ __ __ __   __ __ __ __   __ __ __ __

Expiry date _____   Issue number (Switch only) _____

Signature _____   Tel. No. _____

NAME _____

ADDRESS _____

_____

_____

* Delete as applicable (price includes postage — airmail for Europe/world).

ORDER FORM

LIVING & WORKING SERIES / RETIRING ABROAD

Qty.	Title	Price (incl. p&p)*			Total
		UK	Europe	World	
	Living & Working Abroad	£16.95	£18.95	£22.45	
	Living & Working in America	£14.95	£16.95	£20.45	
	Living & Working in Australia	£14.95	£16.95	£20.45	
	Living & Working in Britain	£14.95	£16.95	£20.45	
	Living & Working in Canada	£16.95	£18.95	£22.45	
	Living & Working in the Far East	Winter 2003			
	Living & Working in France	£14.95	£16.95	£20.45	
	Living & Working in Germany	£16.95	£18.95	£22.45	
	Living & Working in the Gulf States & Saudi Arabia	£16.95	£18.95	£22.45	
	Living & Working in Holland, Belgium & Luxembourg	£14.95	£16.95	£20.45	
	Living & Working in Ireland	£14.95	£16.95	£20.45	
	Living & Working in Italy	£16.95	£18.95	£22.45	
	Living & Working in London	£11.45	£12.95	£14.95	
	Living & Working in New Zealand	£14.95	£16.95	£20.45	
	Living & Working in Spain	£14.95	£16.95	£20.45	
	Living & Working in Switzerland	£14.95	£16.95	£20.45	
	Retiring Abroad	£14.95	£16.95	£20.45	
				Total	

Order your copies today by phone, fax, mail or e-mail from: Survival Books, PO Box 146, Wetherby, West Yorks. LS23 6XZ, UK (☎/▤ +44 (0)1937-843523, ✉ orders@ survivalbooks.net, 💻 www.survivalbooks.net). If you aren't entirely satisfied, simply return them to us within 14 days for a full and unconditional refund.

Cheque enclosed/please charge my Amex/Delta/MasterCard/Switch/Visa* card

Card No. _ _ _ _ _ _ _ _ _ _ _ _ _ _ _ _

Expiry date _____ Issue number (Switch only) _____

Signature _____ Tel. No. _____

NAME _____

ADDRESS _____

_____

_____

* Delete as applicable (price includes postage – airmail for Europe/world).

OTHER SURVIVAL BOOKS

Survival Books publishes a variety of books in addition to the *Living and Working* and *Buying a Home* series (see previous pages). These include:

The Alien's Guides: *The Alien's Guides to Britain* and *France* provide an 'alternative' look at life in these popular countries and will help you to avoid the most serious gaffes and to appreciate more fully the peculiarities (in both senses) of the British and French.

The Best Places to Buy a Home: *The Best Places to Buy a Home in France* and *Spain* are the most comprehensive and up-to-date sources of information available for anyone wanting to research the property market in France and Spain and will save you endless hours choosing the best place for your home.

How to Avoid Holiday and Travel Disasters: This book is essential reading for anyone planning a trip abroad and will help you to make the right decisions regarding every aspect of your travel arrangements and to avoid costly mistakes and the sort of disasters that can turn a trip into a nightmare.

Renovating & Maintaining Your French Home: New for 2003 is the ultimate guide to renovating and maintaining your dream home in France, including essential information, contacts and vocabulary and time and cost-saving tips.

Retiring Abroad: This is the most comprehensive and up-to-date source of practical information available about retiring to a foreign country and will help to smooth your path to successful retirement abroad and save you time, trouble and money.

Wine Guides: *Rioja and its Wines* and *The Wines of Spain* are required reading for lovers of fine wines and are the most comprehensive and up-to-date sources of information available on the wines of Spain and of its most famous wine-producing region.

Broaden your horizons with Survival Books!

Order your copies today by phone, fax, mail or e-mail from: Survival Books, PO Box 146, Wetherby, West Yorks. LS23 6XZ, United Kingdom (☎/🖷 +44 (0)1937-843523, ✉ orders@ survivalbooks.net, 💻 www.survivalbooks.net).